1001 DAYS OUT

Historic Houses, Gardens and Places to Visit

1001 DAYS OUT

Historic Houses, Gardens and Places to Visit

p

This is a Parragon Book
First Published in 2007

Parragon
Queen Street House
4 Queen Street
Bath BA1 1HE, UK

All the information given in this book has come directly from the attractions included and was correct at the time of going to press. The Publishers would be grateful for any information that would assist in keeping future editions up to date. While every care has been taken in the preparation of this book, neither the Compilers nor the Publishers can accept any liability for any consequences arising from the use thereof, or the information contained therein. The prices, times and facilities given should be used as a guide only as they will vary from time to time.

ISBN 978-1-4054-8653-8

Designed by Butler and Tanner
Printed in China

Front cover
Top: St Michael's Mount, courtesy of ©Britain on View
Bottom middle: courtesy of ©Museum of Kent Life
Bottom right: courtesy of ©Beamish

Back cover
Waddesdon Manor, courtesy of ©National Trust/Hugh Palmer

Frontispiece
Coton Manor Garden, courtesy of ©Britain on View

Right
Penmachno, Conwy, courtesy of ©Britain on View

IMPORTANT NOTE FOR THE READER

We have made every effort to ensure the information in this guide is accurate and up to date, but things can change very quickly. Prices and opening times are sometimes altered at short notice, and sadly some venues close unexpectedly. We would therefore urge readers to telephone the venue before setting out on a visit. This will ensure you are aware of any changes in ticket prices or opening times, and will avoid unexpected disappointments or problems.

The contents of this book are believed correct at the time of printing. The Publisher cannot be held responsible for any errors, omissions or changes in the information in this guide or for the consequences of any reliance on the information provided.

Contents

Introduction

Britain is one of the most popular holiday destinations in the world. It's easy to see why. Major cities like London, Glasgow and York with their world-famous museums, palaces and stately architecture attract visitors all year round. There are also Areas of Outstanding Natural Beauty like the Lake District and the Peak District, the Brecon Beacons, the Gower Peninsula in Wales and the Highlands in Scotland – all with their own natural history and wildlife. There are mountains and moors, industrial landscapes, castles, gardens ... all surrounded by more than 3,000 miles of coastline. But with so many places to choose from, it's hard to know where to begin.

1001 Days Out will help you do just that. The book is packed with ideas to form the basis of days out in Britain where you can discover the natural beauty, rich heritage and cultural attractions that England, Scotland and Wales have to offer. This practical guide offers a broad selection of attractions ranging from world-famous castles, stately homes and gardens to carefully restored windmills, ancient ruins and rediscovered gardens. But also included are many small and more unusual places to visit. With 1001 entries, all tastes are catered for.

Of course, at any one time, some attractions may be closed for renovation or refurbishment. For this reason a few of the renowned and popular attractions you may be expecting to see may not have been included in this edition, but as *1001 Days Out* is published annually, these attractions will be considered for inclusion next year.

About this guide

This guide covers England, Scotland (including the Northern and Western Islands) and Wales, and is arranged in regions, shown on the national map on page viii. The counties within each region, the towns within each county and the attractions within each town are all, as far as possible, arranged alphabetically. Each attraction also has a reference number and this is used to identify it on the regional map at the beginning of each section.

Understanding the entries

Coloured bands at the top of each page indicate regions; the numbers in the top corners next to the regional name refer to the numbered range of attractions on the page. The nearest major town or village to the attraction is indicated above the name of the attraction.

Quick-reference icons

an all-weather attraction

an attraction for sunny days only

the expected duration of your visit

when the attraction is open

Description

Each entry has a brief description of the attraction and a flavour of what visitors may expect to find. Additional features are also highlighted beneath the description.

Facilities

WC toilet facilities available

space available for you to eat your own food

restaurant, café or kiosk facilities available

good access for wheelchairs restricted access

dogs allowed, but they may have to be kept on a lead

Disabled visitors

Visitors with mobility difficulties should look for the wheelchair symbol which shows that all or most of the attraction is accessible to wheelchair users. We strongly recommend that visitors telephone in advance of a visit to check exact details, including access to toilets and refreshment facilities. Assistance dogs are usually accepted unless stated otherwise. For the hard of hearing, please check that hearing induction loops are available by contacting the attraction itself.

Location

These are simple directions, usually for motorists (though Underground directions are given for attractions in London) and have been provided by the attraction itself.

Opening times

These times are inclusive, e.g. Apr–Oct indicates that the attraction will be open from the beginning of April to the end of October. Where an attraction has varied opening times, these are indicated, and if it is open seven days a week, this is simply referred to as 'Daily'. Bank Holiday opening is indicated where provided by the attraction.

If you are travelling a long way, please check with the attraction itself to ensure any unexpected circumstances are not going to prevent your entry.

Admission

Wherever possible, the charges quoted are for the 2006–7 season, but please note that prices are subject to change and are correct only at the time of going to print. If no price is quoted, it does not mean that a charge will not be made. Many places that do not charge admission may ask for a voluntary donation. In some instances discounts may be available to families, groups, local residents or members of certain organisations such as English Heritage and The National Trust.

Contact details

We have given details of the administrative address and telephone number for each attraction. While these are usually those of the attraction itself, some properties are administered by an area office, and in these cases relevant details are given (several English Heritage properties fall into this category).

Telephone numbers, and email and website addresses are also included wherever possible.

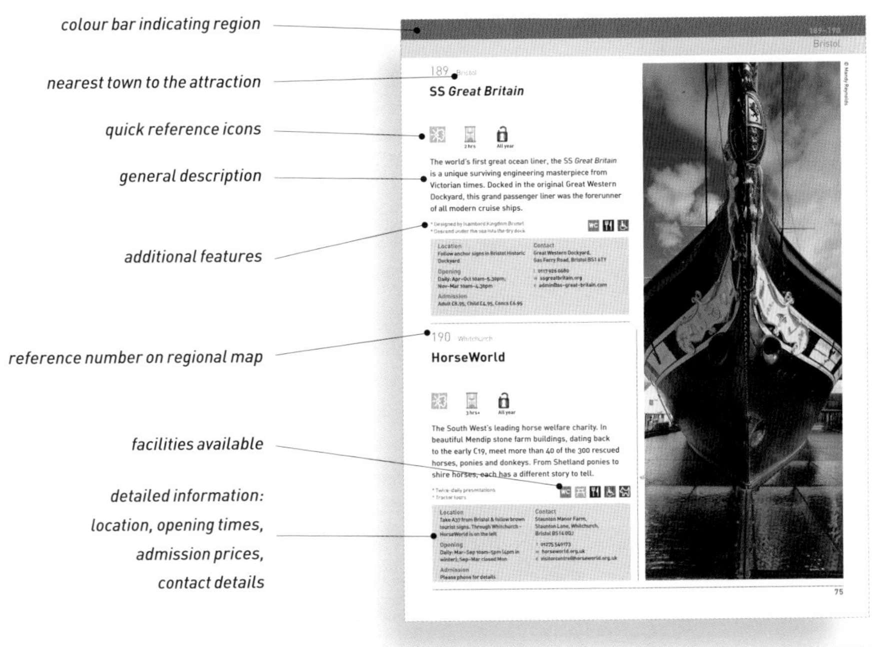

HIGHLANDS & ISLANDS
GRAMPIAN
CENTRAL SCOTLAND
SOUTHERN SCOTLAND
NORTHUMBERLAND
TYNE & WEAR
DURHAM
CUMBRIA
NORTH YORKSHIRE
EAST RIDING OF YORKSHIRE
LANCASHIRE
W. YORKSHIRE
MANCHESTER
MERSEY-SIDE
SOUTH YORKSHIRE
CHESHIRE
DERBYSHIRE
NOTTINGHAMSHIRE
LINCOLNSHIRE
NORTH WALES
STAFFORD-SHIRE
SHROPSHIRE
LEICESTER-SHIRE
RUT-LAND
NORFOLK
WEST MIDLANDS
CENTRAL WALES
WORCESTER-SHIRE
WARWICK-SHIRE
NORTHAMPTON-SHIRE
CAMBRIDGESHIRE
SUFFOLK
HEREFORD-SHIRE
BEDFORD-SHIRE
BUCKING-HAMSHIRE
HERTFORD-SHIRE
ESSEX
GLOUCESTER-SHIRE
SOUTH WALES
OXFORDSHIRE
LONDON
BERKSHIRE
WILTSHIRE
SURREY
KENT
SOMERSET
HAMPSHIRE
WEST SUSSEX
E. SUSSEX
DEVON
DORSET
ISLE OF WIGHT
CORNWALL
Regional colour key
South East
South West
Eastern
East Midlands
West Midlands
Wales
Yorkshire
North West
North East
Scotland

Winchester Cathedral, Hampshire

South East

Berkshire Buckinghamshire East Sussex
Hampshire and Isle of Wight Kent London
Oxfordshire Surrey West Sussex

Great Malvern
612
Pershore
Evesham
Tewkesbury
605-606
273-274
Shipston-on-Stour
551-552
Banbury
129
Moreton-in-Marsh
281-282
Chipping Norton
Stow-on-the-Wold
M5
GLOUCESTERSHIRE
Cheltenham
270-272
289
269
Cotswolds
283
Stroud
Cirencester
287
Tetbury
284-286
Malmesbury
Cricklade
Swindon
325
Faringdon
Carterton
130
Witney
OXFORDSHIRE
Wantage
137
Towcester
013
Brackley
Buckingham
021-022
M40
Bicester
020
Kidlington
138
Oxford
133-136
Abingdon
Didcot
Wallingford
Newport Pagnell
Milton Keynes
339
028
342
341
340
Leighton Buzzard
337
M1
BUCKINGHAMSHIRE
015-019
Aylesbury
030
029
Wendover
Thame
Dunstable
333-334
338
Tring
336
Hemel Hempstead
382
Berkhamsted
380
375-376
Amersham
Chiltern Hills
High Wycombe
023-024
Watford
M25
M40
025-027
Beaconsfield
Marlow
Uxbridge
Maidenhead
Henley-on-Thames
003
Slough
M25
M4
131-132
Reading
A329(M)
Windsor
014
159
BERKSHIRE
M4
LYNEHAM
318
319
Chippenham
Corsham
Calne
Marlborough
Hungerford
Newbury
010-012
Bracknell
Staines
317
291-301
Melksham
Devizes
004-009
001-002
158
Camberley
Woking
M25
141
160
Trowbridge
Kingsclere
Leatherhead
WILTSHIRE
328
Westbury
Salisbury Plain
Basingstoke
M3
Fleet
Aldershot
Guildford
Dorking
Whitchurch
Andover
Farnham
149-153
Warminster
326-327
Amesbury
316
146-147
Godalming
HAMPSHIRE
Alton
142
148
324
329
062
M3
New Alresford
042
Haslemere
Wilton
Winchester
Liphook
Salisbury
320-323
064-065
Petersfield
Billingshurst
Shaftesbury
Midhurst
178
047
Romsey
057-058
Eastleigh
052
177
Pulborough
SOUTHAMPTON
179-180
SOUTHAMPTON
043
WEST SUSSEX
A3(M)
161-164
060
046
Havant
Arundel
Blandford Forum
Ringwood
Lyndhurst
New Forest
Hythe
Chichester
Fawley
Fareham
053-056
Littlehampton
Wimborne Minster
258
Brockenhurst
044
Gosport
061
166-171
176
SET
244
267
New Milton
Lymington
048
Portsmouth
Bognor Regis
261
Poole
245-246
049
Cowes
045
Ryde
Selsey
Christchurch
Newport
Selsey Bill
247
Wareham
254
Bournemouth
Freshwater
ISLE OF WIGHT
050-051
262-264
259
059
Sandown
Shanklin
Swanage
Isle of Wight
066
260
Ventnor
063
St Catherine's Point

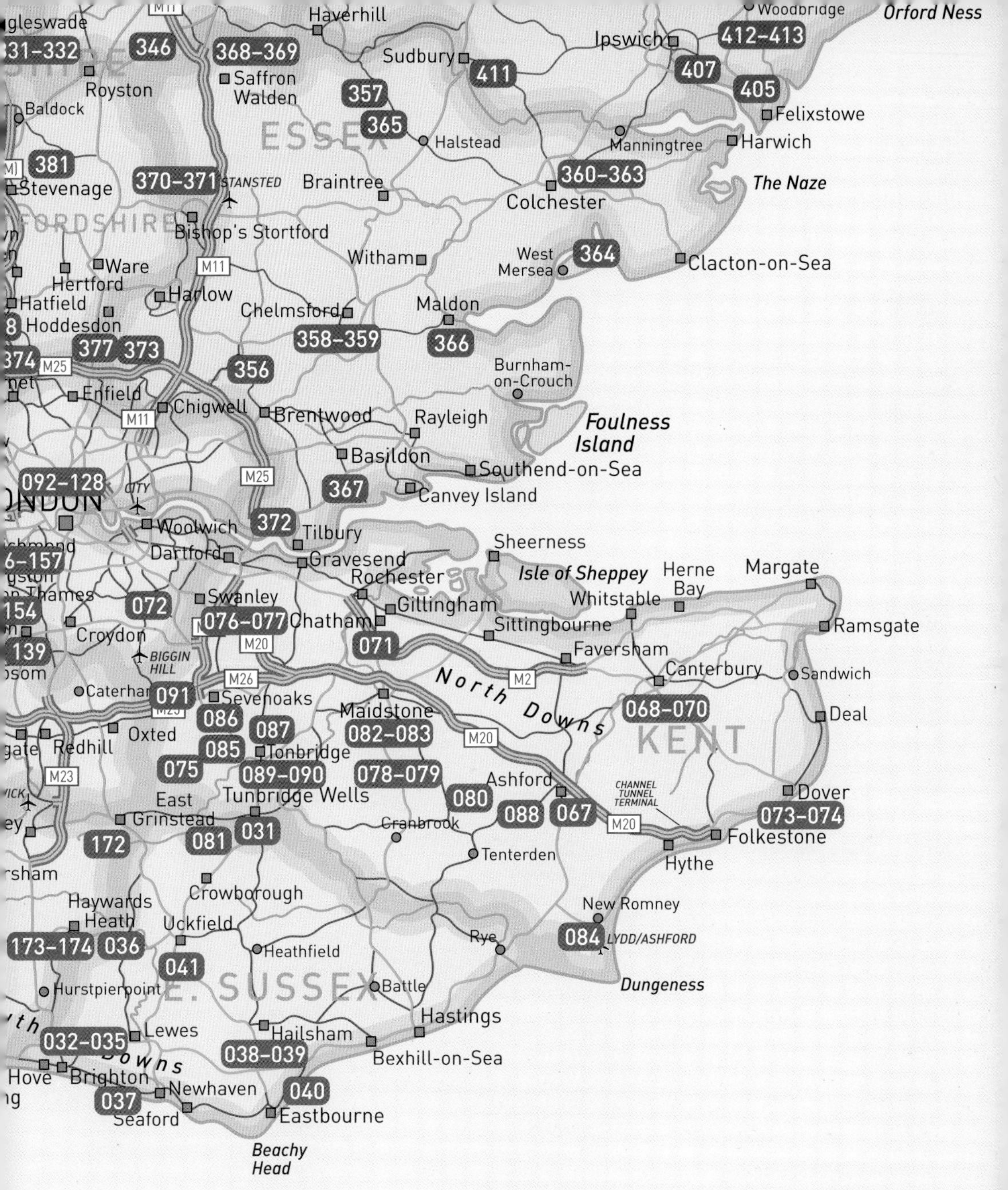
Haverhill
Woodbridge
Orford Ness
Biggleswade
331–332
346
368–369
Ipswich
412–413
Sudbury
411
407
Royston
Saffron Walden
357
405
Baldock
ESSEX
365
Halstead
Felixstowe
Manningtree
Harwich
381
370–371
STANSTED
Braintree
360–363
The Naze
Stevenage
Colchester
HERTFORDSHIRE
Bishop's Stortford
West Mersea
364
Clacton-on-Sea
Ware
Witham
M11
Hertford
Harlow
Hatfield
Chelmsford
Maldon
Hoddesdon
358–359
366
377
373
374
M25
356
Burnham-on-Crouch
Enfield
Chigwell
Brentwood
Rayleigh
M11
Foulness Island
Basildon
Southend-on-Sea
M25
092–128
CITY
367
Canvey Island
LONDON
Woolwich
372
Tilbury
Richmond
Sheerness
Dartford
156–157
Gravesend
Rochester
Isle of Sheppey
Herne Bay
Margate
Kingston upon Thames
Swanley
Whitstable
072
154
076–077
Chatham
Gillingham
Croydon
Sittingbourne
Ramsgate
M20
139
071
Faversham
BIGGIN HILL
Epsom
North Downs
M2
Canterbury
Sandwich
M26
Caterham
091
Sevenoaks
Maidstone
068–070
Deal
086
087
Oxted
082–083
M20
KENT
Redhill
085
Tonbridge
Reigate
M23
075
089–090
078–079
Ashford
CHANNEL TUNNEL TERMINAL
GATWICK
Dover
East Grinstead
Tunbridge Wells
080
088
067
M20
073–074
Crawley
172
081
031
Cranbrook
Folkestone
Tenterden
Hythe
Horsham
Crowborough
Haywards Heath
New Romney
Uckfield
084
LYDD/ASHFORD
173–174
036
Rye
Heathfield
041
Hurstpierpoint
E. SUSSEX
Battle
Dungeness
South Downs
Hastings
Lewes
032–035
Hailsham
038–039
Bexhill-on-Sea
Hove
Brighton
Newhaven
Worthing
040
037
Seaford
Eastbourne
Beachy Head

001 Bracknell

Go Ape!

3 hrs

Mar–Oct

Go Ape! is the ultimate in adrenaline-fuelled adventure, high above the forest floor. Test your nerve exploring the network of rope bridges, trapezes and zip slides that stretches for roughly a mile through the tree canopy.

* 115ft aerial walkway
* Age limit is 10 & a height restriction of 1.4m applies

Location
Follow signs for Go Ape! on A322 S of Bracknell

Opening
Feb half-term & Mar–Oct 9am–5pm; Nov weekends only

Admission
Adult £21, Child £17

Contact
The Look Out, Nine Mile Ride, Swinley Forest, Bracknell RG12 7QW

t 0870 444 5562
w goape.co.uk
e info@goape.co.uk

002 Bracknell

The Lookout Discovery Centre

2 hrs+

All year

A hands-on science exhibition with fun for the entire family. 'Pluck' the laser beams of the Light Harp to make a little light music or put all your energy into launching the Hydrogen Rocket. Explore the wonders of the human body or try the amazing puzzles.

* Children's play area
* 2,600 acres of woodland

Location
Follow signs for Lookout Discovery Centre on A322 S of Bracknell

Opening
Daily: 10am–5pm

Admission
Please phone for details

Contact
Nine Mile Ride, Bracknell RG12 7QW

t 01344 354400
w bracknell-forest.gov.uk/be
e thelookout@bracknell-forest.gov.uk

003 Maidenhead

Cliveden

3 hrs Mar–Dec

This spectacular estate overlooking the River Thames has a series of gardens, each with its own character, featuring topiary, statuary, water-gardens, a formal parterre, informal vistas, woodland and riverside walks. It was once the home of Nancy, Lady Astor.

* Magnificent Italianate palace
* Parks & gardens

Location
2 miles N of Taplow. Take A404 to Marlow & follow brown tourist signs

Opening
House Apr–Oct Thu & Sun 3pm–5.30pm
Estate & Gardens Daily: Mar–Oct 11am–6pm; Nov–Dec 11am–4pm

Admission
Adult £7.50, Child £3.75, £1 extra to view house

Contact
Taplow, nr Maidenhead SL6 0JA

t 01628 605069
w nationaltrust.org.uk
e cliveden@nationaltrust.org.uk

©NTPL/Nick Meers

004 Newbury

Ashdown House

1 hr Apr–Oct

An extraordinary Dutch-style C17 house, famous for its association with Elizabeth of Bohemia, Charles I's sister, to whom the house was consecrated. The interior has a great staircase rising from hall to attic, and important paintings contemporary to the house.

* Spectacular views from the roof over the gardens
* Beautiful walks in neighbouring Ashdown Woods

Location
2 miles S of Ashbury, 3 miles N of Lambourn, on W side of B4000

Opening
House & Gardens Apr–Oct Wed & Sat 2pm–5pm
Tours begin at 2.15pm, 3.15pm & 4.15pm
Woodland All year, closed Fri

Admission
Adult £2.40, Child free

Contact
Lambourn, Newbury RG16 7RE

t 01494 755569
w nationaltrust.org.uk
e ashdownhouse@nationaltrust.org.uk

005 Newbury

Desmoulin

½ hr+ All year

Desmoulin is housed in the granary on the wharf, in one of Newbury's finest old buildings. This contemporary gallery exhibits an ever-changing collection of exquisite art and artefacts – paintings, photographs, furniture, jewellery in silver and gold, glassware and ceramics.

* Café supplies light lunches & caters for vegetarians

Location
In town centre next to Tourist Information Centre

Opening
Mon–Sat 10am–5pm, Sun by appointment

Admission
Free

Contact
The Granary, The Wharf, Newbury RG14 5AS

t 01635 35001
w desmoulin.co.uk
e snail@desmoulin.co.uk

006 Newbury

Donnington Castle

1 hr — All year

Constructed during the late C14, the striking twin-towered gate house of this castle survives amid some impressive earthworks. Originally built as a fortified residence, it was seized by Royalists at the beginning of the English Civil War.

* External viewing only

Location
1 mile N of Newbury off B4494

Opening
Dawn–dusk

Admission
Free

Contact
Newbury RG14 8LT

t 0870 333 1182
w english-heritage.org.uk

007 Newbury

Greenham & Crookham Common

2 hrs+ — All year

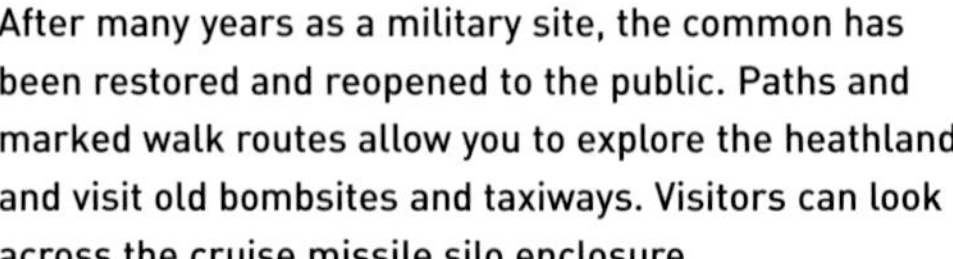

After many years as a military site, the common has been restored and reopened to the public. Paths and marked walk routes allow you to explore the heathland and visit old bombsites and taxiways. Visitors can look across the cruise missile silo enclosure.

* The area is a Site of Special Scientific Interest (SSSI)
* Rare plant communities

Location
Car park at Bury's Bank Road, Greenham

Opening
Daily: *summer* 8am–8pm
winter 8am–4pm

Admission
Free

Contact
West Berkshire Council, Countryside & Environment, Council Offices, Faraday Road, Newbury RG14 2AF

t 01635 519808
w westberks.gov.uk
e tourism@westberks.gov.uk

008 Newbury

Highclere Castle

1 hr — Jul–Aug

Highclere is probably the finest Victorian house in existence. The three men who made Highclere what it is today were the 3rd Earl of Carnarvon who built the new house, Sir Charles Barry who designed it and the 4th Earl of Carnarvon who finished the interiors.

* Georgian pleasure grounds laid out by Robert Herbert
* 5th Earl of Carnarvon found the tomb of Tutankhamun

Location
Off A34, 4½ miles S of Newbury

Opening
Easter school hols & Jun–Aug
Sun–Thu 11am–4pm; all Bank Hols
(last admission 1 hr before close)

Admission
Adult £7.50, Child £4, Concs £6

Contact
Highclere, Newbury RG20 9RN

t 01635 253202
w highclerecastle.co.uk
e theoffice@highclerecastle.co.uk

009 Newbury

The Living Rainforest

  1 hr+  All year

Explore the rainforest and discover its wonders for yourself. This living rainforest aims to promote a sustainable future by providing education on the world's rainforests. It features a tropical rainforest-inspired ecological garden with free-roaming animals.

* Endangered Goeldi's monkeys leap among branches
* Birds, butterflies & lizards roam freely as you explore

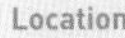

Location
Clearly signed from junction 13 of M4

Opening
Daily: 10am–5.15pm (last admission 4.30pm)

Admission
Please phone or visit the website for details

Contact
Hampstead Norreys RG18 0TN

t 01635 202444
w livingrainforest.org
e enquiries@livingrainforest.org

010 Reading

Basildon Park

  1 hr+  Mar–Oct

Fascinating and beautiful, this C18 Palladian mansion has an extraordinary history. It was used as a hospital during WWI, and as a base for American servicemen during WWII when it was left a near-ruin. It has been lovingly restored by Lord and Lady Iliffe.

* Location for Netherfield in *Pride and Prejudice*
* Pleasure gardens & trails through woodland

Location
A329 between Pangbourne & Streatley

Opening
24 Mar–Oct Wed–Sun & Bank Hols
House 12noon–5pm
Grounds 11am–5pm

Admission
Adult £5, Child £2.65

Contact
Lower Basildon, Reading RG8 9NR

t 0118 984 3040
w nationaltrust.org.uk
e basildonpark@nationaltrust.org.uk

011 Reading

Beale Park

  4 hrs  Mar–Oct

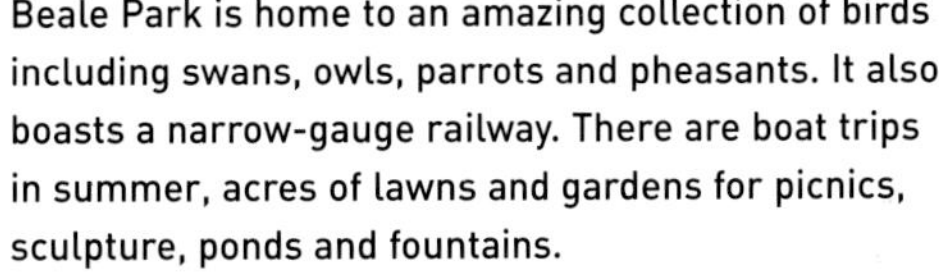

Beale Park is home to an amazing collection of birds including swans, owls, parrots and pheasants. It also boasts a narrow-gauge railway. There are boat trips in summer, acres of lawns and gardens for picnics, sculpture, ponds and fountains.

* The Trust breeds & rears endangered species
* New continental aviaries & jubilee celebration garden

Location
6 miles from Reading on A329 between Pangbourne & Streatley

Opening
Daily: 14 Apr–30 Sep 10am–6pm; 1 Oct–13 Apr 10am–5pm

Admission
Adult £6.50, Child £4.50, Concs £5.50

Contact
Lower Basildon, Reading RG8 9NH

t 0870 777 7160
w bealepark.co.uk
e administration@bealepark.co.uk

012 Reading

Museum of English Rural Life

  1 hr  All year

Founded by the University of Reading in 1951, the museum reflects the changing face of farming and the countryside. It houses collections of national importance, including objects, archives, photographs, film and books.

* Programme of free fun family days
* Part of the university's Museum & Collections Service

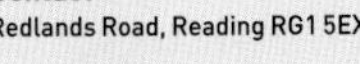

Location
Adjacent to Royal Berkshire Hospital on London Road

Opening
Tue–Fri 10am–4.30pm, Sat–Sun 2pm–4.30pm

Admission
Free

Contact
Redlands Road, Reading RG1 5EX

t 0118 378 8660
w merl.org.uk
e merl@reading.ac.uk

Berkshire

013 Thatcham

Thatcham Nature Discovery Centre

2 hrs+ All year

An exciting place to learn about local wildlife. The wide range of hands-on exhibits in Discovery Hall are set against a dramatic backdrop of giant insect models, colourful banners and wildlife quilts. Visitors can enjoy a walk around the lake and visit the reed-bed bird hide.

* Gallery with changing exhibitions
* Bird hide

Location
Between Thatcham & Newbury, signed from A4

Opening
Mar–Oct Tue–Sun 11am–5pm;
Nov–Feb Tue–Sun 1pm–4pm

Admission
Free

Contact
Muddy Lane, Lower Way, Thatcham RG19 3FU

t 01635 874381
w westberks.gov.uk
e naturecentre@westberks.gov.uk

014 Windsor

Windsor Castle

2 hrs+ All year

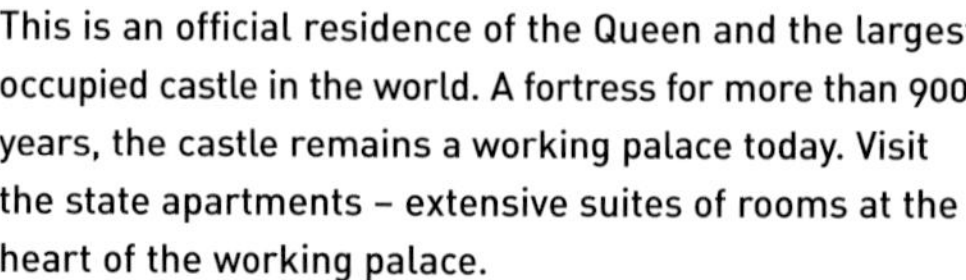

This is an official residence of the Queen and the largest occupied castle in the world. A fortress for more than 900 years, the castle remains a working palace today. Visit the state apartments – extensive suites of rooms at the heart of the working palace.

* The magnificent & beautiful St George's Chapel
* Apr–Jun, Changing of the Guard at 11am (not Sun)

Location
Follow brown tourist signs to central Windsor

Opening
Daily: Mar–Oct 9.45am–5.15pm;
Nov–Feb 9.45am–4.15pm

Admission
Please phone for details

Contact
Ticket Sales & Information Office, The Official Residences of The Queen, London SW1A 1AA

t 0207 766 7304
w royalcollection.org.uk
e information@royalcollection.org.uk

Buckinghamshire

015 Aylesbury

Buckinghamshire County Museum & Roald Dahl Gallery

1 hr+ All year

This award-winning museum is housed in beautifully restored buildings, some dating from the C15. It is a showcase for the county's heritage and runs a varied programme of exhibitions as well as interactive fun in the Roald Dahl Children's Gallery.

* Regular Roald Dahl activities & events
* Varied collections

Location
In town centre

Opening
Museum Mon–Sat 10am–5pm, Sun 2pm–5pm
Roald Dahl Gallery Mon–Fri 3pm–5pm (term time), 10am–5pm (hols), Sat 10am–5pm, Sun 2pm–5pm

Admission
Museum Free
Roald Dahl Gallery Adult & Child £3.50

Contact
Church Street, Aylesbury HP20 2QP

t 01296 331441
w buckscc.gov.uk/museum
e museum@buckscc.gov.uk

016 Aylesbury

Buckinghamshire Railway Centre

2 hrs+ Apr–Oct

A working steam museum where you can experience the sights, sounds and smells of the golden age of steam. Ride behind a full-sized steam engine or aboard the miniature railway. The centre has a large collection of steam locomotives, carriages and wagons.

* See the Royal Train of 1901
* Santa Steaming on 4 weekends before Christmas

Location
Signed from A41 near Waddesdon & A413 at Whitchurch

Opening
Apr–Oct Wed–Fri 10.30am–4.30pm, weekends 10.30am–5.30pm

Admission
Adult £6, Child £4, Concs £5

Contact
Quainton Road Station, Quainton, Aylesbury HP22 4BY

t 01296 655720
w bucksrailcentre.org
e abaker@bucksrailcentre.btopenworld.com

017 Aylesbury

The King's Head

1 hr All year

This is thought to be one of the oldest surviving courtyard inns in the country. Enclosed by the public area and the stable block, it provided services for the many horse-drawn carriages passing through. Excavation has proved activity on the site from the Bronze Age.

* Secondhand bookshop in Great Hall 11am–3pm
* Large mullioned window contains pieces of C15 glass

Location
At NW corner of Market Square in Aylesbury

Opening
Trust Mon–Fri 9am–6pm, Sat 10am–4pm
Bar Mon–Sun licensing hours

Admission
Adult £2, Child £1

Contact
King's Head Passage,
Market Square, Aylesbury HP20 2RW

t 01296 381501
w nationaltrust.org.uk
e kingshead@nationaltrust.org.uk

018 Aylesbury

Tiggywinkles, The Wildlife Hospital Trust

1 hr+ All year

Since opening its doors, the Wildlife Hospital Trust has treated more than 100,000 patients. Watch and learn about a remarkable number of patients including hedgehogs, badgers, rabbits, deer, wild birds and snakes. Virtually all species of British wildlife feature.

* Hedgehog history museum & baby bird viewing area
* New children's play area & CCTV link to animal hospital

Location
Signed off A418 from Aylesbury

Opening
Easter–Sep Mon–Sun 10am–4pm;
Oct–Easter Mon–Fri 10am–4pm

Admission
Adult £3.20, Child & Concs £3

Contact
Aston Road, Haddenham,
Aylesbury HP17 8AF

t 01844 292292
w sttiggywinkles.com
e mail@sttiggywinkles.org.uk

019 Aylesbury

Waddesdon Manor

2 hrs+ All year

A magnificent French Renaissance-style château built for Baron Ferdinand de Rothschild to display his vast collection of C18 art treasures. It has formal gardens, parkland, a fully stocked rococo-style aviary and wine cellars with more than 15,000 bottles of Rothschild wines.

* Highest-quality French furniture, & decorative arts from C18
* Victorian garden is considered one of the finest in Britain

Location
Via Waddesdon village, 6 miles NW of Aylesbury on A41

Opening
House & Grounds Please phone for details

Admission
House & Grounds Please phone for details

Contact
Waddesdon, Aylesbury HP18 0JH

t 01296 653211/653226
w waddesdon.org.uk
e bookings.waddesdon@nationaltrust.org.uk

020 Brill

Boarstall Tower

1 hr Apr–Oct

Visit the C14 gate house and gardens of Boarstall House (demolished 1778). Built by John de Haudlo in 1312, and updated in 1615 for use as a banqueting pavilion or hunting lodge, the tower has retained its medieval belfry, crossloops and crenellations.

* Many rooms remain virtually unchanged since 1615
* Handsome oriel windows

Location
Midway between Bicester & Thame, 2 miles W of Brill

Opening
27 Apr–30 Oct Wed 2pm–6pm, Bank Hol Sat 11am–4pm, Bank Hol Mon 2pm–6pm

Admission
Adult £2.40, Child £1.20

Contact
Boarstall, Aylesbury HP18 9UX

t 01844 239339
w boarstall.com
e boarstall@erros.co.uk

021 Buckingham

The Old Gaol

½ hr+ All year

The Old Gaol is the landmark building in Buckingham town centre. Restored by the Buckingham Heritage Trust, it houses a fascinating museum that reflects the building's history via an audio-visual display and exhibits of Buckingham's past and military history.

* Regular themed exhibitions
* The ancient cells with their double doors still remain

Location
In town centre

Opening
Mon–Sat 10am–4pm

Admission
Adult £2, Child & Concs £1.50

Contact
Market Hill, Buckingham MK18 1JX

t 01280 823020
w mkheritage.co.uk/ogb
e old.gaol@lineone.net

022 Buckingham

Stowe Landscape Gardens

2 hrs+ All year

This is one of the finest Georgian landscape gardens, comprising valleys, vistas, narrow lakes and rivers. You'll also find more than 40 temples and monuments designed by many of the leading architects of the C18. At the centre is Stowe House, now Stowe School.

* Completed restoration of Corinthian art
* Newly discovered C18 pebble alcove

Location
3 miles NW of Buckingham via Stowe Avenue, off A422

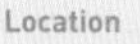

Opening
Feb–Oct Wed–Sun 10.30am–5.30pm; Nov–Feb Weekends 10.30am–4pm

Admission
Adult £6, Child £3

Contact
Buckingham MK18 5EH

 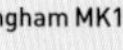

t 01280 822850
w nationaltrust.org.uk
e stowegarden@nationaltrust.org.uk

023 Chalfont St Giles

Chiltern Open-Air Museum

2 hrs+

Apr–Oct

This unusual museum contains more than 30 historic buildings, including a 1940s fully furnished prefab and a working Victorian farm and forge. Set in beautiful open parkland with a nature walk and seat-sculpture trail, the museum is a wonderful place for all ages to visit.

* Explore more than 30 rescued historic buildings
* See hawks and owls in the skipping barn

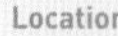

Location
Signposted from A413 at Chalfont St Giles & Chalfont St Peter

Opening
Daily: Apr–Oct 10am–5pm

Admission
Adult £7, Child £4.50, Concs £6

Contact
Newland Park, Gorelands Lane, Chalfont St Giles HP8 4AB

t 01494 871117
w coam.org.uk
e coamuseum@netscape.net

024 Chalfont St Giles

John Milton's Cottage

1 hr+

Mar–Oct

This picturesque late C16 Grade I-listed cottage, set in an attractive garden, is the only surviving building in which the famous writer and parliamentarian lived. It was bought by public subscription in 1887 to celebrate Queen Victoria's jubilee and to preserve it for visitors.

* Milton came here in 1665 to escape the plague
* He completed *Paradise Lost* here

Location
On A40 to Chalfont St Giles, cottage in centre of village

Opening
1 Mar–31 Oct 10am–1pm & 2pm–6pm, closed Mon, except Bank Hol Mon

Admission
Adult £3, Child £1.50

Contact
Chalfont St Giles HP8 4JH

t 01494 872313
w miltonscottage.org
e info@miltonscottage.org

025 High Wycombe

Hellfire Caves

1 hr+

Apr–Oct

These caves were originally excavated in the 1750s by Sir Francis Dashwood on the site of an ancient quarry. It is thought that his inspiration for the design of the caves came from his grand tour of Europe and the Ottoman Empire.

* Sir Francis Dashwood founded the Hellfire Club
* The caves are said to be haunted by Sir Paul Whitehead

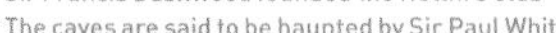

Location
Approximately 3 miles from High Wycombe on A40 towards Oxford

Opening
Apr–Oct Mon–Fri 11am–5.30pm, weekends 11am–5.30pm (last admission 5pm)

Admission
Adult £4, Concs £3

Contact
High Wycombe HP14 3AJ

t 01494 533739
w hellfirecaves.co.uk

026 High Wycombe

Hughenden Manor

2 hrs+

Mar–Oct

The home of Victorian Prime Minister and statesman Benjamin Disraeli from 1848 until his death in 1881. Most of his furniture, books and pictures remain here – his private retreat from parliamentary life in London. There are beautiful walks through the surrounding park.

* Certain rooms have low electric light – avoid dull days
* Events throughout house & park

Location
1 mile N of High Wycombe W of Great Missenden road (A4128)

Opening
House Mar weekends 1pm–5pm; Apr–Oct Wed–Sun 12noon–5pm
Gardens Mar weekends; Apr–Oct Wed–Sun

Admission
Please phone for details

Contact
High Wycombe HP14 4LA

t 01494 755565/755573
w nationaltrust.org.uk
e hughenden@nationaltrust.org.uk

027 High Wycombe

Wycombe Museum

  1 hr+  All year

Trails and special activities combine with imaginative displays to make this a lively museum for visitors. Permanent exhibits, videos and sound recordings tell the story of High Wycombe and the local district.

* Newly refurbished furniture gallery
* Museum art on display

Location
Off A404 towards Amersham

Opening
Mon–Sat 10am–5pm, Sun 2pm–5pm; closed Bank Hols

Admission
Free, donations welcomed

Contact
Priory Avenue,
High Wycombe HP13 6PX

t 01494 421895
w wycombe.gov.uk/museum
e museum@wycombe.gov.uk

028 Milton Keynes

Xscape – Milton Keynes

  7 hrs+  All year

Xscape is a fantastic adrenaline-filled entertainment complex. Try indoor sky-diving in the incredible airkix, learn to ski or snowboard on the UK's longest real-snow slope or test your nerve on Vertical Chill's 13m climbing walls. To relax, enjoy the cinema complex or bowling alley.

* State-of-the-art health & fitness centre
* Wide range of restaurants & bars

Location
Junction 14 of M1 then take A509 & follow signs

Opening
Please phone for details

Admission
Please phone for details

Contact
602 Marlborough Gate,
Milton Keynes MK9 3XS

t 0871 200 3220
w xscape.co.uk
e mkevents@xscape.co.uk

029 Stoke Mandeville

Obsidian Art

1 hr+ All year

This large art gallery houses more than 300 original paintings, ceramics, sculptures, glass and jewellery. It exhibits a wide range of British art, from traditional to modern abstract.

* Regularly changing exhibitions & local artists
* Opportunity to purchase original artwork & gifts

Location
On A4010 S of Stoke Mandeville, follow signs for Goat Centre

Opening
Daily: Mon–Fri 10am–6pm, weekends & Bank Hols 10am–5pm

Admission
Free

Contact
Obsidian Art,
Old Risborough Road,
Stoke Mandeville HP22 5XJ

t 01296 612150
w obsidianart.co.uk
e info@obsidianart.co.uk

030 Wendover

The Chiltern Brewery

1 hr All year

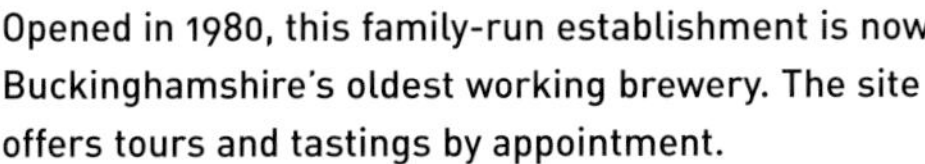

Opened in 1980, this family-run establishment is now Buckinghamshire's oldest working brewery. The site offers tours and tastings by appointment.

* 5 bespoke, award-winning beers are produced here
* Tours on Sat only, booking necessary

Location
On B4009, which joins A413 1 mile from Wendover

Opening
Mon–Sat 9am–5pm

Admission
Free *Tours* £3.95

Contact
Nash Lee Road,Terrick,
Aylesbury HP17 0TQ

t 01296 613647
w chilternbrewery.co.uk
e enquiries@chilternbrewery.co.uk

031 Battle

Battle Abbey & Battlefield

1 hr+ All year

There is almost as much myth surrounding the Battle of Hastings as known fact. The two armies did not even fight at Hastings, but at a place south of the town now named Battle. Visit the ruins of the abbey that William the Conqueror built to commemorate his victory.

* Interactive audio tour recreates the sounds of battle
* Stand on the spot where defeated King Harold fell

Location
In Battle, at S end of high street. Battle is reached by turning off A21 on to A2100 10 mins from Battle station

Opening
Daily: Apr–Sep 10am–6pm; Oct–Mar 10am–4pm

Admission
Adult £6.30, Child £3.20, Concs £4.70

Contact
High Street, Battle TN33 0AD

t 01424 773792
w english-heritage.org.uk

032 Brighton

Brighton Museum & Art Gallery

2 hrs+ All year

The museum has a famous collection of Arts & Crafts, Art Nouveau and Art Deco pieces, Salvador Dali's sofa in the shape of Mae West's lips and stunning gowns from Schiaparelli to Zandra Rhodes. Exhibits include intricate sculptures, decorated masks and beautiful textiles.

* Paintings by Duncan Grant & Edward Lear
* Regularly changing exhibits

Location
In town centre

Opening
Tue 10am–7pm, Wed–Sat 10am–5pm, Sun 2pm–5pm, Bank Hol Mon 10am–5pm

Admission
Free

Contact
Royal Pavilion Gardens,
Brighton BN1 1EE

t 01273 292882
w virtualmuseum.info
e museums@brighton-hove.gov.uk

033 Brighton

Brighton Sea Life Centre

2 hrs+ All year

Originally opened in 1872, the centre combines beautifully restored Victorian architecture with spectacular displays of marine life from shrimps to sharks. It is active in marine conservation projects and in raising awareness about threats to marine life.

* One of the longest underwater tunnels in England
* More than 30 modern marine & freshwater habitats

Location
Take M23/A23 from London or A27 from Portsmouth & Lewes

Opening
Daily: from 10am. Please phone for details of winter opening times

Admission
Please phone for details

Contact
Marine Parade,
Brighton BN2 1TB

t 01273 604234
w sealifeeurope.com
e slcbrighton@merlinentertainment.biz

034 Brighton

The Royal Pavilion

2 hrs+ All year

This former seaside residence of King George IV with its exotic Indian-style exterior boasts myriad domes and minarets. Admire magnificent decorations and furnishings in the Chinese style and gardens replanted to the original Regency scheme. Complete with a superb shop.

* Tactile/Sennheiser tours for partially sighted/hearing
* Audio tours included in admission price

Location
In town centre, 15 min walk from Brighton station

Opening
Daily: Apr–Sep 9.30am–5.45pm (last admission 5pm);
Oct–Mar 10am–5.15pm (last admission 4.30pm)

Admission
Adult £7.50, Child £5, Concs £5.75

Contact
Brighton BN1 1EE

t 01273 290900
w royalpavilion.org.uk
e visitor.services@brightonhove.gov.uk

035 Brighton

University of Brighton Gallery & Theatre

1 hr All year

The presence of some of the country's most innovative artists and students makes this one of the most appealing gallery spaces in the South. The modern gallery presents exhibitions covering many aspects of the arts.

* Frequently changing exhibition programme
* Theatre being renovated late 2006-2007

Location
Grand Parade university campus, central Brighton

Opening
Please phone for details

Admission
Gallery Free
Theatre Please phone for details

Contact
Grand Parade, Brighton BN2 0JY
t 01273 643012
w brighton.ac.uk/gallery-theatre
e c.l.matthews@brighton.ac.uk

036 East Grinstead

Ashdown Forest Llama Park

2 hrs All year

See more than 100 llamas and alpacas! Watch them in the fields or get close to them in the barns. Enjoy farm walks, a museum, a picnic area, a coffee shop, an adventure play area and a lovely shop selling alpaca knitwear and South American crafts.

* Different events throughout the year
* Angora & cashmere goats

Location
Located beside A22, 300 yrds S of junction with A275

Opening
Daily: 10am–5pm

Admission
Adult £4.75, Child & Concs £4

Contact
Wychross, Forest Row RH18 5JN
t 01825 712040
w llamapark.co.uk
e info@llamapark.co.uk

037 Exceat

Seven Sisters Country Park

2 hrs+ All year

Named after the famous Seven Sisters that form part of the Sussex chalk cliffs on Britain's heritage coastline, this site, situated in an Area of Outstanding Natural Beauty, is a popular location for outdoor activities including walking, cycling and canoeing.

* Shop selling leaflets, maps & souvenirs

Location
Off A259 between Eastbourne & Seaford or 12 or 12A bus from Eastbourne

Opening
Easter–Oct daily;
Nov-Oct weekends only

Admission
Free. Car parking fee.

Contact
Exceat, Seaford BN25 4AD
t 01323 870280
w sevensisters.org.uk
e sevensisters@southdowns-aonb.gov.uk

038 Hailsham

Herstmonceux Castle

2–4 hrs Easter–Oct

Herstmonceux is renowned for its magnificent moated castle, beautiful parkland and Elizabethan gardens. Built originally as a country home in the mid-C15, the castle embodies the history of medieval England and the romance of Renaissance Europe.

* Castle is open only to guided tour parties
* Tours last for approximately 1 hour

Location
Off A27 on A22 towards Hailsham

Opening
Castle Please phone for details
Gardens Daily: Easter–Oct 10am–6pm

Admission
Gardens Adult £4.95, Child £3, Concs £3.95 *Castle* £2.50, £1, £2.50

Contact
Hailsham BN27 1RN
t 01323 833816
w herstmonceux-castle.com
e c_dennett@isc.queensu.ac.uk

039 Hailsham

Michelham Priory

2 hrs+ Mar–Oct

England's longest medieval water-filled moat, guarded by a C14 gate house, encloses the remains of an Augustinian priory that incorporates a Tudor mansion. There are 7 acres of picturesque gardens, enhanced by a working watermill and Elizabethan Great Barn.

* House dates back to 1229
* Programme of events throughout the season

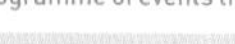

Location
2 miles W of Hailsham. Follow signs from A22 or A27

Opening
Mar–Oct Tue–Sun from 10.30am; daily during August (also open on Bank Hols)

Admission
Adult £5.60, Child £2.90, Concs £4.70

Contact
Upper Dicker, nr Hailsham, East Sussex BN27 3QS

t 01323 844224
w sussexpast.co.uk
e adminmich@sussexpast.co.uk

041 Sheffield Green

Bluebell Railway

1 hr+ All year

This is the UK's first preserved standard-gauge railway, which runs along the Lewes to East Grinstead line of the old London, Brighton and South Coast Railway. It serves to preserve this country branch line, its steam locomotives, coaches and signalling systems.

* Famous Terrier class engines, *Stepney* & *Fenchurch*
* Featured in the film *The Railway Children*

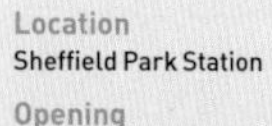

Location
Sheffield Park Station

Opening
Apr–Oct daily 11am–4pm;
Oct–Apr weekends 11am–4pm

Admission
Adult £9.50, Child £4.70, Concs £9

Contact
Sheffield Park Station TN22 3QL

t 01825 720800
w bluebell-railway.co.uk
e info@bluebell-railway.co.uk

040 Pevensey

Pevensey Castle

1 hr All year

The ruins of this medieval castle stand in one corner of a Roman fort, on what was once a peninsula surrounded by the sea and salt marshes. The Roman fort, named Anderida, was built in about AD290. It is one of the largest surviving examples in Britain.

* Britons massacred here by Anglo-Saxons in 491
* William the Conqueror landed his army here in 1066

Location
In Pevensey off A259

Opening
Apr–Sep daily 10am–6pm;
Oct–Mar weekends 10am–4pm

Admission
Adult £3.90, Child £2, Concs £2.90

Contact
High Street, Pevensey BN24 5LE

t 01323 762604
w english-heritage.org.uk

042 Alton

Jane Austen's House

1 hr+

All year

Jane Austen's house is a pleasant C17 house in the pretty village of Chawton, not far from her birthplace of Steventon. The museum houses an attractive collection of items connected with Jane Austen and her family, including the table at which she wrote her novels.

* Pretty garden with varieties of C18 plants & herbs
* Examples of Austen's jewellery & needlework skills

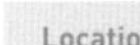

Location
In village of Chawton, 2 miles SW of Alton

Opening
Mar–Dec daily 11am–4.30pm;
Jan–Feb Sat–Sun only 11am–4.30pm

Admission
Adult £4.50, Child £1, Concs £3.50

Contact
Chawton, Alton GU34 1SD

t 01420 83262
w jane-austens-house-museum.org.uk
e enquiries@jahmusm.org.uk

043 Bishop's Waltham

Bishop's Waltham Palace

1 hr

Apr–Sep

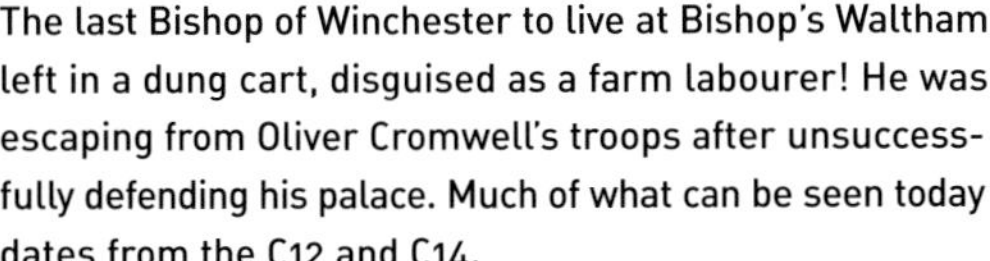

The last Bishop of Winchester to live at Bishop's Waltham left in a dung cart, disguised as a farm labourer! He was escaping from Oliver Cromwell's troops after unsuccessfully defending his palace. Much of what can be seen today dates from the C12 and C14.

* Exhibition on the powerful bishops of Winchester
* Decorative & furnished Victorian farmhouse

Location
5 miles from junction 8 of M27

Opening
Apr–Sep 10am–6pm, closed Sat

Admission
Free Mon–Fri
Sun exhibition Adult £2.80, Child £1.40, Concs £2.10

Contact
Winchester Road,
Bishop's Waltham SO32 1DH

t 01489 892460
w english-heritage.org.uk
e customer@english-heritage.org.uk

044 Brockenhurst

Beaulieu Abbey & National Motor Museum

3 hrs+

All year

Visit the C13 Beaulieu Abbey, Palace House and grounds, and the National Motor Museum. Few car museums in the world can match the unique collection here at Beaulieu, with legendary world-record breakers such as *Bluebird* and *Golden Arrow*.

* Exhibition of James Bond vehicles & props
* Secret Army exhibition, see how Army trained in WWII

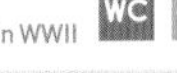

Location
Going W on M27 take A326. Signed Beaulieu or National Motor Museum

Opening
Please phone for details

Admission
Please phone for details

Contact
Brockenhurst SO42 7ZN

t 01590 612123
w beaulieu.co.uk
e info@beaulieu.co.uk

045 East Cowes

Osborne House

3 hrs+ Apr–Sep

Queen Victoria's favourite country home captures the spirit of a world unchanged since the country's longest-reigning monarch died here in 1901. Queen Victoria and Prince Albert rebuilt the original Osborne House in 1845 as a 'modest country home'.

* Indian Durbar Room, with Queen Victoria's gifts from India
* Glorious gardens & Swiss cottage

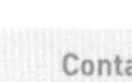

Location
1 mile SE of East Cowes

Opening
Daily: Apr–Sep 10am–4pm

Admission
Please phone for details

Contact
East Cowes, Isle of Wight PO32 6JY

t 01983 200022
w english-heritage.org.uk
e customer@english-heritage.org.uk

046 Fareham

Titchfield Abbey

½ hr All year

An abbey was first founded at Titchfield in the C13 by the Bishop of Winchester. Its history was uneventful until the Dissolution when drastic alterations were made to convert the abbey into a mansion known as Place House. Now a ruin, the remains are magnificent.

* Residents were the Earls of Southampton
* The 3rd Earl was closely connected to Shakespeare

Location
½ mile N of Titchfield off A27

Opening
Daily: Apr–Sep 10am–6pm;
Oct 10am–5pm; Nov–Mar 10am–4pm

Admission
Free

Contact
Mill Lane, Titchfield,
Fareham PO15 5RA

t 01424 775705
w english-heritage.org.uk

047 Fordingbridge

Braemore House & Museum

3 hrs Apr–Sep

This is a large Elizabethan house, set in beautiful parkland, with a Saxon church nearby. Former kitchen gardens house a major countryside museum, village workshops and a reconstructed cottage. Pleasant walks lead to an ancient maze on the Downs.

* Fine collection of pictures & C17 furniture
* Visitors can see displays showing how villages were self-sufficient

Location
3 miles N of Fordingbridge, off A338

Opening
House 2pm–5.30pm (last tour 4.15pm)
Dates vary; please phone for details
Museum 1pm–5.30pm. Dates vary; please phone for details

Admission
Adult £7, Child £5, Concs £6

Contact
nr Fordingbridge SP6 2DF

t 01725 512468
w braemorehouse.com
e braemore@ukonline.co.uk

048 Gosport

Explosion! The Museum of Naval Firepower

2 hrs+ All year

An award-winning visitor experience on the shores of Portsmouth Harbour, Explosion! tells the story of naval warfare from the days of gunpowder to the Exocet. A hands-on, interactive museum set in the historic buildings of the Navy's former armaments depot.

* Trafalgar Gunpowder Trail in main museum

Location
M27 to junction 11. Follow A32 to Gosport & brown tourist signs

Opening
Daily: Apr–Oct 10am–5.30pm; Nov–Mar Thu, Sat & Sun 10am–4.30pm

Admission
Adult £5.50, Child £3.50, Concs £4.50

Contact
Priddy's Hard, Gosport PO12 4LE

t 02392 505600
w explosion.org.uk
e info@explosion.org.uk

049 Lymington

Hurst Castle

3 hrs+ Apr–Oct

Hurst Castle was built by Henry VIII as one of a chain of coastal fortresses and it was completed in 1544. The location was perfect to defend the western approach to the Solent. Charles I was imprisoned here in 1648 before being taken to London for his trial and execution.

* Modernised during the Napoleonic wars
* 2 huge 38-ton guns

Location
By ferry from Keyhaven or on foot from Milford-on-Sea

Opening
Daily: Apr–Sep 10.30am–5.30pm; Oct 10.30am–4pm

Admission
Adult £3, Child £1.80, Concs £2.80

Contact
Hurst Spit, Keyhaven, Lymington SO41 0QU

t 01590 642500
w hurst-castle.co.uk
e info@hurst-castle.co.uk

050 Newport

Carisbrooke Castle

1 hr + All year

Built more than 1,000 years ago, this castle has a rich and varied history. Since time immemorial, whoever controlled Carisbrooke controlled the Isle of Wight. The castle has been a feature of the island since its foundation as a Saxon camp during the C18.

* Remnants of a Saxon wall & a Norman keep
* C15 treadmill operated to this day by donkeys

Location
1 mile SW of Newport on B3323

Opening
Daily: Apr–Sep 10am–5pm;
Oct–Mar 10am–4pm

Admission
Adult £5.50, Child £2.80, Concs £4.10

Contact
Carisbrooke, Newport, Isle of Wight

t 01983 522107
w english-heritage.org.uk

051 Newport

Classic Boat Museum

1 hr Mar–Nov

A fine indoor collection of lovingly restored sailing and motorised classic boats from the C19. Highlights include the ultimate sailing boat, HRH Prince Philip's *Flying 15 Cowslip*, WWII airborne lifeboats and a *Cockleshell Heroes* canoe. Displays of engines, equipment and memorabilia.

* Displays & boats change annually
* Items from *Gypsy Moth IV* on view

Location
Through Sea Close Park

Opening
Daily: Mar–Nov 10am–4.30pm

Admission
Adult £3, Child £1, Concs £2

Contact
Sea Close Wharf, Newport,
Isle of Wight PO30 2EF

t 01983 533493
w classicboatmuseum.org
e cbmiow@fsmail.net

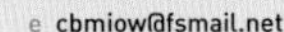

052 Petersfield

Queen Elizabeth Country Park

3 hrs+ All year

This park forms part of the landscape of the South Downs and falls in the East Hampshire Area of Outstanding Natural Beauty. There are 1,400 acres of open access woodland and downland. The park features trackways, barrows, lynchets and the site of a Roman farmstead.

* Visitor centre
* National nature reserve

Location
In SE Hampshire, 4 miles
S of Petersfield

Opening
Daily: Please phone for details

Admission
Car park £1 per day Mon–Sat;
£1.50 per day Sun & Bank Hols

Contact
Gravel Hill, Horndean,
Waterlooville PO8 0QE

t 02392 595040
w hants.gov.uk/countryside/qecp
e info.centres@hants.gov.uk

053 Portsmouth

Charles Dickens' Birthplace Museum

1 hr+ Apr–Oct

Charles Dickens was born in this modest house in Portsmouth in 1812. It is now preserved as a museum furnished in the style of 1809, the year in which Dickens' parents John and Elizabeth began their married life together.

* Regency-style furniture & household objects
* Charles Dickens & Portsmouth exhibition

Location
Just off A3 heading S towards city centre

Opening
Daily: Apr–Sep 10am–5.30pm; Oct 10am–5pm

Admission
Adult £3, Child & Concs £1.80

Contact
393 Old Commercial Road, Portsmouth PO1 4QL

t 02392 827261
w charlesdickensbirthplace.co.uk
e david.evans@portsmouthcc.gov.uk

054 Portsmouth

Portsmouth Historic Dockyard

2 hrs+ All year

This is the home of the Tudor warship *Mary Rose*, Admiral Lord Nelson's flagship HMS *Victory*, the mighty iron-hulled HMS *Warrior* (1860), the Royal Naval Museum and the attraction Action Stations. Together they make Portsmouth Historic Dockyard an essential place to visit.

* Naval Dreadnought exhibition in fiction station
* New interactive gallery

Location
Follow Historic Waterfront & Historic Dockyard signs from junction 12 of M27

Opening
Daily: Apr–Oct 10am–6pm (last admission 4.30pm); Nov–March 10am–5.30pm (last admission 4pm)

Admission
Adult £16, Child &Concs £13

Contact
Visitor Centre, College Road, HM Naval Base, Portsmouth PO1 3LJ

t 02392 839766
w historicdockyard.co.uk
e enquiries@historicdockyard.co.uk

055 Portsmouth

Royal Garrison Church

1 hr

Apr–Sep

This church was constructed around 1212 as a hostel for pilgrims. It was also used as a store for weapons and ammunition before becoming a garrison church in the 1560s. The church was badly damaged in 1941 and modern windows tell the story of the building.

* Charles II married Catherine of Braganza here in 1662
* Once known as the Cathedral Church of the British Army

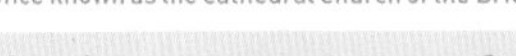

Location
On Grand Parade S of Portsmouth high street

Opening
Apr–Sep Mon–Sat 11am–4pm

Admission
Free

Contact
Grand Parade, Old Portsmouth

t 02392 823973/735521
w english-heritage.org.uk

056 Portsmouth

Spinnaker Tower

1 hr

All year

A contemporary national icon on the South coast, providing a unique 'window on the sea', the Spinnaker Tower is a striking new seamark. Soaring 170 metres above Portsmouth Harbour, it offers visitors spectacular views from a great height.

* Lift to upper levels
* Cross Europe's largest glass floor on Level 1

Location
Come in to Portsmouth on M275 and follow brown tourist signs to Historic Waterfront, then Spinnaker Tower

Opening
Jun–Sep daily 10am–10pm; Oct–May Sun–Fri 10am–5pm; Sat 10am–10pm

Admission
Adult £5.95, Child £4.80, Concs £5.40

Contact
Gunwharf Quays, Portsmouth PO1 3TT

t 02392 857520
w spinnakertower.co.uk
e info@spinnakertower.co.uk

057 Romsey

Mottisfont Abbey

2 hrs+ Mar–Oct

This C12 Augustinian priory boasts sweeping lawns and magnificent old trees, set amid glorious countryside. Medieval monastic remains include a cellarium and original stonework revealed through cut-away sections of the building.

* Unusual *trompe-l'oeil* painting by Rex Whistler
* National Collection of old-fashioned roses

Location
4½ miles NW of Romsey, 1 mile W of A3057

Opening
Mar–May & Sep–Oct 11am–6pm, closed Thu & Fri;
Jun daily 11.30am–8.30pm;
July–Aug 11am–6pm, closed Fri

Admission
Adult £7, Child £3.50

Contact
Mottisfont, nr Romsey SO51 0LP

t 01794 340757
w nationaltrust.org.uk
e mottisfontabbey@nationaltrust.org.uk

058 Romsey

Sir Harold Hillier Gardens

3 hrs+ All year

These gardens, which were formerly known as the Hillier Arboretum, hold the greatest collection of hardy trees and shrubs in the world. Started by the late Sir Harold Hillier in 1953, the gardens now extend to 180 acres.

* Gurkha memorial garden, gift shop & new plant shop
* Largest winter garden of its kind in Europe

Location
Between Ampfield & Braishfield, 2 miles NE of Romsey

Opening
Daily: 10am–6pm

Admission
Adult £7.50, Child free, Concs £6.50

Contact
Jermyns House, Jermyns Lane, Ampfield, Romsey SO51 0QA

t 01794 368787
w hilliergardens.org.uk
e info@hilliergardens.org.uk

059 Shanklin

Shanklin Chine

1 hr Easter–Oct

This historic gorge has formed over the past 10,000 years and boasts a unique collection of flora and fauna, many extremely rare. There is a designated trail with numbered stopping places. The Chine drops 105ft to sea level and covers an area of approximately 3 acres.

* More than 150 varieties of wild plants
* 45ft waterfall

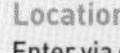    

Location
Enter via old village, off A3055 or through W of Shanklin Esplanade, off Chine Hill

Opening
31 March–25 May 10am–5pm;
26 May–10 Sep 10am–10pm;
11 Sep–29 Oct 10am–5pm

Admission
Adult £3.75, Child £2, Concs £2.75

Contact
12 Ponona Road, Shanklin, Isle of Wight PO37 6PF

t 01983 866432
w shanklinchine.co.uk
e jillshanklinchine@hotmail.co.uk

060 Southampton

Southampton City Art Gallery

2 hrs+ All year

This gallery is internationally renowned for its impressive collection of contemporary works by British artists. A fine selection of works by the Camden Town Group, plus paintings by Sir Stanley Spencer, Matthew Smith and Philip Wilson Steer are brought together.

* Pre-Raphaelite work by Sir Coley-Burne-Jones
* Regular exhibitions throughout the year

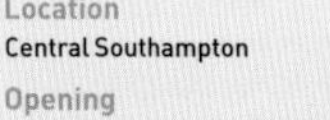

Location
Central Southampton

Opening
Tue–Sat 10am–5pm, Sun 1pm–4pm, closed 21 Dec–2 Jan & Good Friday

Admission
Free

Contact
Civic Centre, Commercial Road, Southampton SO14 7LP

t 02380 832277
w southampton.gov.uk/art
e art.gallery@southampton.gov.uk

061 Southsea

The D-Day Museum & Overlord Embroidery

1 hr+ All year

This museum was established in 1984 to tell the story of Operation Overlord from its origins in the dark days of 1940 to victory in Normandy in 1944. The museum's centrepiece is the Overlord embroidery.

* Audio-visual theatre
* Dawn-to-dusk reconstruction of the Allied landings

Location
On seafront, 2 miles from town centre

Opening
Daily: Apr–Sep 10am–5.30pm; Oct–Mar 10am–5pm

Admission
Adult £6, Child £3.60, Concs £4.50

Contact
Clarence Esplanade, Southsea PO5 3NT

t 02392 827261
w ddaymuseum.co.uk
e museumvisitorcentre@portsmouthcc.gov.uk

062 Stockbridge

Museum of Army Flying

2 hrs+ All year

Celebrating more than 100 years of army aviation, this award-winning museum houses one of the country's finest collections of military kites, gliders, aeroplanes and helicopters. Trace the development of army flying from the Royal Flying Corps to the present day.

* 1940s house, children's centre, rifle range & flight simulator
* Viewing gallery overlooking airfield

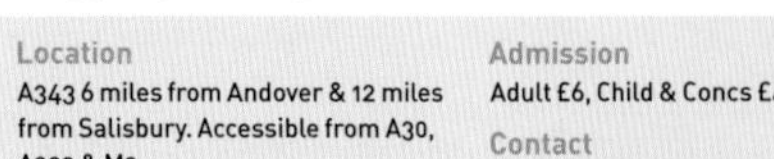

Location
A343 6 miles from Andover & 12 miles from Salisbury. Accessible from A30, A303 & M3

Opening
Daily: 10am–4.30pm

Admission
Adult £6, Child & Concs £4

Contact
Middle Wallop, Stockbridge SO20 8DY

t 01264 784421
w flying-museum.org.uk
e enquiries@flying-museum.org.uk

063 Ventnor

Ventnor Botanic Garden

2 hrs+ All year

This is one of the youngest botanic gardens in Britain. The southern edge of the garden comprises clifftop grassland and cliffs, and the eastern end is backed by a cliff face to the north. Try to identify the large number of native British flowers.

* Japanese plant collection & visitor centre
* Southern hemisphere plant collection

Location
Southern tip of Isle of Wight

Opening
Visitor centre Apr–Jun & Sep daily 10am–5pm; Jul–Aug daily 10am–6pm; Oct–Mar weekends 10am–4pm
Gardens Open all year

Admission
Free

Contact
Undercliff Drive, Ventnor, Isle of Wight PO38 1UL
t 01983 855397
w botanic.co.uk
e simon.goodenough@iow.gov.uk

064 Winchester

INTECH-Hands-on Science & Technology Centre

2 hrs+ All year

This unique hands-on interactive science and technology centre houses more than 100 exhibits designed to amuse and enthuse. Here you will understand how to bend light, create your own tornado spout and vortex and work out how much energy it takes to power a lightbulb.

* Regularly changing exhibitions
* Gift shop with unusual & educational items

Location
Junction 10S & junction 9N on M3 then take A31 & follow signs

Opening
Daily: 10am–4pm

Admission
Adult £6.50, Child £4, Concs £5

Contact
INTECH, Telegraph Way, Morn Hill, Winchester SO21 1HX
t 01962 863791
w intech-uk.com
e htct@intech-uk.com

065 Winchester

Winchester Cathedral

1 hr+ All year

At this 900-year-old cathedral are memorials to Jane Austen and Isaac Walton and a unique collection of chantry chapels. Hear the story of the diver, William Walker, who saved the cathedral in 1906. The crypt boasts the Anthony Gormley Sound II sculpture.

* The longest medieval cathedral
* The Winchester Bible, finest of the great C12 bibles

Location
In town centre

Opening
Daily: Mon–Sat 8.30am–6pm, Sun 8.30am–5pm

Admission
Adult £4, Child free, Concs £3.50, donations welcomed

Contact
Cathedral Office, 1 The Close, Winchester SO23 9LS
t 01962 857200
w winchester-cathedral.org.uk
e cathedral.office@winchester-cathedral.org.uk

066 Wroxall

Appuldurcombe House Owl & Falconry Centre

2 hrs+ Apr–Oct

Visit the ruin of Appuldurcombe, designed by Capability Brown and once the grandest house on the Isle of Wight. A display of prints and photographs depicts the house and its history. The former servants' quarters are now home to an owl and falconry centre.

* Old brew house used for indoor bird flying
* Horseback falconry flying

Location
In Wroxall off B3327 to Ventnor

Opening
Daily: Jul–Aug 10am–5pm; Apr–Jun & Sep–Oct 10am–4pm

Admission
Please phone for details

Contact
Wroxall, Isle of Wight PO38 3EW
t 01983 852484
w appuldurcombe.co.uk
e events@appuldurcombe.co.uk

067 Ashford

Godinton House & Gardens

1 hr+ Mar–Oct

Built in the C14, Godinton House is one of the most fascinating homes in Kent whose history, from its medieval origins to the present day, is revealed through the variety of its style, taste and furnishings. And it is set in glorious gardens.

* Collection of porcelain, pictures & furniture
* 3 stunning delphinium borders best mid-Jun–Jul

Location
Junction 9 off M20 & take A20 towards Ashford

Opening
House 6 Apr–7 Oct Fri–Sun 2pm–5.30pm (last tour at 4.30pm)
Gardens 24 Mar–28 Oct Thu–Mon 2pm–5.30pm

Admission
House & Gardens £6, Child free
Gardens Adult £3, Child free

Contact
Godinton Lane, Ashford TN23 3BP

t 01233 620773
w godinton-house-gardens.co.uk
e ghpt@godinton.fsnet.co.uk

068 Canterbury

Canterbury Cathedral

1 hr+ All year

Founded in AD 597 by St Augustine, a missionary from Rome, the cathedral has been the home of Christianity in England for 1,400 years and has attracted thousands of pilgrims each year since the murder of Archbishop Thomas à Becket in 1170.

* Site of the murder of Archbishop Thomas à Becket
* Stained-glass windows from the C12

Location
In city centre, off high street

Opening
Daily: *summer* 9am–6pm (last admission 5.30pm) *winter* 9am–5.30pm (last admission 4.30pm)

Admission
Adult £6, Child & Concs £4.50

Contact
Cathedral House, 11 The Precinct, Canterbury CT1 2EH

t 01227 762862
w canterbury-cathedral.org
e enquiries@canterbury-cathedral.org

069 Canterbury

The Canterbury Tales

1 hr+ All year

This fascinating audio-visual experience, sited in the centre of Canterbury, is one of the town's most popular visitor attractions. Step back in time to experience the sights, sounds and smells of the Middle Ages in this stunning reconstruction of C14 England.

* Uses headsets with earphones
* Recreates the pilgrimages of Chaucerian England

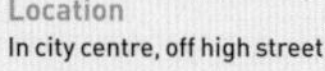

Location
In city centre, off high street

Opening
Daily: Mar–Jun 10am–5pm; Jul–Aug 9.30am–5.30pm; Sep–Oct 10am–5pm; Nov–Jan 10am–4pm

Admission
Adult £7.25, Child £5.25, Concs £6.25

Contact
St Margaret's Street, Canterbury CT1 2TG

t 01227 479227
w canterburytales.org.uk
e info@canterburytales.org.uk

070 Canterbury

Roman Museum

1 hr All year

This underground museum is an exciting mix of excavated real objects, authentic reconstructions and remains of a Roman town house with mosaics. Reconstructions include a Roman market place, with a shoemaker's workshop and fruit and vegetable stall.

* Computer reconstruction shows the Roman house
* Touch-screen computer game on Roman technology

Location
Butchery Lane, close to cathedral

Opening
Mon–Sat 10am–5pm (last admission 4pm); Jun–Oct also open Sun 1.30pm–5pm

Admission
Adult £3, Child & Concs £1.85

Contact
Longmarket, Butchery Lane, Canterbury CT1 2JE

t 01227 785575
w canterburymuseums.co.uk
e museums@canterbury.gov.uk

071 Chatham

The Historic Dockyard, Chatham

4 hrs+ Feb–Nov

Housed in wonderful Victorian and Georgian buildings, the dockyard complex brings 400 years of naval history to life. Attractions include historic warships, the RNLI national collection and the Wooden Walls exhibition with the sights, sounds and smells of the dockyard in 1758.

* Costume guided tour of the Ropery
* Nelson's flagship HMS *Victory* was built here

Location
Leave M2 at junction 1 or 4 & follow signs

Opening
Daily: 10 Feb–24 Mar 10am–4pm; 25 Mar–28 Oct 10am–6pm (last admission 4pm); Nov weekends only 10am–4pm

Admission
Adult £11.50, Child £6.50, Concs £9

Contact
Chatham ME4 4TZ

t 01634 823807
w thedockyard.co.uk
e info@chdt.org.uk

072 Chislehurst

Chislehurst Caves

1 hr All year

Grab a lantern and get ready for an amazing adventure! In these caves the whole family can travel back in time and explore the maze of passageways deep beneath Chislehurst. During a 45-minute guided tour, visit the Caves Church, Druid Altar, Haunted Pool and more.

* Lamp-lit tours & gift shop
* Original WWII air-raid shelter

Location
Take the A222 between A20 & A21. At railway bridge turn into Station Approach then right again to Caveside Close

Opening
School hols daily 10am–4pm (except Christmas). Rest of year Wed–Sun 10am–4pm

Admission
Adult £5, Child £3 & £3

Contact
Old Hill, Chislehurst BR7 5NB

t 020 8467 3264
w chislehurstcaves.co.uk
e enquiries@chislehurstcaves.co.uk

073 Dover

Dover Castle

4 hrs+ All year

Commanding the shortest Channel sea crossing, this site has been the UK's most important defence against invasion since the Iron Age. It was built in the C12 and reinforced by Henry VIII in the 1530s. Underneath the nearby White Cliffs is a series of underground tunnels.

* Reconstruction of Henry VIII's visit in 1539
* Visit the WWII underground hospital

Location
Clearly signed to E of city, on the white cliffs

Opening
Mar–Sep daily 10am–6pm; Oct daily 10am–5pm; Nov–Jan Thu–Mon 10am–4pm; Feb–Mar daily 10am–4pm

Admission
Please phone for details

Contact
Dover CT16 1HU

t 01304 211067
w english-heritage.org.uk

074 Dover

South Foreland Lighthouse

½ hr Mar–Oct

Built in 1843, this distinctive landmark on the white cliffs was the first lighthouse to display an electrically powered signal. It was used by Marconi for his first successful international radio transmission.

* Original 3500-watt lamp on display
* Leaflets on local walks available

Location
2½ miles NE along coast from Dover. 2-mile walk from NT car park

Opening
Guided tour Mar–Oct Mon–Fri 11am–5pm, Sat–Sun 11am–5.30pm; school hols daily

Admission
Adult £3.60, Child £1.80

Contact
The Front, St Margaret's Bay, Dover CT15 6HP

t 01304 852463
w nationaltrust.org.uk
e southforeland@nationaltrust.org.uk

075 Edenbridge

Hever Castle & Gardens

4 hrs Mar–Nov

This romantic C13 castle was the childhood home of Anne Boleyn. It is set in magnificent gardens, which include a formal Italian garden, a lake and a Sunday walk. There is a water maze on Sixteen Acre Island and the Yew Maze Challenge.

* Costumed figure exhibition
* Historic instruments of execution & torture

Location
3 miles SE of Edenbridge off B2026 between Sevenoaks & East Grinstead

Opening
Daily: Mar–Nov
Castle 12noon–6pm (last admission 5pm); Mar & Nov 11am–4pm
Gardens 11am–6pm

Admission
Castle & Gardens Adult £9.80, Child £5.30, Concs £8.20
Gardens £7.80, £5, £6.70

Contact
Edenbridge TN8 7NG

t 01732 865224
w hevercastle.co.uk
e mail@hevercastle.co.uk

076 Eynsford

Eagle Heights Bird of Prey Centre

  4 hrs+  Jan–Nov

With more than 100 birds in indoor and outdoor aviaries, the centre gives visitors the opportunity to see birds of prey in action during flying displays, promoting conservation through education. It also provides sanctuary for injured and unwanted animals.

* 5-day falconry courses available
* Now housing otters

Location
Off M25 at junction 3 on to A20, or M20 at junction 1

Opening
Daily: Mar–Oct 10.30am–5pm; Nov, Jan & Feb weekends 11am–4pm

Admission
Adult £6.95, Child £4.95, Concs £5.95

Contact
Lullingstone Lane, Eynsford DA4 0JB

t 01322 866466
w eagleheights.co.uk
e office@eagleheights.co.uk

077 Eynsford

Lullingstone Roman Villa

  1 hr+  All year

One of the best-preserved Roman villas in England, Lullingstone was built in AD75 and rediscovered in 1949. It is now housed in a modern two-storey building. Renowned for its mosaics, it also features a fresco and a bathing complex.

* Free audio tour
* Gift shop

Location
Off M25 at junction 3, just outside Eynsford on A225

Opening
Please phone for details

Admission
Please phone for details

Contact
Lullingstone Lane, Eynsford DA4 0JA

t 01322 863467
w english-heritage.org.uk
e customers@english-heritage.org.uk

078 Goudhurst

Bedgebury Pinetum

  3 hrs  All year

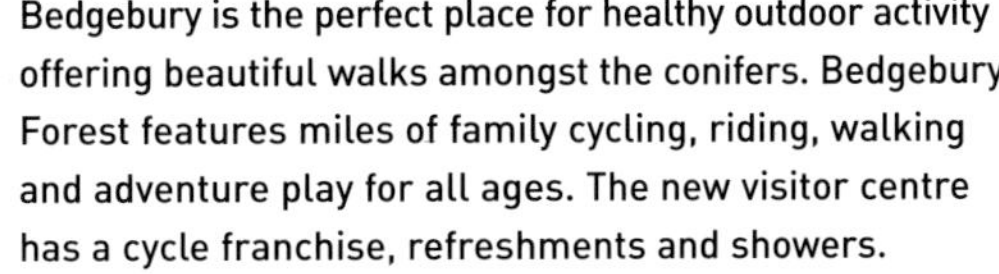

Bedgebury is the perfect place for healthy outdoor activity offering beautiful walks amongst the conifers. Bedgebury Forest features miles of family cycling, riding, walking and adventure play for all ages. The new visitor centre has a cycle franchise, refreshments and showers.

* Come to the Forest for healthy outdoor activity
* Come to the Pinetum for beauty and tranquility

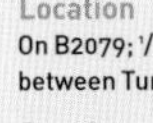

Location
On B2079; ½ a mile from the A21, between Tunbridge Wells & Hastings

Opening
Daily: 8am–7pm (revised seasonally; please phone for details)

Admission
Car parking ticket £5

Contact
Park Lane, Goudhurst TN17 2SL

t 01580 211781
w forestry.gov.uk/bedgebury
e bedgebury@forestry.gov.uk

079 Goudhurst

Finchcocks Living Museum of Music

3 hrs Mar–Sep

This Georgian manor house in the Kent countryside has a huge collection of historical keyboard musical instruments, and contains the world's largest collection of playing instruments. The house is noted for its dramatic brickwork and its beautiful and tranquil garden.

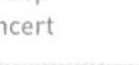     

* Annual music festival & special events in Sep
* All openings include a demonstration concert

Location
Take A262, Goudhurst turning, from A21 & follow signs

Opening
Easter–Sep Sun 2pm–6pm, Mon–Sat by appointment;
Aug Wed –Thu 2pm–6pm;
Bank Hols 2pm–6pm

Admission
House & Gardens Adult £8, Child £4
Gardens only £2.50

Contact
Finchcocks, Goudhurst TN17 1HH

t 01580 211702
w finchcocks.co.uk
e katrina@finchcocks.co.uk

080 Hamstreet

South of England Rare Breeds Centre

3 hrs All year

Here's a chance to meet and pet all your favourite friendly farm animals as you wander around a farm trail. The centre is also home to many endangered and rare British animals. Set in acres of beautiful woodland, there are plenty of places to picnic while the kids play.

* Woodland activity quiz trail
* Piglet racing in season & trailer rides

Location
Leave M20 at junction 10, follow signs to Brenzett and Hamstreet. Situated between Hamstreet & Woodchurch

Opening
Apr–Sep daily 10.30am–5.30pm;
Oct–Mar Tue–Sun 10.30am–4.30pm

Admission
Adult & Child £6.60, Concs £5.50

Contact
Woodchurch, Ashford TN26 3RJ

t 01233 861493
w rarebreeds.org.uk
e visit@rarebreeds.org.uk

081 Lamberhurst

Bewl Water

1 hr+ All year

This reservoir is the largest area of open water in the South East. Set in an Area of Outstanding Natural Beauty, Bewl is home to a huge variety of wildlife. There are many exciting outdoor pursuits here, including windsurfing, fishing, cycling and walking.

* Water-efficient garden
* Interactive exhibition

Location
1 mile S of Lamberhurst, signed from A21

Opening
Daily: Mar–Oct 9am–sunset;
winter 9am–4pm

Admission
Car park Apr–Oct £5, Nov–Mar £2.50

Contact
Bewl Water Reservoir,
nr Lamberhurst TN3 8JH

t 01892 890661
w bewl.co.uk
e bewl@southernwater.co.uk

082 Maidstone

Leeds Castle

3 hrs All year

This medieval castle, situated on two islands in a lake set in 500 acres of parkland, is a popular attraction. Once a Norman stronghold, the castle has since been residence for six of England's medieval queens, a palace for Henry VIII and a retreat for the powerful.

* Open-air concert programme
* Grand Firework spectacular

Location
Leave M20 at junction 8. Castle is 7 miles E of Maidstone

Opening
Daily: Apr–Sep 10am–5pm;
Oct–Mar 10am–3pm

Admission
Adult £13.50, Child £8, Concs £11

Contact
Maidstone ME17 1PL

t 01622 765400
w leeds-castle.com
e enquiries@leeds-castle.co.uk

083 Maidstone

Museum of Kent Life

2 hrs+ Feb–Nov

A unique open-air living museum that celebrates 250 years of Kentish history. Traditional crafts are shown on a working farm. This is one of the only places in England where hops are grown, harvested, dried and packed by hand, using time-honoured techniques.

* Calendar of events throughout the year
* Hop-picking festival in Sep

Location
Off M20 at junction 6. Follow signs

Opening
Daily: Feb–Nov 10am–5pm

Admission
Adult £7, Child £5, Concs £5.20

Contact
Cobtree, Lock Lane, Sandling, Maidstone ME14 3AU

t 01622 763936
w museum-kentlife.co.uk
e enquiries@museum-kentlife.co.uk

084 New Romney

Romney, Hythe & Dymchurch Railway

2 hrs All year

This was the world's smallest public railway when it opened in July 1927. It now runs passenger services covering a distance of 13½ miles from the picturesque Cinque Port of Hythe, near the Channel Tunnel, to the fishermen's cottages and lighthouses at Dungeness.

* Thomas the Tank Engine & Santa specials
* Dining-train specials

Location
The stations at New Romney, Dungeness and Hythe are all on or near A259 trunk road

Opening
Trains run daily Apr–Sep & weekends Oct & Mar. Please phone or visit the website for timetable

Admission
Adult £5–£11, Child half-fare

Contact
New Romney TN28 8PL

t 01797 362353
w rhdr.org.uk
e info@rhdr.org.uk

085 Penshurst

Penshurst Place & Gardens

3 hrs+ Mar–Oct

This medieval manor house was built in 1341. The Great Hall, with its 60ft-high, chestnut-beamed roof and trestle tables, is regarded as one of the world's grandest rooms. Much of the house and the gardens remain unchanged since the days when Elizabeth I made her visits here.

* Includes a fabulous toy museum
* Children's adventure playground

Location
Leave M25 at junction 5 or M20/M26 at junction 2a, follow A21 to Hildenborough, then signs

Opening
Daily: Mar–Oct *House* 12noon–4pm; *Gardens* 10.30am–6pm

Admission
House & Gardens Adult £7, Child £5, Concs £6.50 *Gardens* £5.50, £4.50, £5

Contact
Penshurst TN11 8DG

t 01892 870307
w penshurstplace.com
e enquiries@penshurstplace.com

086 Sevenoaks

Knole

2 hrs+ Mar–Oct

This great house is set in a magnificent deer park. The original C15 house was enlarged and embellished in 1603 and has remained largely unaltered since then. State rooms house a superb collection of furniture, tapestries and paintings.

* Virtual-reality tour of state rooms
* Children's period costume events

Location
Sevenoaks town centre, off A225

Opening
House 25 Mar–29 Oct Wed–Sun 12noon–4pm;
Gardens 25 Mar–29 Oct Wed 11am–4pm

Admission
House Adult £7.50, Child £3.75
Gardens £2, £1

Contact
Sevenoaks TN15 0RP

t 01732 462100
w nationaltrust.org.uk
e knole@nationaltrust.org.uk

087 Sissinghurst

Sissinghurst Castle Garden

2 hrs+ Mar–Oct

This is one of the world's most celebrated gardens, created by Vita Sackville-West and her husband Sir Harold Nicolson, in the ruins of a large Elizabethan house. The library and tower, which are open to the public, include Vita's writing room.

* History of the house & the making of the garden
* Restaurant uses local recipes & produce

Location
1 mile E of Sissinghurst on A262

Opening
Mid-Mar–Oct Mon, Tue & Fri 11am–6.30pm, weekends 10am–6.30pm (last admission 1hr before close)
Woodland walks Open all year

Admission
Please phone for details.
Woodland Free

Contact
Sissinghurst, nr Cranbrook TN17 2AB

t 01580 710701/710700
w nationaltrust.org.uk
e sissinghurst@nationaltrust.org.uk

088 Tenterden

The Chapel Down Winery

2 hrs+ All year

This 25-acre vineyard is at the forefront of the English winemaking industry. Visitors are free to wander around the winery, vineyard and herb garden. Guided tours explain the winemaking process in more detail. A free wine tasting follows each tour.

* Café, wine & gift shop
* Guided tours available during the summer months

Location
From Tenterden (A28), turn on to B2082 to Wittersham & Rye. Vineyard is 2 miles on the right at Small Hythe

Opening
Daily: 10am–5pm

Admission
Free
Tours Adult £6.50, 12–17 yrs £2, Under 12s free, Concs £5.50

Contact
Small Hythe, Tenterden TN30 7NG

t 01580 766111
w englishwinesgroup.com
e tourism@englishwinesgroup.com

089 Tunbridge Wells

Groombridge Place Gardens & The Enchanted Forest

  4 hrs+  Apr–Nov

Groombridge Place's history dates back to medieval times. Flanked by a deep moat, and with a classical C17 manor as its backdrop, the formal gardens boast a rich variety of lawns and flower displays. High above the walled gardens and vineyard lies the Enchanted Forest.

* Bird of prey raptor centre
* Maze & gift shop

Location
A26 towards Tunbridge Wells, turn right on to B2176 towards Penshurst. 3 miles past Penshurst village. Turn left at T junction with A264. Follow signs

Opening
Daily: Apr–Nov 10am–5.30pm

Admission
Adult £8.70, Child & Concs £7.20

Contact
The Estate Office, Groombridge Place, Groombridge, Royal Tunbridge Wells TN3 9QG

t 01892 861444
w groombridge.co.uk
e office@groombridge.co.uk

090 Tunbridge Wells

The Hop Farm

  3 hrs+  All year

Situated among a collection of Victorian oast houses, there is a multitude of attractions and exhibitions to enjoy. Take an interactive look at Kent over the past century, learn about the history of hop-picking and enjoy the impressive military and horse-drawn vehicle collections.

* Special events throughout the year
* Indoor and outdoor adventure play areas

Location
Located on A228 near Paddock Wood, Kent. Follow brown tourist signs from junction 4 of M20 or junction 5 of M25 on to A21 S

Opening
Daily: 10am–5pm (last admission 4pm)

Admission
Adults £7.50, Child (3–15yrs) £6.50, Under-3s free (prices will vary on event days)

Contact
Paddock Wood TN12 6PY

t 0870 027 4166
w thehopfarm.co.uk

©NTPL/Andreas von Einsiedel

091 Westerham

Chartwell

  2 hrs+  Apr–Oct

The home of Winston Churchill for more than 40 years, Chartwell remains as it was in his day. With many personal possessions and reminders of the man voted greatest Briton of all time, the house captures the mood of a key period in British history.

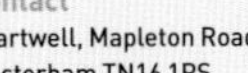
* Exhibition of sound recordings
* Collection of Churchill's paintings

Location
2 miles S of Westerham, turn off A25 on to B2026. Follow signs

Opening
Apr–Oct Wed–Sun 11am–5pm; July–Aug Tue & Bank Hols as well

Admission
Adult £10, Child £5

Contact
Chartwell, Mapleton Road, Westerham TN16 1PS

t 01732 866368
w nationaltrust.org.uk
e chartwell@nationaltrust.org.uk

092 Bloomsbury

The British Museum

2 hrs+ All year

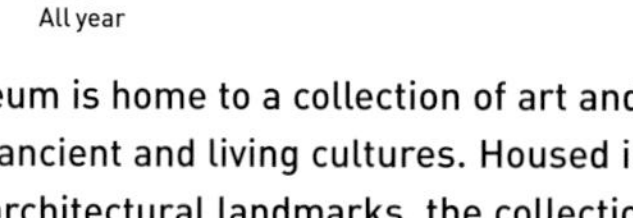

The British Museum is home to a collection of art and antiquities from ancient and living cultures. Housed in one of Britain's architectural landmarks, the collection is one of the finest in existence, spanning two million years of human history.

* Spectacular covered courtyard

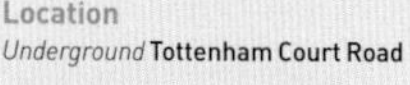

Location
Underground Tottenham Court Road

Opening
Daily: Sat–Wed 10am–5.30pm, Thu–Fri 10am–8.30pm (selected galleries 5.30pm–8.30pm)

Admission
Free, exhibitions may charge

Contact
Great Russell Street, London WC1B 3DG

t 020 7323 8299
w thebritishmuseum.ac.uk
e information@thebritishmuseum.ac.uk

093 Bloomsbury

The Charles Dickens Museum

1 hr All year

Charles Dickens lived in this house between 1837 and 1839 and wrote several of his most famous novels during that time. The house is now the world's foremost repository of Dickens-related material and the headquarters of the Dickens Fellowship.

* Celebrating an 80th anniversary
* Collection of letters, first editions & portraits

Location
Underground Russell Square

Opening
Mon–Sat 10am–5pm, Sun 11am–5pm (last admission 30 mins before close)

Admission
Adult £5, Child £3, Concs £4

Contact
48 Doughty Street, London WC1N 2LX

t 020 7405 2127
w dickensmuseum.com
e info@dickensmuseum.com

094 Chelsea

Chelsea Physic Garden

2 hrs+ Apr–Oct

Founded in 1673 by the Worshipful Society of Apothecaries, this is one of Europe's oldest botanic gardens. Its nearly 4 acres hold a garden showing the history of medicinal plants, a pharmaceutical garden, glasshouses and many rare plants.

* Historical walk
* One of the oldest rock gardens in Europe (1773)

Location
Underground Sloane Square

Opening
Apr–Oct Wed 12noon–5pm, Sun 2pm–6pm

Admission
Adult £6.50, Child £3.50

Contact
66 Royal Hospital Road, Chelsea, London SW3 4HS

t 020 7352 5646
w chelseaphysicgarden.co.uk
e enquiries@chelseaphysicgarden.co.uk

© Chelsea Physic Garden

095 City

Guided Tours of London (Enjayseetours)

2 hrs · All year

Enjaysee invites you to sample the many faces of this great and fascinating city. Journey through 2,000 years of history on walks that will inform, excite and stimulate your curiosity. Your guide is a blue badge tourist guide.

* Programme of fascinating walks all over the city
* Walks are designed throughout London for groups of 20 people

Location
Walks start at different Tube stations every day of the week

Opening
Please phone for details

Admission
Please phone for details

Contact
Please phone for details

t 020 8906 8657
w enjayseetours.com
e nigel.common@btinternet.com

096 City

Museum of London

2 hrs+ · All year

The Museum of London is the world's largest urban museum and presents a quarter of a million years of history. Its collections include more than a million items relating to one of the finest cities in the world.

* Covers the history of the city since it began
* Various exhibitions throughout the year

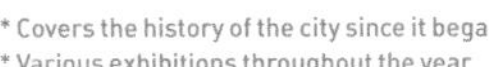   

Location
Underground Barbican & St Paul's

Opening
Mon–Sat 10am–5.50pm,
Sun 12noon–5.50pm

Admission
Free

Contact
London Wall,
London EC2Y 5HN

t 0870 444 3852
w museumoflondon.org.uk
e info@museumoflondon.org.uk

097 City

St Paul's Cathedral

1 hr+ · All year

The distinctive dome of Sir Christopher Wren's magnificent cathedral is prominent in London's skyline. Its monumental interior, sacred tombs and atmospheric crypt ensure it remains one of London's major tourist attractions.

* Newly restored interior
* Climb up to experience the Whispering Gallery

Location
The top of Ludgate Hill
Underground St Paul's

Opening
Mon–Sat 8.30am–4pm.
Special services & events may close all or part of the cathedral

Admission
Guided tours Adult £9, Child £3.50, Concs £8

Contact
The Chapter House, St Paul's Churchyard, London EC4M 8AD

t 020 7236 4128
w stpauls.co.uk
e chapter@stpaulscathedral.org.uk

098 County Hall

London Aquarium

2 hrs

All year

The London Aquarium is for everyone who appreciates the stunning and fascinating natural world. Let your imagination take you on a voyage under the sea, from the beautiful coral reefs and Indian Ocean to the secret depths of the Pacific and Atlantic Oceans.

* Late-night opening times in summer
* Themed activity weeks

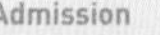

Location
Inside County Hall on South Bank of the Thames by Westminster Bridge
Underground Westminster

Opening
Daily: 10am–6pm (7pm on selected summer evenings)

Admission
Please phone for details

Contact
County Hall, Westminster Bridge Road, London SE1 7PB

t 020 7967 8000
w londonaquarium.co.uk
e info@londonaquarium.co.uk

099 County Hall

London Eye

½ hr

All year

This is the most popular paid-for tourist attraction in the UK. The 443ft observation wheel provides the most spectacular views of one of the biggest cities in the world. On a clear day you can see 25 miles in every direction from a fully enclosed capsule.

* More than 15,000 people a day travel on the Eye
* Views are breathtaking in virtually all conditions

Location
On the South Bank of the Thames by County Hall
Underground Waterloo

Opening
Daily: May–Sep 9.30am–9pm; Oct–Apr 9.30am–8pm

Admission
Adult £13, Child £6.50, Concs £10

Contact
BA London Eye, Riverside Building, County Hall, London SE1 7PB

t 0870 5000 600
w ba-londoneye.com
e customer.services@ba-londoneye.com

100 Fulham

Chelsea FC Museum & Tour

  1 hr+  All year

Visit the home of the Champions! Take the behind-the-scenes tour of London's Premier Club and view the magnificent Chelsea FC dressing rooms, the manager's dug-out, the press room and much, much more! All tours include a visit to the centenary museum.

* Visit the Chelsea Megastore and have your photograph taken with the world-famous Premiership trophy!

Location
Underground Fulham Broadway

Opening
Tours Mon–Fri, 11am, 1pm & 3pm, Sat–Sun 12noon & 2pm
Museum Mon–Fri 10.30am–4.30pm, weekends 11.30am–3.30pm

Admission
Adult £13, Child & Concs £7

Contact
100 Fulham Broadway, London SW6 1HS

t *Enquiries* 0207 957 8278
Booking 0870 603 0005
w chelseafc.com
e tours@chelseafc.com

101 Green Park

Buckingham Palace

  1 hr+  Aug–Sep

The official London residence of Her Majesty The Queen. The state rooms are used extensively to entertain guests of state, and for ceremonial and official occasions but are open to the public during August and September when the Queen makes her annual visit to Scotland.

* The state rooms form the heart of the working palace
* Furnished with treasures from the Royal Collection

Location
Mainline Victoria
Underground Victoria, Green Park & Hyde Park Corner

Opening
Aug–Sep daily 9.45am–6pm (last admission 3.45pm)

Admission
Adult £14, Child £8, Concs £12

Contact
Ticket Sales & Information Office, The Official Residences of The Queen, London SW1A 1AA

t 020 7766 7300
w royalcollection.org.uk
e bookinginfo@royalcollection.org.uk

102 Greenwich

The *Cutty Sark*

  1 hr  Jan–Sep

It's 1880 and the *Cutty Sark*'s Captain has just jumped overboard, you're 1,000 miles from home and there is a 100ft wave in front of you! Actually, you're in Maritime Greenwich overlooking the River Thames, holding the wheel of the fastest tea clipper ever built.

* Experience life on board one of the world's most famous ships
* £25m conservation programme to start end of 2006

Location
Mainline Docklands Light Railway Cutty Sark Station
Underground Canary Wharf
By boat from Westminster Pier

Opening
Daily: 10am–5pm (last admission 4.30pm)

Admission
Adult £4.50, Child £3.25, Concs £3.75

Contact
King William Walk, Greenwich, London SE10 9HT

t 020 8858 3445
w cuttysark.org.uk
e enquiries@cuttysark.org.uk

103 Greenwich

National Maritime Museum

2 hrs+ All year

This is part of a World Heritage site comprising the National Maritime Museum, Royal Observatory and Queen's House. It houses important items on the history of Britain at sea, including maritime art, ship models, plans and navigational and timekeeping instruments.

* 3 marvellous museums in close proximity
* New planetarium opening summer 2007

Location
Mainline Greenwich or Maze Hill
Docklands Light Railway Cutty Sark station. Boat from Embankment or Westminster

Opening
Daily: *summer* 10am–6pm
winter 10am–5pm

Admission
Free, exhibitions may charge

Contact
Park Row, Greenwich SE10 9NF

t 020 8312 6565
020 8858 4422
w nmm.ac.uk

104 Lambeth

Imperial War Museum

3 hrs+ All year

This is the national museum of C20 conflict. It illustrates and records all aspects of modern war and of the individual's experience of it, whether allied or enemy, service or civilian, military or political. Its role embraces the causes, course and consequences of conflict.

* Special Holocaust exhibition
* Cinema shows museum's collection of film & video

Location
Mainline Waterloo & Elephant & Castle
Underground Lambeth North
5 min walk

Opening
Daily: 10am–6pm

Admission
Free, exhibitions may charge

Contact
Lambeth Road, London SE1 6HZ

t 020 7416 5320
w iwm.org.uk
e mail@iwm.org.uk

105 Liverpool Street

Bank of England Museum

1 hr+ All year

This fascinating collection charts the history of the bank from its earliest days to the present. Discover how banknotes are made, take an audio tour, lift a genuine gold bar, and view banknotes (real and forged), coins, books, furniture and pictures.

* Audio tours cost £1
* Special events & activities

Location
Underground Bank & Liverpool Street

Opening
Weekdays 10am–5pm; also open on day of Lord Mayor's Show; closed Sat, Sun & Bank Hols

Admission
Free

Contact
Threadneedle Street, London EC2R 8AH

t 020 7601 5491
w bankofengland.co.uk/museum
e museum@bankofengland.co.uk

106 London Bridge

London Dungeon

1 hr+ All year

Deep in the heart of London, buried beneath the paving stones of historic Southwark, lies the world's most chillingly famous horror attraction. The London Dungeon brings more than 2,000 years of gruesomely authentic history vividly back to life ... and death.

* Traitor boat ride to hell, visit Sweeney Todd the demon barber
* The terrible truth about Jack the Ripper

Location
Underground London Bridge

Opening
Daily: 10am–5.30pm

Admission
Adult £16.95, Child £11.95, Concs £13.95

Contact
28–34 Tooley Street, London SE1 2SZ

t 020 7403 7221
w thedungeons.com
e londondungeon@merlinentertainments.biz

107 Marylebone

Madame Tussaud's

2 hrs+ All year

Not only can you see all the famous people from pop idols to politicians, you can also try out for the England football team, be snapped by the paparazzi and get up close and personal with George Clooney or Kylie.

* Spectacular Hard Man attraction
* World At Your Feet football attraction

Location
Underground Baker Street

Opening
Weekdays 9.30am–5.30pm, weekends 9am–6pm, extended hrs during school hols

Admission
Adult from £19.99, Child from £16.99, Concs from £18.99

Contact
Marylebone Road, London NW1 5LR

t 0870 400 3000
w madame-tussauds.com
e csc@madame-tussauds.com

108 Marylebone

Wallace Collection

2 hrs+ All year

This is both a national museum and the finest private collection of art ever assembled by one family. It is displayed against the opulent backdrop of Hertford House. The collection is best known for its magnificent C18 French paintings, furniture and porcelain.

* Paintings by Titian, Rembrandt & Frans Hals
* Superb new restaurant

Location
Underground Bond Street

Opening
Daily: 10am–5pm

Admission
Free

Contact
Hertford House, Manchester Square, London W1U 3BN

t 020 7563 9500
w wallacecollection.org

109 Regent's Park

London Zoo

4 hrs All year

Come face to face with some of the hairiest, scariest, tallest and smallest animals on the planet. See the Animals in Action presentation and watch some of the finest flying, leaping and climbing animals showing off their skills. Don't miss a visit to B.U.G.S!

* Regular programme of feeding times & special shows
* New komodo dragon, a very impressive predator

Location
At NE corner of Regent's Park on Outer Circle
Underground Camden Town

Opening
Daily: 7 Mar–23 Oct 10am–5.30pm; 24 Oct–31 Oct 10am–4.30pm; Nov–Feb 10am–4pm

Admission
Adult £14.50, Child £11.50, Concs £12.70

Contact
Regent's Park, London NW1 4RY

t 020 7722 3333
w zsl.org

110 Shepherd's Bush

BBC Television Centre Tours

2 hrs All year

Tours of the most famous television centre in the world last up to two hours. You'll see behind the scenes and into studios, visit BBC News, play in the interactive studio and be shown around by well-informed, entertaining guides. No two tours are the same.

* Winner of the 2003 Group Travel Awards
* Also new CBBC tours

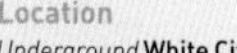

Location
Underground White City

Opening
Tours run 9 times a day Mon–Sat; booking essential

Admission
Adult £8.95, Child £6.50

Contact
BBC Television Centre,
Wood Lane,
London W12 7RJ

t 0870 603 0304 (bookings)
w bbc.co.uk/tours
e bbctours@bbc.co.uk

111 St John's Wood

Lord's Tour & MCC Museum

2 hrs All year

The Lord's Tour is an enjoyable and informative visit to the world-famous home of cricket. The tour includes the Pavilion, Long Room, dressing room and MCC Museum, which houses cricketing memorabilia including bats, balls, paintings and much more.

* Don Bradman's cricket kit
* Home of the Ashes urn, regained by England in 2005

Location
Underground St John's Wood

Opening
Daily: Apr–Sep tours at 10am, 12noon & 2pm; Oct–Mar 12noon & 2pm

Admission
Adult £8, Child £5, Concs £6

Contact
Lord's Cricket Ground, St John's Wood, London NW8 8QN

t 020 7616 8595/8596
w lords.org
e tours@mcc.org.uk

© Sarah Williams

112 South Bank

Clink Prison Museum

  1 hr  All year

On the site of the original Clink prison, this fascinating exhibition examines some of London's unsavoury past. From the C12 until its destruction in 1780 its inmates have ranged from priests to prostitutes.

* The oldest men's prison in London
* Whipping post, torture chair, foot crusher & more

Location
Underground London Bridge

Opening
Daily *winter* 10am–6pm, *summer* 10am–9pm

Admission
Adult £5, Child & Concs £3.50

Contact
1 Clink Street, South Bank, London SE1 9DG

t 020 7403 0900
w clink.co.uk
e museum@clink.co.uk

113 South Bank

Globe Theatre

  1 hr+  All year

The Globe Theatre is a reconstruction of the open-air playhouse, designed in 1599, where Shakespeare worked and for which he wrote many of his greatest plays. You can see a performance or visit the Globe Exhibition, for an introduction to the theatre of Shakespeare's time.

* Annual programme of Shakespeare's plays
* Permanent exhibition & theatre tours

Location
Mainline London Bridge & Waterloo
Underground Southwark

Opening
Theatre Daily: May–Sep 10am–7.30pm
Exhibition Daily: May–Sep 9am–5pm; Oct–Apr 10am–5pm (tours available)

Admission
Exhibition Adult £9, Child £6.50, Concs £7.50

Contact
21 New Globe Walk, London SE1 9DT

t *Enquiries* 020 7902 1400
Box office 020 7401 9919
w shakespeares-globe.org
e info@shakespearesglobe.com

114 South Bank

Tate Modern

  2 hrs+  All year

This spectacular gallery of modern and contemporary art is housed in the old Bankside Power Station on the south side of the River Thames. It is one of the world's most popular modern art galleries,featuring a permanent collection alongside temporary exhibits.

* Superb shop at gallery entrance
* Marvellous river views from the restaurant on Level 7

Location
Opposite St Paul's Cathedral
Underground Southwark & Blackfriars
Boat from Tate Britain to Tate Modern

Opening
Daily: Sun–Thu 10am–6pm, Fri & Sat 10am–10pm

Admission
Free, donations welcomed, exhibitions may charge

Contact
Bankside, London SE1 9TG

t 020 7887 8888
w tate.org.uk
e information@tate.org.uk

115 South Kensington

Natural History Museum

  2 hrs+  All year

The Natural History Museum has hundreds of exciting, interactive exhibits. Highlights include Dinosaurs, Creepy-Crawlies, Human Biology, the must-see exhibition about human beings, and Mammals, with its unforgettable huge blue whale.

* Investigate the wildlife garden
* Special exhibitions throughout the year

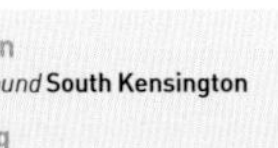

Location
Underground South Kensington

Opening
Mon–Sat & Bank Hols 10am–5.50pm, Sun 11am–5.50pm (last admission 5.30pm)

Admission
Free

Contact
Cromwell Road, London SW7 5BD

t 020 7942 5000
w nhm.ac.uk
e info@nhm.ac.uk

116 South Kensington

Science Museum

  3 hrs+  All year

This museum presents a record of scientific, technological and medical change since the C18. Originally funded by profits from the Great Exhibition of 1851, the museum was intended to improve scientific and technical education, and has done so for more than 150 years.

* Range of interactive exhibits, including new Energy Gallery
* IMAX® cinema

Location
Underground South Kensington

Opening
Daily: 10am–6pm

Admission
Free, donations welcomed, exhibitions may charge

Contact
Exhibition Road, South Kensington, London SW7 2DD

t 0870 870 4868
w sciencemuseum.org.uk
e sciencemuseum@nmsi.ac.uk

117 South Kensington

Victoria & Albert Museum

  2 hrs+  All year

The V&A is widely regarded as the world's greatest museum of art and design. Home to amazing artefacts from the world's richest cultures, the V&A's unsurpassable collection has inspired and informed for more than 150 years.

* A wide choice of special events, exhibitions & activities
* Spend time wandering the 7 miles of corridors

Location
Underground South Kensington

Opening
Daily: 10am–5.45pm, Wed 10am–10pm, last Fri of month 10am–10pm

Admission
Free, exhibitions may charge

Contact
Cromwell Road, South Kensington, London SW7 2RL

t 020 7942 2000
w vam.ac.uk
e vanda@vam.ac.uk

118 Tower Bridge

Design Museum

  1 hr+  All year

The Design Museum is the world's leading museum of industrial design, fashion and architecture. A programme of critically acclaimed exhibitions captures the excitement of design's evolution, ingenuity and inspiration through the C20 and C21.

* Rolling schedule of temporary exhibitions
* Full range of talks, courses & kids' activities

   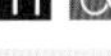

Location
Underground Tower Hill, 10 min walk over Tower Bridge
Docklands Light Railway Tower Gateway

Opening
Daily: 10am–5.45pm

Admission
Adult £7, Child free, Concs £4

Contact
Shad Thames, London SE1 2YD

t 0870 833 9955
w designmuseum.org
e info@designmuseum.org

119 Tower Bridge

HMS *Belfast*

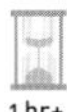

1 hr+ All year

HMS *Belfast* was launched in 1938 and served throughout WWII, playing a leading part in the destruction of the German battle cruiser *Scharnhorst* and in the Normandy landings in 1944. In 1971 she was saved as a unique reminder of Britain's naval heritage.

* Experience what life was like for the crew
* Complete tours of this huge & complex warship

Location
Underground London Bridge

Opening
Daily: Mar–Oct 10am–6pm;
Nov–Feb 10am–5 pm
(last admission 45 mins before close)

Admission
Adult £8.50, Child free, Concs £5.25

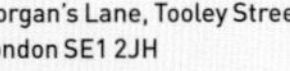

Contact
Morgan's Lane, Tooley Street, London SE1 2JH

t 0207 940 6300
w iwm.org.uk/belfast
e hmsbelfast@iwm.org.uk

120 Tower Bridge

Tower Bridge Exhibition

1 hr All year

This is one of the world's most famous bridges. Visitors can go inside the Gothic towers to discover its history and see the original Victorian engine rooms. From the high-level walkways you can look out across the modern city skyline 42 metres above the Thames.

* New interactive computer displays
* Special ticket rate for Tower Bridge & Monument

Location
Underground Tower Hill & London Bridge. Boat from Tower Pier

Opening
Daily: *summer* 10am–6.30pm *winter* 9.30am–5.30pm (last admission 1hr before close)

Admission
Adult £5.50, Child £3, Concs £4.25

Contact
Tower Bridge, London SE1 2UP

t 020 7403 3761
w towerbridge.org.uk
e enquiries@towerbridge.org.uk

121 Tower Hill

Tower of London

3 hrs All year

Founded by William the Conqueror and modified by successive sovereigns, the Tower of London is one of the world's most famous and spectacular fortresses. Discover its 900-year history as a palace, fortress, prison, mint, arsenal, menagerie and jewel house.

* Beefeater tours all day. See the Crown Jewels
* Constant calendar of special events

Location
Underground Tower Hill

Opening
Mar–Oct Tue–Sat 9am–6pm, Sun–Mon 10am–6pm;
Nov–Feb Tue–Sat 9am–5pm, Sun–Mon 10am–5pm
(last admission 1 hr before close)

Admission
Adult £15, Child £9.50, Concs £12

Contact
Tower Hill, London EC3N 4AB

t 0870 756 6060
w hrp.org.uk

122 Trafalgar Square

National Gallery

 1 hr+
 All year

This gallery houses one of the greatest collections of European painting in the world. The permanent collection spans the period from 1250 to 1900 and includes paintings by artists such as Leonardo da Vinci, Michelangelo, J M W Turner and Vincent van Gogh.

* Selection of courses & lectures available
* Weekend & school holiday family events

Location
Trafalgar Square
Underground Leicester Square & Charing Cross

Opening
Daily: 10am–6pm, Wed 10am–9pm

Admission
Free, donations welcomed, exhibitions may charge

Contact
Trafalgar Square, London WC2N 5DN

t 020 7747 2885
w nationalgallery.org.uk
e information@ng-london.org.uk

123 Trafalgar Square

National Portrait Gallery

 2 hrs+
 All year

Founded in 1856 to collect the likenesses of famous British men and women, the gallery aimed to be about history not art, and this remains its criterion today. The collection is the most comprehensive of its kind in the world.

* Daytime & evening lectures & events & Friday music evenings
* Roof-top restaurant that boasts stunning views

WC

Location
Underground Charing Cross & Leicester Square

Opening
Daily: 10am–6pm, Thu–Fri 10am–9pm

Admission
Free, exhibitions may charge

Contact

St Martin's Place, London WC2H 0HE

t 020 7306 0055/7312 2463
w npg.org.uk

124 Twickenham

Museum of Rugby

2 hrs | All year

More than just a collection of interesting artefacts, this museum is an inspirational journey through the development of this historic team game. Innovative, interactive exhibits bring to life some of the great moments of the international game.

* Finest collection of rugby memorabilia
* Action-packed films show footage of matches

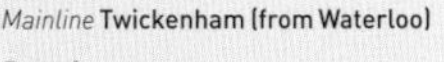

Location
Mainline Twickenham (from Waterloo)

Opening
Tue–Sat 10am–5pm, Sun 11am–5pm

Admission
Adult £9, Child & Concs £6

Contact
Rugby Road, Twickenham,
London TW1 1DZ

t 020 8892 8877
w rfu.com
e museum@rfu.com

125 Westminster

Churchill Museum & Cabinet War Rooms

2 hrs+ | All year

Learn about the man who inspired Britain's finest hour at the interactive and innovative Churchill Museum, the world's first major museum dedicated to the life of the greatest Briton. Discover the secret underground HQ that was the nerve centre of Britain's war effort in WWII.

* New Winston Churchill Museum opened 2005
* Family trail for children

Location
Underground Westminster & St James's Park
Mainline Charing Cross & Victoria

Opening
Daily: 9.30am–6pm (last admission 5pm)

Admission
Adult £11, Child free, Concs £8.50

Contact
King Charles Street,
London SW1A 2AQ

t 020 7930 6961
w iwm.org.uk
e cwr@iwm.org.uk

126 Westminster

Houses of Parliament

2 hrs | Aug–Sep

The House of Commons and House of Lords meet in the Palace of Westminster, beside the River Thames in London. Parliament has met in the Palace of Westminster since around 1550 and it has witnessed many dramatic debates.

* See & hear debates
* When Parliament is sitting, tours must be booked

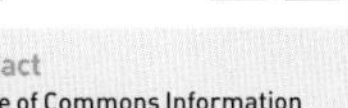

Location
Underground Westminster

Opening
Tours available during summer recess Aug–Sep.
Please phone for details

Admission
Please phone for details

Contact
House of Commons Information Office, Westminster,
London SW1A 0AA

t 020 7219 4272
w parliament.uk
e hcinfo@parliament.uk

127 Westminster

Westminster Abbey

1 hr+ All year

An architectural masterpiece of the C13 to C16, Westminster Abbey presents a unique pageant of British history. It has been the setting for most coronations since 1066 and for numerous royal occasions. Today it is still a church dedicated to regular worship and events.

* The tombs of kings & queens
* Tomb of the Unknown Warrior

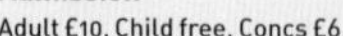

Location
Next to Parliament Square, opposite Houses of Parliament
Underground St James's Park & Westminster

Opening
Mon–Fri 9.30am–3.45pm, Wed 9.30am–7pm, Sat 9.30am–1.45pm, Sun worship only

Admission
Adult £10, Child free, Concs £6

Contact
20 Deans Yard, London SW1 P3PA

t 020 7654 4900
w westminster-abbey.org
e press@westminster-abbey.org

128 Wimbledon

Wimbledon Lawn Tennis Museum

1 hr+ All year

With unique access to the legendary players, the Museum provides a closer view of the living story of tennis than ever before through its artefacts, interactives and films, its amazing 200° cinema taking a 3D look at the Science of Tennis, and a resident 'ghost' of John McEnroe.

* Award-winning tour of the grounds
* Interactives appeal to visitors of all ages

Location
Underground Southfields

Opening
Daily: 10.30am–5pm

Admission
Adult £7.50, Child £4.75, Concs £6.25
Museum & Tour £14.50, £11, £13

Contact
The All England Lawn Tennis Club, Church Road, Wimbledon, London SW19 5AE

t 020 8946 6131
w wimbledon.org/museum
e museum@aeltc.com

129 Banbury

Broughton Castle

1 hr+ May–Sep

This historic C14 moated castle was enlarged in the C16. Home of the family of Lord Saye and Sele for 600 years it has Civil War connections, fine walled gardens, old roses and herbaceous borders. There is also a large area of open parkland.

* Location for the film *Shakespeare In Love*
* Medieval manor house enlarged in 1600

Location
2 miles W of Banbury Cross on B4035 Shipston-on-Stour road

Opening
1 May–15 Sep Wed & Sun 2pm–5pm; Jul & Aug Wed, Thu & Sun 2pm–5pm; Bank Hol Sun & Mon 2pm–5pm

Admission
Adult £6, Child £2.50, Concs £5

Contact
Broughton, Banbury OX15 5EB

t 01295 722547/276070
w broughtoncastle.com
e admin@broughtoncastle.demon.co.uk

130 Burford

Cotswold Wildlife Park & Gardens

3 hrs+ All year

The park, which is set in 160 acres of parkland and gardens around a listed Victorian manor house, has been open to the public since 1970. It is home to a collection of mammals, birds, reptiles and invertebrates, from ants to white rhinos and bats to big cats.

* Insect & reptile houses
* Special events throughout the summer

Location
On A361, 2 miles S of Burford

Opening
Daily: Mar–Sep 10am–5.30pm; Oct–Feb 10am–4.30pm (last admission 1hr before close)

Admission
Adult £9, Child & Concs £6.50

Contact
Burford OX18 4JP

t 01993 823006
w cotswoldwildlifepark.co.uk

131 Henley-on-Thames

Greys Court

1 hr+ Apr–Sep

This intriguing Tudor house is set beside the ruins of C14 fortifications and one surviving tower dating from 1347. It has an interesting history involving Jacobean court intrigue. The outbuildings include a wheel house, a donkey wheel, an ice house and a maze.

* Wisteria walk & ornamental vegetable garden
* Intimate rooms contain beautiful C18 plasterwork

Location
From Henley take A4130 to Oxford. At Nettlebed roundabout take B481

Opening
House Apr–Sep Wed–Fri 2pm–4.30pm; Aug Wed–Sun 12.30–5pm
Gardens Tue–Sat 1pm–5pm

Admission
House Adult £5.40, Child £2.70
Gardens £3.90, £1.90

Contact
Rotherfield Greys, Henley-on-Thames RG9 4PG

t 01491 628529
w nationaltrust.org.uk
e greyscourt@nationaltrust.org.uk

132 Henley-on-Thames

River and Rowing Museum

2 hrs All year

The museum has three main galleries devoted to the River Thames, the international sport of rowing and the town of Henley. Be magically transported, too, into the world of Ratty, Mole, Badger and the irrepressible Toad from Kenneth Grahame's tale *The Wind in the Willows.*

* Exhibits from 400BC to the Sydney 2000 Olympic Games
* Theatrical & audio-visual techniques, models, lighting & sound

Location
Signed from town centre

Opening
Daily: *summer* 10am–5.30pm
winter 10am–5pm

Admission
Adult £7, Child £5, Concs £6

Contact
Mill Meadows,
Henley-on-Thames RG9 1BF

t 01491 415600
w rrm.co.uk
e museum@rrm.co.uk

133 Oxford

The Ashmolean Museum of Art & Archaeology

2 hrs+ All year

This is a museum of the University of Oxford. Founded in 1683, it is one of the oldest public museums in the world. Visitors can now view the Western Art and Egyptians exhibitions and the print room.

* The Treasures exhibition

Location
On Beaumont Street, opposite Randolph Hotel, Oxford

Opening
Tue–Sat 10am–5pm,
Sun 12noon–5pm,
Bank Hol Mon 10am–5pm

Admission
Free

Contact
Beaumont Street, Oxford OX1 2PH

t 01865 278000
w ashmolean.org

134 Oxford

Modern Art Oxford

1 hr All year

One of the UK's leading centres for the presentation of modern and contemporary art. Recent exhibitions have featured Tracey Emin, Jake and Dinos Chapman, Jim Lambie, Mike Nelson, Jannis Kounellis and Cecily Brown.

* Regular & changing programme of events
* Talks & tours, children's events & music evenings

Location
In town centre, 10 mins from railway station

Opening
Tue–Sat 10am–5pm,
Sun 12noon–5pm.
Please phone for details

Admission
Free

Contact
30 Pembroke Street,
Oxford OX1 1BP

t 01865 722733
w modernartoxford.org.uk
e foh@modernartoxford.org.uk

135 Oxford

The Oxford University Museum of Natural History

1 hr+ All year

This museum houses Oxford University's extensive natural history collection in a high-Victorian Gothic building. Exhibits include the remains of the dodo, immortalised in *Alice in Wonderland* and extinct since 1680, and fossil and dinosaur materials.

* The Oxford dinosaurs & other Mesozoic reptiles
* Historic material donated by scientists including Darwin

Location
In Parks Road facing Keble College, signed

Opening
Daily: 12noon–5pm

Admission
Free, donations welcomed

Contact
Parks Road, Oxford OX1 3PW

t 01865 272950
w oum.ox.ac.uk
e info@oum.ox.ac.uk

©Stephen White

136 Oxford

University of Oxford Botanic Garden

1 hr+ All year

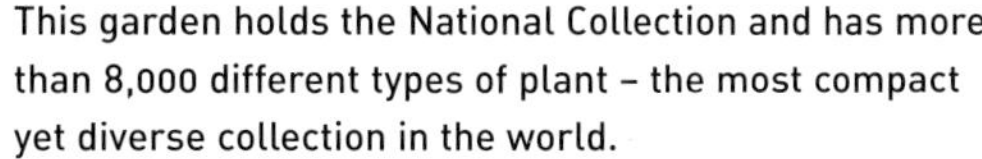

This garden holds the National Collection and has more than 8,000 different types of plant – the most compact yet diverse collection in the world.

* Water-garden, rock garden & Grade I walled garden
* Innovative black border & autumn borders

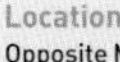

Location
Opposite Magdalen College in centre of Oxford

Opening
Daily: Mar–Apr & Sep–Oct 9am–5pm; May–Aug 9am–6pm; Nov–Feb 9am–4.30pm

Admission
Adult £2.70, Child free, Concs £2

Contact
Rose Lane, Oxford OX1 4AZ

t 01865 286690
w botanic-garden.ox.ac.uk
e postmaster@obg.ox.ac.uk

137 Wantage

The Vale & Downland Museum

2 hrs+

All year

This museum is housed in a converted C17 cloth merchant's house, a fine example of local vernacular architecture. The collections held at the museum contain geological, archaeological and contemporary objects. It is an important record of both natural and social history.

* The story of Victorian rural life in the Vale
* 3D, graphic design & audio-visual presentations

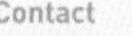

Location
Well signed from Wantage town centre

Opening
Mon–Sat 10am–4.30pm

Admission
Adult £2.50, Child £1, Concs £2

Contact
Church Street, Wantage OX12 8BL

t 01235 771447
w wantage.com/museum
e museum@wantage.com

138 Woodstock

Blenheim Palace

4 hrs

Feb–Dec

This beautiful palace was built for John Churchill, 1st Duke of Marlborough, in 1705. Designed by Sir John Vanbrugh, it is one of the largest private houses in the country and contains a superb collection of tapestries, paintings, sculptures and furniture.

* Birthplace of Sir Winston Churchill
* Set in 2,000 acres of Capability Brown-landscaped park

Location
Signed from junction 9 of M40, 5 miles from Oxford

Opening
Palace Daily: mid-Feb–Oct 10.30am–4.45pm;
Nov–Dec closed Mon–Tue
Park Daily: 9am–4.45pm

Admission
Palace, Park & Gardens Adult £14, Child £8.50, Concs £11.50

Contact
Woodstock OX20 1PX

t 08700 602080
w www.blenheimpalace.com
e administrator@blenheimpalace.com

139 Cheam

Whitehall

1 hr+

All year

A timber-framed Tudor house with additions over the centuries. There is a new virtual computer tour on the ground floor allowing 'access' to the upper floors. Collections include Syntax ware, Nonsuch pottery and a Victorian schoolmaster's room.

* Timber-framed construction
* Audio tour available & touch-screen information system

Location
Off Broadway, in centre of Cheam

Opening
Wed–Fri 2pm–5pm, Sat 10am–5pm, Sun & Bank Hols 2pm–5pm

Admission
Adult £1.30, Child 65p

Contact
1 Malden Road, Cheam SM3 8QD

t 020 8643 1236
w sutton.gov.uk
e curators@whitehallcheam.fsnet.co.uk

140 Chertsey

Chertsey Museum

1 hr+

All year

Reopened in 2003 after a major redevelopment, Chertsey is famous as the site of a medieval abbey and has some of the best-preserved Georgian architecture in the county. The museum has a local research area and includes many items of national interest.

* Hands-on exhibits in Grade II Regency town house
* Nationally famous Olive Matthews costume collection

Location
In town centre

Opening
Tue–Fri 12.30pm–4.30pm, Sat 11am–4pm

Admission
Free

Contact
The Cedars, 33 Windsor Street, Chertsey KT16 8AT

t 01932 565764
w chertseymuseum.org.uk
e enquiries@chertseymuseum.org.uk

141 Cobham

Painshill Park

2 hrs+

All year

Painshill Park was created by Charles Hamilton between 1738 and 1773 as a series of scenes to surprise and mystify. Explore its gothic temple, ruined abbey, chinese bridge, crystal grotto, hermitage, 14-acre serpentine lake, waterwheel and working vineyard.

* Family events throughout the year – fun for everyone
* One of the most important C18 parks in Europe

Location
Off A3 & A245 at Cobham

Opening
Daily: Apr–Oct 10.30am–6pm; Nov–Mar 10.30am–4pm or dusk

Admission
Adult £6.60, Child £3.85, Concs £5.80

Contact
Portsmouth Road, Cobham KT11 1JE

t 01932 868113
w painshill.co.uk
e info@painshill.co.uk

142 Churt

Pride of the Valley Sculpture Park

  2 hrs+  All year

Adjoining Frensham Country Park at the foot of Devil's Jumps, the park has the finest views of the county. Some 100 renowned sculptors exhibit works in a woodland setting. There are acres of hills, valleys, an arboretum and wildfowl-inhabited water-gardens.

* Frensham Country Park provides extensive walks

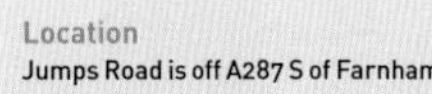

Location
Jumps Road is off A287 S of Farnham

Opening
Tue–Sun 10am–5pm; closed Mon except Bank Hols

Admission
Adult £4.50, Child £2, Concs £2–£3

Contact
Jumps Road, Churt, nr Farnham GU10 2LE

t 01428 605453
w thesculpturepark.com
e eddiepowell@thesculpturepark.co.uk

143 Dorking

Denbies Wine Estate

  2 hrs+  All year

Denbies is one of the largest privately owned vineyards in Europe. A comprehensive tour starts with a 20-minute surround-vision film, followed by a tour through the working winery, finishing in the cellars for a wine tasting. In summer, tours of the vineyard are also available.

* Shop with large selection of wine & gifts
* 2 restaurants, kitchen garden centre & art gallery

Location
On A24, close to M25 & A3 from London (15 min walk from Dorking station)

Opening
Jan–Mar Mon–Sat 10am–5pm, Sun 11.30am–5.30pm; Apr–Dec Mon–Sat 10am–5.30pm, Sun 11.30am–5.30pm

Admission
Free, charges for tours

Contact
London Road, Dorking RH5 6AA

t 01306 876616
w denbiesvineyard.co.uk
e info@denbiesvineyard.co.uk

144 East Molesey

Hampton Court Palace

  3 hrs+  All year

With 500 years of royal history, Hampton Court is one of England's finest attractions. It is a magnificent palace with diverse rooms such as Tudor kitchens and the sumptuous state apartments. The palace is complemented by 60 acres of riverside gardens.

* Horse-drawn carriages through gardens in summer
* World-famous maze in which to get lost

Location
From M25, junction 10 to A307 or junction 12 to A308

Opening
Daily: 24 Mar–27 Oct 10am–6pm; 28 Oct–25 Mar 10am–4.30pm

Admission
Adult £12.30, Child £8, Concs £10

Contact
East Molesey KT8 9AU

t 0870 752 7777
w hamptoncourtpalace.org.uk
e hamptoncourt@hrp.org.uk

145 Esher

Claremont Landscape Garden

  1 hr+  All year

Claremont's creation and development involved some of the great names in garden history. Begun *c.*1715, it became famous throughout Europe. Restoration started in 1975 after years of neglect. The many marvellous features include a lake, grotto and views.

* Design by Capability Brown & Sir John Vanbrugh
* Turf amphitheatre & island with pavilion

Location
1 mile outside Esher on Cobham road, (A307)

Opening
Daily: Apr–Oct 10am–6pm; Nov–Mar Tue–Sun 10am–5pm

Admission
Adult £5, Child £2.50

Contact
Portsmouth Road, Esher KT10 9JG

t 01372 467806
w nationaltrust.org.uk
e claremont@nationaltrust.org.uk

146 Farnham

Farnham Castle Keep

1 hr Apr–Sep

From the C12 until 1920, Farnham Castle was the seat of the Bishop of Winchester. Kings and Queens were entertained here and hunted in the nearby park. Damage was caused during the Civil War, though the medieval shell was maintained.

* Inclusive audio tour available
* Motte & bailey castle design

Location
½ mile N of Farnham on A287

Opening
Apr–Sep Fri–Sun & Bank Hol Mon
12noon–5pm (last admission 4.30pm)

Admission
Adult £2.80, Child £1.40, Concs £2.10

Contact
Castle Street, Farnham GU9 0AG

t 01252 713393
w english-heritage.org.uk

147 Farnham

Rural Life Centre

2 hrs+ All year

The Rural Life Centre is a museum of past village life covering the years from 1750 to 1960. It is set in more than 10 acres of garden and woodland and housed in purpose-built and reconstructed buildings including a chapel, village hall, cricket pavilion and schoolroom.

* Displays show village crafts & trades
* Arboretum with more than 100 species of trees

Location
Off A287, 3 miles S of Farnham

Opening
Mar–Oct Wed–Sun & Bank Hol Mon
10am–5pm;
Nov–Feb Wed & Sun 11am–4pm

Admission
Adult £5.50, Child £3.50, Concs £4.50

Contact
Reeds Road, Tilford,
Farnham GU10 2DL

t 01252 795571
w rural-life.org.uk
e rural.life@lineone.net

148 Godalming

Winkworth Arboretum

2 hrs All year

A hillside woodland, created in the C20 and now containing more than 1,300 different rare shrubs and trees. Delight in displays of magnolias, bluebells and azaleas in spring and stunning colours in autumn. There is a lake and wetland area with wildlife in abundance.

* Trees include Japanese maples & tupelos from USA
* Cool, peaceful walks through woodland

Location
2 miles SE of Godalming, off E side of B2130

Opening
Mar–Nov daily dawn–dusk;
Dec–Feb Sat–Sun dawn–dusk

Admission
Adult £4.50, Child £2

Contact
Hascombe Road,
Godalming GU8 4AD

t 01483 208477
w nationaltrust.org.uk
e winkworthharboretum@nationaltrust.org.uk

149 Guildford

Clandon Park

2 hrs+ Mar–Oct

Built in 1730, this grand Palladian mansion is notable for its magnificent two-storeyed marble hall. The house has a superb collection of C18 furniture and porcelain. The attractive gardens contain a parterre, grotto and Maori meeting house with a fascinating history.

* Home of Queen's Royal Surrey Regiment Museum
* Designed by Venetian architect Giacomo Leoni

Location
Off A247 NE of Guildford

Opening
25 Mar–Oct Tue–Thu & Sun 11am–5pm; museum 12noon–5pm

Admission
Adult £6.50, Child £3.20

Contact
West Clandon, Guildford GU4 7RQ

t 01483 222 482
w nationaltrust.org.uk
e clandonpark@nationaltrust.org.uk

150 Guildford

Guildford House Gallery

1 hr+ All year

Guildford House is a fascinating C17 town house that now contains the council's art gallery showing selections from the borough's collection and varied temporary exhibitions. The house has magnificent plaster ceilings, original panelling and period furniture.

* Constantly changing programme of exhibitions
* Spectacular carved oak staircase

Location
Guildford high street

Opening
Tue–Sat 10am–4.45pm; closed 25–27, 31 Dec & Good Friday

Admission
Free

Contact
155 High Street, Guildford GU1 3AJ

t 01483 444740
w guildfordhouse.co.uk
e guildfordhouse@guildford.gov.uk

151 Guildford

Loseley Park

3 hrs+ May–Sep

Built in 1562, Loseley House is a fine example of Elizabethan architecture, set in acres of peaceful gardens and parklands. Highlights include an award-winning rose garden, a vine walk and an area of native wild flowers. Relax in the serene 'white garden'.

* Herb garden has 6 areas devoted to specific purposes
* Organic vegetable garden, member of the HDRA

Location
A3 SW from Guildford on B3000

Opening
House May–Aug Tue–Thu & Sun 1pm–5pm, Bank Hols 11am–5pm
Gardens May–Sep Tue–Sun 11am–5pm

Admission
House & Gardens Adult £7, Child £3.50, Concs £6.50 *Gardens* £4, £2, £3.50

Contact
Guildford GU3 1HS

t 01483 304440
w loseley-park.com
e enquiries@loseley-park.com

152 Guildford

Hatchlands

2 hrs+ Apr–Oct

Set in the 430-acre Repton Park, Hatchlands is noted for its nautically themed interiors designed by Robert Adam. It is also home to the Cobbe Collection, the world's largest group of keyboard instruments, many associated with famous composers.

* Paintings by Van Dyck & Gainsborough
* Park offers a variety of woodland walks

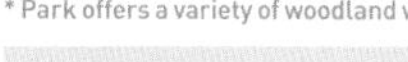

Location
N of A246 Guildford–Leatherhead road

Opening
House Apr–Jun & Sep–Oct Tue–Thu & Sun 2pm–5.30pm; Aug Tue–Fri & Sun Open Bank Hols
Park Daily 11am–6pm

Admission
Adult £6, Child £3

Contact
East Clandon, Guildford GU4 7RT

t 01483 222482
w nationaltrust.org.uk
e hatchlands@nationaltrust.org.uk

©NTPL/Bill Batten

153 Guildford

River Wey & Godalming Navigations & Dapdune Wharf

 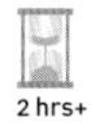  

2 hrs+ Mar–Oct

The Wey was one of the first British rivers to be made navigable (1653). This 15-mile waterway linked Guildford to Weybridge on the River Thames. The visitor centre at Dapdune Wharf in Guildford tells the story of the people who lived and worked on the waterway.

* Boat trips available
* The entire 19-mile towpath is open to walkers

Location
Wharf Road is behind Surrey County Cricket Ground, off Woodbridge Road

Opening
End Mar–end Oct Mon &Thu–Sun 11am–5pm

Admission
Adult £3.50, Child £2

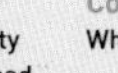

Contact
Wharf Road, Guildford GU1 4RR

t 01483 561389
w nationaltrust.org.uk
e riverwey@nationaltrust.org.uk

154 Morden

Morden Hall Park

2 hrs All year

This oasis in the heart of suburbia covers more than 125 acres of parkland with the River Wandle meandering through. The mill is now used as an environmental centre. The park has a hay meadow and there is an impressive rose garden with more than 2,000 roses.

* Planned walks & monthly programme of events
* Variety of bridges across the river

Location
Off Morden Hall Road

Opening
Daily: 8am–6pm

Admission
Free

Contact
Morden Hall Road, Morden SM4 5JD

t 020 8545 6850
w nationaltrust.org.uk
e mordenhallpark@nationaltrust.org.uk

155 Ockley

The Hannah Peschar Sculpture Garden

2 hrs+ All year

A stunning woodland water-garden is the setting for this specialist exhibition of contemporary sculpture. Hannah Peschar and Anthony Paul are in the vanguard of a C21 revolution in garden design that uses predominantly sculpture and water.

Location
Off A29 to Gatton Manor Road

Opening
May–Oct Fri–Sat 11am–6pm, Sun & Bank Hols 2pm–5pm Tue–Thu by appointment only; Nov–Apr Tue–Thu by appointment only

Admission
Adult £9, Child £6, Concs £7

Contact
Black and White Cottage, Standon Lane, Ockley RH5 5QR

t 01306 627269
w hannahpescharsculpture.com
e hpeschar@easynet.co.uk

©NTPL/Nick Meers

156 Richmond

Ham House & Gardens

2 hrs+ Mar–Oct

This outstanding Stuart house, built in 1610, is famous for its lavish interiors and spectacular collections of fine furniture, textiles and paintings. Restoration of the C17 formal gardens over the last 30 years has influenced similar projects in the great gardens of Europe.

* C18 dairy & gift shop
* Reinstated C17 statuary in wilderness garden

Location
Off A307 W of Richmond

Opening
House 25 Mar–29 Oct Sat–Wed 1pm–5pm
Gardens Sat–Wed 11am–6pm or dusk

Admission
House & Gardens Adult £8, Child £4
Gardens Adult £4, Child £2

Contact
Ham Street, Richmond TW10 7RS

t 020 8940 1950
w nationaltrust.org.uk/hamhouse
e hamhouse@nationaltrust.org.uk

157 Richmond

Royal Botanic Gardens, Kew

3 hrs+

All year

Established in 1759, Kew has developed into 300 acres of garden containing a collection of more than 40,000 varieties of plant. Also see seven spectacular glasshouses and two art galleries, Japanese and rock gardens and a permanent exhibition in the restored museum.

* One of England's top 100 attractions
* Inscribed as a World Heritage Site in 2003

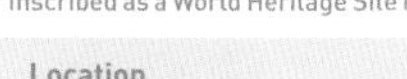

Location
Off A307 at Kew
Underground Kew Gardens

Opening
Daily: 9.30am–sunset

Admission
Adult £11.75, Child free, Concs £8.75

Contact
Kew, Richmond TW9 3AB

t 020 8332 5655
w kew.org
e info@kew.org

158 Weybridge

Brooklands Museum

3 hrs+

All year

Constructed in 1907, Brooklands was the first purpose-built motor-racing circuit in the world, not only the birthplace of British motorsport but also of British aviation. The track and original buildings have been restored, and a motor and aircraft museum added.

* Concorde can now be seen 7 days a week
* Large display of cars, cycles & aircraft

Location
Off B374, A3 to A245. Follow signs

Opening
Daily: *summer* 10am–5pm
winter 10am–4pm

Admission
Adult £7, Child £5, Concs £6

Contact
Brooklands Road,
Weybridge KT13 0QN

t 01932 857381
w brooklandsmuseum.com
e info@brooklandsmuseum.com

159 Windsor

Runnymede

2 hrs+

All year

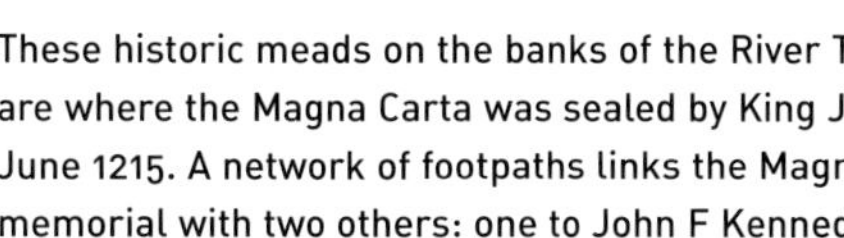

These historic meads on the banks of the River Thames are where the Magna Carta was sealed by King John in June 1215. A network of footpaths links the Magna Carta memorial with two others: one to John F Kennedy and one to the 20,000 RAF airmen killed in WWII.

* Fairhaven Lodges, designed by Lutyens
* Boat trips along the Thames available

Location
6 miles E of Windsor on S side of A308
M25 junction 13

Opening
Daily: *summer* 10am–7pm
winter 9am–5pm

Admission
Charges for parking, fishing & mooring.
Please phone for details

Contact
North Lodge, Windsor Road,
Old Windsor SL4 2JL

t 01784 432891
w nationaltrust.org.uk/runnymede
e runnymede@nationaltrust.org.uk

160 Woking

RHS Garden Wisley

3 hrs+

All year

Wisley is Britain's best-loved garden with 240 acres offering a fascinating blend of beautiful and practical plants plus innovative design and cultivation techniques. It features richly planted borders, luscious rose gardens and the exotica of the glasshouses.

* New plant varieties continuously developed
* Extensive events & educational programmes

Location
Just S of junction 10 of M25

Opening
Mar–Oct Mon–Fri 10am–6pm,
Sat–Sun 9am–6pm;
Nov–Feb Mon–Fri 10am–4.30pm
weekends 9am–4.30pm

Admission
Adult £7.50, Child £2

Contact
Woking GU23 6QB

t 01483 224234
w rhs.org.uk

161 Arundel

Amberley Working Museum

3 hrs+ Mar–Oct

Amberley is a 36-acre open-air museum set in the South Downs. With its historic buildings, working exhibits and demonstrations, the museum aims to show how science, technology and industry have affected people's lives.

* Variety of crafts demonstrated daily
* Trips on vintage bus & narrow-gauge railway

Location
Off B2139 between Arundel & Storrington

Opening
Mar–Oct Wed–Sun 10am–5.30pm (last admission 4.30pm)

Admission
Adult £8.20, Child £5, Concs £7.20

Contact
Amberley, Arundel BN18 9LT

t 01798 831370
w amberleymuseum.co.uk
e office@amberleymuseum.co.uk

162 Arundel

Arundel Castle

1 hr+ Mar–Oct

Originally built in the C11 by the Earl of Arundel, this centre has 1,000 years of fascinating history. There are fabulous displays of furniture, artefacts and paintings by Gainsborough, Reynolds and Van Dyck. The original motte, constructed in 1068, is more than 100ft high.

* Situated in magnificent grounds overlooking River Arun
* Seat of the Dukes of Norfolk for more than 850 years

Location
In Arundel on A27

Opening
24 Mar–27 Oct Sun–Fri 11am–5pm

Admission
Adult £12, Child £7.50, Concs £9.50

Contact
Arundel BN18 9AB

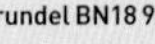

t 01903 882173
w arundelcastle.org
e info@arundelcastle.org

163 Arundel

Denmans Garden

  2 hrs+  All year

This 4-acre garden designed for year-round interest – through use of form, colour and texture – is the home of John Brookes MBE, renowned garden designer and writer. Visit the plant centre and Les Routiers award-winning fully licensed Garden Café.

* Café of the Year 2005 London & South East
* Natural-looking lake is home to moorhens

Location
Off A27 W, between Chichester & Arundel, adjacent to Fontwell Racecourse

Opening
Gardens 9am–5pm (Nov–Feb 9am–dusk)
Plant Centre 9am–5pm
Garden Café 10am–5pm

Admission
Adult £3.95, Child £2.25, Concs £3.25

Contact
Denmans Lane, Fontwell, Arundel BN18 0SU

t 01243 542808
w denmans-garden.co.uk
e denmans@denmans-garden.co.uk

164 Arundel

WWT Arundel

  2 hrs+  All year

Surrounded by ancient woodland and overlooked by the town's historic castle, the wetlands at Arundel are home to many rare species of wetland wildlife. Many of the hundreds of birds you will see are tame enough to eat from your hand.

* Many rare birds regularly sighted

Location
Close to A27 & A29. Follow brown duck signs on approaching Arundel

Opening
Daily: 9.30am–5.30pm;
Winter 9.30am–4.30pm

Admission
Adult £6.95, Child £3.75, Concs £5.25

Contact
Mill Road, Arundel BN18 9PB

t 01903 883355
w wwt.org.uk/visit/arundel
e sarah.fraser@wwt.org.uk

165 Ashington

Holly Gate Cactus Garden

1 hr+ All year

This fascinating garden houses a world-renowned collection of more than 30,000 exotic plants. Rare plants from the arid areas of the world such as the USA, Mexico, South America and Africa are represented, as well as cacti from the Central and South American jungles.

* 10,000 sq ft of glasshouses
* Many plants in flower throughout the year

Location
Off A24 between Horsham & Worthing

Opening
Daily: Feb–Oct 9am–5pm;
Nov–Jan 9am–4pm

Admission
Adult £2, Child & Concs £1.50

Contact
Billingshurst Road,
Ashington RH20 3BB

t 01903 892930
w hollygatecactus.co.uk
e info@hollygatecactus.co.uk

166 Chichester

Chichester Cathedral

1 hr All year

For 900 years Chichester Cathedral has been a landmark from land and sea. Famous for its modern art, it boasts a stunning Chagall window. Its more ancient treasures include the Arundel Tomb that inspired a well-known poem by Philip Larkin.

* C12 sculpture depicting Lazarus
* Newly commissioned icon of St Richard

Location
In town centre

Opening
Daily: subject to services

Admission
Free, donations welcomed

Contact
The Royal Chantry, Cathedral
Cloisters, Chichester PO19 1PX

t 01243 782595
w chichestercathedral.org.uk
e reception@chichestercathedral.org.uk

167 Chichester

Fishbourne Roman Palace & Gardens

2 hrs+ All year

This late C1 palace, discovered in 1960, is the largest Roman residence found to date in Britain. Its treasures include the country's finest collection of Roman mosaic floors and hypocausts. Finds are displayed in a museum, while an audio-visual presentation brings the site to life.

* The remains of more than 20 mosaics are on display
* A new Collections Discovery Centre opened summer 2006

Location
N of A259 off A27 1½ miles W of Chichester

Opening
1 Feb–15 Dec daily from 10am;
16 Dec–31 Jan weekends only from 10am

Admission
Adult £6.50, Child £3.40, Concs £5.50

Contact
Salthill Road, Fishbourne,
Chichester PO19 3QR

t 01243 785859
w sussexpast.co.uk
e adminfish@sussexpast.co.uk

168 Chichester

Military Aviation Museum

4 hrs+ Feb–Nov

Established in 1982, the museum tells the story of military flying from the earliest days, with emphasis on the RAF at Tangmere, and the air war over southern England from 1939 to 1945. Displays include the world speed record-breaking *Meteor* and *Hunter*.

* Opportunity to 'fly' a fighter simulator
* Direct bus service from Chichester to museum, No.55

Location
3 miles E of Chichester off A27

Opening
Daily: Feb & Nov 10am–4.30pm;
Mar–Oct 10am–5.30pm

Admission
Adult £5, Child £1.50, Concs £4

Contact
Military Aviation Museum,
Tangmere, Chichester PO20 6ES

t 01243 775223
w tangmere-museum.org.uk
e tangmeretrust@aol.com

169 Chichester

Goodwood House

2 hrs Mar–Oct

Goodwood House is home to one of the most significant private art collections in the country. The state apartments have been richly refurbished to their original Regency elegance and there is an Egyptian state dining room and magnificent ballroom.

* Curator of the collection is the author Rosemary Baird
* Fine art collection includes Reynolds, Stubbs & Canaletto

Location
3 miles NE of Chichester off A27

Opening
Mar–Oct Sun–Mon 1pm–5pm;
Aug Sun–Thu 1pm–5pm.
Please phone in advance

Admission
Adult £8, Child £4, Concs £7

Contact
Goodwood, Chichester PO18 0PX

t 01243 755040
w goodwood.co.uk
e housevisiting@goodwood.co.uk

170 Chichester

Weald & Downland Open-Air Museum

2 hrs+ All year

This museum, set in the beautiful Sussex countryside, offers a chance to wander through a fascinating collection of original historic buildings dating from the C13 to the C19. Many have period gardens and farm animals. There are also woodland walks and a picturesque lake.

* Leading museum of historic buildings in England
* See food prepared in the working Tudor kitchen

Location
7 miles N of Chichester on the A286

Opening
3 Jan–18 Feb Wed–Sun 10.30am– 4pm;
19 Feb–31 Mar & Nov–23 Dec daily 10.30am–4pm;
Apr–Oct daily 10.30am–6pm

Admission
Adult £7.75, Child £4.25, Concs £6.95

Contact
Singleton, Chichester PO18 0EU

t 01243 811348
w wealddown.co.uk
e office@wealddown.co.uk

171 Chichester

West Dean Gardens

3 hrs+ All year

These Edwardian gardens include 35 acres of ornamental grounds, a 100-yard pergola and herbaceous borders. A 2-mile park walk, walled kitchen and fruit gardens, 16 restored greenhouses and a 49-acre arboretum are additional features.

* New Sussex barn gallery with various exhibitions
* Licensed bar, garden & gift shop at the visitor centre

Location
6 miles N of Chichester on A286

Opening
Daily: May–Sep 10.30am–5pm;
Oct & Mar–Apr 11am–5pm;
Nov–Feb Wed–Sun 10am–4.30pm

Admission
Adult £5.50, Child £2.50, Concs £5

Contact
West Dean, Chichester PO18 0QZ

t 01243 818210
w westdean.org.uk
e gardens@westdean.org.uk

172 East Grinstead

Standen

  2 hrs+  All year

Standen shows off pure Victorian style under the influence of the Arts & Crafts Movement. It's extensively decorated with William Morris carpets, fabrics and wallpaper, and externally finished in sandstone, weatherboard and brick.

* 12-acre garden with fine views over the countryside
* Custom-made furniture from Heal's & William Morris

Location
2 miles S of East Grinstead off B2110

Opening
Mar–Oct 10.30am–5pm;
Nov–Feb Wed–Sun 10.30am–4pm

Admission
Adult £6, Child £2.50, Concs £5.50
Nov–Feb £3, £1.25, £2.75

Contact
West Hoathly Road,
East Grinstead RH19 4NE

t 01342 323029
w nationaltrust.org.uk/standen
e standen@nationaltrust.org.uk

173 Haywards Heath

Borde Hill Gardens

  2 hrs+   Apr–Oct

Borde Hill is set in 200 acres of traditional country estate. The garden was established from 1,900 plants gathered from the Himalayas, China, Burma and Tasmania. Today Borde Hill has one of the most comprehensive collections of trees and shrubs in England.

* Magnificent rhododendrons, azaleas & camellias
* Winner of the HHA Garden of the Year Award 2004

Location
1½ miles N of Haywards Heath

Opening
Daily: Apr–Oct 10am–6pm

Admission
Adult £6, Child £3.50, Concs £5

Contact
Balcombe Road,
Haywards Heath RH16 1XP

t 01444 450326
w bordehill.co.uk
e info@bordehill.co.uk

174 Haywards Heath

Nymans Gardens

  2 hrs  All year

Nymans is one of the great gardens of the Sussex Weald and is internationally famous for its collection of rare plants. Created by three generations of the Messel family over a period of more than a hundred years, Nymans was one of the first gardens given to the National Trust (1953).

* Huge replanting programme followed 1987 storm
* Garden has individually characterised sections

Location
On B2114 at Handcross, 4½ miles S of Crawley, just off M23/A23

Opening
House mid-Mar–Oct 11.30am–5pm
Gardens mid-Feb–Oct Wed–Sun 11am–6pm; Nov–mid-Feb weekends 11am–4pm

Admission
Adult £7, Child £3.50

Contact
Nymans Gardens, Handcross,
nr Haywards Heath RH17 6EB

t 01444 400321
w nationaltrust.org.uk/nymans
e nymans@nationaltrust.org.uk

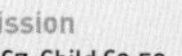

175 Horsham

Leonardslee Lakes & Gardens

3 hrs+

Apr–Oct

A woodland rhododendrons and azaleas garden set in a 240-acre valley with seven lakes, Leonardslee has many features including a rock garden and Alpine House, as well as deer and wallabies roaming in the parkland. It also houses a collection of Victorian motor cars (1889–1900).

* Accolade for most beautiful garden in Europe in May
* Behind the Doll's House exhibition

Location
On junction of A281 & B2110 in Lower Beeding

Opening
Daily: 1 Apr–31 Oct 9.30am–6pm (last admission 4.30pm)

Admission
Apr & Jun–Oct Adult £6, Child £4
May weekdays £8, £4
May weekends £9, £4

Contact
Lower Beeding, Horsham RH13 6PP

t 01403 891212
w leonardslee.com
e gardens@leonardslee.com

176 Littlehampton

Look and Sea!

1 hr+

All year

Explore the geology, geography and history of Littlehampton, finishing in the stunning glass-walled viewing tower with fantastic views across the River Arun out to sea and to Arundel. The attractions include an interactive maritime exhibition and a variety of displays.

* Newly opened riverside walks
* Café overlooking the river & out to sea

Location
By the river, 300 yrds from railway station

Opening
Daily: 9am–5pm

Admission
Adult £1.95, Child & Concs £1.50

Contact
63 Surrey Street, Littlehampton BN17 5AW

t 01903 718984
w lookandsea.co.uk
e info@lookandsea.co.uk

©NTPL

177 Petersfield

Uppark

3 hrs

Apr–Oct

A late C17 house set high on the South Downs with magnificent sweeping views to the sea. It was rescued from a fire in 1989 and the restored Georgian interior houses a famous Grand Tour collection that includes paintings, furniture and ceramics.

* H G Wells's mother was a housekeeper here
* An C18 doll's house is a star of the collection

Location
5 miles SE of Petersfield off B2146

Opening
House Apr–Oct Sun–Thu 12.30–4.30pm
Grounds Apr–Oct Sun–Thu 11.30am–5pm

Admission
Adult £6.50, Child £3.25

Contact
South Harting, Petersfield GU31 5QR

t 01730 825415
w nationaltrust.org.uk/uppark
e uppark@nationaltrust.org.uk

178 Petworth

Petworth House & Park

3 hrs+ All year

A magnificent late C17 mansion set in a park landscaped by Capability Brown and immortalised in Turner's paintings. The house contains the National Trust's finest and largest collection of pictures, with numerous works by J M W Turner, Van Dyck, Reynolds and Blake.

* Ancient & neoclassical sculpture
* Fine furniture & carvings by Grinling Gibbons

    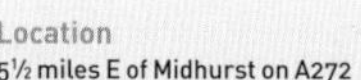

Location
5½ miles E of Midhurst on A272

Opening
House Mar–Oct Wed–Sat 11am–5pm
Park Open all year

Admission
House & Park Adult £8, Child £4
Park £3, £1.50

Contact
Petworth GU28 0AE

t 01798 342207
w nationaltrust.org.uk/petworth
e petworth@nationaltrust.org.uk

©NTPL

179 Pulborough

Bignor Roman Villa

1 hr+ Mar–Oct

Discovered in 1811, the site, which probably dates from the C3, comprises 50 living quarters in the main complex and nine outbuildings. They include a bath house, with one of the best-preserved Roman mosaics in England, and summer and winter dining rooms.

* Spectacular mosaics depicting Venus & Medusa
* One of the largest Roman villas in Britain

Location
6 miles N of Arundel, signed from A29 (Bignor–Billingshurst) and A285 (Chichester–Petworth)

Opening
Mar–Apr Tue–Sun & Bank Hols 10am–5pm;
Daily: May & Oct 10am–5pm;
Jun–Sep 10am–6pm

Admission
Adult £4.35, Child £1.85, Concs £3.10

Contact
Bignor Lane,
Pulborough RH20 1PH

t 01798 869259
w pyrrha.demon.co.uk
e bignorromanvilla@care4free.net

180 Pulborough

Parham House & Gardens

2 hrs+ Easter–Sept

In the Middle Ages Parham House was owned by Westminster Abbey. In 1601 it was sold to Thomas Bysshop and it remained in the family until bought in 1922 by Clive Pearson. He purchased many of the paintings, and added his own *objets d'art* and English furniture.

* Award-winning 4-acre walled garden
* Idyllically sited in the heart of an ancient deer park

Location
Off A283 Pulborough–Storrington road

Opening
House Easter Sun–Sep Wed–Thu Sun & Bank Hol Mon 2pm–6pm
Gardens Easter Sun–Sep Wed–Thu, Sun & Bank Hol Mon (also Tue & Fri in Aug) 12noon–6pm

Admission
House & Gardens Adult £6.80, Child £3, Concs £6
Gardens only £5, £1.50, £4.50

Contact
Parham Park, nr Pulborough RH20 4HS

t 01903 742021
w parhaminsussex.co.uk
e enquiries@parhaminsussex.co.uk

Lyme Regis, Dorset
South West
Bristol Cornwall Devon Dorset
Gloucestershire Somerset Wiltshire

Head
Fishguard
Newcastle Emlyn
659
St David's
PEMBROKESHIRE
CARMARTHE
Carmarthen
656
Haverfordwest
Narberth
St Clears
Milford Haven
662
Neyland
Kidwelly
Pembroke Dock
666–667
Burry Port
Llanelli
M4
Tenby
Pembroke
Caldey Island
St Govan's Head
SWANSEA
SWANSEA
Port Einon
Ilfracombe
Hartland Point
Bideford
Great Torringto
230–231
Bude
Holsworthy
195
Okehampton
233
Tintagel
Launceston
214
196
203
Trevose Head
206
194
Bodmin Moor
237–238
Padstow
Wadebridge
Tavistock
NEWQUAY
CORNWALL
Bodmin
191–193
Liskeard
235–236
PLYMOUTH
Newquay
Saltash
PLYMOU
St Austell
Fowey
Looe
Torpoint
211–212
Truro
215
St Ives
Camborne
Redruth
213
207–208
Dodman Point
197–198
St Just
Penzance
St Mawes
200–201
Falmouth
Sennen
204
Helston
Land's End
205
209–210
199
Lizard
Lizard Point

202
Isles of Scilly

GLOUCESTERSHIRE
OXFORDSHIRE
BERKSHIRE
WILTSHIRE
SOMERSET
DORSET
HAMPSHIRE
MONMOUTHSHIRE
Brecon Beacons
Exmoor
Salisbury Plain
Cotswolds
New Forest
Isle of Wight
Chesil Beach
Bill of Portland
Start Point
CARDIFF
BRISTOL
SOUTHAMPTON
Hereford
Ledbury
Tewkesbury
Cheltenham
Gloucester
Ross-on-Wye
Monmouth
Stroud
Cirencester
Swindon
Chippenham
Bath
Trowbridge
Salisbury
Dorchester
Weymouth
Bournemouth
Poole
Yeovil
Taunton
Exeter
Torquay
Dartmouth
Newport
Swansea

© Mandy Reynolds

181 Bristol

@Bristol

3 hrs+ All year

This is a unique destination bringing science, nature and art to life. It is a place of discovery and home to three attractions: Wildwalk, a living rainforest in the heart of the city, Explore, a C21 science centre, and a giant IMAX® Theatre with digital surround sound.

* Tropical forest with free-flying birds & butterflies
* Bristol's very own planetarium

  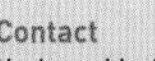

Location
Off Anchor Road in central Bristol

Opening
Daily: 10am–5pm, Sat–Sun & school hols 10am–6pm

Admission
Explore Adult £8, Child £5.50, Concs £6.50
Wildwalk & IMAX® £6.50, £4.50, £5.50

Contact
Harbourside, Bristol BS1 5DB

t 0845 345 1235
w at-bristol.org.uk
e information@at-bristol.org.uk

182 Bristol

Bristol Blue Glass

1 hr All year

Glass-blowing in Bristol was fully established by the mid-C17, when the city was fêted as a centre of excellence for glassmaking and porcelain. See freeblown, handmade glass and watch glass-blowing demonstrations from the public viewing gallery.

* Glass available to puchase in gift shop
* Join in with exciting hands-on activities

Location
From M32 junction 3 then follow signs to A4

Opening
Daily: Mon–Sat 9am–5pm, Sun 10am–4pm

Admission
Adult £3, Child £1, Concs £2

Contact
Unit 7, Whitby Road, Brislington, Bristol BS4 3QF

t 0117 972 0818
w bristol-glass.co.uk
e info@bristolblueglass.co.uk

183 Bristol

Bristol Cathedral

1 hr All year

This fascinating building is a centre for Bristol's history, civic life and culture. Founded as an abbey in 1140, it became a cathedral in 1542 and developed architecturally through the ages. It is one of the finest examples of a 'hall church' anywhere in the world.

* Beautiful examples of Saxon stone carvings
* Expressionist window designed by Keith New in 1965

     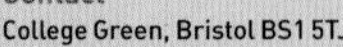

Location
Central Bristol on College Green

Opening
Daily: 8am–6pm

Admission
Donations appreciated, £3 per person

Contact
College Green, Bristol BS1 5TJ

t 0117 926 4879
w bristol-cathedral.co.uk
e reception@bristol-cathedral.co.uk

184 Bristol

Bristol Ferry Boat Company

  2–4 hrs  All year

Enter the exciting world of Bristol's historic harbour – for a round-trip tour or just by visiting one of the many attractions. The journey takes in the Pump House, the Millennium Square and the SS *Great Britain*.

* River trips & pub ferry can be arranged
* Unique view of Bristol past & present

Location
Bristol Harbour

Opening
Daily: Please phone for details

Admission
Multistop day ticket:
Adult £6, Child & Concs £4

Contact
MB *Tempora*, Welsh Back, Bristol BS1 4SP

t 0117 927 3416
w bristolferry.com
e trips@bristolferry.com

185 Bristol

The British Empire & Commonwealth Museum

  2 hrs+  Feb–Dec

This award-winning national museum presents the dramatic 500-year history of the rise and fall of Britain's overseas empire. It is located in Isambard Kingdom Brunel's historic old Bristol station at Temple Meads.

* 16 permanent & interactive galleries
* Special half-term & holiday activities for families

WC

Location
Located next to Temple Meads, Bristol's main railway station

Opening
Feb–Dec daily 10am–5pm
Please phone for details

Admission
Adult £6.95, Child £3.95, Concs £5.95

Contact
Station Approach, Temple Meads, Bristol BS1 6QH

t 0117 925 4980
w empiremuseum.co.uk
e admin@empiremuseum.co.uk

186 Bristol

City Museum & Art Gallery

2 hrs+ All year

Bristol's premier museum and art gallery. This magnificent building houses important collections of minerals and fossils, natural history, Eastern art, archaeology, seven galleries of fine and applied art and ever-changing temporary exhibitions.

* World Wildlife Gallery

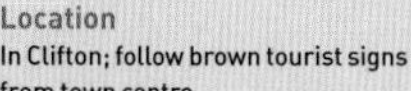

Location
In Clifton; follow brown tourist signs from town centre

Opening
Daily: 10am–5pm

Admission
Free

Contact
Queen's Road, Bristol BS8 1RL

t 0117 922 3571
w bristol-city.gov.uk/museums
e general_museum@bristol-city.gov.uk

188 Bristol

The Georgian House

1 hr All year

This lovely house is an example of Bristol's C18 heritage, illustrating how the city profited from being one of England's premier trading ports. Originally home to John Pinney, a West Indies merchant, the house is displayed as it might have looked in its heyday.

* Home to the slave Pero
* Illustrating life above & below stairs

Location
Just off Park Street, near Cabot Tower

Opening
Sat–Wed 10am–5pm

Admission
Free

Contact
7 Great George Street, Bristol BS1 5RR

t 0117 921 1362
w bristol-city.gov.uk
e general_museum@bristol-city.gov.uk

187 Bristol

CREATE Centre

1 hr All year

CREATE is a showcase of environmental excellence. Bristol's ecological centre is a fount of information on environmental initiatives. Visit the Ecohome, a green home of the future, and learn about meeting the challenge of waste in the recycling exhibition.

* A hands-on journey through waste & recycling
* Themed events throughout the year

Location
Cumberland Basin lies at the far end of the docks. CREATE is in a redbrick warehouse

Opening
Mon–Thu 9am–5pm, Fri 9am–4.30pm

Admission
Free

Contact
Smeaton Road, Bristol BS1 6XN

t 0117 925 0505
w bristol-city.gov.uk/create
e create@bristol-city.gov.uk

© Mandy Reynolds

189 Bristol

SS *Great Britain*

2 hrs

All year

The world's first great ocean liner, the SS *Great Britain* is a unique surviving engineering masterpiece from Victorian times. Docked in the original Great Western Dockyard, this grand passenger liner was the forerunner of all modern cruise ships.

* Designed by Isambard Kingdom Brunel
* Descend under the sea into the dry dock

Location
Follow anchor signs in Bristol Historic Dockyard

Opening
Daily: Apr–Oct 10am–5.30pm; Nov–Mar 10am–4.30pm

Admission
Adult £8.95, Child £4.95, Concs £6.95

Contact
Great Western Dockyard,
Gas Ferry Road, Bristol BS1 6TY

t 0117 926 0680
w ssgreatbritain.org
e admin@ss-great-britain.com

190 Whitchurch

HorseWorld

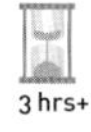
3 hrs+

All year

The South West's leading horse welfare charity. In beautiful Mendip stone farm buildings, dating back to the early C19, meet more than 40 of the 300 rescued horses, ponies and donkeys. From Shetland ponies to shire horses, each has a different story to tell.

* Twice-daily presentations
* Tractor tours

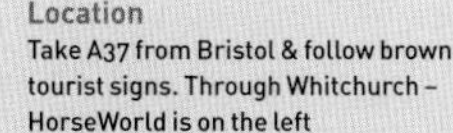

Location
Take A37 from Bristol & follow brown tourist signs. Through Whitchurch – HorseWorld is on the left

Opening
Daily: Mar–Sep 10am–5pm (4pm in winter); Sep–Mar closed Mon

Admission
Please phone for details

Contact
Staunton Manor Farm,
Staunton Lane, Whitchurch,
Bristol BS14 0QJ

t 01275 540173
w horseworld.org.uk
e visitorcentre@horseworld.org.uk

191 Bodmin

Lanhydrock House

  3 hrs+  Apr–Oct

Largely rebuilt in 1881 after a fire, this fascinating C19 home captures the atmosphere and trappings of a high Victorian country house. 'Below stairs' has a huge kitchen, larder, dairy and bake house. The estate is set in 900 acres leading down to the banks of the River Fowey.

* Magnificent gallery with moulded plaster ceiling

Location
2 miles E of Bodmin. Follow signs off either A30 or A38

Opening
Apr–Oct Tue–Sun & Bank Hol Mon 11am–5.30pm (5pm in Oct)

Admission
Please phone for details

Contact
Lanhydrock, Bodmin PL30 5AD
t 01208 265950
w nationaltrust.org.uk
e lanhydrock@nationaltrust.org.uk

192 Bodmin

Military Museum Bodmin

  1 hr+  All year

More than 300 years of regimental history of the Duke of Cornwall Light Infantry is displayed at the museum. The former barracks now houses the regimental museum with uniforms, pictures and medals, and includes one of the country's finest small arms collections.

* General George Washington's Bible, captured 1777
* Events from the capture of Gibraltar in 1704 to WWII

Location
Outskirts of Bodmin

Opening
Mon–Fri 9am–5pm (Sun in Jul–Aug)

Admission
Adult £2.50, Child 50p

Contact
The Keep, Bodmin PL31 1EG
t 01208 72810
e dclimus@talk21.com

193 Bodmin

Pencarrow

  3 hrs+   Apr–Oct

Pencarrow houses a superb collection of pictures, furniture, porcelain and antique dolls. The house sits in 50 acres of Grade II-listed gardens and woodland with a lake, an ice house and a Victorian rockery. There are marked walks through the woodland and gardens.

* Grade II-listed garden & Dogs Trust national award
* Sir Arthur Sullivan composed *Iolanthe* music here

Location
Follow signs off A389, 4 miles NW of Bodmin

Opening
House, Restaurant & Shop 1 Apr–25 Oct Sun–Thu 11am–5pm
Gardens Daily: 1 Mar–31 Oct 9.30am–5.30pm

Admission
House & Gardens Adult £8, Child £4
Gardens £4, £1

Contact
Bodmin PL30 3AG
t 01208 841369
w pencarrow.co.uk
e pencarrow@aol.com

194 Bolventor

Colliford Lake Park

  3 hrs+  Easter–Oct

Acres of indoor and outdoor adventure and fun with a 'Beast of Bodmin Moor' theme. Colliford Lake Park is a farm-based attraction with 8 acres of woodland and 30 acres of farmland stocked with sheep, goats, red deer and other animals.

* Extensive indoor & outdoor play areas
* Nature trails around Colliford Lake

 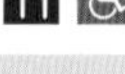 

Location
500 yards off A30 between Launceston & Bodmin

Opening
Daily: Easter–Oct 10.30am–5.30pm

Admission
Adult £6, Child & Concs £6

Contact
Bolventor, Bodmin Moor PL14 6PZ
t 01208 821469
w collifordlakepark.com
e info@collifordlakepark.com

195 Boscastle

Museum of Witchcraft

  1 hr  Easter–Oct

The museum contains the world's largest collection of witchcraft-related artefacts and regalia. With a series of fascinating displays covering everything from stone circles and sacred sites to ritual magic, charms and spells, it is a unique and memorable collection.

* Library with 3,000 books on witchcraft (by appointment only)
* Fresh new displays since the floods of 2004

Location
Located by the Harbour in Boscastle. Boscastle is on the N coast of Cornwall between Tintagel & Bude

Opening
Daily: Easter–Oct Mon–Sat 10.30am–6pm, Sun 11.30am–6pm

Admission
Adults £2.50, Child & Concs £1.50

Contact
The Harbour, Boscastle PL35 0HD

t 01840 250111
w museumofwitchcraft.com
e museumwitchcraft@aol.com

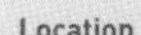

196 Camelford

British Cycling Museum

  1 hr+  All year

An excellent display of cycling history from 1818 to the present day. There are more than 400 machines on display and a large exhibition of cycling memorabilia including the first cycle oil lamps as well as candle lamps. Plus cycling medals, fobs and badges.

* Extensive library of cycling books
* Gallery of cycling pictures & cycle frame donated by Chris Boardman

Location
1 mile N of Camelford on B3266

Opening
Sun–Thu 10am–5pm

Admission
Adult £3.25, Child £1.90

Contact
The Old Station, Camelford PL32 9TZ

t 01840 212811
w chycor.co.uk/britishcycling-museum

197 Falmouth

National Maritime Museum Cornwall

  2 hrs  All year

Enjoy breathtaking views from the 29m tower, one of only three natural underwater viewing locations in the world, hands-on interactives, audio-visual immersive experiences, talks, special exhibitions and the opportunity to get out on to the water.

* Climb to the top of the tower for views over the harbour
* Display of Cornish maritime heritage

Location
SE end of harbourside. Or follow signs from A39 for Park & Float

Opening
Daily: 10am–5pm

Admission
Adult £7, Child & Concs £4.80

Contact
Discovery Quay, Falmouth TR11 3QY

t 01326 313388
w nmmc.co.uk
e enquiries@nmmc.co.uk

© Bob Berry

198 Falmouth

Pendennis Castle

2 hrs | All year

A Cornish fortress, ready for military action since the C16, Pendennis and its sister, St Mawes Castle, face each other across the mouth of the River Fal. Constructed *c.*1540, they are the Cornish end of a chain of castles built by Henry VIII along the south coast.

Location
Pendennis Head, 1 mile S of Falmouth

Opening
Daily: 1 Apr–30 Jun & Sep 10am-5pm;
1 Jul–31 Aug 10am -6pm;
Oct–Mar 10am–4pm;
every Sat 10am–4pm

Admission
Adult £4.80, Child £2.40, Concs £3.60

Contact
Pendennis Head,
Falmouth TR11 4LP

t 01326 316594
w english-heritage.org.uk
e jane.kessell@english-heritage. org.uk

199 Goonhilly

Goonhilly Satellite Earth Station

2 hrs+ | All year

One of the most striking attractions in Cornwall, on the Lizard Peninsula. Visit Goonhilly, the largest satellite station on earth, to learn about space and modern communications through the multimedia visitor centre, interactive exhibits and film shows with tour guides.

* Fastest internet café in the world
* Send email to an alien, 3D virtual head creation

Location
Follow brown tourist signs from Helston

Opening
Tue–Thu & Sat–Sun from 10am
Closing times vary, please phone for details

Admission
Adult £6.50, Child £4.50, Concs £5

Contact
Goonhilly, Helston TR12 6LQ

t 0800 679593
w goonhilly.bt.com
e goonhilly.visitorscentre@bt.com

200 Helston

Godolphin House & Garden

2 hrs | Easter–Oct

This historic landscape includes Godolphin Hill with its wonderful views over west Cornwall. The house has fine C16 and C17 English oak furniture and a collection of superb paintings.

* The Estate has more than 400 archaeological features
* House dates from C15

 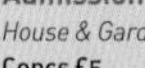

Location
On B3303 turn left to Godolphin Cross. Through Godolphin Cross village & house is on the left with brown tourist signs

Opening
Easter–Oct Tue–Fri & Sun 11am–5pm

Admission
House & Gardens Adult £6, Child £1.50, Concs £5
Gardens Adult £3, Child £1, Concs £2

Contact
Godolphin Cross, Helston TR13 9RE

t 01736 763194
w godolphinhouse.com
e info@godolphinhouse.com

201 Helston

Poldark Mine & Heritage Complex

3 hrs Easter–Oct

This Cornish tin mine has several underground routes with tunnels and stairs and is believed to be Europe's most complete mine workings open to the public. Some machines and water-pumping engines are on display around the garden.

* Entry to the site itself is free
* Family attractions in addition to mine

Location
2 miles from Helston on B3297

Opening
Daily:10am–5.30pm (last tours 4pm)

Admission
Adult £7.50, Child £4.90, Concs £7

Contact
Wendron, Helston TR13 0ES

t 01326 573173
w poldark-mine.co.uk
e info@poldark-mine.co.uk

202 Isles of Scilly

Isles of Scilly Museum

1½ hrs All year

The museum was established after severe gales in the winter of 1962, which yielded up some remarkable Romano-British finds. It now houses an extremely diverse collection including material from wrecks, as well as the original Romano-British artefacts.

* Family history research facility (by appointment)
* Temporary exhibitions throughout the year

Location
5 min walk from Hugh Town harbour

Opening
Easter–Sep Mon–Sat 10am–4.30pm; Oct–Easter Mon–Sat 10am–12noon

Admission
Adult £2.50, Child 50p, Concs £1.50

Contact
Church Street, St Mary's, Isles of Scilly TR21 0JT

t 01720 422337
w iosmuseum.org
e info@iosmuseum.org

203 Launceston

Launceston Castle

1 hr Apr–Oct

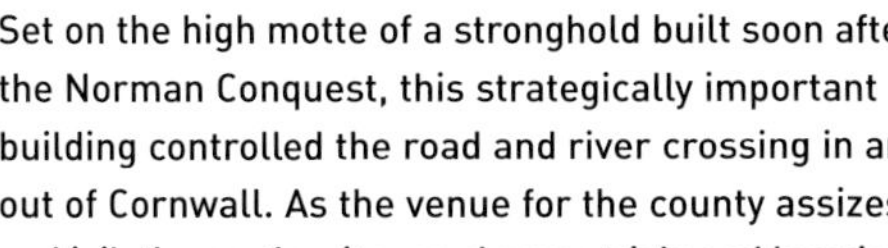

Set on the high motte of a stronghold built soon after the Norman Conquest, this strategically important building controlled the road and river crossing in and out of Cornwall. As the venue for the county assizes and jail, the castle witnessed many trials and hangings.

* Built first as earthwork after Norman Conquest
* Administrative centre for the Earls of Cornwall

Location
In town centre

Opening
Daily: Apr–Jun 10am–5pm; Jul–Aug 10am–6pm; Sep 10am–5pm; Oct 10am–4pm

Admission
Adult £2.30, Child £1.20, Concs £1.70

Contact
Launceston PL15 7DR

t 01566 772365
w english-heritage.org.uk
e launceston.castle@english-heritage.org.uk

204 Marazion

St Michael's Mount

2 hrs+ All year

This former Benedictine priory and castle is one of Britain's most visited properties. It is linked to the mainland when the tide is out by a 500-yard causeway. Beautiful gardens contain many rare plants that are not often found growing out of doors in Britain.

* Once an important harbour & home to 300 people
* Castle is full of history including garrison & armoury

Location
Off coast of Marazion on A394

Opening
26 Mar–29 Oct Sun–Fri 10.30am–5.30pm (last admission 4.45 pm on the island); Nov–end Mar please phone for details
Gardens May & Jun Mon–Fri; Jul–Oct Thu– Fri

Admission
Adult £6, Child £3
Gardens £3

Contact
Marazion TR17 0HT

t 01736 710507
w stmichaelsmount.co.uk
e godolphin@manor-office.co.uk

205 Mawnan Smith

Trebah Gardens

3 hrs

All year

This lovely subtropical ravine paradise winds through huge plantations of 100-year-old giant tree ferns, rhododendrons, magnolias, camellias, palms and 2 acres of massed hydrangeas to a private beach on the Helford River.

* Unique collection of rare plants & trees

Location
Follow signs from junction off A39 & A394

Opening
Daily: Mar–Oct 10.30am–6.30pm (last admission 5pm); Nov–Feb 10.30am–dusk

Admission
Mar–Oct Adult £6.30, Child £2, Concs £5.30; Nov–Feb £3, £1, £2.50

Contact
Mawnan Smith, Falmouth TR11 5JZ

t 01326 252200
w trebah-garden.co.uk
e mail@trebah-garden.co.uk

206 Padstow

Prideaux Place

2 hrs

Apr–Oct

Explore 40 acres of landscaped grounds with terraced walks, a formal garden, a temple, Roman antiquities and the C9 Cornish Cross. An ancient deer park overlooks the estuary of the River Camel. Also see the Elizabethan plastered ceiling in the Great Chamber.

* Treasures include the Prideaux porcelain collection
* Guided tours of the house available

Location
Off B3276, Padstow–Newquay road

Opening
6 Apr–9 Apr & mid-May–early Oct Sun–Thu *House:* 1.30pm–4pm *Grounds:* 12.30pm–5pm

Admission
Adult £6.50, Child £2
Grounds: £2, £1

Contact
Padstow PL28 8RP

t 01841 532411
w prideauxplace.co.uk
e office@prideauxplace.co.uk

207 Penzance

Geevor Tin Mine

  2 hrs  All year

The last working mine in West Penwith and now a mining museum and the largest preserved mining site in the UK, extending a mile inland. Some areas of the mine are 200 years old. The museum provides insight into the history of this traditional Cornish industry.

* Expert guides conduct underground tours
* Display of original mining machinery

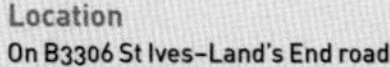

Location
On B3306 St Ives–Land's End road

Opening
Apr–Oct Sun–Fri 10am–5pm;
Nov–Mar Sun–Fri 10am–4pm

Admission
Adult £7.50, Child £4.30, Concs £7

Contact
Pendeen, Penzance TR19 7EW
t 01736 788662
w geevor.com
e bookings@geevor.com

208 Penzance

Land's End Visitor Centre

  2 hrs+  All year

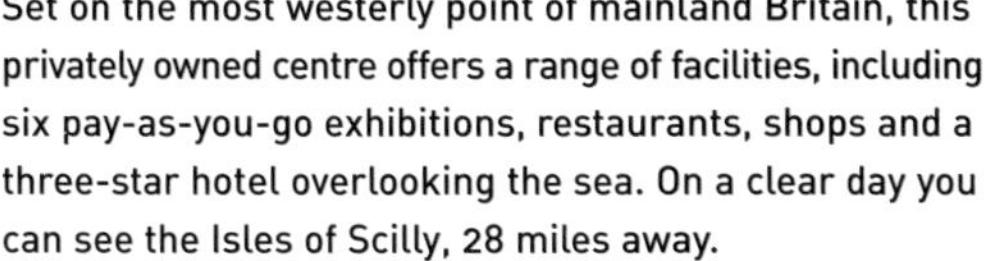

Set on the most westerly point of mainland Britain, this privately owned centre offers a range of facilities, including six pay-as-you-go exhibitions, restaurants, shops and a three-star hotel overlooking the sea. On a clear day you can see the Isles of Scilly, 28 miles away.

* Land's End sweet factory
* Stunning scenery

Location
At end of A30, 12 miles from Penzance

Opening
Daily: From 10am (closing times vary)
Please phone for details

Admission
Adult £9.95, Child £5.95, Concs £7.95

Contact
Land's End, Sennen,
Penzance TR19 7AA
t 01736 871501
w landsend-landmark.co.uk
e info@landsend.landmark.co.uk

209 Porthcurno

Minack Theatre

  2 hrs+  All year

This has to be one of the world's most spectacular theatres – an open-air auditorium carved into the cliffs high above Porthcurno's sandy cove. Founded and largely built by Rowena Cade in the 1930s, it has a remarkable story now told in the visitor centre.

* Full programme of performances through summer
* Fantastic views from the visitor centre

Location
3 miles from Land's End off A30

Opening
Daily: Apr–Sep 9.30am–5.30pm;
Oct–Mar 10am–4pm

Admission
Seasonal charges, please phone for details

Contact
Porthcurno, Penzance TR19 6JU
t 01736 810181
w minack.com
e info@minack.com

210 Porthcurno

Porthcurno Telegraph Museum

2 hrs All year

This award-winning industrial heritage museum explains the development of international telegraphy at the site of the first underground cables that linked Britain to the rest of the world (1870). It is housed in an underground station built for protection during WWII.

* Staff on hand to show how instruments work
* Adjacent to stunning Minack Theatre

Location
3 miles from Land's End off A30

Opening
Easter–Oct daily 10am–5pm
Nov–Easter Sun & Mon 10am–5pm
(last admission 4pm)

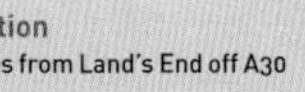

Admission
Adult £4.95, Child £2.75, Concs £4.40

Contact
Porthcurno, Penzance TR19 6JX

t 01736 810966
w porthcurno.org.uk
e mary.godwin@cw.com

211 St Austell

The Eden Project

4 hrs+ All year

The Eden Project is dominated by two huge biomes – effectively the largest greenhouses in the world. The Humid Tropics Biome recreates the conditions and plant life of a lush rainforest while the Warm Temperate Biome has a Mediterranean climate.

* Project has 2 million visitors a year
* See coffee plants, palm trees & pineapples

Location
Follow signs from A390 at St Austell & A30 Bodmin bypass

Opening
Daily: *summer* 9.30am–6pm (last admission 4.30pm)
winter 10am–4.30pm (last admission 3.30pm)

Admission
Adult £13.80, Child £5, Concs £10

Contact
Bodelva, St Austell PL24 2SG

t 01726 811900
w edenproject.com
e info@edenproject.com

212 St Austell

Lost Gardens of Heligan

4 hrs+ All year

These world-renowned gardens comprise 80 acres of pleasure grounds plus a complex of walled gardens. Many spectacular subtropical species thrive in this frost-free Cornish valley. Heligan has undergone one of the largest restoration projects of its kind in Europe.

* Stunning collection of plants from all over the world
* Featured in a major Channel 4 series

Location
From St Austell take Mevagissey road (B3273) & follow brown tourist signs

Opening
Mar–Oct 10am–6pm;
Nov–Feb 10am–5pm

Admission
Adult £7.50, Child £4, Concs £7

Contact
Pentewan,
St Austell PL26 6EN

t 01726 845100
w heligan.com
e info@heligan.com

© Ben Foster

213 St Ives

Tate St Ives

2 hrs All year

St Ives has been famous as an artists' colony since the early C20 and the opening of Tate St Ives in 1993 provided the opportunity to view modern art in the surroundings and atmosphere that inspired them. The gallery also manages the Hepworth Museum and Sculpture Garden.

* Spectacular coastal setting
* Visit Barbara Hepworth's home

Location
Near Porthmeor Beach

Opening
Mar–Oct daily 10am–5.20pm; Nov–Feb Tue–Sun 10am–4.20pm (last admission 30 mins before close)

Admission
Adult £5.75, Child free, Concs £3.25

Contact
Porthmeor Beach, St Ives TR26 1TG

t 01736 796226
w tate.org.uk/stives
e tatestivesinfo@tate.org.uk

© Tate

214 Tintagel

Tintagel Castle

1 hr+ All year

This is the legendary home of King Arthur and Merlin, and its awesome setting with the crashing waves on three sides adds fuel to the story. The ruins that stand today are the remnants of a castle built by Earl Richard of Cornwall, brother of Henry III.

* Short film about the castle
* Put your foot in 'Arthur's Footprint'

Location
Take ½-mile track from village (no vehicles beyond village)

Opening
Daily: Apr–Sep 10am–6pm; Oct 10am–5pm; Nov–Mar 10am–4pm

Admission
Adult £4.30, Child £2.20, Concs £3.20

Contact
Tintagel PL34 0HE

t 01840 770328
w english-heritage.org.uk/membership
e tintagel.castle@english-heritage.org.uk

215 Truro

Royal Cornwall Museum

2 hrs All year

Cornwall's oldest and most prestigious museum, famed for its important collections. See a myriad of minerals, view our unwrapped mummy and discover Cornwall's unique culture. The museum presents an exciting range of changing exhibitions from textiles to contemporary art.

* Diverse range of temporary exhibitions
* *Stingi Lulu's* Pacific-Rim restaurant

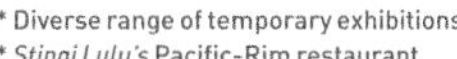   

Location
In town centre

Opening
Mon–Sat 10am–5pm (last admission 4.30pm) (closed Sun & Bank Hols)

Admission
Free

Contact
River Street, Truro TR1 2SJ

t 01872 272205
w royalcornwallmuseum.org.uk
e enquiries@royalcornwallmuseum.org.uk

216 Barnstaple

Arlington Court

3 hrs+ Easter–Oct

Arlington Court houses the treasures amassed during the travels of Miss Rosalie Chichester. These include model ships, tapestries, pewter and shells. The stable block contains a magnificent collection of horse-drawn vehicles offering carriage rides around the grounds.

* 'Batcam' films bat colony May–Sept
* Spectacular gardens & extensive parkland

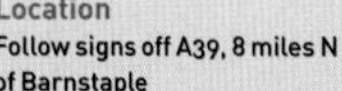

Location
Follow signs off A39, 8 miles N of Barnstaple

Opening
House Easter–Oct 11am–5pm (closed Sat)
Gardens Jul–Aug daily 10.30am–5.30pm

Admission
House & Gardens Adult £7, Child £3.50
Gardens & Parkland £5, £2.50

Contact
Arlington, Barnstaple EX31 4LP

t 01271 850296
w nationaltrust.org.uk
e arlingtoncourt@nationaltrust.org.uk

217 Barnstaple

Marwood Hill Gardens

2 hrs+ All year

Marwood Hill Gardens covers 20 acres and has year-round interest. Camellias and rhododendrons are planted on the walk along the north side of a walled garden, which includes three borders of herbaceous peonies. The Lower Garden has a series of small lakes.

* Bog garden houses a National Collection of astilbes
* Walk between gardens passes plantings of bamboo

Location
4 miles N of Barnstaple

Opening
Daily: 9.30am–5.30pm

Admission
Adult £4, Child free

Contact
Barnstaple EX31 4EB

t 01271 342528
w marwoodhillgarden.co.uk
e marwoodhillgarden@netbreeze.co.uk

218 Beer

Pecorama Millennium Garden

3 hrs+ Easter–Oct

This unusual garden is one of a number of attractions on this hillside site overlooking Beer. Notable designs include a roof garden enclosed by a ruined tower, a moat garden, a rainbow garden and stunning stonework – all with appropriately coloured plants and foliage.

* Miniature railway with steam & diesel locomotives
* Fully restored Pullman carriage from 1950s

Location
Follow signs to Beer turning on A3052

Opening
Easter–Oct Mon–Fri 10am–5.30pm, Sat 10am–1pm, Sun 10am–5.30pm

Admission
Please phone for details

Contact
Beer, nr Seaton EX12 3NA

t 01297 20580
w peco-uk.com
e pecorama@btconnect.com

© Alan Russell

219 Bovey Tracey

Devon Guild of Craftsmen

  2 hrs  All year

These are the South West's leading gallery and craft showrooms with work selected from some 240 makers, many with national and international reputations. Riverside Mill, the Guild's showcase, features frequently changing exhibitions.

* Newly refurbished gallery, extended craft shop
* Riverside Mill dates from 1850

Location
Follow signs for Bovey Tracey, 2 miles from A38

Opening
Daily: *winter* 10am–5.30pm
summer Sun–Thu 10am–5.30pm, Fri–Sat 10am–8pm

Admission
Free, donations welcomed

Contact
Riverside Mill, Bovey Tracey TQ13 9AF
t 01626 832223
w crafts.org.uk
e devonguild@crafts.org.uk

220 Brixham

The Golden Hind

  1 hr  Mar–Oct

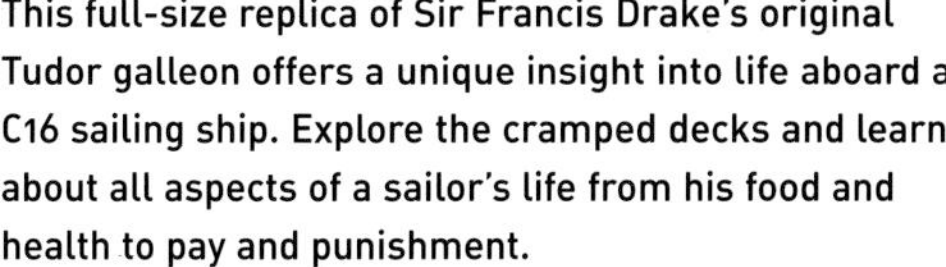
This full-size replica of Sir Francis Drake's original Tudor galleon offers a unique insight into life aboard a C16 sailing ship. Explore the cramped decks and learn about all aspects of a sailor's life from his food and health to pay and punishment.

* Re-enactments & special exhibitions
* Tours for groups & schools

Location
Follow A3022 to town centre. Ship moored in harbour

Opening
Daily: Mar–Jun & Sep–Oct 9.30am–4pm; Jul–Aug 9am–8pm

Admission
Adult £3, Child & Concs £2

Contact
Brixham Harbour, Brixham TQ5 8AW
t 01803 856223
w goldenhind.co.uk
e info@goldenhind.co.uk

221 Buckfastleigh

Buckfast Abbey

  3 hrs+  All year

Buckfast Abbey is the only English medieval monastery to have been restored after the Dissolution and used again for its original purpose. This active Benedictine community provides an insight into monastic life and remarkable church architecture in a peaceful setting.

* Impressive marble flooring
* Original building dates from 1018

Location
Off A38, follow signs on A384

Opening
Daily: *summer* 9am–5.30pm
winter 9am–5pm

Admission
Free

Contact
Buckfastleigh TQ11 0EE
t 01364 645500
w buckfast.org.uk
e enquiries@buckfast.org.uk

222 Buckfastleigh

Buckfast Butterfly Farm & Dartmoor Otter Sanctuary

  2 hrs  Easter–Oct

This unusual attraction offers an educational experience for animal lovers. See free-flying moths and butterflies from around the world in the indoor tropical garden. Otters swim in large glass enclosures ensuring marvellous underwater views.

* Butterfly habitat constructed to maximise viewing
* British, Asian & North American otters on show

Location
Follow signs from A38 at A384 to Buckfastleigh

Opening
Easter–Oct 10am–5.30pm

Admission
Adult £6.25, Child £4.75, Concs £5.75

Contact
Buckfastleigh TQ11 0DZ

t 01364 642916
w ottersandbutterflies.co.uk
e contact@ottersandbutterflies.co.uk

223 Budleigh Salterton

Bicton Park Botanical Gardens

 3 hrs+  All year

Bicton has sweeping lawns, water features, English borders and a formal Italian garden that survived the Capability Brown period. Its palm house is one of the world's most beautiful garden buildings. The museum contains an enormous collection of rural memorabilia.

* Exhibition of traction engines & vintage machinery
* Children's play area & narrow-gauge railway

Location
Off M5 at junction 30. Follow signs via Newton Poppleford

Opening
Daily: *summer* 10am–6pm
winter 10am–5pm

Admission
Adult £5.95, Child & Concs £4.95

Contact
East Budleigh,
Budleigh Salterton EX9 7BJ

t 01395 568465
w bictongardens.co.uk
e info@bictongardens.co.uk

224 Cullompton

Coldharbour Mill & Working Wool Museum

  4 hrs+   All year

This 200-year-old waterside mill houses working spinning and weaving machines, and steam engines restored to their former glory. There are regular exhibitions throughout the year.

* Guided tours available
* Steam engines can be seen running at special events

Location
2 miles off junction 27 of M5. Follow signs to Willand & museum

Opening
Daily: Mar–Oct 10.30am–5pm;
Nov–Feb please phone for details

Admission
Adult £6.25, Child £2.95 Concs £5.75

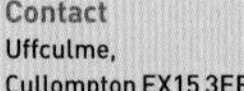

Contact
Uffculme,
Cullompton EX15 3EE

t 01884 840960
w coldharbourmill.org.uk
e info@coldharbourmill.org.uk

225 Dartmouth

Blackpool Sands

  1 hr+  Apr–Oct

This award-winning beach offers superb swimming conditions in clean clear water with a lifeguard on duty during the summer. Facilities include restaurants, a shop selling beach clothes and games, kayak, boogie board and wetsuit and snorkel hire.

* European Blue Flag beach
* Dogs allowed 1 Nov–1 Mar only

Location
On A379, 3 miles from Dartmouth

Opening
Daily: Apr–Oct 9am–7pm

Admission
Free; Car park charges apply
Apr–Oct £2–£5

Contact
Blackpool, Dartmouth TQ6 0RG

t 01803 770606
w blackpoolsands.co.uk
e info@blackpoolsands.co.uk

226 Dartmouth

Dartmouth Castle

1 hr   All year

Built by C14 merchants (led by Mayor John Hawley) to protect themselves from invasion, this brilliantly positioned castle juts out into the narrow entrance to the Dart estuary. It is said that Hawley was the inspiration for Chaucer's Shipman in *The Canterbury Tales*.

* Hands-on exhibition brings 600 years of history to life
* Complete Victorian gun battery

Location
1 mile SE of Dartmouth on B3025

Opening
Daily: Apr–Jun 10am–5pm; Jul–Aug 10am–6pm; Sep 10am–5pm; Oct 10am–4pm; Nov–Mar Sat & Sun 10am–4pm

Admission
Adult £3.70, Child £1.90, Concs £2.80

Contact
Castle Road, Dartmouth TQ6 0JN

t 01803 833588
w english-heritage.org.uk
e dartmouth@english-heritage. org.uk

227 Exeter

Exeter Cathedral

1 hr+   All year

This magnificent Gothic cathedral was largely rebuilt in the C13, though the imposing towers remain from the earlier Norman structure. The cathedral has played an important historical role through the ages, particularly in the C17.

* Elaborately carved choir stalls of particular note
* Visited by William the Conqueror

Location
Just off high street in city centre

Opening
Daily: Guided tours Apr–Oct

Admission
Free, donations encouraged
Charge for group visits

Contact
The Cloisters, Exeter EX1 1HS

t 01392 285983
w exeter-cathedral.org.uk
e visitors@exeter-cathedral.org.uk

228 Exeter

Killerton House

 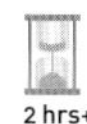  

2 hrs+   Mar–Oct

An elegant C18 house in a hillside garden. The house has many treasures including the famous Killerton costume collection. The garden features a Victorian rock garden, an interesting ice house and a rustic Bear's Hut. There are fine views across the Devon countryside from the lawns.

* Costume collection extends to more than 9,000 items
* Costume display changes every year

Location
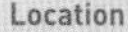
6 miles from Exeter off B3181

Opening
Mid-Mar–Jul & Sep Wed–Mon 11am–5pm; Aug daily 11am–5pm; Oct Wed–Sun 11am–5pm

Admission
House & Gardens
Adult £7.30, Child £3.50

Contact
Broadclyst, Exeter EX5 3LE

t 01392 881345
w nationaltrust.org.uk

229 Exeter

Powderham Castle

  3 hrs+  Easter–Oct

Built in 1390, the Courtenay family home is occupied by the 18th Earl of Devon. It has rich history and architecture (a music room by Wyatt), fine views of the deer park and Exe estuary and animals in the secret garden, a miniature train and new Courtenay fort.

* Fabulous grand staircase once part of medieval hall
* Children's secret garden

Location
8 miles from Exeter on A379 to Dawlish

Opening
Easter–Oct Sun–Fri 10am–5.30pm

Admission
Adult £7.95, Child £5.95 Concs £7.50

Contact
Kenton, Exeter EX6 8JQ

t 01626 890243
w powderham.co.uk
e castle@powderham.co.uk

231 Great Torrington

RHS Garden Rosemoor

  3 hrs+  All year

RHS Garden Rosemoor is a garden of great importance. To the huge range of plants collected by its former owner, the RHS has added features such as the formal garden, herbaceous borders, herb, fruit, vegetable and cottage gardens, and Mediterranean and winter gardens.

* Extensive rose garden is most popular feature
* Extensive stream & lakeside planting

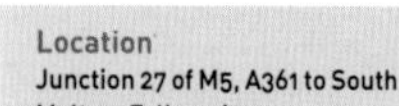

Location
Junction 27 of M5, A361 to South Molton. Follow signs

Opening
Daily: Apr–Sep 10am–6pm; Oct–Mar 10am–5pm

Admission
Adult £5.50, Child £1.50

Contact
Great Torrington EX38 8PH

t 01805 624067
w rhs.org.uk/rosemoor
e rosemooradmin@rhs.org.uk

230 Great Torrington

Dartington Crystal

  3 hrs+  All year

Discover the history of glass and the Dartington company, internationally known for handmade contemporary glassware, in the visitor centre, and watch craftsmen at work in the factory. The factory shop is thought to be the biggest glass shop in the world.

* See Dartington's innovative glass designs
* Have your hand or foot cast

Location
In town centre off A386

Opening
Daily: Mon–Fri 9am–5pm, Sat 10am–5pm, Sun 10am–4pm (last tour 3.15pm)
No factory tour at weekends

Admission
Please phone for details

Contact
Great Torrington EX38 7AN

t 01805 626242
w dartington.co.uk
e tours@dartington.co.uk

232 Newton Abbott

Tuckers Maltings

2 hrs+ Easter–Oct

Britain's only working malt house open to the public, making malt from barley for beer. With its working Victorian machinery, Tuckers Maltings is an education for all ages with video and audio. See and taste real ale from the inhouse brewery.

* Guided tours last 1 hour
* Speciality beer shop open all year

Location
3 min walk from Newton Abbot railway station

Opening
Easter–Oct 10am–5pm (closed Sun)
Please phone for tour times

Admission
Adult £5.75, Child £3.45, Concs £4.95

Contact
Teign Road,
Newton Abbott TQ12 4AA

t 01626 334734
w tuckersmaltings.com
e info@tuckersmaltings.com

233 Okehampton

Okehampton Castle

3 hrs+ Apr–Sep

The impressive ruins of the largest castle in Devon stand on the banks of a river in the foothills of Dartmoor. The central keep is still impressive atop its motte, and there are excellent walks through the woodlands surrounding the castle.

* Free audio-tape tour available
* Beautiful picnic grounds

Location
1 mile SW of town centre

Opening
Daily: Apr–Jun & Sep 10am–5pm; Jun–Aug 10am–6pm

Admission
Adult £3, Child £1.50, Concs £2.30

Contact
Castle Lodge,
Okehampton EX20 1JA

t 01837 52844
w english-heritage.org.uk
e okehampton@english-heritage.org.uk

234 Paignton

Paignton Zoo Environmental Park

3 hrs+ All year

Home to some of the world's most endangered plants and animals, the zoo has hundreds of different animals and birds, including tigers, rhinos and giant tortoises. They are grouped into different climate zones that reflect the world's major habitats.

* 1,500 different animals from around the world
* Great day out for all the family

Location
Situated on A3022 Totnes road, 1 mile from Paignton town centre

Opening
summer daily 10am–6pm
winter daily 10am–dusk

Admission
Please phone for details

Contact
Totnes Road, Paignton TQ4 7EU

t 01803 697500
w paigntonzoo.org.uk
e info@paigntonzoo.org.uk

235 Plymouth

The National Marine Aquarium

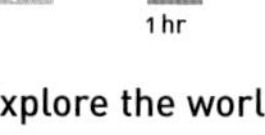

1 hr All year

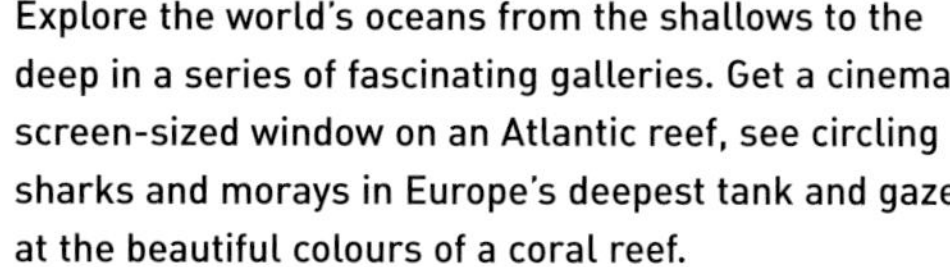

Explore the world's oceans from the shallows to the deep in a series of fascinating galleries. Get a cinema screen-sized window on an Atlantic reef, see circling sharks and morays in Europe's deepest tank and gaze at the beautiful colours of a coral reef.

* 'Meet the expert' sessions in the Discovery Theatre
* Café with panoramic views of the harbour

Location
Take A38 to Marsh Mills then along A374 Embankment Road. Follow brown & white fish signs

Opening
Daily: Nov–Mar 10am–5pm; Apr–Oct 10am–6pm

Admission
Adult £9.50, Child £5.75, Concs £8

Contact
Rope Walk, Coxside,
Plymouth PL4 0LF

t 01752 600 301
w national-aquarium.co.uk

236 Plymouth

Royal Albert Memorial Museum

2 hrs All year

This outstanding collection of local and national importance ranges from local archaeological finds to natural history displays from around the world as well as works of art. The impact of geology on Devon and its people is explored in the Geology at Work Gallery.

* Fascinating building to commemorate Prince Albert
* Display of clocks, watches & timekeeping

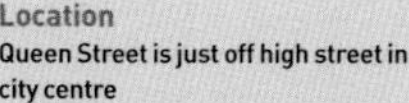

Location
Queen Street is just off high street in city centre

Opening
Mon–Sat 10am–5pm (closed Sun & Bank Hols)

Admission
Free

Contact
Queen Street,
Exeter EX4 3RX

t 01392 665858
w exeter.gov.uk/museums
e ramm@exeter.gov.uk

237 Tavistock

Morwellham Quay

4 hrs+ All year

Despite being 23 miles from the sea, Morwellham Quay was the Empire's greatest copper port in the time of Queen Victoria. Today the 1860s are recreated with a Tamar ketch moored at the quay, shops, cottages and costumed staff to act as guides.

* Take a tram underground to explore a copper mine
* Explore the farm, wildlife reserve & parkland

Location
4 miles from Tavistock on River Tamar

Opening
Daily: Easter–Oct 10am–5.30pm;
Nov–Easter 10am–4.30pm

Admission
Adult £8.90, Child £6, Concs £7.80
Reduced prices in winter

Contact
Morwellham, Tavistock PL19 8JL

t 01822 832766
w morwellham-quay.co.uk
e enquiries@morwellham-quay.co.uk

238 Tiverton

Tiverton Castle

1 hr Easter–Oct

Originally built in 1106 as the home of the Earl of Devon, the building now exhibits aspects of architecture from medieval to modern. Visitors can climb to the roof for views of the town and surrounding hillside, try on some English Civil War armour, and stroll round the gardens.

* Celebrating 900th anniversary
* Superb holiday accommodation, please phone for details

Location
A361 to Tiverton. Follow signs

Opening
Easter–Oct Sun, Thu & Bank Hols
2.30–5.30pm

Admission
Adult £4, Child £2

Contact
Park Hill,
Tiverton EX16 6RP

t 01884 253200
w tivertoncastle.com
e tiverton.castle@ukf.net

239 Torquay

Bygones

2 hrs+ All year

This life-size Victorian street with shops and period rooms also features a giant model railway and railwayana collection, an interactive and illuminated children's fantasy land, a multisensory WWI trench with militaria collection and a real Anderson shelter.

* Housed in a former cinema
* Christmas is a winter wonderland in a Victorian street

Location
Well signed from Torquay harbour

Opening
Daily: Apr–Jun & Sep 10am–6pm;
Nov–Mar 10am–5pm;
Jul–Aug Wed–Thu 10am–9.30pm,
Fri–Tue 10am–6pm

Admission
Adult £5.50, Child £3.50, Concs £4.95

Contact
Fore Street, St Mary Church,
Torquay TQ1 4PR

t 01803 326108
w bygones.co.uk

240 Torquay

Living Coasts

2 hrs+ All year

A unique aquatic visitor attraction, focusing on the conservation of coastal and marine life around the globe. The spacious interior of the meshed aviary allows free flight for the birds and access for visitors, enabling an intimacy unusual in seabird exhibits in this country.

* Adopt an animal & underwater viewing
* Special events throughout the year

Location
In town centre on the harbourside

Opening
Daily: Mar–Sep 10am–6pm; Oct–Feb 10am–5pm

Admission
Adult £6.75, Child £4.70, Concs £5.25

Contact
Torquay Harbourside, Beacon Quay, Torquay TQ1 2BG

t 01803 202470
w livingcoasts.org.uk
e info@livingcoasts.org.uk

241 Torquay

Torquay Museum

1 hr All year

Devon's oldest established museum takes you on a journey through time, exploring local history through prehistoric artefacts from Kents Cavern to WWII. Discover the story of Torquay's famous resident Agatha Christie and see a giant replica of a Japanese man-flying kite.

* Don't miss the fantastic new Explorers Gallery, opens spring 2007
* More than 300,000 natural history specimens in store

Location
Near Torquay harbour, a short walk from clocktower

Opening
Mon–Sat 9.30am–5pm, Sun & mid-Jul–Sep 1.30pm–5pm

Admission
Adult £3, Child £1.50, Concs £2

Contact
529 Babbacombe Road, Torquay TQ1 1HG

t 01803 293975
w torquaymuseum.org

242 Totnes

Totnes Castle

1 hr Apr–Oct

Totnes Castle sits high on a hill above the town, commanding the approaches from three valleys. One of the best surviving examples of a Norman motte and bailey castle, its C11 wood structure was replaced by a stone keep in the C13 and C14.

* Keep has survived in excellent condition
* Keep surrounded by a curtain wall

Location
On a hill overlooking Totnes

Opening
Daily: Apr–Jun & Sep 10am–5pm; Jul–Aug 10am–6pm; Oct 10am–4pm

Admission
Adult £2.40, Child £1.20, Concs £1.80

Contact
Castle Street, Totnes TQ9 5NU

t 01803 864406
w english-heritage.org.uk

243 Beaminster

Mapperton Gardens

  1 hr+  Mar–Oct

These terraced valley gardens surround a delightful Tudor/Jacobean manor house, stable blocks, dovecote and All Saints church. They featured in dramatisations of Jane Austen's *Emma*, Rose Tremain's *Restoration* and Henry Fielding's *Tom Jones*.

* Shop with plants, pots and gift items; charming café
* Spring plant sale

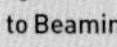

Location
15 mins from Crewkerne via A303 to Beaminster on B3163

Opening
House Please phone for details
Gardens Mar–Oct Sun–Fri 11am–5pm

Admission
Please phone for details

Contact
Mapperton,
Beaminster DT8 3NR

t 01308 862645
w mapperton.com
e office@mapperton.com

244 Blandford

Hall & Woodhouse Brewery

  1 hr   All year

The brewery visitor centre tells the story of Hall & Woodhouse through the ages. Devise your own beer recipes, enjoy a virtual tour of the brewery, read the guide to beer tasting and view a personal collection of brewery artefacts and old advertising materials.

* Fascinating insight into this 225-year-old brewery
* Beer can be bought at the brewery shop

Location
Follow signs from centre of Blandford

Opening
Visitor centre Mon–Sat 10.30am–5.30pm, Sun Easter–Oct 10am–2.30pm
Brewery tours Please phone for details

Admission
Free to visitor centre, charge for tour

Contact
Blandford, St Mary DT11 9LS

t 01258 452141
w hall-woodhouse.co.uk
e enquiries@hall-woodhouse.co.uk

245 Bournemouth

Dorset Belle Cruises

  1 hr+  Apr–Oct

Take a glorious coastal and harbour cruise on one of the routes linking Bournemouth, Swanage and Poole Quay as well as Brownsea Island and the Isle of Wight. Specialist cruises are also available along this stunning coastline. Dogs are not allowed on Brownsea Island.

* Ride in the shockwave speedboat
* Fireworks & magnificent sunset cruises

Location
Boats depart from Bournemouth pier, Swanage or Poole

Opening
Daily: Apr–Oct please phone for details of trips; Nov–Mar 10.30am–6pm

Admission
Adult from £7, Child from £2

Contact
Pier Approach,
Bournemouth BH2 5AA

t 01202 558550
w dorsetcruises.co.uk
e thedorsetbelle@aol.com

246 Bournemouth

Oceanarium Bournemouth

2 hrs All year

A visit to the oceanarium provides an encounter with marine life from across the globe. This is a fully interactive experience with feeding demonstrations and talks, a walk-through underwater tunnel and exhibits to help you discover more about this fascinating underwater world.

* Gift shop & café

Location
Follow signs to Bournemouth beaches & piers

Opening
Please phone for details

Admission
Adult £7.50, Child £5, Concs £6.50

Contact
Pier Approach,
Bournemouth BH2 5AA

t 01202 311993
w oceanarium.co.uk
e info@oceanarium.co.uk

248 Dorchester

The Dinosaur Museum

1 hr+ All year

The award-winning museum dedicated to dinosaurs combines life-size reconstructions of dinosaurs with fossils and skeletons to create an exciting hands-on experience. Multimedia displays tell the story of these giant prehistoric animals.

* Award-winning hands-on museum
* Top 10 Hands-on Museum

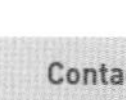

Location
In town centre

Opening
Daily: Easter–Oct 9.30am–5.30pm; Nov–Mar 10am–4.30pm

Admission
Adult £6.50, Child £4.75, Concs £5.50

Contact
Icen Way,
Dorchester DT1 1EW

t 01305 269880
w thedinosaurmuseum.com
e info@thedinosaurmuseum.com

247 Bovington

Tank Museum

3 hrs+ All year

There are few places in the world where you can touch a WWII tank. There are even fewer that have tanks that are in fully restored, running condition. Here are examples of tanks from both world wars to the modern day, along with a good deal of post war equipment.

* Indoor collection of 250 vehicles from 26 countries
* Vehicle rides & live demonstrations

Location
Off A352, between Dorchester & Wareham, near Wool. Follow signs from Bere Regis

Opening
Daily: 10am–5pm

Admission
Adult £10, Child £7, Concs £9

Contact
Bovington BH20 6JG

t 01929 405096
w tankmuseum.org
e info@tankmuseum.org

249 Dorchester

Dorset County Museum

  1 hr+  All year

Visit Dorset's main general museum with 16 display rooms exploring aspects of local history, literature, geology, archaeology, fine art and natural science. Winner of the Best Museum of Social History category in the 1998 Museum of the Year awards.

* Interactive audio guide
* New Jurassic Coast Geology Gallery

Location
In town centre. Follow museum signs

Opening
Oct–Jun Mon–Sat 10am–5pm;
Jul–Sep daily 10am–5pm

Admission
Adult £6, Child free, Concs £5

Contact
High West Street,
Dorchester DT1 1XA

t 01305 262735
w dorsetcountymuseum.org
e secretary@dor-mus.demon.co.uk

250 Dorchester

The Keep Military Museum of Devon & Dorset

  1 hr+  All year

Learn stories of courage, tradition and sacrifice of those who served in the regiments of Devon and Dorset over 300 years. Climb up to the battlements for spectacular views of Dorchester and the surrounding countryside, evoked in the novels of Thomas Hardy.

* Modern interactive & creative displays

Location
On A35 Bridport road on W edge of Dorchester

Opening
Apr–Sep Mon–Sat 9.30am–5pm;
Oct–Mar Tue–Sat 9am–5pm

Admission
Adult £4, Child & Concs £3

Contact
Bridport Road, Dorchester DT1 1RN

t 01305 264066
w keepmilitarymuseum.org
e curator@keepmilitarymuseum.org

251 Dorchester

Kingston Maurward Gardens

 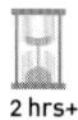 2 hrs+   All year

Kingston Maurward Gardens are set deep in Hardy's Dorset and are listed on the English Heritage register of gardens. The 35 acres of Georgian and Edwardian parkland and lawns sweep majestically down to the lake from the Georgian house (house not open to the public).

* National Collections of penstemons & salvias
* Edwardian formal & walled demonstration gardens

Location
1 mile E of Dorchester off A35

Opening
Daily: 5 Jan–21 Dec 10am–5.30pm or dusk if earlier

Admission
Adult £5, Child £3, Concs £4.50

Contact
Dorchester DT2 8PY

t 01305 215003
w kmc.ac.uk
e administration@kmc.ac.uk

252 Dorchester

The Tutankhamun Exhibition

  1 hr  All year

This exhibition recreates the original Tutankhamun artefacts found when the pharaoh's tomb was reopened. The artefacts are displayed in a model of the tomb chamber as it looked in 1922 when local archaeologist Howard Carter unearthed it.

* A permanent exhibition of the World Heritage Organisation
* Death of Tutankhamun exhibition

Location
3 min walk from town centre

Opening
Daily: Easter–Oct 9.30am–5.30pm;
Nov–Easter Mon–Fri 9.30am–5pm,
Sat 10am–5pm, Sun 10am–4.30pm

Admission
Adult £6.50, Child £4.75, Concs £5.50

Contact
High West Street,
Dorchester DT1 1UW

t 01305 269571
w tutankhamun-exhibition.co.uk
e info@tutankhamun-exhibition.co.uk

253 Dorchester

Zorb South UK

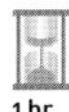
1 hr

Apr–Oct

Zorbing is the latest adrenaline-surging fix of fun. Ride within the gigantic 3 metre-high PVC ball down the 200-metre run – the world's longest. Options include tandem and triple-harnessed rides and hydro-zorbing in a water-filled zorb.

* Booking essential
* Under-6 age restriction

Location
Follow A35 NE of Dorchester at Stinsford roundabout & take the road signed Bockhampton/Tincleton. Situated approximately 1 mile on the left

Opening
Please phone for details

Admission
Please phone for details

Contact
Pine Lodge Farm, Bockhampton, Dorchester DT2 8QL

t 01929 426595
w zorbsouth.co.uk
e info@zorbsouth.co.uk

254 Poole

Brownsea Island National Trust

3 hrs+

Mar–Oct

Just a short boat journey (not National Trust) from Poole or Sandbanks, the island offers glorious views, a peaceful setting for walks and picnics, a rich variety of habitats for wildlife including the rare red squirrel, and a varied and colourful history.

* Birthplace of Scout & Guide movements
* Dorset Wildlife Trust Reserve (Adult £2, Child £1)

Location
By boat from Poole, Sandbanks, Bournemouth or Swanage

Opening
25 Mar–Oct from 10am (closing time varies)

Admission
Adult £4.40, Child £2.20

Contact
Poole Harbour, BH13 7EE

t 01202 707744
w nationaltrust.org.uk/brownsea
e brownseaisland@nationaltrust.org.uk

255 Portland

Portland Castle

1 hr+

Apr–Oct

Portland Castle was built by Henry VIII as part of his ambitious scheme of coastal defences against the French and Spanish. It has survived largely unaltered since the C16, making it one of the best-preserved examples of Henry's castles.

* Audio guides around the castle
* 70% of the attraction now has disabled access

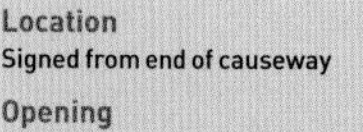
Location
Signed from end of causeway

Opening
Daily: Apr–Jun & Sep 10am–5pm; Jul–Aug 10am–6pm; Oct 10am–4pm

Admission
Adult £3.70, Child £1.90, Concs £2.80

Contact
Castletown, Portland Harbour, Weymouth DT5 1AZ

t 01305 820539
w english-heritage.org.uk/portland
e customers@english-heritage.org.uk

256 Sherborne

Sherborne Abbey

1 hr+

All year

This former cathedral is home to a flourishing community of Benedictine monks. It was the monks who carried out a major rebuilding in the C15 and gave the abbey one of its chief glories, the earliest great fan-vaulted roof in Europe.

* Sherborne School is part of the abbey complex
* Tours are free

Location
Centre of Sherborne

Opening
summer daily 8am–6pm
winter daily 8am–4pm

Admission
Free, donations encouraged

Contact
Parish Office, 3 Abbey Close, Sherborne DT9 3LQ

t 01935 812 452
w sherborneabbey.com
e parishsecretary@sherborneabbey.com

257 Sherborne

Sherborne Castle

2 hrs+

Apr–Oct

Built by Sir Walter Raleigh in 1594 and set in 30 acres of beautiful landscaped gardens around a 50-acre lake, Sherborne Castle has been home to the Digby family since 1617 and contains a fine collection of pictures, porcelain, furniture and decorative arts.

* Capability Brown lake
* Special events throughout the season

Location
½ mile E of Sherborne. Follow signs from A30

Opening
Castle & Gardens Apr–Oct 11am–4.30pm, closed Mon & Fri (House may be shut on Sat)

Admission
Adult £8, Child free, Concs £7.50

Contact
Sherborne Castle, New Road, Sherborne DT9 5NR

t 01935 813182
w sherbornecastle.com
e enquiries@sherbornecastle.com

258 St Leonards

Avon Heath Country Park

4 hrs+

All year

Dorset's largest country park has nearly 600 acres of heathland with stands of pine trees and birch woodland. Special events include pond-dipping, Easter egg trails, bug hunts, den-building, orienteering, animal tracks and signs, and dawn-chorus walks.

* Barbecue hire available
* Birthday parties & school visits

Location
On A31, 2 miles W of Ringwood

Opening
Park Daily: Apr–Sep 8am–7.30pm; Oct–Mar 8.30am–5.30pm
Visitor centre Daily: 11am–4pm

Admission
Free. Car park charge

Contact
Brocks Pine, St Leonards, Ringwood BH24 2DA

t 01425 478470

259 Studland

Studland Beach & Nature Reserve

3 hrs+ All year

Fine sandy beaches stretch for 3 miles from South Haven Point to the chalk cliffs of Handfast Point and Old Harry Rocks. Along the way are Shell Bay and a designated naturist area. The heathland behind the beach is a National Nature Reserve.

* Restrictions apply to dogs in summer

Location
Across Bournemouth & Swanage motor road ferry or via Corfe Castle on B3351

Opening
Daily: Please phone for details

Admission
Parking charges vary through seasons
Please phone for details

Contact
Countryside Office, Studland, Swanage BH19 3AX

t 01929 450259
w nationaltrust.org.uk
e studlandbeach@nationaltrust.org.uk

260 Swanage

Swanage Railway

2 hrs+ All year

This award-winning railway currently operates on the 6-mile track between Swanage and Norden, through the beautiful Isle of Purbeck, passing the magnificent ruins of Corfe Castle. At present there is extension work taking place to the north of Norden.

* Special events including Santa's Christmas train
* Train-driving lessons

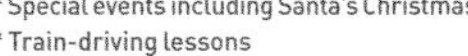    

Location
Station is in centre of Swanage, a few mins walk from the beach

Opening
Trains daily Apr–Oct. Weekends only rest of the year. Daily 26–31 Dec

Admission
Adult £7.50, Child & Concs £5.50

Contact
Station House, Swanage BH19 1HB

t 01929 425800
w swanagerailway.co.uk
e general@swanrail.freeserve.co.uk

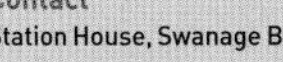

261 Tolpuddle

The Tolpuddle Martyrs Museum

 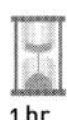 

1 hr All year

Learn the harrowing tale of the Martyrs' arrest, trial and punishment, leading to the foundation of modern-day trade unionism. The museum has a modern, informative, and educational exhibition, using interactive touch screen displays telling the story in text and images.

* Tolpuddle Martyrs Festival on 3rd Sun in Jul
* Souvenir shop

Location
On edge of Tolpuddle in W of village

Opening
Please phone for details

Admission
Free

Contact
Tolpuddle, Dorchester DT2 7EH

t 01305 848237
w tolpuddlemartyrs.org.uk
e tolpuddle@tuc.org.uk

262 Wareham

Corfe Castle

1 hr+ All year

One of Britain's most majestic ruins, this castle once controlled the gateway through the Purbeck Hills and in its time served as a fortress, prison and home. Many fine Norman and early English features remain.

* Special events including historical re-enactments
* Guided tours available

    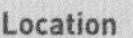

Location
On A351 Wareham–Swanage road

Opening
Daily: Mar & Oct 10am–5pm; Apr–Sep 10am–6pm; Nov–Feb 10am–4pm

Admission
Adult £5, Child £2.50

Contact
Corfe Castle, Wareham BH20 5EZ

t 01929 481294
w nationaltrust.org.uk
e corfecastle@nationaltrust.org.uk

263 Wareham

Lulworth Castle

3 hrs+ All year

Lulworth Castle was built between 1608 and 1610 but caught fire in 1929 and was all but ruined. In the 1970s careful restoration work began and the exterior is now as it was before the fire. This is a unique building with a rich history to discover.

* Open-air theatre & concerts, Spirit of Countryside Fayre
* Jousting shows throughout Aug

    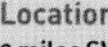

Location
3 miles SW of Wareham. Follow signs

Opening
summer Sun–Fri 10.30am–6pm
winter Sun–Fri 10.30am–4pm (closed Sat)

Admission
Adult £7, Child £4, Concs £6

Contact
East Lulworth, Wareham BH20 5QS

t 01929 400352
w lulworth.com
e estate.office@lulworth.com

264 Wareham

Monkey World

2 hrs+ All year

Monkey World is a sanctuary for more than 160 rescued primates from all over the world. Living at the park is the largest group of chimpanzees outside Africa. Orang-utans, gibbons and many more primates inhabit spacious enclosures in a natural woodland setting.

* Adoption scheme
* UK's great ape play area for kids

Location
Between Bere Regis & Wool, 1 mile from Wool railway station

Opening
Daily: 10am–5pm (6pm Jul–Aug)

Admission
Adult £9, Child & Concs £6.50

Contact
Longthorns, Wareham BH20 6HH

t 01929 462537
w monkeyworld.org
e apes@monkeyworld.org

265 Weymouth

Brewers Quay

3 hrs+ All year

This redeveloped Victorian brewery is at the heart of Weymouth's Old Harbour, offering speciality shopping, entertainment and eating out. Step back in time at the Timewalk and Brewery Days attraction.

* Events held throughout the year

Location
On harbour, 5 min from town centre

Opening
Daily: 10am–5.30pm

Admission
Free entry to complex
Timewalk attraction Adult £4.75, Child £3.50, Concs £4.25

Contact
Hope Square, Weymouth DT4 8TR

t 01305 777622
w brewers-quay.co.uk
e brewersquay@yahoo.co.uk

266 Weymouth

Deep Sea Adventure

 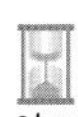 

3 hrs All year

Experience the exciting world of underwater exploration from the C17 to the high-tech equipment used today. Children of all ages will love to swing, slide and climb all four floors of this fantastic fun-filled play warehouse.

* Sharkey's Play & Party Warehouse for children up to 11 yrs
* Laser shoot-out nights available

Location
A35 into Weymouth. Follow signs

Opening
Daily: 9.30am (please phone for details of closing times)

Admission
Adult £3.95, Child £2.95, Concs £3.45

Contact
9 Custom House Quay, Old Harbour, Weymouth DT4 8BG

t 0871 222 5760
w deepsea-adventure.co.uk
e enquiries@deepsea-adventure.co.uk

267 Wimborne

Kingston Lacy House

 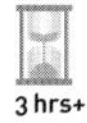 

3 hrs+ Mar–Dec

Kingston Lacy was home to the Bankes family for more than 300 years. All four floors are open to visitors and contain lavish interiors. The Edwardian laundry gives a fascinating insight into life below stairs 100 years ago. Formal gardens and parkland surround the house.

* Special snowdrop days in Jan
* Events throughout the year

Location
1½ miles from Wimborne on B3082

Opening
House & gardens Mar–Oct Wed–Sun & Bank Hols 11am–5pm (last admission 4pm)
Gardens Daily: Mar–Oct 10.30am–6pm; Nov–mid Dec 10.30am–4pm

Admission
House & Gardens Adult £9, Child £4.50
Gardens £4.50, £2.30

Contact
Wimborne BH21 4EA

t 01202 883402
w nationaltrust.org.uk
e kingstonlacy@nationaltrust.org.uk

268 Berkeley

Edward Jenner Museum

  1 hr+  Mar–Oct

This was the beautiful Queen Anne home of Edward Jenner (1749–1823), who discovered the smallpox vaccine and also studied birds, fossils and ballooning. There is an exhibition of modern immunology with the aim of promoting wider public understanding.

* Share your views on today's vaccination issues
* See how smallpox has been eradicated

Location
Junction 13/14 on M5. Follow brown tourist signs on A38

Opening
Mar–Oct Tue–Sat & Bank Hol Mon 12.30pm–5.30pm, Sun 1pm–5.30pm; Oct Sun only 1pm–5.30pm

Admission
Adult £4.25, Child £2.50, Concs £3.50

Contact
Church Lane, Berkeley GL13 9BN

t 01453 810631
w jennermuseum.com
e manager@jennermuseum.com

269 Bourton-on-the-Water

Cotswold Motor Museum & Toy Collection

  1 hr+  Feb–Nov

A veritable treasure of yesteryear. Although the main focus is on motoring, with a fine collection of classic cars, motorcycles and caravans, the museum has its very own toy collection – including teddy bears and aircraft plus a rare collection of pedal cars.

* Large collection of historic motoring signs
* Home to the children's TV character Brum

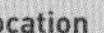

Location
In town centre at junction with Sherbourne Street

Opening
Daily: Feb–Nov 10am–6pm

Admission
Adult £3.50, Child £2.45

Contact
The Old Mill, Sherbourne Street, Bourton-on-the-Water, Cheltenham GL54 2BY

t 01451 821255
w cotswold-motor-museum.com
e motormuseum@csma-netlink.co.uk

270 Cheltenham

Chedworth Roman Villa

  2 hrs   Mar–Nov

The site comprises over a mile of walls, several fine mosaics, two bath houses, hypocausts, a water-shrine and latrine. Set in a wooded Cotswold combe, the site was excavated in 1864 and still has a Victorian atmosphere. The museum houses objects found on site.

* National Trust property
* One of the largest Roman villas in the country

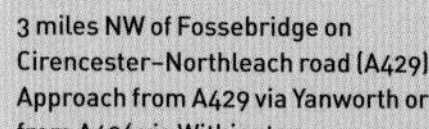

Location
3 miles NW of Fossebridge on Cirencester–Northleach road (A429). Approach from A429 via Yanworth or from A436 via Withington

Opening
Mar & 1 Nov–mid-Nov Tue–Sun 11am–4pm; Apr–Oct Tue–Sun 10am–5pm; Bank Hol Mon 10am–5pm

Admission
Adult £5.50, Child £3

Contact
Yanworth, nr Cheltenham GL54 3LJ

t 01242 890256
w nationaltrust.org.uk
e chedworth@nationaltrust.org.uk

271 Cheltenham

Cheltenham Art Gallery & Museum

  1 hr  All year

This collection has been built up over the past 100 years by generous residents who have donated their collections and items. There is a nationally important Arts & Crafts collection and one room is dedicated to Edward Wilson, who travelled with Scott to Antarctica.

* Started with donation of 43 important paintings in 1897
* Oriental gallery with Chinese pottery & costume

Location
In town centre

Opening
Mon–Sat 10am–5.20pm (closed Bank Hols)

Admission
Free, donations appreciated

Contact
Clarence Street, Cheltenham GL50 3JT

t 01242 237431
w cheltenham.artgallery.museum
e artgallery@cheltenham.gov.uk

272 Cheltenham

Holst Birthplace Museum

1 hr Feb–Dec

This Regency terrace house is where Gustav Holst, composer of *The Planets Suite,* was born in 1874. The story of the man and his music is told alongside a fascinating display of personal belongings, including his piano.The museum is also a fine period house.

* Working Victorian kitchen & laundry
* Regency drawing room & Edwardian nursery

Location
In Pitville area of Cheltenham, opposite Pitville Park

Opening
Feb–Dec Tue–Sat 10am–4pm (tours by appointment)

Admission
Adult £3.50, Child & Concs £3

Contact
4 Clarence Road, Cheltenham GL52 2AY

t 01242 524846
w holstmuseum.org.uk
e holstmuseum@btconnect.com

273 Chipping Campden

Hidcote Manor Gardens

2 hrs+ Apr–Sep

One of England's great gardens created early in the C20 by the horticulturalist Major Lawrence Johnston. A series of small gardens are separated by walls and hedges of different species. The varied style of the outdoor 'rooms' ensures an interesting visit at any time.

* Rare & unusual plants from around the world
* Shop & plant centre

Location
4 miles NE of Chipping Campden, off B4081

Opening
Please phone for details

Admission
Please phone for details

Contact
Hidcote Bartrim, Chipping Campden GL55 6LR

t 01386 438333
w nationaltrust.org.uk/hidcote
e hidcote@nationaltrust.org.uk

274 Chipping Campden

Kiftsgate Court Garden

1 hr Apr–Sep

A series of interconnecting gardens each with a distinct character, including a sheltered Mediterranean garden. There are many unusual plants that have been collected by the garden's creators – three generations of women.

* Newly added water garden
* Views stretch to the Bredon & Malvern Hills

Location
SE of Mickleton & 4 miles NE of Chipping Campden off B4081

Opening
Apr & Aug–Sep Sun, Mon & Wed 2pm–6pm; May–July Sat–Wed 12noon–6pm

Admission
Adult £5.50, Child £1.50

Contact
Chipping Campden GL55 6LN

t 01386 438777
w kiftsgate.co.uk
e kiftsgate@aol.com

275 Cinderford

Dean Heritage Centre

2 hrs+ All year

This is the museum of the Forest of Dean, situated by a mill pond in a wooded valley, with woodland walks, adventure playground and picnic site. There are exhibits reflecting the area's social and industrial history, including a beam engine and a water-wheel.

* Traditional charcoal-burning demonstrations annually
* Special events throughout the year (please phone for details)

Location
In Forest of Dean on B4227 at Soudley

Opening
Daily: British Summer Time 10am–5.30pm;
British Winter Time 10am–4pm

Admission
Adult £4.50, Child £2.50, Concs £3.50

Contact
Camp Mill, Soudley,
Cinderford GL14 2UB

t 01594 822170
w deanheritagemuseum.com
e deanmuse@btinternet.com

276 Gloucester

Clearwell Caves – Ancient Iron Mines

2 hrs All year

Mining in the Forest of Dean is believed to have started more than 7,000 years ago as people migrated back into the area after the last Ice Age. Large-scale iron-ore mining continued until 1945. Visitors are able to walk into some of the oldest underground mines in Britain.

* See how mine-extracts coloured iron oxides for paint
* 9 caverns open (deep-level visits by appointment)

Location
1½ miles S of Coleford

Opening
Mid-Feb–Oct 10am–5pm; Nov–Dec Christmas Fantasy, phone for details; Jan–Feb weekends only 10am–5pm

Admission
Adult £4.50, Child £2.80, Concs £4

Contact
Clearwell Caves & Ancient Iron Mines, nr Coleford, Royal Forest of Dean, Gloucester GL16 8JR

t 01594 832535
w clearwellcaves.com
e jw@clearwellcaves.co.uk

277 Gloucester

Gloucester City Museum & Art Gallery

1 hr All year

This museum is nearly 150 years old and in that time it has acquired a fine collection of art, plus archaeological, geological and natural history items. Many local people have donated their collections. Special treasures include paintings by Rembrandt and Turner.

* Hands-on & interactive computer displays
*Special exhibitions, activities & events

Location
In city centre at junction with Parliament Street

Opening
Tue–Sat 10am–5pm

Admission
Free

Contact
Brunswick Road GL1 1HP

t 01452 396131
w livinggloucester.co.uk
e citydockmuseum@gloucester.gov.uk

278 Gloucester

Gloucester Folk Museum

1 hr+ All year

In splendid Tudor and Jacobean buildings that date from the C16 and C17 are local history displays of Severn fishing, farming and craft industries, including pinmaking and shoemaking. There is also a children's gallery with toys and games.

* Exhibition of domestic life – kitchen & laundry
* Displays of a dairy, ironmonger's & carpenter's

Location
Signed from city centre

Opening
Tue–Sat 10am–5pm

Admission
Free

Contact
99–103 Westgate Street GL1 2PG

t 01452 396868/396869
w livinggloucester.co.uk
e folk.museum@gloucester.co.uk

279 Gloucester

National Waterways Museum

 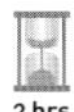 

2 hrs · All year

Housed in the historic Gloucester docks, the museum charts the story of Britain's canals with a nationally important collection. You enter through a replica lock complete with running water and the exhibits show what it was like to live and work on the waterways.

* Discover Gloucester's role as an important historical dock
* For boat trips please phone to check availability

Location
Follow signs for Historic Docks

Opening
Daily 10am–5pm

Admission
Adult £5.95, Child & Concs £4.75
Occasionally subject to change, please phone for details

Contact
Llanthony Warehouse,
Gloucester Docks GL1 2EH

t 01452 318200
w nwm.org.uk
e 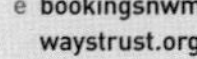bookingsnwm|@thewater waystrust.org

280 Gloucester

Soldiers of Gloucestershire Museum

1 hr+ · All year

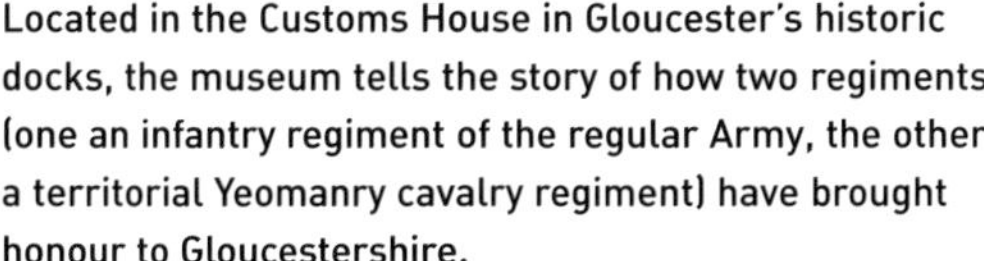

Located in the Customs House in Gloucester's historic docks, the museum tells the story of how two regiments (one an infantry regiment of the regular Army, the other a territorial Yeomanry cavalry regiment) have brought honour to Gloucestershire.

* The Gloucestershire Regiment (regular Army)
* The Royal Gloucestershire Hussars (territorials)

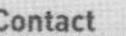

Location
Follow signs to Historic Docks

Opening
Daily 10am–5pm; closed winter Mons (last admission 4.30pm)

Admission
Adult £4.25, Child £2.25, Concs £3.25

Contact
Gloucester Docks GL1 2HE

t 01452 522682
w glosters.org.uk
e regimental-secretary@rgbw.army.mod.uk

281 Moreton-in-Marsh

Sezincote Gardens

1 hr+ · Jan–Nov

Built in a Moghul architectural style, a mixture of Hindu and Muslim, Sezincote is a very unusual English house. The gardens are fascinating and include canals, Moghul paradise gardens and a small Indian-style pavilion. The water-gardens contain many rare plants.

* Indian bridge decorated with Brahmin bulls
* Sezincote comes from Cheisnecote, 'the home of the oaks'

Location
1½ miles W of Moreton-in-Marsh on A44

Opening
House May–Jul & Sep Thu–Fri 2.30pm–6pm
Gardens Jan–Nov Thu, Fri & Bank Hol Mon 2pm–6pm or dusk if earlier

Admission
House & Gardens £6 (no children)
Gardens Adult £4, Child £1.50

Contact
nr Moreton-in-Marsh GL56 9AW

t 01386 700444

282 Moreton-in-Marsh

Wellington Aviation Museum

1 hr All year

Near a training school for Bomber Command during WWII, the museum contains an extensive collection of artefacts from the war years including a Vickers-Armstrong Wellington tail section that demonstrates the Barnes-Wallis design used to strengthen bombers.

* New exhibition of flight car mascots
* Collection of aviation & military history relating to the local area

Location
On A44 NE of Cheltenham

Opening
Tue–Sun 10am–12noon & 2pm–5pm; Jan–Feb Sat–Sun only

Admission
Adult £2, Child £1

Contact
British School House, Moreton-in-Marsh GL56 0BG

t 01608 650323
w wellingtonaviation.org

284 Tetbury

Chavenage House

1 hr+ May–Sep

This wonderful Elizabethan manor house, with Cromwellian connections, has changed little in 400 years. The house is noted for Cromwell's room, the main hall with its magnificent stained-glass windows, the ballroom and the Oak Room.

* Set in beautiful gardens
* A favourite with film makers

Location
On B4014, 1½ miles NW of Tetbury

Opening
May–Sep Thu, Sun & Bank Hols 2pm–5pm

Admission
Adult £6, Child £3

Contact
nr Tetbury GL8 8XP

t 01666 502329
w chavenage.com
e info@chavenage.com

283 Painswick

Painswick Rococo Garden

2 hrs Jan–Oct

The rococo style was a short but important design period more often associated with art or architecture. Few such gardens survive and its mixture of formal and informal creates a unique effect. Characterised by winding paths, the garden is full of fascinating features.

* Geometric kitchen garden, maze & snowdrops
* Interesting mixture of building styles

Location
Off A46, then B4073 ½ mile N of Painswick

Opening
Daily: Jan–Oct 11am–5pm

Admission
Adult £5, Child £2.50, Concs £4

Contact
Painswick GL6 6TH

t 01452 813204
w rococogarden.co.uk
e info@rococogarden.co.uk

285 Tetbury

Tetbury Police Museum

 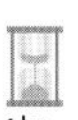 1 hr  All year

This museum is in the town's original police station and cells of a former magistrates' court. The building is Victorian with an interesting collection of artefacts from the Gloucestershire Constabulary. An under-courtroom display demonstrates what a trial would have been like.

* See early police batons, helmets & gas masks
* Visit Fred in the cells

Location
5 min walk from town centre

Opening
Mon–Fri 10am–3pm (closed Bank Hols)

Admission
Free, donations appreciated

Contact
The Old Court House, 63 Long Street, Tetbury GL8 8AA

t 01666 504670
w tetbury.org/policemuseum
e tetburycouncil@virgin.net

286 Tetbury

Westonbirt Arboretum

 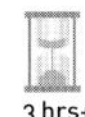 3 hrs+  All year

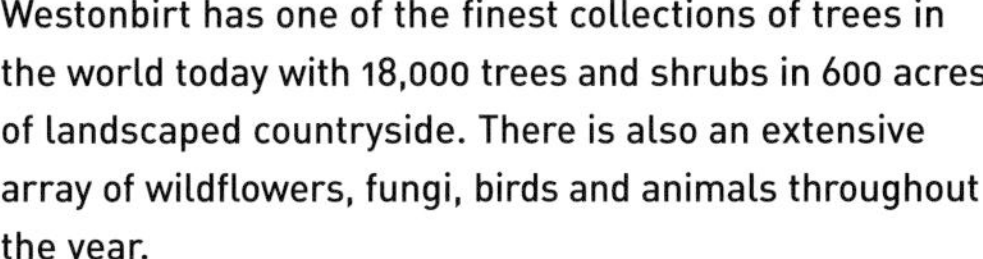

Westonbirt has one of the finest collections of trees in the world today with 18,000 trees and shrubs in 600 acres of landscaped countryside. There is also an extensive array of wildflowers, fungi, birds and animals throughout the year.

* Many events & concerts throughout the year
* Restaurant, café, forest shop & plant centre

Location
3 miles S of Tetbury on A433 to Bath

Opening
Daily: 10am–8pm or dusk if earlier

Admission
Prices change with the seasons
Adult £5–7.50, Child £1, Concs available, please phone for details

Contact
Westonbirt, nr Tetbury GL8 8QS

t 01666 880220
w forestry.gov.uk/westonbirt
e westonbirt@forestry.gsi.gov.uk

287 Uley

Owlpen Manor House & Gardens

  1 hr+  May–Sep

This Tudor manor house (1450–1616) has a splendid great hall and stands at the centre of a clutch of medieval buildings. The terraced garden is a rare survival of an early formal garden with magnificent yew topiary, old roses and box parterres.

* Queen Margaret of Anjou is said to haunt the manor
* Contains a fine collection of furniture, textiles & paintings

Location
1 mile E of Uley, off B4066

Opening
May–Sep Tue, Thu & Sun 2pm–5pm

Admission
House & Gardens Adult £5.25, Child £2.25
Gardens only £3.25, £1.25

Contact
nr Uley, Dursley GL11 5BZ

t 01453 860261
w owlpen.com
e sales@owlpen.com

288 Westbury-on-Severn

Westbury Court Garden

  1 hr  Mar–Oct

Originally laid out at the turn of the C17, this is the only restored Dutch water-garden in the country. It was also the National Trust's first garden restoration, completed in 1971, and is planted with species predating 1700.

* Replica C17 panelling installed in pavilion
* Parterre & vegetable plots reinstated to C17 style

Location
9 miles SW of Gloucester on A48

Opening
Mar–Jun Wed–Sun 10am–5pm;
Jul–Aug daily 10am–5pm;
Sep–Oct Wed–Sun 10am–5pm

Admission
Adult £4, Child £2

Contact
Westbury-on-Severn GL14 1PD

t 01452 760461
w nationaltrust.org.uk
e westburycourt@nationaltrust.org.uk

289 Winchcombe

Sudeley Castle & Gardens

  2 hrs+  Mar–Oct

Nestled in the Cotswold Hills, set in 14 acres of magnificent gardens, Sudeley Castle Gardens offers various exhibitions that give an insight into Sudeley through the ages. There are also seasonal exhibitions, The Pheasantry, a coffee shop, plant centre and picnic area.

* Programme of special events throughout the season
* Groundbreaking contemporary art exhibition returns

Location
8 miles NE of Cheltenham on B4632

Opening
Please phone for details

Admission
Please phone for details

Contact
Winchcombe GL54 5JD

t 01242 602308
w sudeleycastle.co.uk
e enquiries@sudeley.org.uk

290 Barrington

Barrington Court

2 hrs+ Mar–Oct

An enchanting formal garden laid out in a series of walled rooms, including the white garden, the rose and iris garden and the lily garden. The working kitchen garden has espaliered apple, pear and plum trees trained along high stone walls.

* Special events throughout the year

Location
5 miles NE of Ilminster in village of Barrington

Opening
Mar & Oct Thu–Tue 11am–4.30pm; Apr–Sep Thu–Tue 11am–5pm; Sat–Sun in Dec 11am–4pm

Admission
Please phone for details

Contact
Barrington TA19 0NQ

t 01460 241938
w nationaltrust.org.uk
e barringtoncourt@nationaltrust.org.uk

291 Bath

The American Museum & Gardens

2 hrs Mar–Oct

Learn how Americans lived from the time of the early European settlers to the American Civil War. Rooms include a replica C18 tavern where all visitors are given a piece of home-cooked gingerbread. Admire a wonderful collection of quilts, Native American objects and folk art.

* Events throughout the year
* Beautiful skyline walls & stunning American arboretum

Location
Off A36 S of Bath at Claverton (5 min drive from city)

Opening
18 Mar–29 Oct 12noon–5pm (last admission 4pm); closed Mon; open Bank Hols; Aug open daily

Admission
Adult £6.50, Child £3.50, Concs £6

Contact
Claverton Manor, Bath BA2 7BD

t 01225 460503
w americanmuseum.org
e info@americanmuseum.org

292 Bath

Bath Abbey – Heritage Vaults Museum

1 hr All year

Situated on the south side of Bath's C15 abbey (itself built on the site of a Saxon abbey), the vaults have been beautifully restored. They provide an atmospheric setting for objects that have survived from the abbey's fascinating past.

Location
S side of abbey, in city centre

Opening
Daily: Apr–Oct 9am–6pm; Nov–Mar 9am–4.30pm
Please phone in advance for group bookings

Admission
Free, donations welcomed

Contact
Bath BA1 1LT

t 01225 422462
w bathabbey.org
e office@bathabbey.org

293 Bath

Bath Aqua Theatre of Glass

 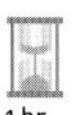 

1 hr All year

In this living/working museum, glass is produced for church windows, art projects and private commissions. You can see the beautiful aquamarine glass being blown in the theatre during regular public demonstrations.

* Signed & dated pieces available in shop
* Exhibition of old & new stained glass

Location
10 min walk W out of city centre

Opening
Shop May–Sep daily 9.30am–5pm; Apr–Oct Mon–Sat 9.30am–5pm
Viewing times Please phone for details

Admission
Adult £3.50, Child & Concs £2

Contact
105–107 Walcot Street, Bath BA1 5BW
t 01225 428146
w bathaquaglass.com

294 Bath

Bath Balloons

3–4 hrs Apr–Oct

Balloons launch from Royal Victoria Park, close to the city centre. Booking ahead is essential and all flights are subject to suitable weather conditions. Flight direction is wind-dependent, but the central start point ensures fantastic views of the city and its surroundings.

* Bookings available for singles, couples & groups
* Champagne served during flight

Location
Royal Victoria Park is 5 min walk from city centre

Opening
Apr–Oct (office open all year)

Admission
Please phone for details

Contact
8 Lambridge, London Road, Bath BA1 6BJ
t 01225 466888
w balnet.co.uk
e sales@balnet.co.uk

295 Bath

Bath Postal Museum

1 hr All year

The first letter sent with a stamp (the Penny Black) was sent from this building in 1840. The former post office now illustrates 4,000 years of communication, including Egyptian clay tablets, various writing implements and the story of the first air mail sent from Bath to London.

* Special exhibitions
* Pillar boxes through the ages

Location
Next to main post office

Opening
Mon–Sat 11am–5pm

Admission
Adult £2.90, Child £1.50, Concs £2.40

Contact
27 Northgate Street, Bath BA1 1AJ
t 01225 460333
w bathpostalmuseum.org
e info@bathpostalmuseum.org

296 Bath

Holburne Museum of Art

  1 hr+  All year

This jewel among Bath's splendid array of museums and galleries displays the treasures collected by Sir William Holburne: superb English and continental silver, porcelain, majolica, glass and Renaissance bronzes, and paintings including works by Gainsborough and Turner.

* Regular specialist exhibitions & lectures
* Book & gift shop

Location
5 min walk from Pulteney Bridge at end of Great Pulteney Street

Opening
Tue–Sat 10am–5pm, Sun 11pm–5pm; open Bank Hols

Admission
Adult £5.50, Child free, Concs £4.50

Contact
Great Pulteney Street, Bath BA2 4DB
t 01225 466669
w bath.ac.uk/holburne
e holburne@bath.ac.uk

297 Bath

The Jane Austen Centre

  1 hr  All year

Jane Austen is perhaps the best loved of Bath's many famous residents and visitors. She spent two long periods here at the end of the C18 and start of the C19 and the city featured in her work. There are period costumes and exhibits that explore Jane's life in Bath.

* New Regency tea room

Location
In city centre N of Queen Square

Opening
Daily: Apr–Oct 10am–5.30pm; Nov–Mar 10am–4.30pm, Sat 10am–5.30pm

Admission
Adult £5.95, Child £2.95, Concs £4.50

Contact
40 Gay Street, Bath BA1 2NT
t 01225 443000
w janeausten.co.uk
e info@janeausten.co.uk

298 Bath

Museum of Costume & Assembly Rooms

  2 hrs  All year

The story of fashion over the past 400 years is brought to life with one of the world's finest collections of fashionable dress. There are more than 150 dressed figures illustrating changing styles for both men and women. Each of the museum's 30,000 items is original.

* Combined ticket savings with Roman Baths
* Fashion flower prints & treasures exhibition

Location
In city centre, just off The Circus

Opening
Daily: Nov–Feb 11am–4pm; Mar–Oct 11am–5pm

Admission
Adult £6.50, Child £4.50, Concs £5.50

Contact
Bennett Street, Bath BA1 2QH
t 01225 477173
w museumofcostume.co.uk
e costume_bookings@bathnes.gov.uk

299 Bath

Roman Baths & Pump Rooms

2 hrs All year

This is Bath's most famous attraction. Britain's only natural hot spring flourished between the C1 and the C5 and the remains are among the finest in Europe. Walk where Romans walked on ancient stone pavements around the steamy pool.

* Taste the water in the C18 Pump Room above the Temple
* Combined ticket savings with Museum of Costume

Location
In city centre near the abbey

Opening
Jan–Feb & Nov–Dec 9.30am–4.30pm; Mar–June & Sep–Oct 9am–5pm; July–Aug 9am–9pm (last exit 1 hr after close)

Admission
Adult £10, Child £6, Concs £8.50
Jul–Aug £11, £6, £8.50

Contact
Abbey Church Yard, Bath BA1 1LZ

t 01225 477785
w romanbaths.co.uk
e romanbath_bookings@bathsnes.gov.uk

300 Bath

Sally Lunn's Refreshment House & Museum

1 hr All year

Sally Lunn's famous bun is still served from Bath's oldest house (*c*.1482). The museum shows remains of Roman, Saxon and medieval buildings on the site. The ancient kitchen used by Sally Lunn in the late C17 can also be seen.

* 3 themed refreshment rooms
* Historic Trencher Dinner is served from 5pm

Location
Between Abbey Green & North Parade

Opening
Daily: Mon–Sat 10am–10pm, Sun 11am–10pm

Admission
Adult 30p, Child & Concs free

Contact
4 North Parade Passage, Bath BA1 1NX

t 01225 461634
w sallylunns.co.uk
e info@sallylunns.co.uk

301 Bath

William Herschel Museum & Star Vault Astronomy Auditorium

1 hr+ Feb–Dec

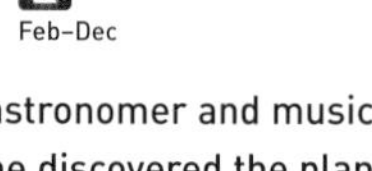

The home of C18 astronomer and musician William Herschel, where he discovered the planet Uranus in 1781. The museum is furnished in the style of the period and is representative of Bath's famous mid-Georgian town houses.

* Georgian garden & audio tours
* Education programmes available on request

Location
5 min walk W of city centre

Opening
Feb–mid-Dec Mon–Tue, Thu–Fri 1pm–5pm Sat–Sun 11am–5pm

Admission
Adult £3.50, Child £2, Concs £3

Contact
19 New King Street, Bath BA1 2BL

t 01225 446865
w bath-preservation-trust.org.uk
e admin@herschelbpt.fsnet.co.uk

302 Chard

The Wildlife Park at Cricket St Thomas

3–5 hrs All year

This park is home to more than 600 animals, including lemurs, monkeys, leopards, oryx, camels, wallabies, cheetahs and birds. Through its captive breeding programmes the park plays an important part in the conservation of rare and endangered species.

* Licensed for civil marriages
* New meerkat enclosure

  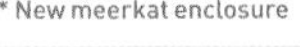

Location
3 miles from Chard on A30. Signed from M5 junction 25 & A303

Opening
summer Mon–Sun 10am–6pm
winter Mon–Sun 10am–4.30pm

Admission
Please phone for details

Contact
Chard, Somerset TA20 4DB

t 01460 30111
w wild.org.uk
e wildlifepark.cst@bourne-leisure.co.uk

303 Cheddar

Cheddar Gorge & Caves

3 hrs+ All year

The highest inland limestone cliffs in Britain and the famous cathedral-like caves form a 360-acre nature reserve owned by Lord Bath (of Longleat). The gorge walk is worth the effort for the fantastic views across Somerset from the top.

* New Cheddar Man & the Cannibals attraction
* Open-top bus tour runs through gorge Apr–Sep

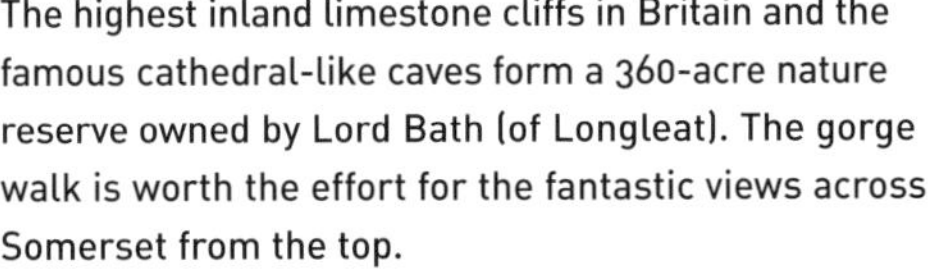

Location
Follow signs from junction 22 on M5 & A38 or take B3135 from A37 & follow brown tourist signs

Opening
Jul–Aug 10am–5pm;
Sep–Jun 10.30am–4.30pm

Admission
Explorer ticket for all attractions
Adult £11.50, Child £8.50

Contact
Cheddar BS27 3QF

t 01934 742343
w cheddarcaves.co.uk
e info@cheddarcaves.co.uk

304 Dunster

Dunster Castle

2 hrs Mar–Nov

Dramatically sited on top of a wooded hill, there has been a castle here at least since Norman times. The present building was remodelled between 1868 and 1872. A sheltered terrace to the south is home to the National Collection of strawberry trees.

* C13 gate house survives
* Surrounded by beautiful parkland for walking

Location
Off A39, 3 miles SE of Minehead

Opening
Castle 4 Mar–4 Nov Sat–Wed 11am–5pm
Gardens & Park Daily 10am–5pm

Admission
Castle Adult £7.20, Child £3.60
Gardens & Park £3.90, £1.70

Contact
Dunster, nr Minehead TA24 6SL

t 01643 821314
w nationaltrust.org.uk
e dunstercastle@nationaltrust.org.uk

305 Farleigh Hungerford

Farleigh Hungerford Castle

  2 hrs  All year

The ruins of this C14 castle lie in the beautiful valley of the River Frome. A free audio guide tells the story of the castle, its sinister past and its occupants during the Middle Ages. The impressive castle has a chapel that contains wall-paintings and stained glass.

* Important collection of death masks in chapel crypt
* Programme of living history throughout the year

Location
9 miles SE of Bath off A36

Opening
Daily: Apr–Jun & Sep–Oct 10am–5pm; Jul–Aug 10am–6pm; Nov–Mar Sat–Sun 10am–4pm

Admission
Adult £3.50, Child £1.80, Concs £2.60

Contact
Farleigh Hungerford, nr Trowbridge BA2 7RS

t 01225 754026
w english-heritage.org.uk/farleigh hungerford
e customers@english-heritage.org.uk

306 Glastonbury

Glastonbury Abbey

  2 hrs  All year

The abbey is set in 36 acres of peaceful parkland in the centre of this ancient market town. One of the oldest religious sites in Great Britain visited, so legend has it, by Joseph of Arimathea, St David and St Patrick. It is believed by many to be the burial site of King Arthur.

* Visitor centre with award-winning museum
* Period-dressed guides in summer

Location
Take A39 from junction 23 of M5. Follow signs once in Glastonbury

Opening
Daily: Jun–Aug 9am–6pm; Mar–May & Sep–Nov 9.30am–6pm or dusk if earlier; Dec–Feb 10am–dusk

Admission
Adult £4.50, Child £3, Concs £4

Contact
Abbey Gatehouse, Magdalene Street, Glastonbury BA6 9EL

t 01458 832267
w glastonburyabbey.com
e info@glastonburyabbey.com

307 Langport

Muchelney Pottery

  1 hr  All year

John Leach, grandson of illustrious potter Bernard Leach, continues the family tradition at Muchelney, in the beautiful Somerset Levels. Visit the gallery for collectable ceramics, art, sculpture and woodwork and the shop for kitchenware. Workshop tours by prior appointment.

* Take a walk round the pond, a County Wildlife site
* Twice-yearly Kiln Opening events – visit the website for details

Location
1 mile S of Muchelney village, nr Langport

Opening
Mon–Sat 9am–1pm, 2pm–5pm

Admission
Free

Contact
Muchelney, nr Langport TA10 0DW

t 01458 250324
w johnleachpottery.co.uk
e enquiry@johnleachpottery.co.uk

308 Sparkford

Haynes Motor Museum

 3 hrs
 All year

Haynes Motor Museum is the UK's largest exhibition of great cars from around the world and the perfect all-weather attraction. A working museum, with more than 350 amazing cars and motorcycles, from nostalgic classics of the 1950s and 1960s, to supercars of today.

* Fabulous collection of American sports cars
* 70-seat video theatre

Location
½ mile N of Sparkford on A359

Opening
Daily: Apr–Oct 9.30am–5.30pm;
Nov–Mar 10am–4.30pm

Admission
Adult £7.50, Child £4.50, Concs £6.50

Contact
Sparkford BA22 7LH

t 01963 440804
w haynesmotormuseum.co.uk
e info@haynesmotormuseum.co.uk

309 Taunton

Hestercombe Gardens

 2 hrs+
 All year

Hestercombe is a unique combination of a Georgian landscape created by Bampfylde in the 1750s, Victorian terraces and Edwardian gardens by Lutyens and Jekyll. The landscaped gardens (40 acres) have walks, lakes, temples, woods and stunning views.

* Jekyll's original planting faithfully restored
* Visitor centre & gift shop

Location
4 miles N of Taunton & 1 mile NW of Cheddon Fitzpaine

Opening
Daily 10am–6pm (last admission 5pm)

Admission
Please phone for details

Contact
Cheddon Fitzpaine, Taunton TA2 8LG

t 01823 413923
w hestercombegardens.com
e info@hestercombegardens.com

310 Weston-super-Mare

The Helicopter Museum

  2 hrs  All year

Marvel at more than 80 helicopters from Britain, Europe and the USA. A team of conservationists restore the aircraft and prepare them for show. The museum organises special events throughout the year, including open-cockpit days and Air Experience flights.

* World's largest helicopter museum
* Weston-super-Mare's largest all-weather attraction

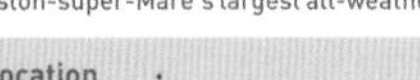   

Location
On A371, off M5 (junction 21)

Opening
Apr–Oct Wed–Sun 10am–5.30pm;
Nov–Mar 10am–4.30pm;
Easter & summer school hols daily 10am–5.30pm

Admission
Adult £5.30, Child £3.30, Concs £4.30

Contact
The Heliport, Locking Moor Road, Weston-super-Mare BS24 8PP

t 01934 635227
w helicoptermuseum.co.uk

311 Williton

The Bakelite Museum

  1 hr+  Mar–Sep

Set in peaceful Somerset countryside, and housed within a historic watermill, this is the largest collection of vintage plastics in Britain. See exhibits from the interwar period, stylish Art Deco and hundreds of interesting domestic items.

* Thousands of quirky & rare items on show
* Before Bakelite – a display of Victorian plastics

Location
Williton is at junction of A39 & A358, NW of Taunton

Opening
Mar–Sept 10.30am–6pm;
Thu–Sun only in school term time

Admission
Adult £3.50, Child £2, Concs £3

Contact
Orchard Mill, Williton TA4 4NS

t 01984 632133
w bakelitemuseum.co.uk
e info@bakelitemuseum.co.uk

312 Wookey Hole

Wookey Hole Caves & Papermill

  4 hrs  All year

Cut into the Mendip Hills by the River Axe, these are some of Britain's most spectacular caves. The story of the famous Witch of Wookey is a highlight of the cave tour. The C19 papermill has demonstrations of papermaking with the opportunity for visitors to make their own.

* Magical mirror maze & penny arcade
* King Kong & the Valley of Dinosaurs

Location
Junction 22 of M5, then follow signs A39 from Bath to Wells

Opening
Daily: Apr–Oct 10am–5pm;
Nov–Mar 10am–4pm

Admission
Adult £10.90, Child & Concs £8.50

Contact
Wookey Hole, nr Wells BA5 1BB

t 01749 672243
w wookey.co.uk
e witch@wookey.co.uk

313 Yeovil

Fleet Air Arm Museum

3 hrs+ All year

The Fleet Air Arm Museum is one of the 'must-see' attractions when in the South West. Among Europe's largest collections of naval aircraft, see Concorde, Harriers, helicopters and the award-winning Aircraft Carrier Experience. There is even a nuclear bomb.

* *Ark Royal* Aircraft Carrier Experience
* Many events throughout the year

WC

Location
1 mile off A303/A37 roundabout

Opening
Daily: Apr–Oct 10am–5.30pm; Nov–Mar Wed–Sun 10am–4.30pm; open Bank Hols & school hols

Admission
Adult £10, Child £7, Concs £8

Contact
PO Box D6, RNAS, Yeovilton, Ilchester BA22 8HT

t 01935 840565
w fleetairarm.com
e info@fleetairarm.com

314 Yeovil

Montacute House & Gardens

 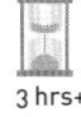  

3 hrs+ Mar–Oct

A glittering Elizabethan house with splendid Renaissance features. The magnificent state rooms, including a long gallery (the largest of its type in England), are full of fine C17 and C18 furniture and period portraits from the National Portrait Gallery.

* Featured in the film *Sense and Sensibility*
* Parkland & gardens including historic rose garden

Location
Signed from A303 W of Yeovil

Opening
House 21 Mar–28 Oct Wed–Mon 11am–5pm
Gardens Mar–Oct Wed–Mon 11am–6pm; Nov–Mar please phone for details

Admission
Please phone for details

Contact
Montacute TA15 6XP

t 01935 823289
w nationaltrust.org.uk
e montacute@nationaltrust.org.uk

315 Yeovil

Tintinhull House & Gardens

1 hr Mar–Sep

This small manor house (a C17 farmhouse with Queen Anne façade) stands in a beautiful formal garden created by Mrs Phyllis Reiss. The garden is divided into seven 'rooms' by clipped yew hedges and walls, and comprises a pool garden, fountain garden and kitchen garden.

* Striking mixed borders & colour schemes

Location
Tintinhull is just off A303 S of Yeovil. Follow signs from village

Opening
21 Mar–28 Oct Wed–Sun 11am–5pm; open Bank Hols

Admission
Please phone for details

Contact
Montacute, Yeovil TA15 6XP

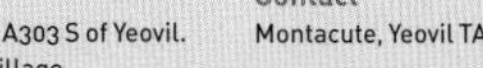

t 01935 822545
w nationaltrust.org.uk
e montacute@nationaltrust.org.uk

316 Amesbury

Stonehenge

  1 hr  All year

Stonehenge is a ring of upright stones set in a circle – each stone towering about 19 feet. Its original purpose is unclear, but theories range from a temple for the worship of ancient deities to an astronomical observatory. Others claim it was a sacred burial site.

* World Heritage Site
* Audio tours in 9 languages

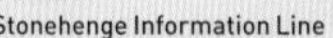

Location
2 miles W of Amesbury on junction of A303 & A360

Opening
Daily: Please phone for details

Admission
Adult £5.90, Child £3, Concs £4.40

Contact
Stonehenge Information Line

t 0870 333 1181
w english-heritage.org.uk/stonehenge
e customers@english-heritage.org.uk

317 Avebury

Avebury

  2 hrs+   All year

One of the most important megalithic monuments in Europe dating back to *c.*3000BC. The great stone circle, encompassing part of the village of Avebury, is roughly a quarter of a mile across. It encloses an area of about 28 acres and has two smaller circles within it.

* World Heritage Site
* World's biggest megalithic monument

Location
6 miles W of Marlborough, 1 mile N of Bath road (A4) on A4361 & B4003

Opening
Daily: Apr–Oct 10am–6pm; Nov–Mar 10am–4pm

Admission
Adult £4.20, Child £2.10

Contact
nr Marlborough SN8 1RF

t 01672 539250
w nationaltrust.org.uk
e avebury.estateoff@nationaltrust.org.uk

318 Chippenham

Lacock Abbey & Fox Talbot Museum

2 hrs+ Mar–Oct

Founded in 1232 and converted into a country house *c.*1540, the medieval cloisters, sacristy, chapter house and monastic rooms of the abbey have survived largely intact. The museum commemorates the achievements of William Henry Fox Talbot, photographic pioneer.

* Harry Potter films filmed here
* Beautiful Victorian woodland garden

Location
3 miles S of Chippenham, just E of A350

Opening
Abbey Mar–Oct Wed–Mon 1pm–5.30pm
Museum Mar–Oct 11am–5.30pm;
winter Sat–Sun only

Admission
Adult £7.80, Child £3.90

Contact
Chippenham SN15 2LG

t 01249 730141
w nationaltrust.org.uk

319 Corsham

Corsham Court

1 hr+ All year

Corsham Court is based on an Elizabethan house dating from 1582. It was bought by Paul Methuen to house a collection of C16 and C17 paintings and, after alterations to the house in C19, more Italian Old Masters and works of art were added.

* Works by Van Dyck, Carlo Dolci & Reynolds
* Picture gallery boasts a rare ornate ceiling

Location
Signed 4 miles W of Chippenham from Bath road (A4)

Opening
20 Mar–30 Sep daily (closed Mon & Fri) open Bank Hols 2pm–5.30pm;
1 Oct–19 Mar Sat & Sun 2pm–4.30pm (last entry 30 mins before close)

Admission
House & Gardens Adult £6.50, Child £3, Concs £5 *Gardens* £2.50, £1.50, £2

Contact
Corsham SN13 0BZ

t 01249 701610
w corsham-court.co.uk
e staterooms@corsham-court.co.uk

320 Salisbury

Larmer Tree Gardens

2 hrs Apr–Oct

These gardens were created by General Pitt Rivers in 1880 and have been restored over the past 10 years. An open-air theatre, Roman temple, Nepalese carved buildings and water features cover the land. Free-flying macaws and peacocks roam the gardens.

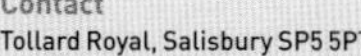

* Site available for events & weddings
* Victorian tea room open on Sun only

Location
On B3081 off A354 Salisbury–Blandford road

Opening
Apr–Oct Sun–Thu 11am–4.30pm

Admission
Adult £3.75, Child £2.50, Concs £3

Contact
Tollard Royal, Salisbury SP5 5PT

t 01725 516228
w larmertreegardens.co.uk
e larmer.tree@rushmore estate.co.uk

321 Salisbury

Old Sarum

1 hr+ All year

This great earthwork, with more than 2,000 years of history, and its huge banks and ditches were created by Iron Age people around 500BC, and later occupied by Romans, Saxons and Normans. See the remains of the prehistoric fortress, the palace, castle and cathedral.

* William the Conqueror paid off his army here in 1070
* Beautiful views to surrounding chalk downs

Location
2 miles N of Salisbury off A345

Opening
Apr–Jun & Sep 10am–5pm;
Jul–Aug 9am–6pm;
May & Oct 10am–4pm;
Nov–Feb 11 am–3pm

Admission
Adult £2.90, Child £1.50, Concs £2.20

Contact
English Heritage, Castle Road, Salisbury SP1 3SD

t 01722 335398
w english-heritage.org.uk/oldsarum
e old_sarum.castle@english-heritage.org.uk

322 Salisbury

Salisbury & South Wiltshire Museum

  1 hr+  All year

The museum holds material from major archaeological sites in Salisbury and south Wiltshire. In addition to the archaeology, the galleries display fine and decorative arts, ceramics, costume and local history.

* Temporary exhibitions all year round & gift shop
* Collection of Turner watercolours

Location
In Cathedral Close, opposite the West Front

Opening
Mon–Sat 10am–5pm;
Jul–Aug Sun 2pm–5pm

Admission
Adult £4, Child £1.50, Concs £3

Contact
The King's House, 65 The Close, Salisbury SP1 2EN

t 01722 332151
w salisburymuseum.org.uk
e museum@salisburymuseum.org.uk

323 Salisbury

Salisbury Cathedral

  1 hr   All year

Salisbury Cathedral is one of the finest medieval cathedrals in Britain. Started in 1220, it was completed by 1258, with the spire, the tallest in England (404ft) added a generation later. It also boasts the largest and best-preserved cathedral close in Britain.

* Voluntary guided tours of cathedral & chapter house
* Chapter house has the finest preserved 1215 Magna Carta

Location
In city centre

Opening
Daily: 7.15am–6.15pm
Times vary depending on services, please phone for details

Admission
Recommended voluntary donations
Adult £4.50, Child £2.50, Concs £4.00

Contact
Visitor Services, 33 The Close, Salisbury SP1 2EJ

t 01722 555120
w salisburycathedral.org.uk
e visitors@salcath.co.uk

324 Stourhead

Stourhead Gardens

  3 hrs+  All year

The gardens were designed by Henry Hoare II. Classical temples, including the Pantheon and the Temple of Apollo, are set around the central lake. Vistas change as the visitor walks around the paths and through the magnificent mature woodland.

* Palladian mansion & gift shop
* King Alfred's Tower, a 50m redbrick folly

  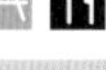 

Location
At Stourton, off B3092, 3 miles NW of Mere (A303)

Opening
House Mar–Oct (closed Wed–Thu) 11.30am–4.30pm
Gardens All year daily 9am–7pm

Admission
Gardens or House Adult £6.20, Child £6.40 *Both* £10.40, £5.20

Contact
Stourhead Gardens, nr Warminster BA12 6QD

t 01747 842020
w nationaltrust.org.uk
e stourhead@nationaltrust.org.uk

325 Swindon

STEAM – Museum of the Great Western Railway

2 hrs All year

This museum tells the story of the men and women who built, operated and travelled on the Great Western Railway. The museum celebrates Isambard Kingdom Brunel and the thousands of ordinary people who made the GWR one of the world's greatest railways.

* Special events running throughout the year
* World-famous GWR locomotives

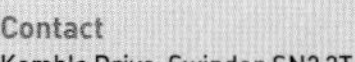

Location
Follow signs from town centre

Opening
Daily: 10am–5pm

Admission
Adult £5.95, Child & Concs £3.95

Contact
Kemble Drive, Swindon SN2 2TA

t 01793 466646
w swindon.gov.uk/steam
e steampostbox@swindon.gov.uk

326 Warminster

Longleat

4 hrs+ Feb–Nov

Longleat is set in more than 900 acres of Capability Brown-landscaped parkland with further woodlands, lakes and farmland. Longleat House is one of the best examples of high Elizabethan architecture, and there are the safari park, mazes and murals to explore, too.

* Longleat hedge maze
* Featured in the BBC programme *Animal Park*

Location
Off A36 between Bath & Salisbury (A362 Warminster–Frome road)

Opening
Daily: Feb–Nov
Times vary, please phone for details

Admission
Please phone for details

Contact
The Estate Office, Longleat, Warminster BA12 7NW

t 01985 844400
w longleat.co.uk
e enquiries@longleat.co.uk

327 Warminster

Shearwater Lake

2 hrs All year

Surrounded by woodland, Shearwater Lake is one of the finest waterways in west Wiltshire. The 37-acre lake, which is part of the Longleat Estate, was designed in 1791 by Francis Drake of Bridgwater. It is known for its fishing and sailing.

* 20-mile cycleway to Salisbury begins here
* Regular fishing & sailing competitions

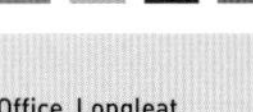     

Location
1 mile off A350 at Crockerton

Opening
Daily: *summer* 7am–8pm
winter 8am–5pm

Admission
Car park £1

Contact
The Estate Office, Longleat, Warminster BA12 7NW

t 01985 844400
w longleat.co.uk
e enquiries@longleat.co.uk

328 Westbury

Westbury White Horse & Bratton Camp

3 hrs+ All year

This famous landmark in west Wiltshire has fine views of the Wiltshire and Somerset countryside. Cut into a chalk hillside in 1778, the White Horse is thought to rest on the site of an older horse that commemorated the defeat of the Danes by King Alfred at Ethandun in AD 878.

*Neolithic barrow or burial mound

  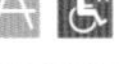

Location
Between Westbury & B3098

Opening
Daily: Please phone for details

Admission
Free

Contact
Westbury Tourist Information Centre

t 01373 827158
w english-heritage.org.uk

329 Wilton

Wilton House

2 hrs Easter–Oct

Wilton House contains many state rooms, including the Double Cube Room, which houses a world-famous collection of Van Dyck paintings. Other attractions include the old riding school, a Tudor kitchen and a Victorian laundry.

* Gardens & parkland bordered by the River Nadder
* A location for the film *Pride and Prejudice*

Location
3 miles W of Salisbury, situated on A30, off A36. 10 miles from A303

Opening
Please phone or visit the website for details

Admission
House & Grounds Adult £9.75, Child £5.50, Concs £8
Grounds only £4.50, £3.50

Contact
The Estate Office, Wilton, Salisbury SP2 0BJ

t 01722 746720
w wiltonhouse.com
e tourism@wiltonhouse.com

Stacey Arms Windmill, Norfolk

Eastern

Bedfordshire Cambridgeshire Essex
Hertfordshire Norfolk Suffolk

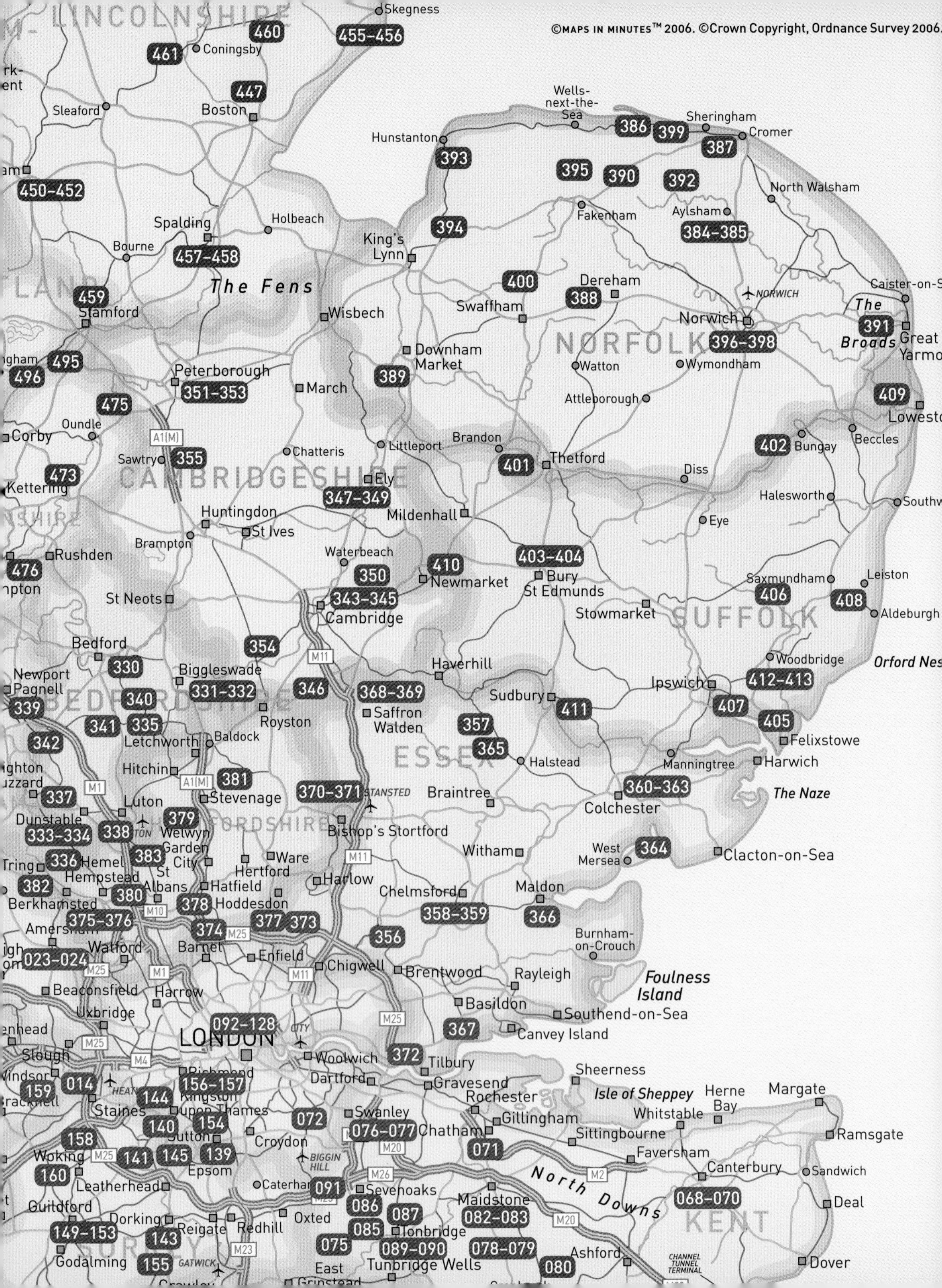

LINCOLNSHIRE
Skegness
460
455-456
461
Coningsby
447
Sleaford
Boston
Wells-next-the-Sea
386
399
Sheringham
Cromer
387
Hunstanton
393
395
390
392
North Walsham
450-452
Spalding
Holbeach
Fakenham
Aylsham
384-385
394
King's Lynn
Bourne
457-458
The Fens
400
Dereham
388
NORWICH
Caister-on-S
459
Stamford
Wisbech
Swaffham
Norwich
The Broads
391
Great Yarmo
NORFOLK
396-398
495
496
Peterborough
Downham Market
Watton
Wymondham
351-353
389
March
475
Attleborough
409
Lowesto
Corby
Oundle
A1(M)
Chatteris
Littleport
Brandon
Bungay
402
Beccles
Sawtry
355
401
Thetford
473
Kettering
CAMBRIDGESHIRE
Ely
Diss
347-349
Halesworth
Southw
Huntingdon
Mildenhall
Eye
St Ives
Brampton
Rushden
Waterbeach
403-404
476
410
Saxmundham
Leiston
350
Newmarket
Bury St Edmunds
406
408
St Neots
343-345
Aldeburgh
Cambridge
Stowmarket
SUFFOLK
Bedford
354
M11
Woodbridge
Orford Nes
330
Biggleswade
Haverhill
Newport Pagnell
Ipswich
412-413
331-332
346
368-369
Sudbury
339
340
Saffron Walden
411
407
BEDFORDSHIRE
Royston
405
341
335
357
Felixstowe
342
Letchworth
Baldock
365
Halstead
Manningtree
Harwich
Hitchin
ESSEX
A1(M)
381
M1
The Naze
337
Luton
Stevenage
370-371
STANSTED
Braintree
360-363
Colchester
Dunstable
379
Welwyn Garden City
HERTFORDSHIRE
Bishop's Stortford
333-334
338
LUTON
364
West Mersea
336
Hemel Hempstead
383
Ware
Witham
Clacton-on-Sea
Tring
St Albans
Hertford
M11
382
380
Hatfield
Harlow
Chelmsford
Maldon
Berkhamsted
M10
378
Hoddesdon
358-359
366
375-376
374
377
373
Amersham
M25
356
Burnham-on-Crouch
Watford
Barnet
023-024
M25
Enfield
Chigwell
M1
M11
Brentwood
Rayleigh
Foulness Island
Beaconsfield
Harrow
Basildon
Uxbridge
M25
Southend-on-Sea
092-128
CITY
367
Canvey Island
LONDON
M25
Slough
M4
Woolwich
372
Tilbury
Sheerness
Windsor
Richmond
Dartford
159
014
HEATHROW
156-157
Gravesend
Isle of Sheppey
Herne Bay
Margate
Kingston upon Thames
Rochester
144
Whitstable
Staines
154
072
Swanley
Gillingham
140
076-077
Chatham
Sittingbourne
Ramsgate
158
Sutton
M20
Croydon
071
Faversham
Woking
M25
141
145
139
BIGGIN HILL
North Downs
M2
Canterbury
Sandwich
160
Epsom
M26
Leatherhead
Caterham
091
Sevenoaks
Maidstone
068-070
Deal
Guildford
086
087
082-083
Dorking
Reigate
Redhill
Oxted
Tonbridge
M20
KENT
149-153
143
085
075
089-090
078-079
Ashford
SURREY
M23
Godalming
155
GATWICK
East Grinstead
Tunbridge Wells
080
CHANNEL TUNNEL TERMINAL
Dover

BURE VALLEY
BOAT TRAIN

330 Bedford

Cecil Higgins Art Gallery

  2 hrs+  All year

The gallery is housed in a Victorian mansion, once home to wealthy brewers, the Higgins family. Adjoining this is a modern gallery that boasts an internationally renowned collection of watercolours, prints and drawings, ceramics, glass and lace.

* Rooms include items from the Handley-Read Collection
* Furniture by Victorian architect William Burges

Location
Just off Embankment & high street

Opening
Tue–Sat 11am–4.45pm, Sun & Bank Hols 2pm–4.45pm

Admission
Free, donations welcomed

Contact
Castle Lane, Bedford MK40 3RP

t 01234 211222
w cecilhigginsartgallery.org
e chag@bedford.gov.uk

331 Biggleswade

The English School of Falconry

  3 hrs+  Feb–Oct

This family-run centre is sited in Shuttleworth Old Warden Park to provide a woodland setting as near as possible to the birds' natural surroundings. The centre is home to more than 300 birds of various species, including falcons, hawks, eagles, vultures and owls.

* 3 flying displays daily
* New reptile house

Location
Old Warden is 2 miles W of A1 where it bypasses Biggleswade

Opening
Daily: Feb–Oct 10am–5pm

Admission
Adult £8, Child £5, Concs £7

Contact
Old Warden Park, Biggleswade SG18 9EX

t 01767 627527
w birdsofpreycentre.co.uk
e falconry.centre@virgin.net

332 Biggleswade

Shuttleworth Collection

2 hrs+ All year

This world-famous collection of aircraft, started by Richard Shuttleworth, depicts the history of flight from 1900 to the 1940s and ranges from a 1909 Blériot to a WWII Spitfire. Cars, motorcycles and carriages are exhibited alongside the aircraft in eight hangars.

* Regular flying displays in summer
* Clayton & Shuttleworth steam-traction engine

Location
Shuttleworth Old Warden Aerodrome is 2 miles W of A1 where it bypasses Biggleswade

Opening
Daily: Apr–Oct 10am–5pm; Nov–Mar 10am–4pm

Admission
Adult £8, Child Free, Concs £7

Contact
Old Warden Aerodrome, nr Biggleswade SG18 9EP

t 01767 627927
w shuttleworth.org

e collection@shuttleworth.org

333 Dunstable

Leighton Buzzard Railway

2 hrs Mar–Oct

One of the few narrow-gauge light railways to survive in England. Built more than 85 years ago to transport sand, the line has run a steam-hauled passenger train service since 1968, and passengers can now make a 70-minute round trip from Page's Park to Stonehenge Works.

* Children's play area
* Explore the Guntry terminus

    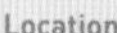

Location
Off A4146 on edge of Leighton Buzzard, close to junction with A505 Dunstable–Aylesbury road

Opening
Please phone for timetable details

Admission
Adult £6, Child (2–15) £3, Concs £5

Contact
Billington Road, Leighton Buzzard LU7 4TN

t 01525 373888
w buzzrail.co.uk
e info@buzzrail.co.uk

334 Dunstable

Whipsnade Tree Cathedral

2 hrs+ All year

Planted as an act of 'faith, hope and reconciliation' after WWI, the cathedral covers 9.5 acres with grass paths forming the chancel, nave, transepts, chapels and cloisters. With many different tree species and a small pond, it is a very tranquil space to explore.

* Wide variety of tree & shrub species
* Guided tours by arrangement

Location
4 miles S of Dunstable, off B4540

Opening
Daily: dawn–dusk

Admission
Free

Contact
Trustees c/o Chapel Farm, Whipsnade, Dunstable LU6 2LL

t 01582 872406
w nationaltrust.org.uk
e dunstabledowns@nationaltrust.org.uk

335 Henlow

Stondon Motor Museum

2 hrs All year

This museum houses one of the largest private collections in the country, with more than 400 exhibits. It includes veteran cars from 1890 to 1993, in eight different halls, some of which are for sale. An exclusive collection of Rolls-Royce and Bentley vehicles is a special feature.

* Full-size replica of Captain Cook's *Endeavour*
* Large free car park

  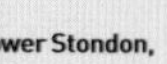

Location
At Lower Stondon near Henlow, off A600

Opening
Daily: 10am–5pm

Admission
Adult £6, Child £3, Concs £5

Contact
Station Road, Lower Stondon, Henlow SG16 6JN

t 01462 850339
w transportmuseum.co.uk
e info@transportmuseum.co.uk

336 Kensworth

Dunstable Downs Countryside Centre & Whipsnade Estate

2 hrs+ All year

Dunstable Downs and Whipsnade cover 510 acres of grassland and farmland, where the steep slopes are rich in flora and associated fauna. With outstanding views, it's a great place to walk, fly kites or watch paragliders. The centre has exhibits and kites for sale.

* New visitor facility & annual kite festival
* Designated Area of Outstanding Natural Beauty

Location
4 miles NE of Ashridge between B4540 & B4541

Opening
Downs All year
Centre Apr–Oct daily 10am–5pm; Nov–Apr Sat–Sun 10am–4pm

Admission
Free

Contact
Whipsnade Road, Kensworth, Dunstable LU6 2TA

t 01582 608489
w nationaltrust.org.uk
e dunstabledowns@nationaltrust.org.uk

337 Leighton Buzzard

Ascott House

 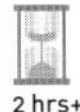 

2 hrs+ Mar–Aug

Ascott is a black-and-white C19 house set in 30 acres of grounds. It houses Anthony de Rothschild's collection of art, French and English furniture and Oriental porcelain. The garden has unusual trees, flower borders, topiary, a sundial, a Dutch garden and fountain statuary.

* Houses one of the foremost collections of Chinese three-colour-ware ceramics in the world

Location
On A418 between Aylesbury & Leighton Buzzard, E of Wing

Opening
15 Mar–30 Apr & 1–31 Aug Tue–Sun 2pm–6pm;
2 May–29 Jul Tue–Thu 2pm–6pm

Admission
Adult £7, Child £3.50

Contact
Wing, Leighton Buzzard LU7 0PP

t 01296 688242
w ascottestate.co.uk
e info@ascottestate.co.uk

338 Luton

Stockwood Craft Museum & Gardens

1 hr+ Apr–Oct

This award-winning museum covers nine centuries of garden history. There are displays on rural life and crafts, the Mossman Collection of horse-drawn vehicles, stunning period gardens and a programme of events that changes throughout the year.

* Conservatory tearoom set in C18 walled garden
* Largest display of horse-drawn carriages in the UK

Location
2 miles S of town centre, close to junction 10 of M1

Opening
Daily: Apr–Oct 10am–5pm

Admission
Free, donations welcomed

Contact
Farley Hill, Luton LU1 4BH

t 01582 738714
w lutonline.gov.uk
e museum.gallery@luton.gov.uk

339 Milton Keynes

Woburn Safari Park

6 hrs All year

Enjoy a Safari Adventure! Experience the thrill of being alongside rhinos, lions, giraffe and more. The excitement continues with close encounters in walkthroughs with wallabies, squirrel monkeys and lemurs, playgrounds, trains, boats and keeper talks and demonstrations.

* Tour the animal reserves as often as you wish
* See bears & wolves running together

Location
5 min off M1 (junction 13). Follow signs

Opening
Feb half-term & Mar–Oct daily 10am–5pm; Nov–Feb Sat–Sun 11am–3pm

Admission
Please phone for details

Contact
Woburn MK17 9QN

t 01525 290407
w discoverwoburn.co.uk
e info@woburnsafari.co.uk

340 Shefford

Hoo Hill Maze

1 hr+ All year

Set within an orchard, this hedge maze measures 300 square feet by 7 feet high (30 square metres x 2 metres). Visitors are invited to picnic in the orchard, where there are tables and plenty of space to play games.

* 3 children's play houses
* All 3 species of woodpecker present

Location
Off A507 & A600 close to Shefford

Opening
Mon–Fri: Please phone for details; Sat–Sun, Bank Hol Mon & school hols 10am–6pm

Admission
Adult & Child £3, under-5s £2

Contact
Hoo Hill Maze, Hitchin Road, Shefford SG17 5JD

t 01462 813475

341 Silsoe

Wrest Park Gardens

2 hrs+ Apr–Oct

Come and marvel at the magnificent gardens inspired by the great gardens of Versailles and the Loire Valley in France. Woodland walks and stunning formal gardens are complemented by the reflective expanses of water and wonderful stone and lead statuary.

* Domed baroque pleasure pavilion
* Chinese & Roman architecture

Location
In Silsoe village, 10 miles S of Bedford

Opening
Please phone for details

Admission
Adult £4.50, Child £2.30, Concs £3.40

Contact
Silsoe MK45 4HS

t 01525 860152/860000
w english-heritage.org.uk

342 Woburn

Woburn Abbey

3 hrs+ Apr–Sep

A palatial C18 mansion built originally in 1145 as a religious house for a group of Cistercian monks. In 1547 Edward VI gave Woburn Abbey to Sir John Russell who became the 1st Earl of Bedford. Tours include Queen Victoria's bedroom and the state dining room.

* Woburn's treasures are acknowledged worldwide
* Home to the Dukes of Bedford for more than 400 years

Location
On edge of Woburn village

Opening
Daily: Apr–Sep 11am–4pm

Admission
Adult £10.50, Child £6, Concs £9.50

Contact
Woburn MK17 9WA

t 01525 290333
w discoverwoburn.co.uk
e admissions@woburnabbey.co.uk

343 Cambridge

Cambridge University Botanic Garden

3 hrs All year

This tranquil 40-acre garden offers year-round interest to visitors. More than 10,000 labelled plant species grow in beautifully landscaped settings, including rock garden, lake, winter garden, woodland walk and glasshouses. There are nine National Collections to admire.

* Important collections of native English plants
* Founded by mentor of Charles Darwin

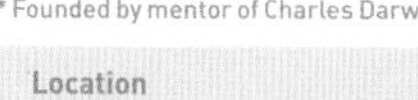

Location
1 mile S of city centre

Opening
Daily: Nov–Jan 10am–4 pm;
Feb & Oct 10am–5pm;
Mar–Sep 10am–6pm

Admission
Adult £3, Child (accompanied) free, Concs £2.50

Contact
Cory Lodge, Bateman Street, Cambridge CB2 1JF

t 01223 336265
w botanic.cam.ac.uk
e enquiries@botanic.cam.ac.uk

344 Cambridge

Fitzwilliam Museum

 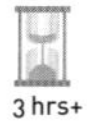  

3 hrs+ All year

This is the art museum of the University of Cambridge with public access to its collection of international repute. See antiquities from ancient Egypt, rare printed books, Chinese jades and Japanese ceramics, plus paintings by Titian, Canaletto, Rubens, Monet and Picasso.

* Fine collection of C20 art
* Exhibition of medals from the Renaissance onwards

Location
Approximately 500 yrds from city centre

Opening
Tue–Sat 10am–5pm, Sun 12noon–5pm. Closed Mon except summer Bank Hols

Admission
Free, donations welcomed

Contact
Trumpington Street, Cambridge CB2 1RB

t 01223 332900
w fitzmuseum.cam.ac.uk
e fitzmuseum-enquiries@lists.cam.ac.uk

345 Cambridge

King's College

1 hr+ All year

King's is one of the oldest colleges in Cambridge, founded in 1441 by Henry VI. It is also the premier tourist attraction, thanks primarily to the stunning architecture of its perpendicular chapel and its impressive interior that houses the painting *Adoration of the Magi* by Rubens.

* Home to the world-famous King's College choir

Location
Take junction 11 or 12 off M11; follow signs for centre parking or park+ride

Opening
Daily: term time, Mon–Fri 9.30am–3.30pm, Sat 9.30am–3.15pm, Sun 1.15pm–2.15pm;
out of term Mon–Sat 9.30am–4.30pm, Sun 10am–5pm

Admission
Adult £4.50, Child £3

Contact
King's College, Cambridge CB2 1ST

t 01223 331212
w kings.cam.ac.uk/visitors
e visitor.manager@kings.cam.ac.uk

346 Duxford

Imperial War Museum Duxford

3 hrs+ All year

This former Battle of Britain airfield is now home to 200 historic aircaft including biplanes, Spitfires, Concorde and Gulf War jets – many of which still fly regularly. The 7 acres of indoor exhibition space also houses one of the country's finest collections of military vehicles.

* Normandy Experience complete with video story
* Flying displays held throughout summer

Location
Off junction 10 of M11

Opening
Daily: mid-Mar–mid-Oct 10am–6pm; *winter* 10am–4pm

Admission
Adult £13, Child Free, Concs £11

Contact
Duxford CB2 4QR

t 01223 835000
w iwm.org.uk/duxford
e duxford@iwm.org.uk

347 Ely

Ely Cathedral

3 hrs+ All year

Begun by William the Conqueror, this magnificent cathedral stands on the site of a monastery founded in AD673 by St Ethelreda. Essentially Romanesque, there is a blend of architectural styles complemented by many beautiful objects in stone, wood and glass.

* Extensive renovation completed in 2000
* Tower tours available. West tower & octagonal tower

Location
In city centre

Opening
Daily: *summer* 7am–7pm
winter Mon–Sat 7.30am–6pm, Sun 7.30am–5pm

Admission
Adult £5.20, Concs £4.50, free on Sun

Contact
Chapter House, The College, Ely CB7 4DL

t 01353 667735
w cathedral.ely.anglican.org
e receptionist@cathedral.ely.anglican.org

348 Ely

Oliver Cromwell's House

 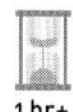 

1 hr+ All year

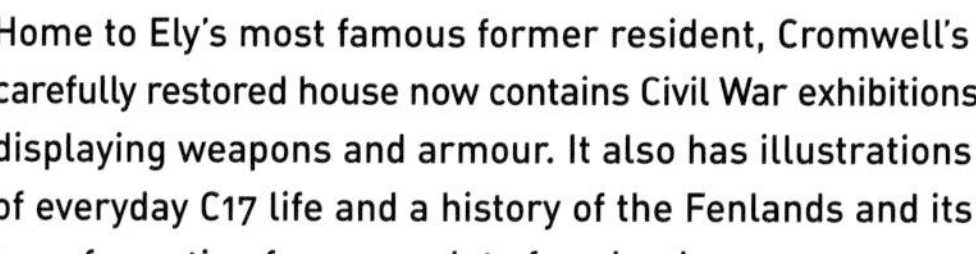

Home to Ely's most famous former resident, Cromwell's carefully restored house now contains Civil War exhibitions displaying weapons and armour. It also has illustrations of everyday C17 life and a history of the Fenlands and its transformation from marsh to farmland.

* C15 inglenook fireplace restored to working order
* Kitchen area has display of C17 recipes & ingredients

Location
In town centre next to St Mary's church

Opening
Apr–Oct daily 10am–5.30pm;
Nov–Mar Sun–Fri 11am–4pm,
Sat 10am–5pm

Admission
Adult £3.95, Child £2.70, Concs £3.45

Contact
29 St Mary's Street, Ely CB7 4HF

t 01353 662062
w ecambs.gov.uk
e tic@ely.org.uk

349 Ely

Stained Glass Museum

1 hr All year

The museum offers a unique insight into the story of stained glass, an artform practised in Britain for at least 1,300 years. This Trust, set up in the 1970s to rescue and preserve stained glass, now houses a National Collection of British stained glass.

* Work by William Morris on display
* One-day workshop for glass-painting, fusing and glazing

Location
Inside Ely Cathedral

Opening
Daily: Mon–Fri 10.30am–5pm,
Sat 10.30am–5.30pm (5pm in winter),
Sun 12noon–6pm (4.30pm in winter)

Admission
Adult £3.50, Child & Concs £2.50

Contact
Ely Cathedral, Ely CB7 4DL

t 01353 660347
w stainedglassmuseum.com
e info@stainedglassmuseum.com

350 Lode

Anglesey Abbey

1 hr+ All year

This site of a former Augustinian priory (many C12 stonework features remain) was brought to its current splendour by Lord Fairhaven in the first half of the C20. He purchased the mill and the vast collection of paintings, and planned the elaborate gardens.

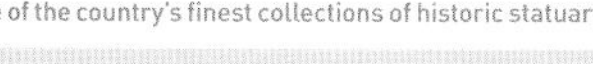

* Watermill can be seen working on 1st & 3rd Sats

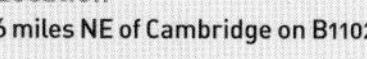

* One of the country's finest collections of historic statuary

Location
6 miles NE of Cambridge on B1102

Opening
House & Mill Mar–Oct Wed–Sun 1pm–5pm
Gardens Mar–Oct Wed–Sun & some Tues, 10.30am–5.30pm
Winter Garden Nov–Mar Wed–Sun & some Tues 10.30am–4.30pm

Admission
summer House & Gardens Adult £8, Child £4 *Gardens only* £4.50, £2.25
winter Adult £4, Child £2

Contact
Lode CB5 9EJ

t 01223 810080
w nationaltrust.org.uk
e angleseyabbey@nationaltrust.org.uk

©NTPL/Andreas von Einsiedel

351 Peterborough

Flag Fen Bronze Age Centre

4 hrs All year

Travel back in time to the Bronze Age and see how people lived more than 3,000 years ago. Discover tools, technology, clothes and food from 1000BC. The museum displays artefacts including swords, daggers and axes, and the earliest wheel ever discovered in England.

* Featured on the Channel 4 programme *Time Team*
* Set within a 20-acre park, a haven for wildlife

Location
NE of Peterborough, off A1139 or A605

Opening
Daily: 10am–5pm (last admission 4pm)

Admission
Adult £4.75, Child £3.50, Concs £4.25

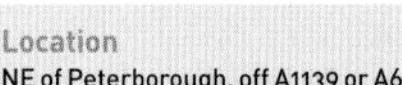

Contact
The Droveway, Northey Road, Peterborough PE6 7QJ

t 01733 313414
w flagfen.com
e office@flagfen.co.uk

352 Peterborough

Nene Valley Railway

3 hrs+ All year

Embark on a 15-mile round trip through the beautiful Nene Park from Wansford to Peterborough. One of Britain's leading steam railways, it is home to a wide range of British and European engines and carriages, both steam and diesel.

* Children's play area
* Talking Timetable 01780 784404

Location
Off southbound A1 at Stibbington between A47 & A605 junctions

Opening
Daily: 9am–4.30pm

Admission
Adult £10.50, Child £5.50, Concs £8

Contact
Wansford Station, Stibbington, Peterborough PE8 6LR

t 01780 784444
w nvr.org.uk
e nvrorg@aol.com

353 Peterborough

Peterborough Cathedral

1 hr All year

Today's cathedral is essentially the third abbey, founded in 1118 (the first dates from 655). It suffered badly at the hands of Oliver Cromwell, but many of its unique features remain to be admired today. The west front is a remarkable example of medieval architecture.

* Interior has remained largely unchanged through 800 years
* Burial place for 2 queens

Location
Follow signs for city centre from junction 16/17 of A1M

Opening
Daily: Mon–Fri 9am–6.30pm, Sat 9am–5pm, Sun visitors 12noon–5pm, services 7.30am–5pm

Admission
Free, donations encouraged

Contact
Little Prior's Gate, Minster Precincts, Peterborough PE1 1XS

t 01733 355300
w peterborough-cathedral.org.uk
e a.watson@peterborough-cathedral.org.uk

354 Royston

Wimpole Estate

 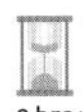  

3 hrs+ Mar–Nov

First built in 1643 and much altered by subsequent owners, Wimpole has developed into the largest country house in Cambridgeshire. The 360 acres of beautiful parkland is the work of four celebrated designers including Capability Brown.

* Parkland includes restored lakes & Gothic tower
* Walks available through woodland & rolling hills

Location
8 miles SW of Cambridge junction 12 of M11/junction 9 of A1(M)

Opening
Mar–Nov Sat–Wed (Thu during Aug & Good Friday) 1pm–5pm (Bank Hol Mon 11am–5pm) *Farm & Gardens* Sat–Wed 10.30am–5pm

Admission
Hall Adult £7.50, Child £4
Farm & Gardens Adult £6, Child £4

Contact
Wimpole Hall, Arrington, Royston SG8 0BW
t 01223 206000
w wimpole.org
e wimpolehall@nationaltrust.org.uk

355 Sawtry

Hamerton Zoo Park

2 hrs+ All year

Opened as a conservation sanctuary in 1990, Hamerton's 15 acres of parkland provides a safe home for a fascinating array of beautiful creatures from around the world, including many endangered species and some that are extinct in the wild.

* New outdoor tiger paddock
* Undercover walkways, picnic area & children's play area

Location
Follow brown and white signs from A1M at junction 15, or B660 turn off A14.

Opening
Daily: 10.30am–6pm (4pm in winter)

Admission
Please phone for details

Contact
Hamerton, nr Sawtry PE28 5RE
t 01832 293362
w hamertonzoopark.com
e office@hamertonzoopark.com

356 Brentwood

Kelvedon Hatch Secret Nuclear Bunker

2 hrs+ All year

Explore the biggest and deepest bunker in South-East England, built as a shelter for more than 600 people in the event of nuclear attack. An interactive tour takes you through numerous rooms including the power plant, surgery, plotting room and broadcasting centre.

* Try out authentic military uniforms & gasmasks

Location
Access is from A128 Chipping Ongar–Brentwood road at Kelvedon Hatch

Opening
Mar–Oct Mon–Fri 10am–4pm, Sat–Sun & Bank Hols 10am–5pm; Nov–Feb Thu–Fri 10am–4pm, Sat–Sun 10am–5pm

Admission
Adults £6, Child £4

Contact
Crown Buildings, Kelvedon Hall Lane, Brentwood CM14 5TL
t 01277 364883
w secretnuclearbunker.co.uk
e bunkerInfo@japar.demon.co.uk

357 Castle Hedingham

Colne Valley Railway

2 hrs+ Mar–Oct

Take a ride on a period country railway with a pretty line, relocated station buildings, signal boxes and bridges all lovingly restored and rebuilt. A large collection of vintage steam and diesel engines, carriages and wagons are waiting to be explored.

* 7 steam engines & 14 carriages & wagons
* Colne Valley Farm Park

Location
On right-hand side of A1017 1 mile from Castle Hedingham

Opening
Please phone or visit the website for details

Admission
Steam train Adult £6, Child £3, Concs £5
Diesel train Please phone for details

Contact
Yeldham Road, Castle Hedingham CO9 3DZ
t 01787 461174
w colnevalleyrailway.co.uk
e info@colnevalleyrailway.co.uk

358 Chelmsford

Chelmsford Museum & Essex Regiment Museum

1 hr+ All year

The museum is set in a Victorian mansion where visitors can follow the story of Chelmsford from the Ice Ages, via the Roman town, to the present day. See the superb Essex Regiment Museum which houses many military artefacts as well.

* Bright & colourful Victorian pottery from Hedingham
* Period dress & room settings

Location
In Oaklands Park, off Moulsham Street

Opening
Daily: Mon–Sat 10am–5pm,
Sun 2pm–5pm (winter 1pm–4pm)

Admission
Free, donations welcomed

Contact
Oaklands Park,
Chelmsford CM2 9AQ

t 01245 605700
w chelmsfordmuseums.co.uk
e oaklands@chelmsfordbc.gov.uk

359 Chelmsford

RHS Garden Hyde Hall

3 hrs All year

RHS Garden Hyde Hall in Essex is a wonderful experience whatever the time of year. Each season offers its own inspirational beauty, from the frosty mornings of winter to the first sweet flush of spring, the heady delights of summer to the shedding of leaves in autumn.

* Rope walk of climbing & pillar roses
* Ornamental ponds with lilies & fish

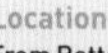

Location
From Rettendon follow flower signs

Opening
Daily: Oct–Mar 10am–dusk;
Apr–Sep 10am–6pm

Admission
Adult £5, Child £1

Contact
Rettendon,
Chelmsford CM3 8ET

t 01245 400256
w rhs.org.uk/gardens/hydehall
e hydehall@rhs.org.uk

360 Colchester

Beth Chatto Gardens

2 hrs+ All year

These gardens began in 1960 when the site was an overgrown wasteland between two farms. Faced with difficult conditions and with dry and damp soil in both sun and shade, the owners have put into practice what is now referred to as ecological gardening.

* Remarkable drought-resistant garden
* Water garden & woodland

Location
On A133. Approximately 4 miles E of Colchester and ¼ mile E of Elmstead Market

Opening
Mar–Oct Mon–Sat 9am–5pm;
Nov–Feb Mon–Fri 9am–4pm

Admission
Adult £4.50, Child free

Contact
Elmstead Market, Colchester CO7 7DB

t 01206 822007
w bethchatto.co.uk
e info@bethchatto.fsnet.co.uk

361 Colchester

Colchester Castle Museum

2 hrs All year

The museum covers 2,000 years of the most important events in British history. Once the capital of Roman Britain, Colchester has experienced devastation by Boudicca, invasion by the Normans and a siege during the English Civil War.

* Year-round events that bring history to life
* 2250BC Dagenham idol

Location
In Castle Park at E end of High Street

Opening
Daily: Mon–Sat 10am–5pm,
Sun 11am–5pm

Admission
Adult £4.90, Child & Concs £3.10

Contact
High Street, Castle Park, Colchester CO1 1TJ

t 01206 282939 Minicom 01206 507806
w colchestermuseums.org.uk
e museums@colchester.gov.uk

362 Colchester

Colchester Zoo

6 hrs All year

Colchester Zoo has some of the best cat and primate collections in Europe. Come face-to-face with a white tiger in White Tiger Valley, or get closer to the zoo's chimpanzees at Chimp World. Other enclosures include Penguin Shores, and Lions Rock for African lions.

* Playa Patagonia – sealion underwater experience
* Spirit of Africa: elephants, giraffes, rhinos, etc

Location
Take A1124 exit from A12

Opening
Daily: from 9.30am (closing times vary)

Admission
Please phone or visit the website for details

Contact
Maldon Road, Stanway, Colchester CO3 0SL

t 01206 331292
w colchester-zoo.co.uk
e enquiries@colchester-zoo.co.uk

363 Colchester

High Woods Country Park

2 hrs+ All year

This country park boasts areas of woodland, wetland and grassland. Numerous footpaths provide an opportunity to see a wide range of wildlife. A visitor centre houses exhibits of local history and natural history.

* Quality Assured Visitor Attraction
* Award-winning Green Flag park

Location
Accessible from Mile End Road & Ipswich Road, travelling N from Colchester

Opening
Visitor centre 1 Apr–30 Sep daily Mon–Sat 10am–4.30pm, Sun & Bank Hols 11am–5.30pm; 1 Oct–31 Mar Sat–Sun only 10am–4pm

Admission
Free

Contact
Turner Road, Colchester CO4 5JR

t 01206 853588
w colchester.gov.uk
e countryside@colchester.gov.uk

364 East Mersea

Cudmore Grove Country Park

1 hr All year

Cudmore Grove is at the eastern end of Mersea Island, with fine views across the Colne and Blackwater estuaries. Walk the sea wall, explore the shore and watch for wildlife. Behind the sandy beach is a tranquil area of cliff top and grassland perfect for relaxing.

* Wildside walk & bird hides
* Ranger-led guided walks available by request

    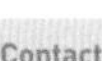

Location
Take B1025 S of Colchester & Mersea Island. Take left-hand fork to East Mersea – signed

Opening
Daily: 8am–dusk

Admission
£1 per hour per car, £2 per day per car

Contact
Bromans Lane, East Mersea CO5 8UE

t 01206 383868
w essexcc.gov.uk
e cudmoregrove@essexcc.gov.uk

365 Halstead

Hedingham Castle

1 hr+ Apr–Sep

This is one of the best-preserved Norman keeps in England. Built in 1140, it possesses four floors including a magnificent banqueting hall with a minstrels' gallery and Norman arch. It is approached by a Tudor bridge, built in 1496 to replace the drawbridge.

* Special events weekends, please visit the website
* 1920s bog garden contains camellias & azaleas

Location
In Castle Hedingham, ½ mile from A1017 between Cambridge & Colchester

Opening
Apr–Sep Sun 10am–5pm

Admission
Adult £4.50, Child £3.50, Concs £4

Contact
Halstead CO9 3DJ

t 01787 460261
w hedinghamcastle.co.uk
e hedinghamcastle@aspects.net.co.uk

366 Maldon

Combined Military Services Museum

2 hrs All year

This museum, uniquely, covers the history of all the armed forces. There is a fascinating array of equipment and weaponry used by soldiers from the Civil War to the present day. Many items in the secret service collection are the only examples on display worldwide.

* See rare RAF escape & survival equipment
* Captured Iraqi personnel carrier

Location
Half a mile from Maldon's High Street, it is most easily reached via A130/A414, then follow the Maldon's ring road

Opening
Wed–Sun 10.30am–5pm

Admission
Adult £3.50, Child £2, Concs £2.75, Family £10

Contact
Station Road, Maldon CM9 4LQ

t 01621 841826
w cmsm.co.uk
e cmsm@btopenworld.com

367 Pitsea

The Motorboat Museum

2 hrs+ All year

This museum is devoted to the history and evolution of sports and leisure motorboats, with more than 30 exhibits of motorboats from 1873 to the present day. From state-of-the-art offshore powerboats to the early days of steamers, trace the history of these wonderful craft.

* Model boat pond
* Carstais Collection

Location
Well signed from Pitsea

Opening
Thu–Mon 10am–4.30pm, daily during school hols

Admission
Free

Contact
Wat Tyler Country Park, Basildon SS16 4UH

t 01268 550077
w motorboatmuseum.org.uk

368 Saffron Walden

Audley End House & Gardens

3 hrs+ Mar–Oct

The house was built by the first Earl of Suffolk, Lord Treasurer to James I, on the scale of a great royal palace. Parts of the house were demolished in the early C18 but what remains is one of the most significant Jacobean houses in England.

* Historic kitchen & dry laundry
* Landscaped garden walks

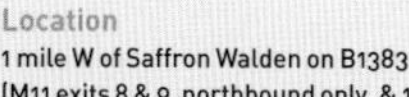

Location
1 mile W of Saffron Walden on B1383 (M11 exits 8 & 9, northbound only, & 10)

Opening
Mar–Oct Wed–Sun 10am–6pm

Admission
Adult £8.95, Child £4.50, Concs £6.70

Contact
Saffron Walden CB11 4JT

t 01799 522399
w english-heritage.org.uk

369 Saffron Walden

Mole Hall Wildlife Park

2 hrs All year

This family-owned wildlife park was first opened to the public in 1963 and has continued to grow. The collection of animals and birds includes many exotic species, primates (including chimpanzees) as well as otters and owls.

* Tropical butterfly pavilion & animal adoption scheme
* Café & gift shop closed during winter months

Location
Signed from B1383 & junction 8 of M11

Opening
Daily: Easter–Oct 10.30am–5.30pm
Nov–Spring 10.30am–4pm (or dusk if earlier)
Please note: not all attractions are available during winter. Please phone for details.

Admission
Adult £6.30, Child £4.30, Concs £5

Contact
Widdington, nr Saffron Walden CB11 3SS

t 01799 540400
w molehall.co.uk
e enquiries@molehall.co.uk

370 Stansted

Mountfitchet Castle & Norman Village

  2 hrs  Mar–Nov

This is a Norman motte and bailey castle and village, reconstructed on its original ancient site. A vivid exhibition of village life at the time of the Norman Conquest includes houses, a seige tower and a church. Animated figures give historical information.

* Iron Age fort, Roman, Saxon & Viking settlements

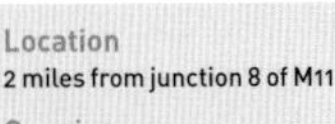

Location
2 miles from junction 8 of M11

Opening
Daily: Mar–Nov 10am–5pm

Admission
Adult £6.50, Child £5, Concs £5.50

Contact
Stansted CM24 8SP

t 01279 813237
w mountfitchetcastle.com
e info@mountfitchetcastle.com

371 Stansted Mountfitch

The House on the Hill Toy Museum

  2 hrs  All year

The largest private collection in Europe with more than 80,000 items will rekindle the child in everyone. The display covers toys from Victorian times to the present day, with everything from vintage slot machines to modern Barbie and Cindy dolls.

* Large collection of Rock n'Roll memorabilia
* Shop selling reproduction wall machines

WC

Location
In Stansted Mountfitchet village, 3½ miles from junction 8 of M11

Opening
Daily: Apr–Oct 10am–5pm;
Nov–Mar 10am–4pm

Admission
Adult £4, Child £3.30, Concs £3.50

Contact
Stansted, Essex CM24 8SP

t 01279 813237
w stanstedtoymuseum.com
e info@stanstedtoymuseum.com

372 Tilbury

Tilbury Fort

  2 hrs  All year

The finest surviving example of C17 military engineering in England, Tilbury Fort remains largely unaltered. Today exhibitions, the powder magazine and bunker-like casemates demonstrate how the fort protected the city. Visitors can even fire an anti-aircraft gun.

* Designed by Charles II's chief engineer

Location
5 miles E of Tilbury off A126

Opening
Apr–Nov daily 10am–5pm;
Dec–Mar Wed–Sun 10am–4pm

Admission
Adult £3.40, Child £1.70, Concs £2.60

Contact
Tilbury RM18 7NR

t 01375 858489
w english-heritage.org.uk

373 Waltham Abbey

Royal Gunpowder Mills

  3 hrs+  Apr–Sep

The world of explosives is uncovered with a range of interactive and static displays following the trail back to the C17. This unique museum traces the evolution of gunpowder technology and reveals the impact it had on the history of Great Britain.

* Muskets, rifles, pistols & machine guns
* Munitionettes – photo exhibits of women workers in WWII

Location
1 mile from junction 26 of M25 & A121

Opening
Apr–Sep Sat–Sun & Bank Hols only
11am–5pm (last admission 3.30pm)

Admission
Adult £6, Child £3.25, Concs £5

Contact
Beaulieu Drive, Waltham Abbey
EN9 1JY

t 01992 707370
w royalgunpowdermills.com
e info@royalgunpowdermills.com

374 Barnet

Museum of Domestic Design & Architecture

1 hr All year

The museum (MoDA) houses one of the most important and comprehensive collections of late C19 and C20 decorative design for the home. MoDA offers a wide-ranging programme alongside its permanent exhibition, Exploring Interiors: Decoration of the Home 1900–1960.

* Wallpapers & textiles from 1870s to 1960s
* Crown Wallpaper archive

Location
Underground to Oakwood, MODA 15 min walk away; or take a 298, 299 and 307 bus to Cat Hill roundabout; or M25 junction 24 on to A111 for 3 miles to Cat Hill

Opening
Tue–Sat 10am–5pm, Sun 2pm–5pm

Admission
Free, donations welcomed

Contact
Middlesex University, Cat Hill, Barnet EN4 8HT

t 020 8411 5244
w moda.mdx.ac.uk
e moda@mdx.ac.uk

375 Berkhamsted

Ashridge Estate

1 hr+ All year

This estate, covering 5,000 acres along the main ridge of the Chiltern Hills, offers a variety of picturesque walks, supporting a variety of wildlife in the commons, woodlands and chalk downland. The focal point is the Duke of Bridgewater monument, erected in 1832.

* Splendid views from Ivinghoe Beacon
* Visitor centre with exhibition room

Location
Between Northchurch & Ringshall just off B4506

Opening
All year
Visitor centre 17 Mar–16 Dec 12noon–5pm
Duke of Bridgewater monument 17 Mar–28 Oct, 12noon–5pm

Admission
Estate Free
Monument Adult £1.30, Child 60p

Contact
Ringshall, Berkhamsted HP4 1LT

t 01442 851227
w nationaltrust.org.uk
e ashridge@nationaltrust.org.uk

376 Berkhamsted

Berkhamsted Castle

2 hrs+

All year

Berkhamsted Castle is a good example of a motte and bailey castle where the original wooden defences were later rebuilt in stone. It consists of a large bailey and a motte to one side, on which there are traces of a stone tower. The only double-moated Norman castle in the UK.

* Built in late C11 by Robert of Mortain
* Further improvements were made by King John

Location
Next to Berkhamsted railway station

Opening
Daily: Apr–Oct 10am–6pm;
Nov–Mar 10am–4pm

Admission
Free

Contact
Berkhamsted HP4 1LJ

t 01442 871737
w english-heritage.org.uk
e customers@english-heritage.org.uk

377 Broxbourne

Paradise Wildlife Park

2 hrs+

All year

The park is a special place, with a relaxed and friendly atmosphere. It has a range of animals from monkeys to lions, zebras to tigers, cheetahs to camels. What makes it rare is the fact that you can get really close, meeting and feeding many of the animals.

* On Safari crazy golf & Wild West parrot show

Location
Junction 25 of M25 on to A10, signed from Broxbourne

Opening
Daily: Mar–Oct 9.30am–6pm;
Nov–Feb 10am–5pm

Admission
Adult £11, Child & Concs £8

Contact
White Stubbs Lane,
Broxbourne EN10 7QA

t 01992 470490
w pwpark.com
e info@pwpark.com

378 Hatfield

Hatfield House

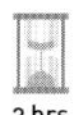
3 hrs

Easter–Sep

Visit this stunning Jacobean house within its own Great Park and see the surviving wing of the Tudor royal palace, where Elizabeth I spent much of her childhood. Home of the Cecil family for 400 years, the house is steeped in Elizabethan and Victorian political history.

* Beautifully carved wooden grand staircase
* Rare stained-glass window in private chapel

Location
Close to A1 (M) & M25. Entrance opposite Hatfield railway station

Opening
House Easter–Sep Wed–Sun & Bank Hol Mon 12noon–4pm *Gardens* daily 11am–5.30pm. Tours of house & garden available; please phone for details

Admission
Adult £8, Child £4

Contact
Hatfield AL9 5NQ

t 01707 287010
w hatfield-house.co.uk
e visitors@hatfield-house.co.uk

379 Knebworth

Knebworth House

3 hrs+

Apr–Sep

Knebworth House is a beautiful Gothic mansion set in 250 acres of parkland with formal gardens, a dinosaur trail, children's outdoor adventure playground, miniature railway, licensed tearoom and gift shop. It is also now the stately home of rock music.

* Constance Lytton, of Knebworth's Lytton family fought for votes for women in 1900s

Location
29 miles N of London off junction 7 of the A1(M) at Stevenage

Opening
House & Exhibition 12noon–5pm
Park & Gardens 11am–5.30pm
Opening times vary, please phone for details

Admission
House Adult £9, Child & Concs £8.50
Gardens £7

Contact
Knebworth SG3 6PY

t 01438 812661
w knebworthhouse.com
e info@knebworthhouse.com

380 St Albans

Verulamium Museum

1 hr+

All year

Explore the life and times of the major Roman city of St Albans at this museum of everyday Roman Britain. Displays and activities include recreated Roman rooms, hands-on discovery areas and some of the best mosaics and wall plasters outside the Mediterranean.

* Excavation video & accessible collections
* Roman mosaic & hypocaust building

Location
Approach via M1 junction 6 or M25 Junction 21A. Museum is just off A4147, 1 mile from St Albans centre

Opening
Daily: Mon–Sat 10am–5.30pm, Sun 2pm–5.30pm (last admission 30 min before close)

Admission
Adult £3.30, Child & Concs £2

Contact
St Michaels, St Albans AL3 4SW

t 01727 751810
w stalbansmuseums.org.uk
e museums@stalbans.gov.uk

381 Stevenage

Fairlands Valley Park

  4 hrs+  All year

This beautiful 120-acre park boasts an 11-acre lake used for a range of watersport courses whose waters are kept well stocked for anglers. There is a kids' area with paddling pool and play equipment. The park is also home to a wide selection of wildlife and wildfowl.

* Children's play area
* Paddling pools open during summer

Location
On Six Hills Way, 1 mile E of Stevenage

Opening
Daily: 8am–dusk

Admission
Park Free
Charges for water sports, boat hire, etc

Contact
Six Hills Way,
Stevenage SG2 0BL

t 01438 353241
w stevenage-leisure.co.uk/fairlands
e fairlands@stevenage-leisure.co.uk

382 Tring

Walter Rothschild Zoological Museum

  1 hr+  All year

This collection, started in 1890 by Walter Rothschild, contains thousands of birds, mammals, reptiles, fish, insects and even dressed fleas. The Victorian setting gives it a unique atmosphere and it is a fascinating insight into the life of a classic English eccentric.

* Come face to face with a giant anaconda
* Part of the Natural History Museum since 1937

Location
Tring is on A41, 12 miles W of Hemel Hempstead & 33 miles N of London. Museum is off Tring high street

Opening
Daily: Mon–Sat 10am–5pm, Sun 2pm–5pm

Admission
Free

Contact
Akeman Street,
Tring HP23 6AP

t 020 7942 6171
w nhm.ac.uk/tring
e tring-enquiries@nhm.ac.uk

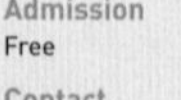

383 Welwyn

Shaw's Corner

  1 hr+  Mar–Oct

This Edwardian villa was the home of George Bernard Shaw from 1906 until his death in 1950. The rooms remain much as he left them, with many literary and personal effects and many touches evoking the individuality and genius of this great dramatist.

* Edwardian Arts & Crafts-influenced house
* Kitchen & outbuildings evocative of early C20 life

Location
Junction 4 of A1(M), signed from B653 & B656

Opening
17 Mar–Oct Wed–Sun & Bank Hols
House 1pm–5pm (last admission 4.30pm)
Gardens 12noon–5.30pm

Admission
Adult £4.20, Child £2.10

Contact
Ayot St Lawrence,
Welwyn AL6 9BX

t 01438 820307
w nationaltrust.org.uk/shawscorner
e shawscorner@nationaltrust.org.uk

384 Aylsham

Blickling Hall, Garden & Park

3 hrs+ Mar–Nov

One of England's great Jacobean houses, it is famed for its spectacular long gallery, superb library and fine collections of furniture, pictures and tapestries. The gardens are full of colour all year, and the extensive parkland features a lake and a series of beautiful walks.

* Superb Jacobean plaster ceiling in long gallery
* Formal woodland, parterre & wilderness garden

Location
N of B1354, 1½ miles NW of Aylsham on A140

Opening
Hall 24 Mar–28 Oct Wed–Sun 1pm–4.30pm
Garden & Park 24 Mar–28 Oct Wed–Sun 10.15am–5.15pm, 29 Oct–23 Mar Thu–Sun 11am–4pm

Admission
Adult £8, Child £4
Garden only £5, £2.50

Contact
Blickling, Norwich NR11 6NF

t 01263 738030
w nationaltrust.org.uk
e blickling@nationaltrust.org.uk

385 Aylsham

Bure Valley Railway

2 hrs+ All year

Bure Valley Railway is one of England's premier narrow-gauge railways serving enthusiasts, travellers and tourists. Its steam and diesel trains pass through scenery that is as varied, interesting and beautiful as any to be seen on a railway journey in England.

* 2 main stations at Aylsham & Wroxham
* Easy to combine with a cruise on the Norfolk Broads

Location
Aylsham railway station is midway between Norwich & Cromer on A140

Opening
Railway Mar–Sep 10am–5.30pm plus school hols
Please phone for details of other opening times

Admission
Please phone for details

Contact
Norwich Road, Aylsham, Norfolk NR11 6BW

t 01263 733858
w bvrw.co.uk
e info@bvrw.co.uk

386 Blakeney

Blakeney Point

4 hrs+ All year

One of Britain's foremost bird sanctuaries, the Point is a 4-mile sand and shingle spit, noted for its colonies of breeding terns and for the rare migrants that pass through in spring and autumn. Both common and grey seals can also be seen.

* Information centre at Morston Quay provides further details
* Restricted access during main bird breeding season

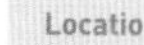

Location
Morston Quay, Blakeney & Cley are all off A149 Cromer–Hunstanton road

Opening
Daily: All reasonable times

Admission
Free

Contact
Friary Farm, Cley Road, Blakeney, Holt NR25 7NW

t 01263 740241
w nationaltrust.org.uk
e blakeneypoint@nationaltrust.org.uk

©NTPL/Joe Cornish

387 Cromer

Norfolk Shire Horse Centre

2 hrs+ Apr–Oct

See magnificent heavy shire horses working just as they did in days gone by. Take time to look around the rural museum and at the video show, see the small farm animals and the mares with their foals, and join in with feeding times.

* Displays twice daily
* Special events include blacksmith demonstrations

Location
Rail & bus services to West Runton

Opening
Apr–Oct Sun–Fri 10am–5pm (closed Sat except Bank Hols)

Admission
Adult £6, Child £4, Concs £5

Contact
West Runton, nr Cromer NR27 9QH

t 01263 837339
w norfolk-shirehorse-centre.co.uk
e bakewell@norfolkshirehorse.fsnet.co.uk

388 Dereham

Gressenhall Museum & Workhouse

4 hrs+ Mar–Oct

Set in 50 acres of beautiful countryside, this exhibition of Norfolk rural life is housed in a Georgian workhouse dating from 1777. There is a traditional farm, worked by heavy horses. Explore village life, agriculture and the workhouse through hands-on displays.

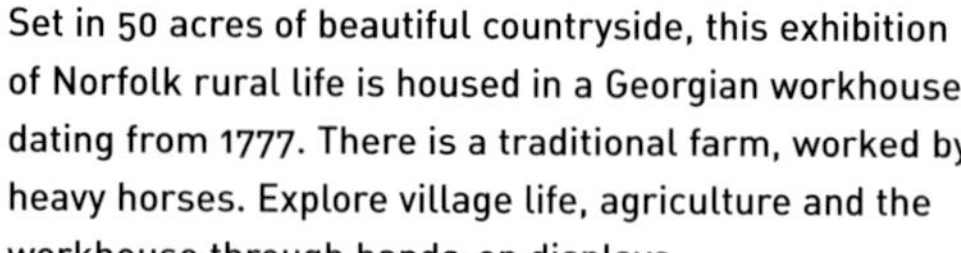

* Exciting woodland playground
* Family-friendly displays

Location
3 miles NW of Dereham. Follow signs

Opening
Daily: Mar–Oct 10am–5pm

Admission
Adult £7, Child £4.65, Concs £5.95

Contact
Gressenhall, Dereham NR20 4DR

t 01362 860563
w museums.norfolk.gov.uk
e gressenhall.museum@norfolk.gov. uk

389 Downham Market

Denver Windmill

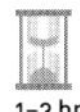
1–3 hrs

All year

Visit a working windmill set on the edge of the Fens. Recently restored, this unique set of buildings allows visitors to explore the story of windmilling in England and of the people who have lived and worked at the windmill since it was built in 1835.

* Tours to very top of windmill tower
* See mill working – wind & miller permitting

Location
Signed from A10

Opening
Daily: Apr–Oct Mon–Sat 10am–5pm, Sun 12noon–5pm;
Nov–Mar Mon–Sat 10am–4pm, Sun 12noon–4pm

Admission
Adult £3.50, Child £2, Concs £3

Contact
Denver, Downham Market PE38 0EG

t 01366 384009
w denverwindmill.co.uk
e enquiries@denverwindmill.fsnet.co.uk

390 Fakenham

Thursford Collection

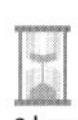
2 hrs

Easter–Sep

An Aladdin's cave of old road engines and mechanical organs of magical variety, all gleaming with colour. Live musical shows feature nine mechanical pipe organs and Robert Wolfe stars in the Wurlitzer Show. Old farm buildings are transformed into a small village.

* 4 gift shops open all year

Location
On A148 between Fakenham & Holt

Opening
6 Apr–Sep Sun–Fri 12noon–5pm

Admission
Adult £5.75, Child £3.25, Concs £5.45

Contact
Thursford, Fakenham NR21 0AS

t 01328 878477
w thursford.com
e admin@thursfordcollection.co.uk

391 Great Yarmouth

Tolhouse Museum

1 hr+

Apr–Oct

This C13 museum is one of the oldest civic buildings in the country. Once Great Yarmouth's court-room and gaol, it illustrates aspects of local history, including the dungeons in which Victorian figures can be seen lurking in their cells. Brass rubbings can be made and costumes worn.

* Audio guide brings to life the stories & characters
* Museum of local history

Location
Great Yarmouth, near Historic South Quay

Opening
Daily: 1 Apr–29 Oct Mon–Fri 10am–5pm, Sat–Sun 1.15pm–5pm

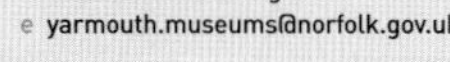

Admission
Adult £3, Child £1.60, Concs £2.50

Contact
Tolhouse Street, Great Yarmouth NR30 2SH

t 01493 858900
w museums.norfolk.gov.uk
e yarmouth.museums@norfolk.gov.uk

392 Holt

Baconsthorpe Castle

1 hr+

All year

Reached via a maze of tiny lanes are the remains of this C15 castle, built by Sir John Heydon as a manor house and wool-processing factory during the Wars of the Roses. In the 1560s Sir John's grandson added the outer gate house, which was inhabited until the 1920s.

* English Heritage property

Location
Off A148 & B1149, ¾ mile N of Baconsthorpe village, off an unclassified road. 3 miles E of Holt

Opening
Daily: All reasonable times

Admission
Free

Contact
Baconsthorpe, Holt

t 01223 582700
w english-heritage.org.uk

393 Hunstanton

Hunstanton Sea Life Centre

1 hr+

All year

At this sanctuary you will see otters, penguins and more than 30 permanent displays all showcasing the diversity of life under the waves. The centre also provides a safe haven for sick, injured or orphaned seal pups that are cared for at the sanctuary.

* Penguin sanctuary, home to rare Humboldt penguins
* Marine Hospital

Location
Take A149 from King's Lynn to Hunstanton. Follow signs

Opening
Daily: 10am–4pm
Times may vary during winter, please phone for details

Admission
Adult £9.50, Child £6.95, Concs £7.50

Contact
Southern Promenade, Hunstanton PE36 5BH

t 01485 533576
w sealsanctuary.co.uk
e hunstantonsealifecentre@merlinentertainments.biz

394 King's Lynn

Sandringham

3 hrs

Apr–Oct

The country retreat of Her Majesty The Queen and His Royal Highness The Duke of Edinburgh. Sandringham is a friendly and informal place and tours include ground-floor rooms within the house, a museum within the stable blocks and beautiful grounds.

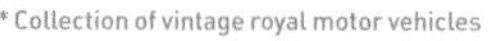
* Nature trails & woodland walks in the country park
* Collection of vintage royal motor vehicles

Location
Signed from King's Lynn

Opening
Daily: Apr–Sep
House 11am–4.45pm, Oct 11am–3pm
Museum 11am–5pm, Oct 11am–4pm
Gardens 10.30am–5pm; Oct 10.30am–4pm

Admission
House, Gardens & Museum Adult £8, Child £5, Concs £6.50
Gardens & Museum £5.50, £3.50, £4.50

Contact
Estate Office, Sandringham PE35 6EN

t 01553 612908
w sandringhamestate.co.uk
e visits@sandringhamestate.co.uk

395 Little Walsingham

Walsingham Shirehall Museum & Abbey Grounds

 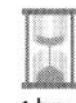 

1 hr+ All year

Walsingham is one of the main centres for Christian pilgrimage in England. It has been an important site since 1061 and in 1153 an Augustinian priory was founded in the village. It was destroyed in 1538, but the remains and site of the original shrine can still be seen.

* Picturesque tranquil grounds & snowdrop walks
* Shirehall Museum – unaltered hands-on courtroom

Location
4 miles NE of Fakenham off A149

Opening
Daily: 10am–4.30pm

Admission
Adult £3, Child & Concs £2

Contact
Common Place, Little Walsingham NR22 6BP

t 01328 820510/820259
e walsingham.museum@farmline.com

396 Norwich

Felbrigg Hall, Garden & Park

2 hrs+ Mar–Oct

This handsome house owes much of its splendour to William Windham II. The interior was remodelled in the 1750s to provide a sumptuous setting for his art treasures. The state rooms contain C18 furniture and paintings, and there is an outstanding library.

* Orangery has a fine display of camellias in spring
* Walled garden, extensive parkland, lake & woods

Location
In Felbrigg, 2 miles SW of Cromer, off B1346. Signed from A140 & A148

Opening
Mar–Oct Sat–Wed
Hall 1pm–5pm
Gardens 11am–5pm

Admission
Please phone for details

Contact
Felbrigg, Norwich NR11 8PR

t 01263 837444
w nationaltrust.org.uk
e felbrigg@nationaltrust.org.uk

397 Norwich

Norwich Cathedral

1 hr+ All year

This is a magnificent Norman building. The nave roof bosses, illustrating Bible scenes from Creation to the Day of Judgement, and the Saxon bishop's throne, are unique features. The cloisters are the largest monastic cloisters in the country, and the spire the second highest.

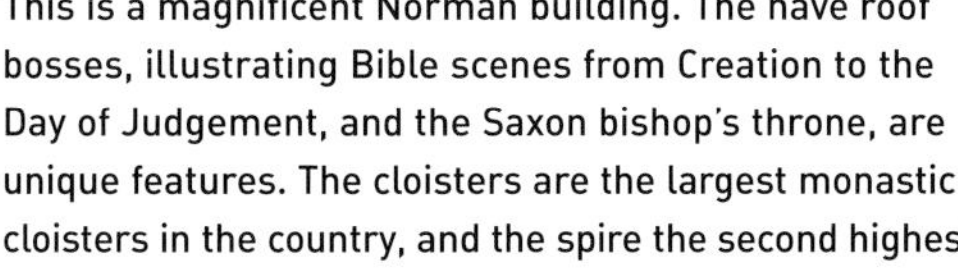

* Nurse Edith Cavell buried here
* Famous collection of medieval carvings

Location
Signed from city centre

Opening
Daily: *summer* 7am–7pm
winter 7am–6pm

Admission
Free, donations welcomed

Contact
62 The Close, Norwich NR1 4EH

t 01603 218321/218300
e vis-proffice@cathedral.org.uk
w cathedral.org.uk

398 Norwich

Sainsbury Centre for Visual Arts

2 hrs All year

In an internationally renowned building designed by Norman Foster, discover the delights of the Robert and Lisa Sainsbury art collection. There are more than 1,200 items, spanning thousands of years and many cultures. Alongside African masks are works by Picasso and Bacon.

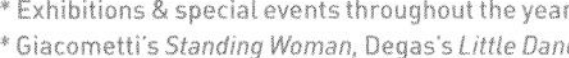

* Exhibitions & special events throughout the year
* Giacometti's *Standing Woman*, Degas's *Little Dancer*

Location
On university campus. Signed

Opening
Tue–Sun 10am–5pm, Wed 10am–8pm
Please phone for details

Admission
Free, some charges for temporary exhibitions & events

Contact
University of East Anglia, Earlham Road, Norwich NR4 7TJ

t 01603 593199
w scva.ac.uk
e scva@uea.ac.uk

Norfolk

399 Sheringham

The Muckleburgh Collection

  2 hrs  Feb–Oct

This is a collection of military vehicles, many of which are in full working order. Further displays feature the Royal Flying Corps and the modern armed forces. Several aero engines and missiles are on show, and frequent tank demonstrations take place.

* The Meteor on loan from Imperial War Museum
* Gama Goat Rides – in a US personnel carrier

Location
Signed from A149 W of Cromer, 3 miles W of Sheringham

Opening
12–19 Feb daily 10am–5pm;
26 Feb–26 Mar Sun 10am–5pm;
Apr–Oct daily 10am–5pm

Admission
Adult £5.50, Child £3, Concs £4.50

Contact
Weybourne Military Camp,
Holt NR25 7EG

t 01263 588210
w muckleburgh.co.uk
e info@muckleburgh.co.uk

400 Swaffham

Castle Acre Priory

  1 hr   All year

The priory's ruins span seven centuries and include a C12 church with an elaborately decorated great west front that still rises to its full height, a C15 gate house and a porch and prior's lodging. Visit the recreated herb garden, growing both culinary and medicinal herbs.

* Regular events held throughout the year
* One of the first Cluniac priories in England

Location
¼ mile W of village of Castle Acre, 5 miles N of Swaffham

Opening
Apr–Sep daily 10am–6pm;
Oct–Mar Thu–Mon 10am–4pm

Admission
Adult £4.50, Child £2.30, Concs £3.40

Contact
Stocks Green PE32 2AF

t 01760 755394
w english-heritage.org.uk
e castleacre-priory@english-heritage.org.uk

Suffolk

401 Brandon

High Lodge Forest Centre

 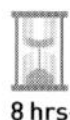 8 hrs+  All year

This centre in the heart of Thetford Forest offers walks, cycle trails, cycle hire, an adventure playground, a ropes course, one of the largest mazes of Scots pine in Europe, and a giant sculpture trail. Special events include bird walks, a deer safari and family-fun walks.

* Events throughout the year

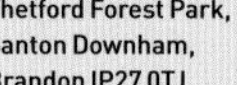

Location
Just off A11 on B1107 midway between Thetford & Brandon

Opening
Daily: 9am–dusk
Please phone for details

Admission
£5 per car

Contact
Thetford Forest Park,
Santon Downham,
Brandon IP27 0TJ

t 01842 815434 (High Lodge Centre)
01842 810271 (Forestry Commission)
w forestry.gov.uk
e e.anglia.fdo@forestry.gsi.gov.uk

402 Bungay

Norfolk & Suffolk Aviation Museum

 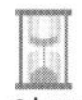 

2 hrs+ All year

The museum contains an impressive collection of aircraft and equipment. It also houses the Royal Observer Corps Museum, the 446th (H) Bomb Group Museum, the RAF Bomber Command Museum and the Air Sea Rescue and Coastal Command Museum.

* 40 aircraft within 7 hangars
* Aircraft from pre-WWI to the present day

Location
On B1062, off A143, 1 mile W of Bungay

Opening
Apr–Oct Sun–Thu 10am–5pm;
Nov-Mar Tue–Wed & Sun 10am–4pm
(closed 15 Dec–15 Jan)

Admission
Free, donations welcomed

Contact
The Street, Flixton NR35 1NZ

t 01986 896644
w aviationmuseum.net
e lcurtis@aviationmuseum.net

403 Bury St. Edmunds

Greene King Brewery Tour & Tasting

2 hrs All year

Greene King has been brewing on this site since 1799. Its fascinating museum traces the history of brewing in Bury St Edmunds, and the company's development. The tour of the brew house explains how its famous ales are made and gives you the chance to sample them.

* Shop with wide array of merchandise, souvenirs & beer
* Over-12s only on tours, Evening tours must be prebooked

Location
1 mile from A14, in town centre

Opening
summer Mon–Sat 10am–5pm,
Sun 11am–3.30pm
winter Mon–Sat 10am–5pm

Admission
Daytime tours £8, *Evening tours* £10

Contact
Westgate Street,
Bury St Edmunds IP33 1QT

t 01284 714297
w greeneking.co.uk
e brewerymuseum@greeneking.co.uk

404 Bury St Edmunds

Ickworth House

 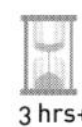  

3 hrs+ Mar–Dec

Ickworth is an elegant Italianate house set amid spectacular English parkland. The central rotunda and curving wings were intended to house treasures collected from all over Europe. Today the state rooms display works by Titian, Velasquez and Gainsborough.

* Noted for its Georgian silver & Regency furniture
* Enchanting gardens & woodland walks

Location
On A143, 2 miles S of Bury St Edmunds, signed from A14

Opening
House & Gardens Opening times vary, please phone for details
Gardens Daily: Opening times vary, please phone for details

Admission
Please phone for details

Contact
Bury St Edmunds IP29 5QE

t 01284 735 270
w nationaltrust.org.uk
e julia.vinson@nationaltrust.org.uk

©NTPL/Ian Shaw

405 Felixstowe

Landguard Fort

1 hr Apr–Oct

Guarding the Orwell Estuary since the mid-C16, Landguard Fort is the site of the last opposed invasion of England in 1667 where the Royal Marines won their first land battle. The current fort was built in the C18, modified in the C19 and has substantial C19/C20 outside batteries.

* Guided tours, free audio tours & a DVD presentation
* Visit the website for re-enactments & other special events

Location
On Viewpoint Road, Landguard Point, off A14

Opening
Daily: Apr 10am–5pm; May–Sep 10am–6pm; Oct 10am–5pm (last admission 1 hr before close)

Admission
Adult £3, Child £1, Concs £2.50

Contact
Viewpoint Road, Landguard Point IP11 3TX

t 07749 695523
w landguard.com

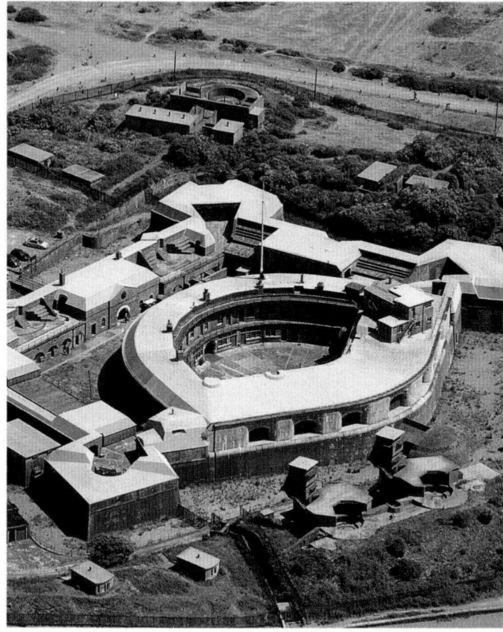

406 Framlingham

Framlingham Castle

1 hr+ All year

This is a fine example of a late C12 castle. It has 13 hollow towers connected by a large curtain wall, 42 feet high and 8 feet thick (13 x 2.5 metres), similar to those at Dover and Windsor castles. The castle has fulfilled a number of roles including fortress, prison, poor house and school.

* Gift shop, museum & audio tours
* Explore the outer courts, moat & mere

Location
In Framlingham on B1116

Opening
Daily: Apr–Sep 10am–6pm; Oct 10am–5pm; Nov–Mar 10am–4pm

Admission
Adult £4.50, Child £2.30, Concs £3.40

Contact
Framlingham, Woodbridge IP13 9BP

t 01728 724189
w english-heritage.org.uk

407 Ipswich

Ipswich Transport Museum

 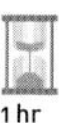 

1 hr Mar–Nov

This museum has the largest collection of transport items in Britain devoted to just one town. Everything was either made or used in and around Ipswich. The collection, started in 1965, consists of around 100 major exhibits, and numerous smaller transport-related items.

* Timetables, photographs, maps, tickets & uniforms
* Varied programme of events as advertised

   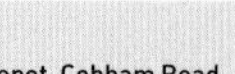

Location
SE of Ipswich near junction 57 of A14

Opening
Mar–Nov Sun & Bank Hols 11am–4pm; school hols Mon–Fri 1pm–4pm

Admission
Adult £3.50, Child £2.50, Concs £3

Contact
Old Trolleybus Depot, Cobham Road, Ipswich IP3 9JD

t 01473 715666
w ipswichtransportmuseum.co.uk
e enquiries@ipswichtransportmuseum.co.uk

408 Leiston

Long Shop Museum

1 hr+ Apr–Oct

The Long Shop was built in 1852 as Britain's first production line for steam engines. Traction engines, steamrollers, electric trolleybuses and even ammunitions were also produced here. Learn how the Victorians worked and explore our industrial heritage.

* Discover the amazing range of Garrett products
* Collection of unique & fascinating exhibits

Location
Turn off A12 at Saxmundham and follow signs to town centre

Opening
Daily: Apr–Oct Mon–Sat 10am–5pm, Sun 11am–5pm

Admission
Adult £4, Child £2, Concs £3.50

Contact
Main Street, Leiston IP16 4ES

t 01728 832189
w longshop.care4free.net
e longshop@care4free.net

409 Lowestoft

Lowestoft Maritime Museum

1 hr+ Easter–Oct

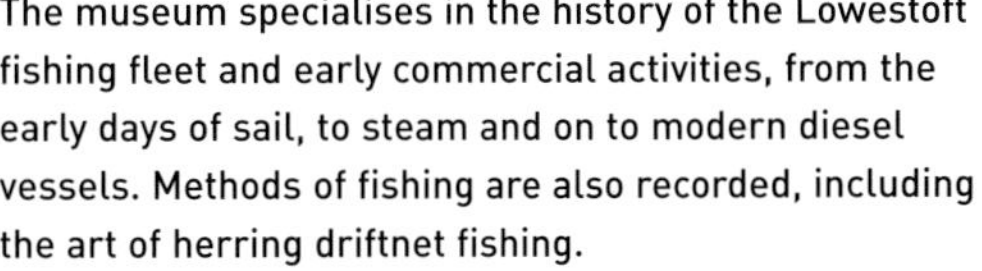

The museum specialises in the history of the Lowestoft fishing fleet and early commercial activities, from the early days of sail, to steam and on to modern diesel vessels. Methods of fishing are also recorded, including the art of herring driftnet fishing.

* Fine exhibition of evolution of lifeboats
* Collection of shipwrights' & coopers' tools

Location
Under Lighthouse on Whaplode Road in Sparrow's Nest Park

Opening
Daily: 6–15 Apr & 29 Apr–28 Oct 10am–5pm

Admission
Adult 75p, Child 25p, Concs 50p

Contact
Whapload Road, Lowestoft NR32 1XG

t 01502 561963

410 Newmarket

National Horseracing Museum

1 hr+ Apr–Oct

The story of the people and horses involved in racing – from royal origins to Lester Piggott, Frankie Dettori and other modern-day heroes. Highlights include the head of Persimmon, a great Royal Derby winner in 1896, and the colourful jackets of 'Prince Monolulu'.

* Gift shop well stocked with a range of unusual souvenirs
* Minibus tours – behind the scenes at Newmarket

Location
In town centre, well signed

Opening
Daily: Apr–Oct 11am–4.30pm (last admission 4pm), 10am–4.30pm on race days

Admission
Adult £4.50, Child £2.50, Concs £3.50

Contact
99 High Street, Newmarket CB8 8JH

t 01638 667333
w nhrm.co.uk
e museum@nhrm.freeserve.co.uk

411 Sudbury

Gainsborough's House

1 hr

All year

This is the birthplace of Thomas Gainsborough RA (1727–88). The Georgian-fronted town house with attractive walled garden displays more of the artist's work than any other gallery. The collection is shown together with C18 furniture and memorabilia.

* Varied exhibitions of contemporary art
* Includes works by Hubert Gravelot & Francis Hayman

Location
In town centre

Opening
Mon–Sat 10am–5pm

Admission
Please phone for details

Contact
46 Gainsborough Street, Sudbury CO10 2EU

t 01787 372958
w gainsborough.org
e mail@gainsborough.org

412 Woodbridge

Orford Castle

1 hr+

All year

Originally a keep and bailey castle with a walled enclosure and a great tower, the building we see today was constructed by Henry II as a coastal defence during the C12. The unique polygon keep survives almost intact with three immense towers.

* Building records are the earliest in the UK
* 50-minute audio tours & gift shop

Location
In Orford on B1084, 20 miles NE of Ipswich

Opening
Apr–Sep daily 10am–6pm;
Oct daily 10am–4pm;
Nov–Mar Thu–Mon 10am–4pm

Admission
Adult £4, Child £2, Concs £3

Contact
Orford, Woodbridge IP12 2ND

t 01394 450472
w english-heritage.org.uk

413 Woodbridge

Sutton Hoo

2–3 hrs

All year

Excavations here in 1939 revealed a burial chamber containing a 90ft ship, filled with treasures including a warrior's helmet, weapons, armour, ornaments, tableware and a purse with gold coins from *c.*AD 620. The exhibition hall houses a full-size reconstruction of the chamber.

* Most important archaeological find in the UK
* Largest Anglo-Saxon ship ever discovered

Location
On B1083 Melton-Bawdsey road. Signed from A12 N of Woodbridge

Opening
Jan–24 Mar, Nov–17 Dec Sat–Sun 11am–4pm; Apr, Jul–Sep daily 11am–5pm; 25 Mar–2 Apr, May–Jul, Sep–Oct Wed–Sun 11am–5pm; 27 Dec–31 Dec Wed–Sun 11am–4pm

Admission
Adult £5.50, Child £2.50

Contact
Tranmer House, Sutton Hoo, Woodbridge IP12 3DJ

t 01394 389700
w nationaltrust.org.uk
e suttonhoo@nationaltrust.org.uk

Lincoln Cathedral, Lincolnshire

East Midlands

Derbyshire Leicestershire Lincolnshire
Northamptonshire Nottinghamshire Rutland

LEEDS
Garforth
Selby
HULL
M621
719-721
722-727
M62
Hessle
Withernsea
Castleford
675-679
Goole
Batley
M62
Pontefract
Barton-upon-Humber
728-730
Wakefield
M18
454
Hemsworth
Thorne
Immingham
Scunthorpe
Grimsby
Spurn Head
M1
M181
M180
M180
453
Cleethorpes
Barnsley
Brigg
448
Penistone
Doncaster
SOUTH YORKSHIRE
Caistor
711
Stocksbridge
A1(M)
Bawtry
The Wolds
Rotherham
Gainsborough
SHEFFIELD
712
713
449
Market Rasen
Louth
714-717
SHEFFIELD CITY
Mablethorpe
19-421
Peak District
Dronfield
M1
Worksop
Retford
446
Staveley
718
491-493
422-423
Chesterfield
Lincoln
Horncastle
Bakewell
478
487-488
Washingborough
Ingoldmells
416
429
417
Ollerton
DERBYSHIRE
Skegness
Clay Cross
Mansfield
NOTTINGHAMSHIRE
LINCOLNSHIRE
Matlock
Sutton in Ashfield
479
460
455-456
430-431
480
Alfreton
414
Kirkby in Ashfield
461
Coningsby
Wirksworth
424
489-490
Newark-on-Trent
432
Belper
Ripley
447
425
477
Hucknall
Sleaford
Boston
Ashbourne
481-486
Ilkeston
NOTTINGHAM
Hunstanton
DERBY
Stapleford
Beeston
Uttoxeter
Grantham
426-428
Long Eaton
450-452
530
546
418
Burton upon Trent
EAST MIDLANDS
Melton Mowbray
Spalding
Holbeach
Loughborough
Bourne
King's Lynn
532
415
M1
457-458
434
442
433
Ashby-de-la-Zouch
The Fens
Coalville
RUTLAND
459
535-537
445
497-498
Stamford
Wisbech
Lichfield
435-436
438-441
Oakham
M42
LEICESTERSHIRE
494
Tamworth
LEICESTER
Uppingham
495
437
543-545
559
Oadby
Peterborough
389
Sutton Coldfield
496
570
Hinckley
Blaby
March
351-353
M69
475
588
Nuneaton
M1
Oundle
Market Harborough
444
BIRMINGHAM
Bedworth
Corby
A1(M)
Littleport
468
464-465
Chatteris
594
596
Sawtry
355
577-578
589-590
Rothwell
473
CAMBRIDGESHIRE
M6
443
Kettering
Ely
COVENTRY
469
347-349
561
466
Huntingdon
Mildenhall
553
Rugby
NORTHAMPTONSHIRE
St Ives
558
556
Brampton
M40
463
M45
560
Leamington Spa
Wellingborough
Rushden
Waterbeach
555
Warwick
476
350
462
Daventry
571-574
WARWICKSHIRE
Northampton
St Neots
343-345
562-569
470-472
Cambridge
Stratford upon Avon
575-576
467
554
Bedford
354
474
M1
557
M11
Towcester
330
Newport Pagnell
Biggleswade
551-552
Banbury
Milton Keynes
340
BEDFORDSHIRE
346
368-369
331-332
273-274
Shipston-on-Stour
013
339
Royston
Saffron Walden
129
Brackley
341
335
Buckingham
028
Baldock
342
Letchworth
Moreton-in-Marsh

DERBYSHIRE

LEICESTERSHIRE

LINCOLNSHIRE

414 Alfreton

Wingfield Manor

1 hr+ All year

Mary, Queen of Scots was imprisoned three times in this C15 manor house. Now an imposing ruin, the building was begun by Ralph, Lord Cromwell, Chancellor of England, around 1429. Over the entrance are carved twin money bags, symbolising Cromwell's status.

* Impressive undercroft of the hall, with vaulted roof
* The ITV series *Peak Practice* & Zeffirelli's *Jane Eyre* were filmed here

Location
On B5035, 5 miles S of South Wingfield

Opening
Pre-booked tours only. Please phone for details
Apr Sun only;
May–Mar Sat–Sun

Admission
Adult £3.40, Child £1.70, Concs £2.60

Contact
Garner Lane, South Wingfield
DE55 7NH

t 01773 832060
w english-heritage.org.uk

415 Ashby-de-la-Zouch

Conkers

4 hrs+ All year

Located at the heart of the national forest, Conkers offers a great mix of hands-on activities, from four indoor discovery zones for all ages to 23 outdoor activities, including lakeside walks, sculpture and nature trails, an assault course, and train rides.

* Visitor Attraction of the Year finalist
* Summer shows in our covered amphitheatre

Location
5 miles from M42

Opening
Daily: *summer* 10am–6pm
winter 10am–5pm

Admission
Adult £6.50, Child £4.50, Concs £5.25

Contact
Rawden Road, Moira,
nr Ashby-de-la-Zouch,
Derbyshire DE12 6GA

t 01283 216633
w visitconkers.com
e info@visitconkers.com

416 Bakewell

Haddon Hall

2 hrs+ Apr–Oct

Once home to William the Conqueror's illegitimate son, Peverel, little now remains of the original building (1087) but major restoration work undertaken from 1370 onwards means visitors can now experience what this fine hall and beautiful gardens were like in their heyday.

* location for the BBC drama *Jane Eyre*
* Film location for *Pride and Prejudice*

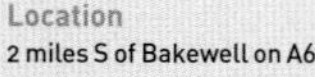

Location
2 miles S of Bakewell on A6

Opening
Please phone or visit the website for details

Admission
Adult £7.75, Child £4, Concs £6.75

Contact
Bakewell, Derbyshire DE45 1LA

t 01629 812855
w www.haddonhall.co.uk
e info@haddonhall.co.uk

417 Bolsover

Bolsover Castle

1 hr+ All year

Bolsover Castle is a C17 house, built on the site of a Norman fortress, and is a wonderful place to meander and muse in. Sir Charles Cavendish, son of Bess of Hardwick, began the construction of the little castle in 1612.

* Shop, visitor centre & audio tours
* Venus fountain garden has been restored

Location
In Bolsover, on A632, 6 miles E of Chesterfield

Opening
Sep–Apr Sun–Mon & Thu–Fri 10am–5pm, Sat 10am–4pm;
May–Aug Sun–Fri 10am–6pm, Sat 10am–4pm

Admission
Adult £6.60, Child £3.30, Concs £5

Contact
Castle Street, Bolsover S44 6PR

t 01246 822844
w english-heritage.org.uk
e bolsover.castle@english-heritage.org.uk

418 Castle Donington

Donington Grand Prix Collection

2–4 hrs All year

Take a spin around the world's largest collection of Grand Prix cars and journey through motor sport history. Exhibits include Schumacher's 1999 Williams, Coulthard's McLaren from 1997 and the car in which Senna won the 1993 European Grand Prix at Donington Park.

* World's only complete collection of Vanwalls
* Henry Seagrave's 1922 3-litre GP Sunbeam

Location
M1 junction 23a/24, access from NW via A50

Opening
Daily: 10am–5pm (last admission 4pm)

Admission
Adult £7, Child £2.50, Concs £5

Contact
Donington Park, Castle Donington DE74 2RP

t 01332 811027
w doningtoncollection.com
e enquiries@doningtoncollection.co.uk

419 Castleton

Blue John Cavern

1 hr All year

A historic cavern containing eight of the 14 known veins of Blue John Stone for which the area is famous. It was worked by the Romans more than 2,000 years ago. Tours take visitors through many colourful caves, including the crystallised and waterfall caverns.

* Exhibition of C19 miners' working implements

Location
2 miles W of Castleton

Opening
Daily: *summer* 9.30am–5.30pm
winter 9.30am–dusk

Admission
Adult £7, Child £3.50, Concs £5

Contact
Castleton S33 8WP

t 01433 620638/620642
w bluejohn-cavern.co.uk
e lesley@bluejohn.gemsoft.co.uk

420 Castleton

Peak Cavern

1 hr All year

Explore the mystery of the Great Cave and step into the unique world of Peak Cavern, with its unusual rock formations, eerie sounds of running water and echoes of a bygone age. The cavern's imposing entrance chamber is the largest natural cave entrance in the British Isles.

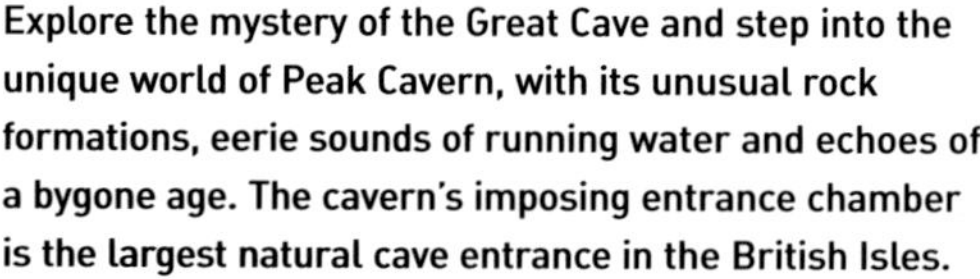

* Riverside walk past historic miners' cottages
* Guided tours & rope-making demonstrations

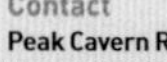

Location
On A6187, between Hathersage & Whaley Bridge

Opening
Daily: 10am–5pm (last admission 4pm)

Admission
Adult £6.25, Child £4.25, Concs £5.25

Contact
Peak Cavern Road, Castleton, Hope Valley S33 8WS

t 01433 620285
w www.peakcavern.co.uk
e info@peakcavern.co.uk

421 Castleton

Peveril Castle

1 hr All year

Built shortly after the Norman Conquest of 1066 by one of William I's most trusted knights, the elegant tower of this stronghold still stands to its original height. The castle, perched high above the pretty village of Castleton, offers breathtaking views of the Peak District.

* Some of the earliest herringbone masonry
* Sir Walter Scott based one of his novels on the castle

Location
On S side of Castleton, on A6187, 15 miles W of Sheffield

Opening
Apr & Sep–Oct daily 10am–5pm;
May–Aug daily 10am–6pm;
Nov–Mar Thu–Mon 10am–4pm

Admission
Adult £3.50, Child £1.80, Concs £2.60

Contact
Market Place, Castleton S33 8WQ

t 01433 620613
w english-heritage.org.uk

422 Chesterfield

Chesterfield Parish Church & Crooked Spire

1 hr | All year

This fabulous twisting, leaning spire has been astonishing visitors since it was first constructed in 1362. Built by unskilled craftsmen who used unseasoned timbers and neglected to use cross-bracing, the spire distorted and now leans at a bizarre angle.

* Guided tours of tower by appointment
* Coffee shop

Location
In the centre of Chesterfield, on St Mary's Gate road

Opening
Daily: 10am–4pm

Admission
Free

Contact
Church Way, Chesterfield, Derbyshire S40 1XJ

t 01246 206506
w chesterfieldparishchurch.org.uk

423 Chesterfield

Stainsby Mill: Hardwick Estate

2 hrs+ | Mar–Oct

This stunning watermill has an idyllic setting in the heart of the Hardwick estate and beautifully evokes the life of a C19 miller. The massive 17ft waterwheel powers the fully working grinding millstones producing flour that is for sale.

* Weigh yourself on the flour scales
* National mill days

Location
From M1 exit 29 take A6175 signed to Clay Cross, then first left & left again to Stainsby Mill

Opening
Mar–Jun Wed–Thu & Sat–Sun 11am–4.30pm; Jul–Aug Wed–Sun 11am–4.30pm; Sep–Oct Wed–Thu & Sat–Sun 11am–4.30pm

Admission
Adult £2.60, Child £1.30

Contact
Doe Lea, Chesterfield S44 5QJ

t 01246 850430
w nationaltrust.org.uk
e stainsbymill@nationaltrust.org.uk

424 Crich

The National Tramway Museum

 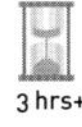 

3 hrs+ | Mar–Dec

Visit the museum to see a variety of trams, including open, closed, double-deck, single-deck, horse-drawn, steam and vintage electric from all four corners of the globe. Electric trams also run through Period Street, and on to open countryside, giving panoramic views.

* Exhibition hall houses impressive displays
* Dramatic Tram at Night Experience

Location
8 miles from M1 junction 28, via A38, A6, A61 & A52

Opening
Apr–Oct daily 10am–5.30pm; Nov–Dec & Mar Sat–Sun 10.30am–4pm

Admission
Adult £9, Child £4.50, Concs £8

Contact
Crich Tramway Village, Matlock DE4 5DP

t 01773 854321
w tramway.co.uk
e enquiry@tramway.co.uk

425 Denby

Denby Pottery Visitor Centre

1 hr+ All year

Admire and compare examples of Denby ware from early salt-glazed bottles and jars to the distinctive tableware of recent years. You can also see how Denby ware is made and have a go at painting a plate. There are extra activities for children during school holidays.

* Watch free cookery demonstrations
* New flagship store & tours of glass studio

Location
Next to Denby Pottery on B6179, off A38, 8 miles N of Derby

Opening
Daily: Mon–Sat 9.30am–5pm, Sun 10am–5pm

Admission
Factory tour Adult £5.25, Child & Concs £4.25

Contact
Derby Road, Denby, nr Ripley DE5 8NX

t 01773 74799
w denbyvisitorcentre.co.uk
e visitor.centre@denby.co.uk

426 Derby

Derby Museum of Industry & History

 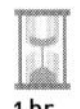 

1 hr All year

Built on the site of one of the world's oldest factories, dating from 1723, the museum tells the story of the industrial heritage and achievement of Derby and its people. There is a special emphasis on the development of Rolls-Royce aero engines and the railway industry.

* On site of Derby's first silk mill
* History of Midland Railway

Location
Off A6, near Derby Cathedral

Opening
Daily: Mon 11am–5pm, Tue–Sat 10am–5pm, Sun & Bank Hols 1pm–4pm
Please phone to confirm holiday opening times

Admission
Free

Contact
Silk Mill Lane, off Full Street, Derby DE1 3AF

t 01332 255308
w derby.gov.uk/museums

427 Derby

Melbourne Hall & Gardens

 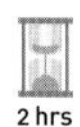  

2 hrs Apr–Sep

A historic house and garden that was once the home of Prime Minister William Lamb, who as Lord Melbourne gave his name to the Australian city. It has interesting and extensive gardens that contain a wrought-iron arbour made around 1710 by Robert Bakewell of Derby.

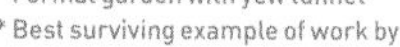

* Formal garden with yew tunnel
* Best surviving example of work by London & Wise

Location
7 miles S of Derby in Melbourne village off B587

Opening
House Aug daily 2pm–5pm except first 3 Mons (last admission 4.15pm)
Gardens Apr–Sep Wed, Sat–Sun & Bank Hols 1.30pm–5.30pm

Admission
House & Gardens Adult £5.50, Child £3.50, Concs £4.50
Gardens £3, Child & Concs £2.50

Contact
Church Square, Melbourne DE73 8EN

t 01332 862502/864224
w melbournehall.com
e melbhall@globalnet.co.uk

428 Derby

Royal Crown Derby Visitor Centre

2 hrs All year

Tour the working factory and watch the production of tableware and giftware, from clay through to the finished hand-decorated product. The museum is full of treasures dating back to 1750 and there are demonstrations of skills such as flowermaking, painting and gilding.

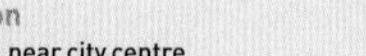

* Working factory tour available on weekdays
* Museum, demonstration studio & factory shop

Location
On A415, near city centre

Opening
Daily: Mon–Sat 9.30am–4pm, Sun 10.30am–4pm

Admission
Adult £2.95, Child & Concs £2.75
Tour £4.95, £4.75

Contact
194 Osmaston Road, Derby DE23 8JZ

t 01332 712800
w royalcrownderby.co.uk
e enquiries@royalcrownderby.co.uk

429 Matlock

Chatsworth House

 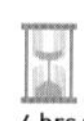 4 hrs+  Mar–Dec

The 'Palace of the Peak' contains one of Europe's finest collections of treasures, displayed in more than 30 rooms, from the grandeur of the 1st Duke's hall and state apartments with their rich decoration and painted ceilings, to the C19 library and dining room.

* Kids' farmyard & woodland adventure playground
* Maze, rose, cottage & kitchen gardens

Location
8 miles N of Matlock, off B6012

Opening
Mid-Mar–mid-Dec
House 11am–4.30pm
Gardens 11am–6pm

Admission
Please phone for details

Contact
Bakewell DE45 1PP

t 01246 565300
w chatsworth.org
e visit@chatsworth.org

430 Matlock Bath

Heights of Abraham

  2 hrs+   Feb–Oct

Since 1780 people have been visiting the Heights of Abraham. Your journey starts with a spectacular scenic cable-car ride to the summit station. From here you can take a tour of the caverns, wander through the woods or simply enjoy the views.

* 2 adventure play areas
* Exhibition centre

Location
Off A6 in Matlock Bath

Opening
Feb half-term daily 10am–4.30pm;
Mar Sat–Sun 10am–4.30pm;
Apr–Oct daily 10am–5pm

Admission
Adult £9.50, Child £6.50, Concs £7

Contact
Matlock Bath DE4 3PD

t 01629 582365
w heights-of-abraham.co.uk
e office@heights-of-abraham.co.uk

431 Matlock Bath

Masson Mills Working Textile Museum

   1 hr+  All year

Sir Richard Arkwright built these mills as his showpiece on the banks of the River Derwent in 1783. Beautifully restored, Masson Mills house a working textile museum containing a unique and comprehensive collection of authentic historic working textile machinery.

* Internationally famous Grade II-listed buildings
* Experience more than 200 years of industrial history

Location
On A6, ½ mile S of Matlock Bath

Opening
Daily: Mon–Fri 10am–4pm,
Sat 11am–5pm, Sun 11am–4pm

Admission
Adult £2.50, Child £1.50, Concs £2

Contact
41 Derby Road, Matlock Bath DE4 3PY

t 01629 581001
w massonmills.co.uk

432 Middleton by Wirksworth

National Stone Centre

 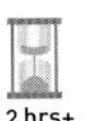  

2 hrs+ All year

In the heart of the Derbyshire Dales, this dramatic site is steeped in industrial history, but the centre tells the full story of stone. The history and science of stone is illustrated with displays of tropical reefs and 330 million-year-old fossils, and its use in art is beautifully demonstrated.

* Gem-panning and fossil-rubbing
* Millennium Wall – 19 different sections of dry stone wall

Location
On B5035, S of Matlock, between Cromford & Carsington

Opening
Daily: *summer* 10am–5pm
winter 10am–4pm

Admission
Site Free *Discovery centre* Adult £1.80, Child 90p

Contact
Porter Lane, Wirksworth DE4 4LS

t 01629 824833
w nationalstonecentre.org.uk
e nsc@nationalstonecentre.org.uk

433 Swadlincote

Beehive Farm Woodland Lakes

4 hrs+ All year

Using specially laid-out trails, visitors can explore the beauty of this woodland landscape on foot or horseback. Alternatively, they can simply enjoy the atmosphere of the three tranquil fishing lakes – Horseshoe, Botany Bay and Jubilee.

* Woodland, meadow, wetland habitats & animal farm
* Caravan & camping park

Location
In Rosliston, near Burton upon Trent

Opening
Daily: Mon–Sat 9.30am–5pm, Sun 9.30–4pm; Closed Mon–Tue in winter

Admission
Adult £2, Child £1

Contact
Lullington Road, Rosliston, Swadlincote DE12 8HZ

t 01283 763981/763980
w beehivefarm-woodlandlakes.co.uk
e info@beehivefarm-woodlandlakes.co.uk

434 Ashby-de-la-Zouch

Ashby-de-la-Zouch Castle

1 hr+ All year

In the C15 Edward IV gave this property to Lord Hastings, who converted what was then a Norman manor house into a grand castle, adding a chapel and the Hastings Tower. Now partly ruined, the tower still soars to the great height of 80 feet.

* Wonderful views across Leicestershire
* The setting for jousting scenes in the book *Ivanhoe*

Location
In Ashby-de-la-Zouch, 12 miles S of Derby, on A511

Opening
Please phone for details

Admission
Adult £3.40, Child £1.70, Concs £2.60

Contact
South Street, Ashby-de-la-Zouch LE65 1BR

t 01530 413343
w english-heritage.org.uk
e customers@english-heritage.org.uk

435 Coalville

Manor House at Donington

  1 hr+  All year

Donington-le-Heath Manor House was built in the late C13 and renovated early in the C17. Visitors can see the restored rooms and displays on medieval life. It is set in recently recreated C17-style gardens with herbaceous borders, herb gardens, an orchard and a maze.

* Audio & virtual tours
* Temporary exhibitions on a wide range of subjects

Location
1 mile S of Coleville, signed from M1 junction 22

Opening
Mar–Dec daily 11am–4pm;
Jan–Feb Sat–Sun 11am–4pm

Admission
Free

Contact
Donington-le-Heath,
Coalville LE67 2FW

t 01530 831259
w leics.gov.uk/museums
e dlhmanorhouse@leics.gov.uk

436 Coalville

Snibston Discovery Park

 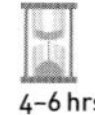 4–6 hrs  All year

Visit Snibston and see the £1.4 million makeover. Try to lift a Mini Cooper in the brand-new interactive gallery Extra Ordinary, see the amazing selection of costumes in the Fashion Gallery or join real-life miners on a tour of Snibston colliery.

* Brand-new colliery-themed outdoor play area
* Train ride along the newly restored colliery railway

Location
On A511, on edge of Coalville town centre

Opening
Daily: 10am–5pm (closed in early Jan)
Please phone for details

Admission
Adult £5.70, Child £3.60, Concs £3.90

Contact
Ashby Road, Coalville LE67 3LN

t 01530 278444
w leics.gov.uk/museums
e snibston@leics.gov.uk

437 Desford

Tropical Birdland

2 hrs+ All year

Created in 1982, this exotic bird lover's dream is set in beautiful surroundings and features more than 85 species of birds. You can walk through aviaries, visit the chick room, see spectacular free-flying birds, take a woodland stroll and visit the koi carp ponds.

* Take tea with free-to-fly birds in the café
* Boarding service for pet birds when you go on holiday

Location
Just off M1 at junction 22

Opening
Daily: 10am–5pm

Admission
Adult £5, Child & Concs £3.50

Contact
Lindridge Lane, Desford,
Leicester LE9 9GN

t 01455 824603
w tropicalbirdland.co.uk
e info@tropicalbirdland.co.uk

438 Leicester

Jewry Wall

  1 hr  All year

One of Leicester's most famous landmarks, this rare example of Roman walling has survived for nearly 2,000 years. Originally part of the Roman public baths, it separated the exercise hall, which stood on the site of St Nicholas Church, from the rest of the baths.

* Archaeologists discovered remains of Roman baths
* Museum tells the story of Leicester from the Iron Age

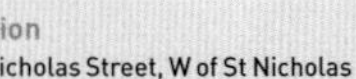

Location
In St Nicholas Street, W of St Nicholas Church in town centre

Opening
Sat 11am–4.30pm, Sun 11am–4.30pm; school hols Mon–Fri 11am–4.30pm

Admission
Free

Contact
St Nicholas Circle, Leicester LE1 4LB

t 0116 225 4971
w english-heritage.org.uk

439 Leicester

The National Gas Museum, Leicester

  1 hr  All year

Established in 1977 to preserve the knowledge and skills of the gas industry during a period of rapid technological and economic change, the museum contains many artefacts, collected during the conversion to natural gas and tells the story of gas from 1667 to the present day.

* Largest collection of gas-related artefacts in the world

Location
Off A426, S of city centre

Opening
Tue–Thu 12noon–4.30pm; closed Bank Hols
Open at other times by special arrangement

Admission
Free

Contact
195 Aylestone Road, Leicester LE2 7QH

t 0116 250 3190
w gasmuseum.co.uk
e information@gasmuseum.co.uk

440 Leicester

National Space Centre

  4 hrs+   All year

This centre is dedicated to astronomy and space science. From its futuristic Rocket Tower discover the history of our relationship with space, the personalities involved, our space technology, past and present, and find out where our space exploration is now headed.

* 6 themed galleries with hands-on activities
* Space theatre show

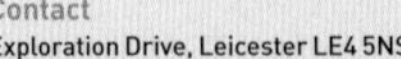

Location
Just off A6, 2 miles N of city centre

Opening
Tue–Sun 10am–5pm; school hols daily 10am–5pm
Please phone for details

Admission
Adult £11, Child & Concs £9

Contact
Exploration Drive, Leicester LE4 5NS

t 0870 607 7223
w spacecentre.co.uk
e info@spacecentre.co.uk

441 Leicester

New Walk Museum

 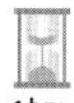 

1 hr+ All year

The museum's permanent collections include the Ancient Egypt Gallery and the Natural History Room, the latter housing dinosaur skeletons and interesting fossils. It is also a major art gallery, with a collection of German Expressionist art and European art dating from the C15.

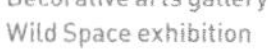

* Decorative arts gallery
* Wild Space exhibition

Location
Short walk from city centre

Opening
Daily: Mon–Sat 10am–5pm
Sun 11am–5pm

Admission
Free

Contact
53 New Walk, Leicester LE1 7EA

t 0116 225 4900
w leicester.gov.uk/museums
e museums@leicester.gov.uk

443 Lutterworth

Stanford Hall

1 hr Easter–Sep

Stanford, on the River Avon, has been the home of the Cave family since 1430. In the 1690s Sir Roger Cave commissioned Smiths of Warwick to pull down the old manor house and build the present hall, which is a superb example of their work.

* Collection of Stuart royal portraits

Location
Just off M1/M6 interchange, near A14

Opening
Easter–Sep Sun & Bank Hol Mon only
House 1.30pm–5pm
Grounds 12noon–5.30pm

Admission
House & Grounds Adult £5, Child £2
Grounds £3, £1

Contact
Lutterworth LE17 6DH

t 01788 860250
w stanfordhall.co.uk
e enquiries@stanfordhall.co.uk

442 Loughborough

Great Central Railway

2 hrs+ All year

Mainline steam trains run every weekend throughout the year. Experience the famous expresses of the steam age. Relax in the comfort of classic corridor trains, which are steam-heated in winter; buffet and griddle carriages are available on all trains.

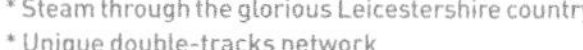

* Steam through the glorious Leicestershire countryside
* Unique double-tracks network

Location
SE of town centre

Opening
Trains run at weekends all year & midweek Jun–Aug
Please phone for details

Admission
Adult £12, Child & Concs £8

Contact
Great Central Road, Loughborough LE11 1RW

t 01509 230 726
w gcrailway.co.uk
e booking_office@gcrailway.co.uk

444 Market Harborough

Rockingham Castle

3 hrs Easter–Sep

Built by William the Conqueror more than 900 years ago, the castle stands in beautiful grounds, with superb views across the Welland Valley. As well as being a stronghold, it was an important seat of government. It is now home to the Saunders Watson family.

* Best Small Visitor Centre in Excellence in England Award
* Regular events including kite & Viking days

Location
Off A6003, 1 mile N of Corby

Opening
Easter–May Sun & Bank Hol Mons 12noon–5pm; Jun–Sep Sun, Tue & Bank Hols 12noon–5pm

Admission
Adult £7.50, Child £4.50, Concs £6.50

Contact
Rockingham, Market Harborough, Leicestershire LE16 8TH

t 01536 770240
w rockinghamcastle.com
e estateoffice@rockinghamcastle.com

445 Newtown Linford

Bradgate Country Park

3 hrs+ All year

With 850 acres of heathland, small woods, herds of deer and the River Lin, this is Leicestershire's largest country park. It also includes the ruins of Bradgate House, the birthplace of Lady Jane Grey, who was famously Queen of England for just nine days.

* Old John Tower folly

Location
3 miles from M1 junction 22, signed on A50

Opening
Daily: dawn–dusk

Admission
Park Free. Car park fees
Visitor centre Adult £1.20, Child 60p

Contact
Deerbarn Buildings, Newtown Linford LE6 0HE

t 0116 236 2713

446 Alford

Claythorpe Watermill & Wildfowl Gardens

 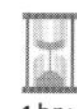 

1 hr+ Easter–Oct

At the tip of the Lincolnshire wolds, Claythorpe is home to more than 500 animals and birds, and visitors are able to experience their environment and habitat. Visit the bygone exhibit area, which depicts the history of the site's milling and baking industry.

* Enchanted woods in which fairytales come to life
* Otters, red squirrels & wallabies

Location
Signed off A16

Opening
Daily: Easter–Oct 10am–5pm; early & late season 10am–4pm

Admission
Adult £4.25, Child £3.25, Concs £3.75

Contact
Aby, nr Alford LN13 0DU

t 01507 450687
w claythorpewatermill.fsbusiness.co.uk
e info@claythorpewatermill.co.uk

447 Boston

Sibsey Trader Windmill

1 hr All year

Built in 1877 in typical Lincolnshire style, to replace a small post mill, this is one of the few six-sailed mills remaining in England. It's not exceptionally tall, but the slender tower and surrounding flat landscape create the impression that it's bigger than it really is!

* Grade I -listed working windmill
* Range of fresh, organic, stoneground flour available

Location
Off A16, 5 miles N of Boston, ½ mile W of Sibsey

Opening
Apr–Sep Tue, Sat & Bank Hol Mon 10am–6pm, Sun 11am–6pm; Oct–Mar Sat 11am–5pm

Admission
Adult £2, Child £1, Concs £1.50

Contact
Frith Ville Road, Sibsey PE22 0SY

t 01205 750036/460647
w sibsey.fsnet.co.uk
e traderwindmill@sibsey.fsnet.co.uk

448 Cleethorpes

Cleethorpes Humber Estuary Discovery Centre

1 hr All year

Located on the boating lake, surrounded by fantastic views and friendly wildlife, the hands-on exhibition explores Cleethorpes's Victorian seaside history, the seaside and nature. The second-floor observatory has outstanding views over the Humber Estuary.

* On the edge of an important wildlife habitat

Location
From A180 & A16 follow signs for lakeside

Opening
Daily: Jan–Jun & Sep–Oct 10am–5pm; Jul–Aug 10am–6pm; Nov–Dec 10am–4pm

Admission
Adult £1.95, Child £1.30

Contact
Lakeside, Kings Road, Cleethorpes DN35 0AG

t 01472 323232
w cleethorpesdiscoverycentre.co.uk
e lynne.emeny@nelincs.gov.uk

449 Gainsborough

Gainsborough Old Hall

2 hrs All year

This is a large C15 timber-framed medieval house, with a magnificent great hall and brick tower, built on the site of an earlier C13 manor house. In 1483 Richard III stayed at the Old Hall and in 1541 Henry VIII was a guest.

* Special events throughout the year
* Most parts of house have disabled access

Location
In town centre, off Parnell Street

Opening
Easter–Oct daily Mon–Sat 10am–5pm, Sun 1pm–4.30pm,
Nov–Easter Mon–Sat 10am–5pm

Admission
Adult £3.70, Child &Concs £2.50

Contact
Parnell Street, Gainsborough DN21 2NB

t 01427 612669
w lincolnshire.gov.uk/gainsborougholdhall
e gainsborougholdhall@lincolnshire.gov.uk

450 Grantham

Belton House

6 hrs Mar–Dec

A stunning example of Restoration country house architecture, Belton was built in 1685–88 and later altered by James Wyatt. The interiors contain fine plasterwork and wood carving, as well as collections of paintings, furniture, tapestries and silverware.

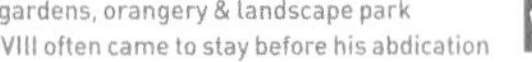

* Formal gardens, orangery & landscape park
* Edward VIII often came to stay before his abdication

Location
On A607 3 miles NE of Grantham, signed from A1

Opening
House Mar–Oct Wed–Sun 12.30pm–5pm
Gardens Mar–Oct Wed–Sun 11am–5.30pm;
Nov–Dec Fri–Sun 12noon–4pm

Admission
Adult £8, Child £4.50

Contact
Grantham NG32 2LS

t 01476 566116
w nationaltrust.org.uk
e belton@nationaltrust.org.uk

451 Grantham

Grantham Museum

1 hr All year

The museum interprets the archaeology and social history of Grantham and includes exhibits on famous residents such as Sir Isaac Newton and Margaret Thatcher, who has donated many personal items. There is also a section on the Dambusters.

* Dambusters mission planned here
* 1851 Great Exhibition gold medal-winning doll

Location
In central Grantham

Opening
Mon–Sat 10am–5pm

Admission
Free

Contact
St Peter's Hill, Grantham NG31 6PY

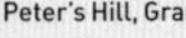

t 01476 568783
w lincolnshire.gov.uk/granthammuseum
e grantham.museum@lincolnshire.gov.uk

452 Grantham

Woolsthorpe Manor

2 hrs Mar–Oct

This C17 manor house was the birthplace and home of the scientist Sir Isaac Newton. Visitors can see his childhood scribblings on the walls. A gnarled old apple tree in the garden may be a descendant of the famous specimen that inspired Newton in his work.

* An interactive science discovery centre
* Replica of Newton's *Principia*

Location
From A1 take B676 at Colsterworth roundabout, turn right at 2nd cross-roads & follow signs

Opening
3 Mar–25 Mar Sat–Sun 1pm–5pm; 31 Mar–30 Sep Wed–Sun 1pm–5pm; 6 Oct–28 Oct Sat–Sun 1pm–5pm

Admission
Adult £4.50, Child £2.20

Contact
23 Newton Way, Woolsthorpe-by-Colsterworth, nr Grantham NG33 5NR

t 01476 860338
w nationaltrust.org.uk
e woolsthorpemanor@nationaltrust.org.uk

453 Grimsby

National Fishing Heritage Centre

2 hrs All year

The centre tells the story of the area's fishermen, their trawlers and the waters they fished in. The dangers and hardships of life at sea are explained and there is a reconstruction of a 1950s sea voyage, complete with authentic aromas and a moving deck.

* Tours of working 1950 trawler
* Reconstruction of streets & alleys of 1950s Grimsby

Location
Next to Alexandra Dock, 2 min walk from town centre

Opening
Apr–Oct Mon–Fri 10am–5pm, Sat–Sun & Bank Hols 10.30am–5.30pm; Nov–Mar Mon–Fri 10am–4pm, Sat–Sun 11am–3pm

Admission
Adult £6, Child £2, Concs £4

Contact
Alexandra Dock, Grimsby DN31 1UZ

t 01472 323345
w nelincs.gov.uk
e ann.hackett@nelincs.gov.uk

454 Scunthorpe

Normanby Hall Country Park

4 hrs All year

Set in the heart of tranquil North Lincolnshire, 300 acres of country park provide the perfect day out for all the family. Learn about Lincolnshire's rich rural heritage in the fascinating Farm Museum or step back in time in the award-winning Victorian walled garden.

* Extensive woodland with a wealth of wildlife
* Adventure playground for younger children

Location
4 miles N of Scunthorpe on B1430

Opening
Hall & Museum Easter–Sep 1pm–5pm
Gardens All year 10.30am–4pm
Park All year 9am–dusk

Admission
Adult £4.40, Child £2.20, Concs £4

Contact
Normanby, Scunthorpe DN15 9HU

t 01724 720588
w northlincs.gov.uk/normanby
e normanby.hall@northlincs.gov.uk

455 Skegness

Gibraltar Point National Nature Reserve & Visitor Centre

2 hrs+ All year

This area of unspoilt coastline comprises sand dunes, saltmarshes and freshwater habitats for rare plants, and animals including seals, water voles and pygmy shrews. There are five bird-watching hides, a nature trail, an interpretation centre, and various activities and events.

* Area of International Scientific Interest
* Home to many rare plants, insects & animals

Location
3 miles S of Skegness, signed from town centre

Opening
Daily, please phone for details

Admission
Free

Contact
Gilbraltar Road, Skegness PE24 4SU

t 01507 526667
w lincstrust.org.uk
e info@lincstrust.co.uk

456 Skegness

Skegness Natureland Seal Sanctuary

2 hrs All year

The sanctuary houses seals, penguins and tropical birds. There are reptiles in a tropical house and a display of free-flying tropical butterflies. Natureland is well known for rescuing abandoned seal pups and visitors can view the hospital unit and large seascape pool.

* Family Attraction of the Year 2004
* New Blue Lagoon restaurant

Location
Signed from town centre

Opening
Daily: Jun–Sep 10am–5pm;
Oct–May 10am–4pm

Admission
Adult £5.50, Child £3.60, Concs £4.40

Contact
North Parade, Skegness PE25 1DB

t 01754 764345
w skegnessnatureland.co.uk
e natureland@fsbdial.co.uk

457 Spalding

Baytree Garden Centre & Owl Centre

2 hrs+ All year

Set in 16 acres, this garden centre and nursery has something for all gardeners, including bulbs, plants, pets and aquatics. The centre is also home to more than 100 owls and birds of prey, including very rare Mexican striped owls. There are regular flying displays.

* Discover Britain's No. 1 grotto
* See tropical owls in the Hot House

Location
On main A151 at Weston between Spalding & Holbeach

Opening
Please phone for details

Admission
Please phone for details

Contact
High Road Weston, Spalding, Lincolnshire PE12 6JU

t *Garden centre* 01406 370242
Owl centre 01406 372840
w baytree-gardencentre.com
e info@baytree-gardencentre.com

458 Spalding

The Butterfly & Wildlife Park

4 hrs Mar–Oct

Set in the heart of the Fens, the park has a tropical house, a reptile area with crocodiles and snakes, a creepy-crawly house and an ant room. Outdoor attractions include a birds of prey centre that runs twice-daily flying displays, an animal centre and an adventure playground.

* Quality Assured Visitor Attraction
* Lincolnshire Family Attraction of the Year 2003

Location
Signed off A17 at Long Sutton

Opening
Daily: end Mar–end Oct from 10am
Please phone for details

Admission
Please phone for details

Contact
Long Sutton, Spalding
PE12 9LE

t 01406 363833
w butterflyandwildlifepark.co.uk
e butterflypark@hotmail.com

459 Stamford

Burghley House

3 hrs Mar–Oct

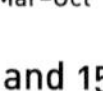

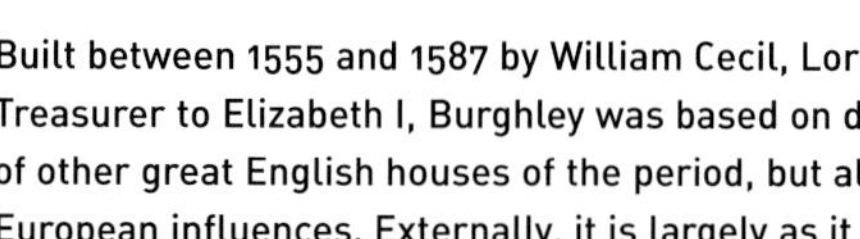

Built between 1555 and 1587 by William Cecil, Lord Treasurer to Elizabeth I, Burghley was based on designs of other great English houses of the period, but also had European influences. Externally, it is largely as it was when completed by Cecil's masons.

* Paintings include work by John Frederick Herring
* Sculpture park

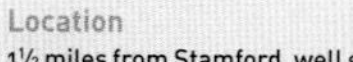

Location
1½ miles from Stamford, well signed

Opening
House Mar–Oct Sun–Thu 11am–5pm
Sculpture Park All year Sun–Thu 10am–5pm

Admission
Adult £9, Child £4, Concs £8

Contact
Stamford PE9 3JY

t 01780 752451
w burghley.co.uk
e burghley@burghley.co.uk

460 Spilsby

Lincoln Aviation Heritage Centre

4 hrs All year

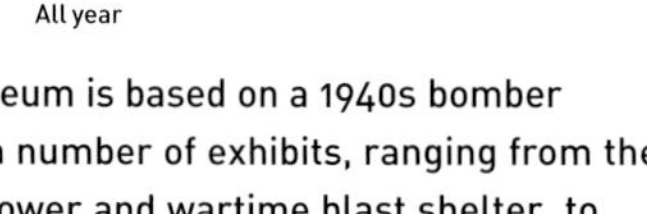

This aircraft museum is based on a 1940s bomber airfield and has a number of exhibits, ranging from the original control tower and wartime blast shelter, to Barnes Wallis's bouncing bomb, and squadron and airfield photographs.

* Avro Lancaster bomber NX611 *Just Jane*
* RAF Escaping exhibition

Location
Off A16 N of Boston

Opening
Easter–Oct Mon–Sat 9.30am–5pm;
Nov–Easter Mon–Sat 9.30am–4pm

Admission
Adult £6.75, Child £2.50, Concs £5.75

Contact
East Kirkby Airfield, nr Spilsby
PE23 4DE

t 01790 763207
w lincsaviation.co.uk
e enquiries@lincsaviation.co.uk

461 Tattershall

Tattershall Castle

1 hr Mar–Dec

A large medieval fortified and moated redbrick tower, built, in the C15 for Ralph Lord Cromwell, Chancellor of England. The building was restored by Lord Curzon in 1911–14 and contains four great chambers with enormous Gothic fireplaces, tapestries and brick vaulting.

* Spectacular views from the battlements
* Special events throughout the year

Location
On S side of A153, 15 miles NE of Sleaford, 10 miles SW of Horncastle

Opening
Apr–Oct Mon–Wed & Sat–Sun 11am–5pm; Mar & Nov–Dec Sat–Sun 12noon–4pm

Admission
Adult £4, Child £2

Contact
Tattershall, Lincoln LN4 4LR

t 01526 342543
w nationaltrust.org.uk
e tattershallcastle@nationaltrust.org.uk

462 Althorp

Althorp House

 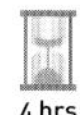 

4 hrs Jul–Aug

The home of the Spencer family since 1508. The park came to world attention on 6 September 1997, when Diana, Princess of Wales was laid to rest here. See her final resting place on the island in the Round Oval, surrounded by her family's ancestral heritage.

* Magnificent Palladian stable block for 100 horses
* One of the world's finest collections of portraiture

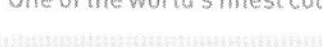

Location
7 miles W of Northampton off A428. Clearly signed from junction 16 of M1

Opening
Daily: Jul–Aug 11am–5pm

Admission
Adult £12, Child £6, Concs £10

Contact
The Stables, Althorp, Northampton NN7 4HQ

t 01604 770107
w althorp.com
e mail@althorp.com

463 Brixworth

Brixworth Country Park

 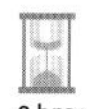 

2 hrs+ All year

The park has many facilities including a café, cycle hire, play area, sensory garden and waymarked trails. It is now the main gateway to Pitsford Water and the 10km safe walking/cycling route called the Pitsford Water Trail. The park is also linked with the Brampton Valley Way.

* Take a walk along our sculpture trail
* Watch birds from our bird hide

Location
Close to Brixworth village & 7 miles N of Northampton on A508 Northampton –Market Harborough road

Opening
Daily: dawn–dusk

Admission
Free. Car park fees

Contact
Northampton Road, Brixworth NN6 9DG

t 01604 883920
w northamptonshire.gov.uk/countryside
e brixworth@northamptonshire.gov.uk

464 Corby

Deene Park

2 hrs Jun–Aug

Deene Park is a largely C16 house incorporating an earlier medieval manor. It's built around a courtyard and had important rooms added during the reign of George III. It was the seat of the 7th Earl of Cardigan, who led the Charge of the Light Brigade at Balaclava in 1854.

* Crimean War exhibition of uniforms & memorabilia
* Beautiful gardens & parkland

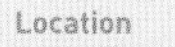

Location
6 miles NE of Corby, off A43

Opening
Jun–Aug Sun & Bank Hols 2pm–5pm

Admission
Adult £6.50, Child £2.50, Concs £5.50

Contact
Corby NN17 3EW

t 01780 450278
w deenepark.com
e admin@deenepark.com

465 Corby

Kirby Hall

1 hrs All year

Featuring decorative carving and ornate gardens fit for a queen, Kirby Hall is one of the great Elizabethan houses, built in the hope of a royal visit. The great hall and state rooms have recently been refitted and redecorated to authentic C17 and C18 designs.

* Special events throughout the year

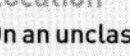

Location
On an unclassified road off A43, 4 miles NE of Corby

Opening
23 Mar–30 Jun Thu–Mon 10am–5pm;
1 Jul–31 Aug daily 10am–6pm;
1 Sep–31 Oct Thu–Mon 10am–5pm;
1 Nov–31 Mar Thu–Mon 10am–4pm

Admission
Adult £4.50, Child £2.30, Concs £3.40

Contact
Kirby Hall Deene, nr Corby NN17 5EN

t 01536 203230
w english-heritage.org.uk

466 Cottesbrooke

Cottesbrooke Hall & Gardens

2 hrs+ May–Sep

An architecturally magnificent Queen Anne house with a renowned picture collection featuring sporting and equestrian subjects. Other collections include fine furniture and porcelain. Cottesbrooke is reputed to be the model for Jane Austen's Mansfield Park.

* HHA/Christie's Garden of the Year 2000
* Guided tours of the house available

Location
At A14 junction 1 head S on A5199, signed for Cottesbrooke

Opening
May–Jun Wed–Thu & Bank Hols 2pm–5.30pm;
Jul–Sep Thu & Bank Hols 2pm–5.30pm

Admission
Hall & Gardens Adult £7.50, Child £3.50, Concs £6
Gardens £5, £2.50, £4

Contact
Cottesbrooke, Northampton NN6 8PF

t 01604 505808
w cottesbrookehall.co.uk
e enquiries@cottesbrooke.co.uk

467 Daventry

Canons Ashby House

 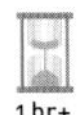 

1 hr+ Apr–Oct

Constructed in the mid-C16, this charming house has remained largely unaltered since 1710. The interior contains wall paintings and Jacobean plasterwork, with rich panelling in the Winter Parlour. Edward Dryden's formal gardens have been restored.

* Remains of an Augustinian priory
* Orchard containing varieties of typical C16 apple trees

Location
Between Northampton & Banbury

Opening
Apr–Sep Sat–Wed 1pm–5pm;
Oct Sat–Wed 1pm–4pm

Admission
House Adult £6.10, Child £3.10
Gardens £2.20, children free

Contact
Daventry NN11 3SD

t 01327 860044
w nationaltrust.org.uk
e canonsashby@nationaltrust.org.uk

468 Kettering

Rushton Triangular Lodge

1 hr Apr–Oct

This triangular building was designed and built by Sir Thomas Tresham in 1593 as a testament to his Catholicism, for which he had been imprisoned. Consequently, the lodge is emblazoned with references to the Holy Trinity and the number three.

* Colourful house adorned with dates & emblems
* 3 windows, 3 floors, 3 roof gables

Location
1 mile W of Rushton, on A6, on an unclassified road 3 miles from Desborough

Opening
Apr–Oct Thu–Mon 10am–5pm

Admission
Adult £2.40, Child £1.20, Concs £1.80

Contact
Rushton, Kettering NN14 1RP

t 01536 710761
w english-heritage.org.uk

469 Market Harborough

Kelmarsh Hall & Gardens

2 hrs+ Easter–Sep

This early C18 Palladian-style house was designed by James Gibbs and includes a Chinese room with handpainted wallpaper. Interesting gardens, a lake and woodland walks can be enjoyed outside. A herd of British white cattle roam the parkland.

* Managed by Kelmarsh Trust
* Regular events throughout the season

Location
On A508 in Kelmarsh

Opening
House Easter–2 Sep Tue, Sun & Bank Hols 2pm–5.30pm
Gardens Sun, Tue–Thu & Bank Hol Mon 2pm–5.30pm

Admission
House & Gardens Adult £4.50, Child £2.50, Concs £4
Gardens £3.50, £2, £3

Contact
Kelmarsh, Northampton NN6 9LY

t 01604 686543
w kelmarsh.com
e enquiries@kelmarsh.com

470 Northampton

Holdenby House, Gardens & Falconry Centre

2 hrs Apr–Sep

Across the fields from Althorp lies Holdenby, a house whose royal connections go back more than 400 years. Its history is complemented by a regal collection of birds of prey which visitors can see soaring high in the sky over the grounds.

* Based on remaining kitchen wing of old palace
* Built in 1583 by Sir Christopher Hatton

Location
6 miles NW of Northampton, off A5199 or A428

Opening
Gardens & Falconry centre Easter–Sep Sun & Bank Hols 1pm–5pm
House Easter Mon & Spring Bank Hol, pre-booked tours on other days

Admission
Gardens & Falconry centre Adult £4.50, Child £3, Concs £4

Contact
Holdenby, Northampton NN6 8DJ

t 01604 770074
w holdenby.com
e enquiries@holdenby.com

471 Northampton

Northampton Museum & Art Gallery

1 hr All year

Showcasing one of the world's largest collections of footwear, the museum celebrates shoe fashions and the history of shoe making. Other displays include fine Italian and British paintings, British and Oriental ceramics and glass, and the history of Northampton.

* A dynamic programme of temporary exhibitions & events
* The town's history from the Stone Age to the present day

Location
In town centre

Opening
Daily: Mon–Sat 10am–5pm, Sun 2–5pm

Admission
Free

Contact
4–6 Guildhall Road, Northampton NN1 1DP

t 01604 838111
w northampton.gov.uk/museums
e museums@northampton.gov.uk

472 Northampton South

Abington Museum

3 hrs+ All year

Housed in a C15 manor house that was once the home of Shakespeare's granddaughter, Elizabeth Bernard, the museum is now home to displays of Victorian curiosities and Northamptonshire local and military history, a costume gallery and a leathercraft gallery.

* C17 oak-panelled room
* C19 fashion gallery

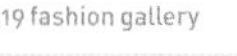

Location
Approximately 1½ miles E of town centre

Opening
March–Oct Sun–Tue 1pm–5pm; Nov–Feb Sun–Tue 1pm–4pm; Bank Hol Mon 1pm–5pm

Admission
Free

Contact
Abington Park, Park Avenue, South Northampton NN1 5LW

t 01604 838110
w northampton.gov.uk/museums

474 Towcester

Canal Museum

2 hrs All year

Housed in an old corn mill on the Grand Union Canal are exhibits from two centuries of canal history, including a reconstructed narrowboat with all its traditional furniture and equipment. Trips can be taken through the 1.75 mile-long Blisworth Tunnel.

* Cruise along Grand Union Canal
* Gift shop & cafeteria

Location
S of Northampton, 10 min from both M1 junction 15 & A5, just off the A508, on Grand Union Canal S of Blisworth Tunnel

Opening
Daily: Oct–Mar 10am–4pm; Apr–Sep 10am–5pm

Admission
Adult £3.75, Child & Concs £3.25

Contact
Stoke Bruerne, Towcester NN12 7SE

t 01604 862 229
w waterwaystrust.org.uk
e canal.museum@waterwaystrust.org

473 Oundle

Lyveden New Bield

1 hr+ Feb–Nov

This incomplete Elizabethan garden lodge remains unaltered since building work stopped 400 years ago.- Designed in the shape of a cross, with fascinating architectural stonework, the lodge is set in beautiful countryside adjoining the remains of a moated garden.

* Designed by Sir Thomas Tresham
* Elizabethan water-gardens

Location
4 miles SW of Oundle on A427, 3 miles E of Brigstock, leading off A6116

Opening
Good Fri & Bank Hol Mons 10.30am–5pm; Apr–Jul & Sep–Oct Wed–Sun 10.30am–5pm; Aug daily 10.30am–5pm; Nov & Feb–March Sat–Sun 10.30am–4pm

Admission
Adult £3.50, Child free

Contact
nr Oundle, Peterborough PE8 5AT

t 01832 205358
w nationaltrust.org.uk/lyveden
e lyveden@nationaltrust.org.uk

475 Wansford

Prebendal Manor House

2 hrs+ Easter–Sep

This C13 Grade I-listed manor house is the oldest surviving dwelling in Northamptonshire and is steeped in history. The recreated medieval gardens are unique to the area and are the largest in Europe. Visit the C16 dovecote and the large C18 tithe barn museum.

* Rare breeds of sheep & pigs, & medieval farming
* Explore the history of the Prebends

Location
A few miles from A1 & A605, signed from nearby villages

Opening
Easter–Sep Sun, Wed & Bank Hols 1pm–5.30pm

Admission
Adult £5.50, Child £3, Concs £5

Contact
Nassington, Peterborough PE8 6QG

t 01780 782575
w prebendal-manor.co.uk
e info@prebendal-manor.co.uk

476 Wellingborough

Irchester Country Park

4 hrs+ All year

Explore a network of trails running across 83 hectares of mixed woodland and observe the wealth of wildlife, including woodpeckers and sparrowhawks. A Forestry Centre of Excellence, the park balances conservation with timber production and recreation.

* Park shop
* Accessible trails & orienteering trail

Location
2 miles S of Wellingborough, on B570, off A509, in the Nene Valley

Opening
Park Daily: 24 hrs
Car park Daily: 24 hrs
Lower car park Daily: 9am–6pm

Admission
Free. Car park fees

Contact
Gypsy Lane, Little Irchester, Wellingborough NN29 7DL

t 01933 276866
w northamptonshire.gov.uk
e irchester@northamptonshire.gov.uk

477 Eastwood

D H Lawrence Birthplace Museum

2 hrs+ All year

The carefully restored birthplace and early home of D H Lawrence gives a fascinating glimpse into the cramped realities of a Victorian mining family. The museum also uses an interactive wash house, exhibition room and video to interpret the writer's roots and his community.

* Combine with a visit to Durban House Heritage Centre
* See the style in which the local mineowner lived

Location
From M1 junction 26 or 27 follow signs towards Eastwood, then signed

Opening
Daily: Apr–Oct 10am–5pm; Nov–Mar 10am–4pm

Admission
Mon–Fri free; Sat, Sun & Bank Hols Adult £2, Child £1.20, Concs £1.20

Contact
Mansfield Road, Eastwood, Nottingham NG16 3DZ

t 01773 717353
w broxtowe.gov.uk
e culture@broxtowe.gov.uk

478 Edwinstowe

Sherwood Forest Country Park & Visitor Centre

2 hrs All year

A good place to begin any exploration of Sherwood Forest is the visitor centre. Find out what life would have been like for outlaws, kings and commoners in Sherwood Forest during the Middle Ages. Enjoy the-trails and discover the forest yourself.

* See the Major Oak, Robin Hood's hiding place
* National Nature Reserve

   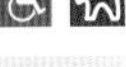

Location
In Edwinstowe, off B6034

Opening
Visitor centre Daily: summer 10am–5pm, winter 10am–4.30pm
Park Daily: dawn–dusk

Admission
Free. Car park £3

Contact
Edwinstowe, nr Mansfield NG21 9HN

t 01623 823202
w nottinghamshire.gov.uk/countryparks
e sherwood.forest@nottscc.gov.uk

479 Mansfield

Mansfield Museum & Art Gallery

1 hr All year

Explore the history of Mansfield and the surrounding area. Permanent displays illustrate the social, industrial and natural history of the area. Enjoy the Xplorative hands-on environmental exhibition.

* Pottery pieces from Derby, Pinxton & Mansfield
* Varied programme of temporary exhibitions

Location
5 min walk from market place

Opening
Mon–Sat 10am–5pm (closed Bank Hols)

Admission
Free

Contact
Leeming Street, Mansfield NG18 1NG

t 01623 463088
w mansfield.gov.uk/museum
e mansfieldmuseum@mansfield.gov.uk

480 Newark-on-Trent

Newark Air Museum

2 hrs All year

The museum's impressive collection currently stands at more than 70 aircraft and cockpit sections, including those from transport, training and reconnaissance aircraft and helicopters and a diverse selection of jet fighters and bombers.

* Postwar air-to-air missile display
* History of RAF Winthorpe, wartime bomber training

Location
Easily accessible from A1, A46, A17, A1133 & Newark-on-Trent bypass

Opening
Daily: Mar–Oct 10am–5pm; Nov–Feb 10am–4pm

Admission
Please phone for details

Contact
Winthorpe Showground, Newark on-Trent NG24 2NY

t 01636 707170
w newarkairmuseum.co.uk
e newarkair@onetel.com

481 Nottingham

Angel Row Gallery

1 hr+ All year

This is one of the region's leading contemporary art galleries, with a programme of exhibitions covering a wide range of art, including painting, photography, video and installations. The gallery also runs workshops and hosts talks by leading artists.

* Temporary exhibitions change throughout the year

Location
In central Nottingham

Opening
Mon, Tue & Thu–Sat 10am–5pm, Wed 10am–7pm

Admission
Free

Contact
Central Library Building, 3 Angel Row, Nottingham NG1 6HP

t 0115 915 2869
w angelrowgallery.com
e angelrow.info@nottinghamcity.gov.uk

482 Nottingham

City of Caves

  1 hr+  All year

Descend under the city in man-made Anglo-Saxon tunnels to discover an enchanted well, a medieval tannery that includes a pillar cave (AD1250), original Victorian slums and the Anderson shelter, used during the Blitz. Learn more about ongoing archaeological digs.

* Visit our Rock Shop
* Special events throughout the year

Location
In city centre. Inside Broadmarsh shopping centre on upper level

Opening
Daily: 10.30am–4.30pm

Admission
Adult £4.95, Child & Concs £3.95
Combined ticket with NCCL Galleries available

Contact
Drury Walk, Broadmarsh Centre, Nottingham NG1 7LS

t 0115 988 1955
w cityofcaves.com
e info@cityofcaves.com

483 Nottingham

NCCL Galleries of Justice

  2 hr+  All year

A tour through three centuries of crime, punishment and law. Located in the Shire Hall, it includes a Victorian street, courtrooms, an C18 prison, an exercise yard, cave cells, a women's prison with bath house and laundry, a medieval cave system and an Edwardian police station.

* Costumed interpreters bring the experience to life
* Narrow Marsh Victorian adventure for children

Location
In central Nottingham, near Broadmarsh shopping centre

Opening
Tue–Sun & Bank Hols 10am–5pm, daily during school hols. Please phone for details

Admission
Adult £7.95, Child & Concs £5.95

Contact
High Pavement, Lace Market, Nottingham NG1 1HN

t 0115 952 0555
w nccl.org.uk
e info@nccl.org.uk

484 Nottingham

Nottingham Castle

  1 hr+  All year

Looming high above the city and set in scenic Victorian gardens, Nottingham Castle, a ducal mansion built over the originally medieval site, has a turbulent history. The castle has displays about its history, and a fine collection of paintings, sculptures and china.

* Network of caves & passageways beneath the castle
* Robin Hood statue

Location
In central Nottingham

Opening
Daily: Mar–Oct 10am–5pm;
Nov–Feb 10am–4pm

Admission
Adult £3, Child & Concs £1.50

Contact
Lenton Road, Nottingham NG1 6EL

t 0115 915 3700
w nottinghamcity.gov.uk/museums
e helens@ncmg.demon.co.uk

485 Nottingham

Tales of Robin Hood

1 hr+ All year

The swashbuckling adventures of Robin Hood have inspired storytellers for more than 700 years. Explore the world of this notorious, endearing outlaw and experience medieval life, legend and adventure by fleeing through the forest to escape the evil Sheriff.

* Regular Robin Hood events
* Medieval banquets held on Fri & Sat

Location
In city centre, next to castle, signed from M1

Opening
Daily: 10am–5.30pm (last admission 4.30pm)

Admission
Adult £8.95, Child £6.95, Concs £7.95

Contact
30–38 Maid Marian Way, Nottingham NG1 6GF

t 0115 948 3284
w robinhood.uk.com
e robinhoodcentre@mail.com

486 Nottingham

Wollaton Hall Museum

 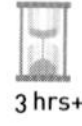 

3 hrs+ All year

Set in more than 500 acres of historic deer park, Wollaton Hall is a spectacular Tudor building, designed by Robert Smythson and completed in 1588. It is now home to the city's natural history museum, an industrial museum, a visitor centre and a gallery.

* Steam-engine house
* Parts under restoration & closed until Easter 2007

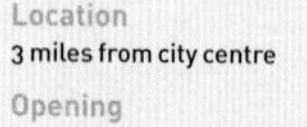

Location
3 miles from city centre

Opening
Natural History Museum, Industrial Museum & Yard Gallery
Daily: Oct–Mar 11am–4pm; Apr–Sep 11am–5pm

Admission
Mon–Fri Free, Sat–Sun each museum Adult £1.50, Child & Concs £1

Contact
Wollaton Park, Nottingham NG8 2AE

t 0115 915 3900
w nottinghamcity.gov.uk
e carolb@ncmg.demon.co.uk

487 Ollerton

Holocaust Centre, Beth Shalom

2 hrs+ All year

Beth Shalom is set in 2 acres of beautiful gardens and provides a range of facilities for visitors to explore the history and implications of the Holocaust. The main features are its redbrick memorial building, permanent exhibition on the Nazi period and memorial gardens.

* Survivors regularly speak at the centre

Location
Large buildings on right between Laxton & Ollerton

Opening
Apr–Sep daily 10am–5pm; Oct–March Mon–Fri 10am–5pm (last admission 3.30pm)

Admission
Adult £6, Child & Concs £4

Contact
Laxton, nr Ollerton NG22 0PA

t 01623 836627
w bethshalom.com
e office@bethshalom.com

488 Ollerton

Rufford Abbey & Country Park

  4 hrs  All year

This site was originally that of a C12 Cistercian monastery, dissolved by Henry VIII in 1536, and granted to George Talbot, 4th Earl of Shrewsbury. The Talbot family then went on to transform the buildings into a country house.

* Stable block houses a contemporary craft exhibition
* Gardens re established in late 1970s

Location
2 miles S of Ollerton, off A614

Opening
Daily: Apr–Oct 10am–5pm;
Nov–Mar 10am–4pm

Admission
Free. Car park fees Sat–Sun & Bank Hols

Contact
Ollerton, nr Newark NG22 9DF

t 01623 822944
w nottinghamshire.gov.uk/country-parks
e rufford.park@nottscc.gov.uk

489 Southwell

Southwell Minster

  2 hrs   All year

Southwell Minster, with its majestic Norman nave and glorious C13 chapter house, is one of the least known jewels in the crown of Nottinghamshire. Nearby is the Minster Centre with an audio-visual theatre showing a film on the life of the Minster, a library, gallery and bookshop.

* Dedicated education officer organises events & talks for children

Location
In town centre

Opening
Minster Daily
Minster centre Mon–Fri 9am–5pm, Sat–Sun times vary, please phone for details

Admission
Free but donations welcomed

Contact
Southwell, Nottinghamshire

t 01636 812649
w southwellminster.org.uk
e office@southwellminster.org.uk

490 Southwell

Southwell Workhouse

  1 hr+  Mar–Oct

The lives of the poor and destitute in the C19 and C20 are revealed at Southwell Workhouse. Explore the building and its history, including the segregated staircases and rooms, and unlock the stories of the people who lived and worked there.

* Play the Master's Punishment game
* Meet some of the 'characters' who lived here

 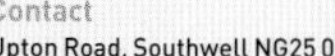

Location
13 miles from Nottingham on A612, 8 miles from Newark on A617 & A612

Opening
Please phone for details

Admission
Adult £4.90, Child £2.40

Contact
Upton Road, Southwell NG25 0PT

t 01636 817250
w nationaltrust.org.uk
e theworkhouse@nationaltrust.org.uk

491 Workshop

Clumber Park

2 hrs+ All year

Part of Nottinghamshire's famed 'Dukeries', at Clumber Park there are more than 3,800 acres of parkland, woods, open heath and rolling farmland with a superb serpentine lake at their heart. Although the house was demolished in 1938, many features of the estate remain.

* Walled kitchen garden & interpretation centre
* Bicycle hire available

Location
4 miles SE of Worksop

Opening
Park Daily: dawn–dusk
Gardens Daily: Mar–Oct 10am–5.30pm, Sat–Sun 10am–6pm

Admission
£4.30 per car

Contact
The Estate Office, Clumber Park, Worksop S80 3AZ

t 01909 476592
w nationaltrust.org.uk/clumberpark
e clumberpark@nationaltrust.org.uk

492 Worksop

Harley Gallery

1 hr All year

The award-winning Harley Gallery was built in 1994 on the site of the original C19 gasworks at the Welbeck Estate. It offers displays of contemporary art, crafts and design, with the museum displaying fine and decorative arts from the Portland Collection.

* Stylish café with freshly prepared bistro-style menu
* Neighbours a large garden centre

Location
5 miles S of Worksop on A60

Opening
Mid-Jan–Dec Tue–Sun & Bank Hols 10am–5pm

Admission
Free

Contact
Welbeck, Worksop S80 3LW

t 01909 501700
w harleygallery.co.uk
e info@harley-wellbeck.co.uk

493 Worksop

Mr Straw's House

1 hr+ Apr–Oct

This modest semi-detached Edwardian house provides an intriguing insight into early C20 everyday life. The interior has remained unaltered since the 1930s and features contemporary wallpaper, Victorian furniture and household objects.

* Learn about the Straw family history in new exhibition
* A typical suburban garden

WC

Location
Follow signs to Bassetlaw General Hospital, signed from Blyth Road

Opening
Apr–Oct Tue–Sat 11am–4pm booking essential

Admission
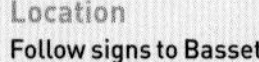
Pre-booked timed ticket only
Adult £5, Child £250

Contact
5 Blyth Grove, Worksop S81 0JG

t 01909 482380
w nationaltrust.org.uk
e mrstrawshouse@nationaltrust.org.uk

494 Barnsdale

Drought Garden & Arboretum

  1 hr  All year

Designed by the late Geoff Hamilton with refurbishment by Nick Hamilton, this garden – on a south-facing clay slope at Barnsdale – has survived dry summers and penetrating frost. The arboretum shows the species of trees planted around the reservoir.

* Accolade Winner 2002
* The Best of its Kind 2003

Location
Accessed from A606 Oakham–Stamford road

Opening
Daily: All reasonable times

Admission
Free

Contact
Barnsdale, Rutland Water
t 01572 653026
w anglianwaterleisure.co.uk
e tic@anglianwater.co.uk

495 Clipsham

Clipsham Yew Tree Avenue

 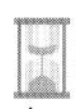 1 hr+  All year

The Yew Tree Avenue is a unique collection of 150 clipped yew trees, most more than 200 years old, once the drive to Clipsham Hall. The topiary was begun in 1870 by Amos Alexander, the estate's head forester, who lived in the gate lodge at the foot of the avenue.

* Clipping each autumn by Forestry Commission
* Muntjac deer may be seen crossing the avenue

Location
Less than 1 mile E of Clipsham on Castle Bytham road

Opening
Daily: All reasonable times

Admission
Free

Contact
Forestry Commision, North Hants
Top Lodge, Fineshade NN17 3BB
t 01780 444920
w forestry.gov.uk
e northants@forestry.gsi.gov.uk

496 Lyddington

Lyddington Bede House

  1 hr  Apr–Oct

Lyddington Bede House was originally a wing of a medieval rural palace belonging to the bishops of Lincoln. In 1600 the building was converted into an alms house and it remained a home for pensioners until the 1930s.

* Great chamber features a beautiful ceiling cornice
* Bedesmen's rooms with tiny windows & fireplaces

Location
In Lyddington, 6 miles N of Corby, 1 mile E of A6003, next to church

Opening
Apr–Oct Thu–Mon 10am–5pm

Admission
Adult £3.30, Child £1.70, Concs £2.50
Prices for events vary

Contact
Bluecoat Lane, Lyddington LE15 9LZ

t 01572 822438
w english-heritage.org.uk

497 Oakham

Rutland County Museum

  1 hr+  All year

Rutland Museum is a perfect introduction to England's smallest county. The new Welcome to Rutland Gallery is a guide to the house of Rutland and leads into displays of local archaeology and history, and an extensive rural life collection.

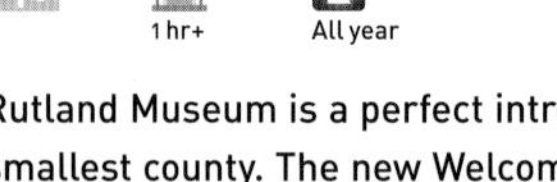

* Newly refurbished courtyard containing agricultural machinery
* Rare Saunderson tractor

Location
Off A603, near town centre

Opening
Daily: Mon–Sat 10.30am–5pm, Sun 2pm–4pm

Admission
Free

Contact
Catmose Street, Oakham LE15 6HW

t 01572 758440
w rutnet.co.uk/rcc/rutlandmuseums
e museum@rutland.gov.uk

498 Oakham

Rutland Water

  2 hrs+  All year

The largest man-made lake in western Europe, this attractive 3,100-acre reservoir has an international reputation for balancing leisure activities with wildlife conservation. Visitors may windsurf, rock-climb or canoe, hire a dinghy, bike or fishing boat, or just relax.

* Butterfly & Aquatic Centre & bird-watching
* Range of craft available for hire or launch your own

Location
Just off A606, signed from A1

Opening
Daily: 10am–5pm

Admission
Free. Car park fee

Contact
Tourist Information Centre, Sykes Lane, Empingham, Rutland LE15 8PX

t 01572 653026
w anglianwaterleisure.co.uk
e tic@anglianwaterleisure.co.uk

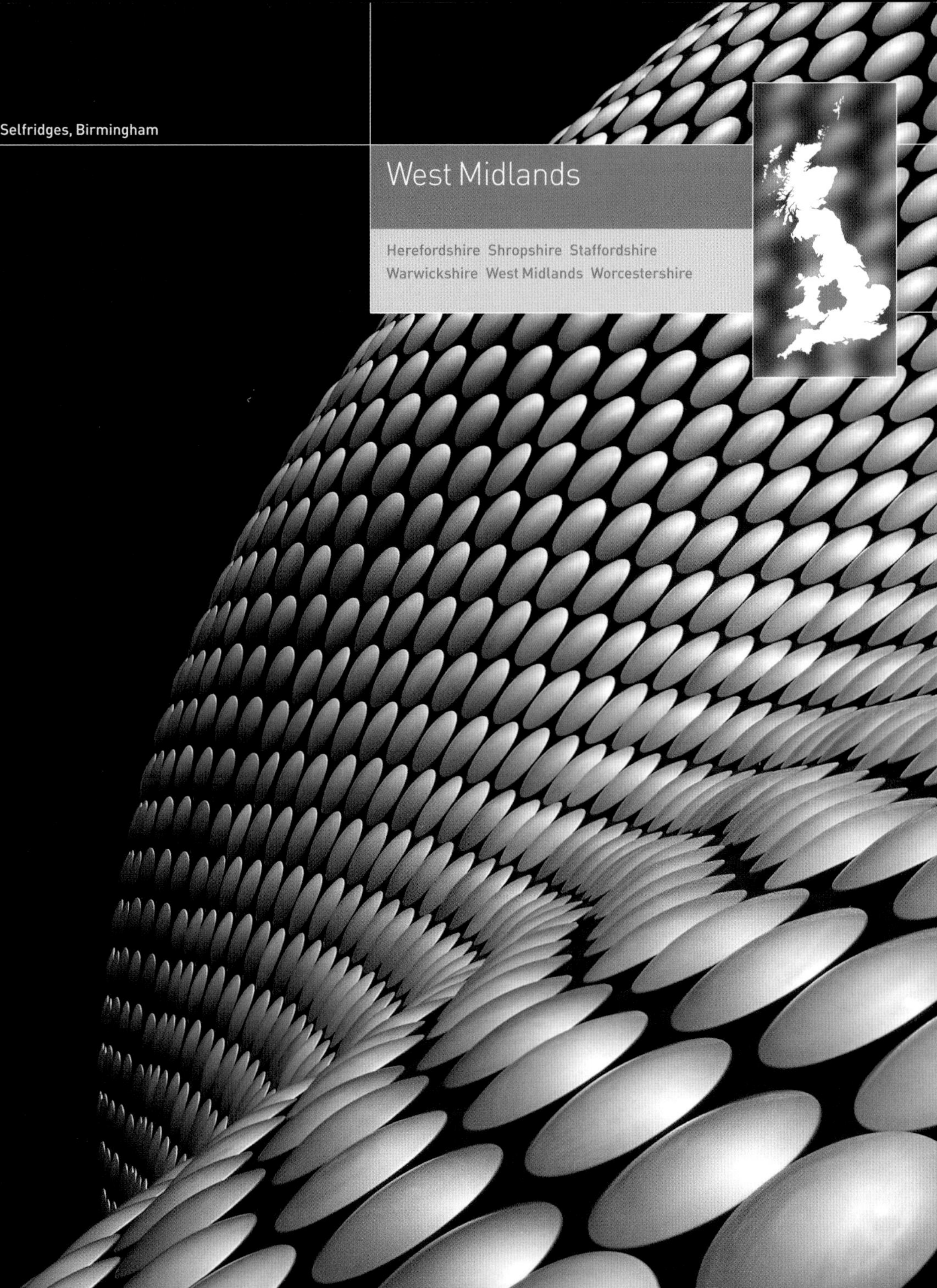
Selfridges, Birmingham
West Midlands
Herefordshire Shropshire Staffordshire
Warwickshire West Midlands Worcestershire

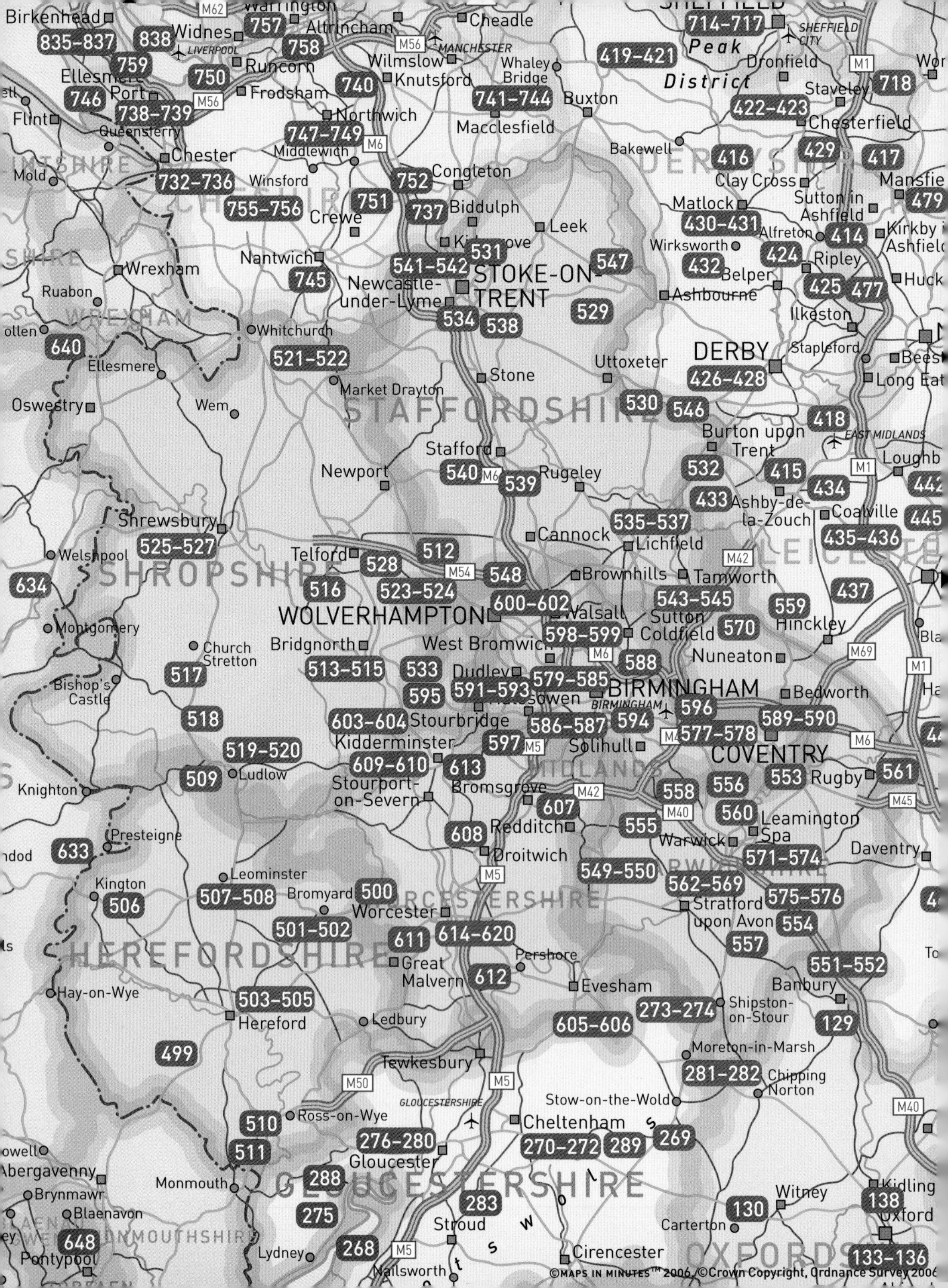

Birkenhead
835-837
838
Widnes
LIVERPOOL
757
Warrington
M62
Altrincham
758
M56
MANCHESTER
Cheadle
714-717
SHEFFIELD
SHEFFIELD CITY
Peak
District
419-421
Wor
759
Ellesmere Port
750
Runcorn
740
Wilmslow
Knutsford
Whaley Bridge
Dronfield
M1
718
746
Frodsham
M56
741-744
Buxton
Staveley
Flint
738-739
Northwich
Macclesfield
422-423
Chesterfield
Queensferry
747-749
M6
Chester
Middlewich
Bakewell
416
429
417
Mold
732-736
Winsford
752
Congleton
Clay Cross
Mansfie
479
755-756
751
737
Biddulph
Matlock
Sutton in Ashfield
Crewe
Leek
430-431
Alfreton
414
Kirkby in Ashfield
Kidsgrove
531
Wirksworth
424
Nantwich
541-542
547
432
Belper
Ripley
Wrexham
745
Newcastle-under-Lyme
STOKE-ON-TRENT
Hucknall
425
477
Ruabon
Ashbourne
529
534
538
Ilkeston
WREXHAM
Whitchurch
Llangollen
640
Ellesmere
521-522
Uttoxeter
DERBY
Stapleford
Beeston
426-428
Stone
Long Eaton
Market Drayton
Oswestry
Wem
STAFFORDSHIRE
530
546
418
Burton upon Trent
EAST MIDLANDS
Stafford
Newport
540
M6
539
Rugeley
532
415
M1
Loughborough
433
Ashby-de-la-Zouch
434
442
Shrewsbury
Coalville
535-537
Cannock
445
525-527
Lichfield
435-436
Welshpool
Telford
512
M42
LEICESTERSHIRE
SHROPSHIRE
528
M54
548
Brownhills
Tamworth
634
516
523-524
600-602
543-545
437
559
WOLVERHAMPTON
Walsall
Sutton Coldfield
570
Hinckley
Montgomery
598-599
Church Stretton
Bridgnorth
West Bromwich
M6
588
Nuneaton
M69
Blaby
M1
517
513-515
533
Dudley
579-585
BIRMINGHAM
Bishop's Castle
595
591-593
Halesowen
BIRMINGHAM
Bedworth
518
603-604
Stourbridge
586-587
594
596
589-590
Kidderminster
597
M5
Solihull
M42
577-578
M6
519-520
COVENTRY
609-610
613
MIDLANDS
Knighton
509
Ludlow
Stourport-on-Severn
Bromsgrove
M42
558
556
553
Rugby
561
607
M40
M45
560
Leamington Spa
Redditch
555
Presteigne
608
Warwick
Daventry
633
Llandod
Droitwich
571-574
Leominster
M5
549-550
WARWICKSHIRE
Kington
562-569
507-508
Bromyard
500
WORCESTERSHIRE
Stratford upon Avon
575-576
506
Worcester
554
501-502
611
614-620
557
HEREFORDSHIRE
Great Malvern
Pershore
551-552
612
Banbury
Hay-on-Wye
Evesham
503-505
273-274
Shipston-on-Stour
Hereford
Ledbury
605-606
129
499
Tewkesbury
Moreton-in-Marsh
281-282
Chipping Norton
M50
M5
GLOUCESTERSHIRE
Stow-on-the-Wold
M40
510
Ross-on-Wye
Cheltenham
276-280
270-272
289
269
Crickhowell
511
Abergavenny
Gloucester
288
Monmouth
GLOUCESTERSHIRE
Kidlington
Brynmawr
Witney
283
138
Blaenavon
275
130
Oxford
BLAENAU GWENT
MONMOUTHSHIRE
Stroud
Carterton
648
Pontypool
Lydney
268
M5
Cirencester
OXFORDSHIRE
133-136
Nailsworth
©MAPS IN MINUTES™ 2006. ©Crown Copyright, Ordnance Survey 2006

WARWICKSHIRE

WEST MIDLANDS

WORCESTERSHIRE

499 Abbeydore

Dore Abbey

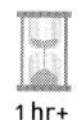
1 hr+

All year

Founded by French monks in 1147, Dore Abbey is remarkable for its wealth of features dating back to the C12. Today only the chancel area and transepts remain but the foundations of the nave, cloisters, chapter house and domestic buildings are all still in evidence.

* The only Cistercian monastery in Britain founded from Morimond, France, & in continuous use

Location
In Abbeydore on B4347

Opening
Daily

Admission
Free

Contact
Abbeydore, Hereford, Herefordshire HR2 0AD

t 01981 570251
w doreabbey.org.uk

500 Bringsty

The Garden at The Bannut

2 hrs

Easter–Sep

Set in the Herefordshire countryside with beautiful views of the Malvern Hills, this magnificent garden has been developed over the past 22 years by one couple. Manicured hedges divide the garden into formal and informal rooms, each with its own specific interest.

* Laburnum Walk & intriguing Secret Garden
* Plants for sale & light lunches & tea in tearooms

Location
On A44 2½ miles E of Bromyard, near entrance to Brockhampton

Opening
Easter–Sep 12.30pm–5pm

Admission
Adult £3, Child £1.50

Contact
Bringsty, WR6 5TA

t 01885 482206
w bannut.co.uk
e everettbannut@zetnet.co.uk

501 Bromyard

Brockhampton Estate

  1 hr  All year

This 1,700-acre estate still maintains farms and has extensive areas of woodland, which include ancient oak and beech. Visitors can enjoy a variety of walks through the park and woodland. At the heart of the estate lies Lower Brockhampton House, a late C14 moated manor house.

* Timber-framed gate house & ruined chapel
* Woodland is home to interesting range of wildlife

Location
2 miles E of Bromyard on A44

Opening
House Mar Sat–Sun 12noon–4pm; Apr–Sep Wed–Sun 12noon–5pm; Oct Wed–Sun 12noon–4pm
Estate All year. Daily dawn–dusk

Admission
Adult £4, Child £2

Contact
Greenfields, Bringsty WR6 5TB

t 01885 488099/482077
w nationaltrust.org.uk
e brockhampton@nationaltrust.org.uk

©NTPL/Paul Harris

502 Bromyard

Shortwood Family Farm

 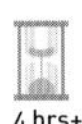 4 hrs+   Easter–Oct

Ideal for all the family, this organic farm offers visitors the opportunity to collect eggs, feed animals, see at first hand the benefits of organic farming, buy fresh produce, visit Mini-Farm World and the pets' corner, follow the farm trail, and take a trailer ride.

* Milk a cow by hand

Location
Signed from A417 between Burley Gate & Bodenham from Pencombe

Opening
Daily: Easter–Oct from 10am

Admission
Adult £5.50, Child £3.50

Contact
Pencombe,
Bromyard HR7 4RP

t 01885 400205
w shortwoodfarm.co.uk

503 Hereford

The Cider Museum

  1 hr  All year

Learn the story of traditional cidermaking: how apples were harvested, milled and pressed, and how the resulting juice was fermented to produce cider. You can also walk through a reconstructed farm cider house and see the 300-year-old travelling cidermaker's 'tack'.

* Visit original champagne cider cellars
* Distillery viewing window & Pomona Gallery

Location
In W Hereford, off A438

Opening
Apr–Oct Tue–Sat & Bank Hols 10am–5pm; Nov–Mar, please phone for details

Admission
Adult £3, Child £2, Concs £2.50

Contact
21 Ryelands Street, Hereford HR4 0LW

t 01432 354207
w cidermuseum.co.uk
e enquiries@cidermuseum.co.uk

504 Hereford

Hereford Cathedral, Mappa Mundi & Chained Library

2 hrs All year

Housed within the cathedral's C15 south-west cloister and the new library building is an exhibition that uses models and original artefacts to reveal the secrets of the Mappa Mundi, the largest and most elaborate complete pre-C15 world map in existence.

* The world's largest chained library – 1,500 rare books
* Working stonemason's yard & cathedral shop

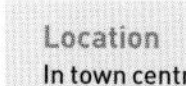

Location
In town centre

Opening
Cathedral daily 7.30am–evensong
Mappa Mundi & Chained Library
summer Mon–Sat 10am–4.30pm, Sun 11am–3.30pm
winter Mon–Sat 10am–3.30pm

Admission
Mappa Mundi & Chained Library
Adult £4.50, Child &Concs £3.50

Contact
5 College Cloisters, Cathedral Close, Hereford HR1 2NG
t 01432 374200
w herefordcathedral.org
e visits@herefordcathedral.org

© The Dean and Chapter of Hereford

505 Hereford

The Weir

2 hrs+ Jan–Oct

A delightful riverside garden, particularly spectacular in early spring, with fine views over the River Wye and the Black Mountains. The late C18 house (not open to the public) sits at the top of steep slopes that fall away to the river.

* Walks through beech woodland high above river
* Created by the Parr family in 1920s

Location
5 miles W of Hereford, signed from A438

Opening
Daily: Mar–Apr 11am–5pm. For all other times please phone for details

Admission
Adult £3.80, Child £1.90

Contact
National Trust Estate Office, Swainshill, nr Hereford HR4 7QF
t 01981 590509
w nationaltrust.org.uk
e theweir@ntrust.org.uk

506 Kington

Hergest Croft Gardens

 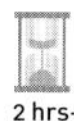 

2 hrs+ Mar–Oct

In the heart of the Welsh Marches, with stunning views towards the Black Mountains, Hergest Croft was created over 100 years by three generations of the Banks family. There are hidden valleys, woodland glades, open parkland and flower borders for year-round beauty.

* National Collection of birch & maples
* Rhododendrons & azaleas

Location
Signed on A44 from Kington

Opening
Mar Sat–Sun 12.30pm–5pm;
Apr & Jul–Oct daily 12.30pm–5.30pm;
May–Jun daily 12noon–6pm

Admission
Adult £5, Child free

Contact
Kington HR5 3EG
t 01544 230160
w hergest.co.uk
e gardens@hergest.co.uk

507 Leominster

Berrington Hall

2 hrs Mar–Oct

With sweeping views to the Brecon Beacons, this elegant Henry Holland house was built in the late C18 and is set in parkland designed by Capability Brown. A rather austere external appearance belies a surprisingly delicate interior.

* Beautiful ceilings & a spectacular staircase hall
* Good collection of furniture & paintings

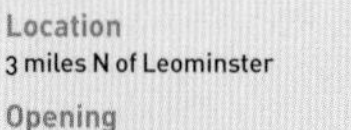

Location
3 miles N of Leominster

Opening
Times vary, please phone for details

Admission
Adult £5.30, Child £2.65

Contact
Leominster HR6 0DW

t 01568 615721
w nationaltrust.org.uk
e berrington@nationaltrust.org.uk

©English Heritage Photographic Library/Jonathan Bailey

508 Leominster

Croft Castle

2 hrs Apr–Oct

Croft Castle has an extensive range of showrooms to complement the fine Georgian interior and period furnishings. The gardens and park offer pleasant walks and magnificent views.

* Joint tickets with Berrington Hall available
* Beautiful period walled garden

Location
5 miles NW of Leominster

Opening
1 Apr–30 Sep Wed–Sun 1pm–5pm;
1 Oct–31 Oct Sat–Sun 1pm–5pm

Admission
House & Gardens Adult £5, Child £2.50
Gardens £2.50, £1.70

Contact
nr Leominster HR6 9PW

t 01568 780246
w nationaltrust.org.uk
e croftcastle@nationaltrust.org.uk

509 Ludlow

Wigmore Castle

2 hrs All year

One of the most remarkable ruins in England, Wigmore Castle hasn't been occupied since the C17, and over time has collapsed into ruin. However, despite the first floor having been buried by fallen upper floors, its towers and curtain walls survive to their full height.

*WARNING: Castle has steep steps to the summit that are hazardous in icy conditions

Location
8 miles W of Ludlow on A4110

Opening
Daily: All reasonable times

Admission
Free

Contact
English Heritage West Midlands,
112 Colmore Row,
Birmingham B3 3AG

t 0121 625 6820
w english-heritage.org.uk
e customers@englishheritage.org.uk

510 Ross-on-Wye

Goodrich Castle

1 hr

All year

This fortified baronial palace stands majestically on a red sandstone crag, commanding the passage of the River Wye into the picturesque wooded valley of Symonds Yat. Much of the stone used was quarried from the rock around the base of the castle, creating a deep moat.

* Cannon that destroyed the castle in 1645 is now on display
* Views over River Wye & Symonds Yat

Location
5 miles S of Ross-on-Wye off A40

Opening
Mar–May & Sep–Oct daily 10am–5pm;
Jun–Aug daily 10am–6pm;
Nov– Feb Thu–Mon 10am–4pm

Admission
Please phone for details

Contact
Ross-on-Wye HR9 6HY

t 01600 890538
w english-heritage.org.uk

511 Symonds Yat

Amazing Hedge Puzzle

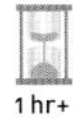
1 hr+

All year

Planted more than 20 years ago by brothers Lindsay and Edward Heyes, the Amazing Hedge Puzzle is one of Herefordshire's most popular and fun private tourist attractions. Learn about mazes through the history and myths surrounding them in the maze museum.

* Hands-on displays allow you to build your own maze
* Amazing Puzzle Shop – great fun!

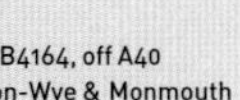

Location
Follow signs on B4164, off A40 between Ross-on-Wye & Monmouth

Opening
Daily: Jan–Feb & Nov–Dec 11am–3pm;
Apr–Sep & half-terms 11am–5pm;
Mar & Oct 11am–4pm

Admission
Please phone for details

Contact
Jubilee Park, Symonds Yat West, Ross-on-Wye HR9 6DA

t 01600 890360
w mazes.co.uk
e info@mazes.co.uk

512 Bishop's Wood

Boscobel House & The Royal Oak

2 hrs+

Apr–Oct

A refuge for Charles II before he fled to France, this timber-framed farmhouse was later converted into a hunting lodge. It was called Boscobel after the Italian '*bosco bello*', meaning 'in the midst of fair woods' a reference to the woodland that once surrounded it.

* Its true use is thought to have been to hide Catholics
* Escape from Worcester and farm exhibition

Location
8 miles NW of Wolverhampton, on minor road between A41 & A5

Opening
Daily: Apr–Sep 10am–6pm;
Oct 10am–5pm

Admission
Adult £4.60, Child £2.30, Concs £3.50

Contact
Brewood, Bishop's Wood ST19 9AR

t 01902 850244
w english-heritage.org.uk
e boscobelhouse@english-heritage.org.uk

513 Bridgnorth

Dudmaston

2 hrs+

Apr–Sep

A late C17 house with intimate family rooms, containing fine furniture and Dutch flower paintings, as well as a fabulous collection of important contemporary paintings and sculpture. The gardens are a mass of colour in spring and include a wooded valley or dingle.

* C20 art includes Nicholson, Moore & Hepworth

Location
4 miles SE of Bridgnorth, on A442

Opening
House Apr–Sep Tue–Wed & Sun 2pm–5.30pm
Gardens Apr–Sep Mon–Wed & Sun 12noon–6pm

Admission
House & Gardens Adult £5, Child £2.50
Gardens only £4, £2

Contact
Quatt, nr Bridgnorth WV15 6QN

t 01746 780866
w nationaltrust.org.uk
e dudmaston@nationaltrust.org.uk

514 Bridgnorth

Rays Farm Country Matters

  2 hrs  Mar–Oct

Animals both large and small and woodland walks with mystical moments are the main attractions at Rays Farm. There are also more than 40 owls on display, many of whom have been rescued from the wild, plus llamas, reindeer, red deer, axis deer and many more.

* Pull 'Excalibur' from its stone
* Many varieties of deer & goats

Location
Signed off B4363 near Billingsley between Bridgnorth & Cleobury Mortimer

Opening
Daily: Mar–Oct 10am–5.30pm

Admission
Adult £5.50, Child £4, Concs £5

Contact
Billingsley, Bridgnorth, Shropshire WV16 6PF

t 01299 841255
w raysfarm.com

515 Bridgnorth

Severn Valley Railway

 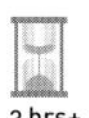 3 hrs+  All year

A full-size standard-gauge line running regular steam-hauled passenger trains between Kidderminster and Bridgnorth, a distance of 16 miles. For most of the way, the route closely follows the meandering course of the River Severn.

* Crosses impressive Victoria Bridge
* Passengers may break the journey at any station

Location
Stations in Kidderminster, Bridgnorth & Bewdley

Opening
Daily: May–Sep & Oct–Apr Sat–Sun
Full timetable on website

Admission
Please visit the website for full details

Contact
The Railway Station, Bewdley DY12 1BG

t 01299 403816
w svr.co.uk

516 Broseley

Benthall Hall

   1 hr+   Apr–Sep

Situated on a plateau above the gorge of the Severn, this C16 stone house has mullioned and transomed windows and a stunning interior with carved oak staircase, decorated plaster ceilings and oak panelling. There is also an interesting Restoration church.

* Carefully restored plantsman's garden
* George Moore's genus crocus book

Location
On B4375, 1 mile NW of Broseley, 1 mile SW of Ironbridge

Opening
Apr–Jun Tue–Wed, Bank Hols & Sun of Bank Hols; Jul–Sep Tue, Wed, Sun & Bank Hols
House 2pm–5.30pm
Gardens 1.30pm–5.30pm

Admission
Please phone for details

Contact
Broseley TF12 5RX

t 01952 882159
w nationaltrust.org.uk

517 Church Stretton

Acton Scott

  3 hrs  Apr–Oct

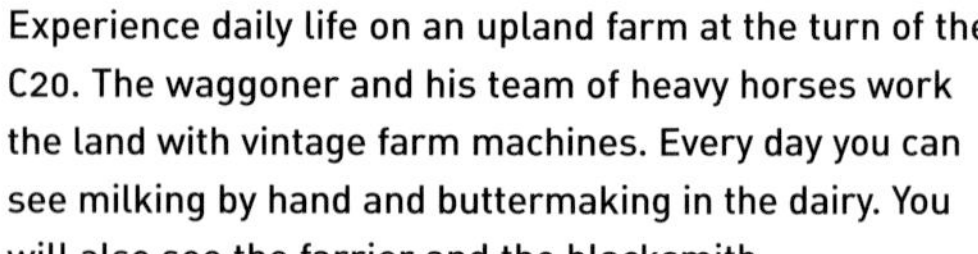

Experience daily life on an upland farm at the turn of the C20. The waggoner and his team of heavy horses work the land with vintage farm machines. Every day you can see milking by hand and buttermaking in the dairy. You will also see the farrier and the blacksmith.

* Lambing, shearing, cidermaking, etc in season
* Children's holiday activities

Location
Off A49, 17 miles S of Shrewsbury, 14 miles N of Ludlow

Opening
Apr–Oct Tue–Sun & Bank Hols
10am–5pm

Admission
Adult £4.85, Child £2.50, Concs £4.25

Contact
nr Church Stretton SY6 6QN

t 01694 781306
w actonscottmuseum.co.uk
e acton.scott.museum@shropshire-cc.gov.uk

518 Craven Arms

Secret Hills – Shropshire Hills Discovery Centre

 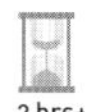 

2 hrs+ All year

A stylish and imaginative new building with a grass roof set within 30 acres of the Onny Meadows. Designed to improve understanding of the landscape, culture and heritage of the area, the centre provides a base for year-round entertainment and hands-on activities.

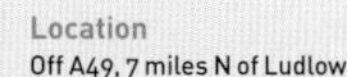
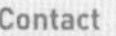

* Craft gallery & activities area
* Find out about earthquakes

Location
Off A49, 7 miles N of Ludlow

Opening
Daily: Apr–Oct 10am–5.30pm;
Nov–Mar 10am–4.30pm

Admission
Adult £4.50, Child £3, Concs £4

Contact
School Road, Craven Arms SY7 9RS

t 01588 676000/676040
w shropshire-cc.gov.uk/discover.nsf
e secrethills@shropshire-cc.gov.uk

519 Ludlow

Angel Gardens

1 hr+ Easter–Sep

Angel Gardens are spectacular, landscaped ornamental gardens at 1,000 feet, with magnificent views over Stretton and the Welsh hills. Take lunch or afternoon tea in the lakeside pavilion tearooms and admire other harmonious design structures.

* Exotic planting & fernery
* Chinese seat swing & minute children's cottage

Location
Between Kidderminster & Ludlow on A4117

Opening
Easter–Sep Sun–Tue 12noon–5pm

Admission
Adult £3.50, Child free

Contact
Springfield, Angel Lane, Bitterley, Ludlow SY8 3HZ

t 01584 890381
w stmem.com/angelgardens
e angelgardens@sy83hz.fsnet.co.uk

520 Ludlow

Stokesay Castle

1 hr All year

Strength and elegance are united in this fortified medieval manor house, built by renowned wool merchant Lawrence of Ludlow. In 1291 a 'licence to crenellate' was obtained from Edward I for the three-storey south tower.

* Magnificent great hall largely untouched
* Timber-framed Jacobean gate house

Location
Off A49, 7 miles NW of Ludlow

Opening
Mar–Apr Sep–Oct Thu–Mon 10am–5pm; May–Jun daily 10am–5pm; Jul–Aug daily 10am–6pm; Nov–Feb Fri–Mon 10am–4pm

Admission
Adult £4.80, Child £2.40, Concs £3.60

Contact
Craven Arms SY7 9AH

t 01588 672544
w english-heritage.org.uk

521 Market Drayton

Dorothy Clive Garden

1 hr+ Mar–Oct

A wide range of unusual plants can be seen in this lovely garden. Features include a quarry garden with a waterfall, a woodland garden and a scree and water-garden. The summer borders are spectacular, the autumn crocus and dwarf cyclamen stunning.

* Lovely views of 3 counties
* Japanese maples add to autumn colours

Location
On A51, between Nantwich & Stone

Opening
Daily: Mar–Oct 10am–5.30pm

Admission
Adult £4.20, Child (0–11yrs) free, Child (11–16yrs) £1, Concs £3.60

Contact
Willoughbridge, Market Drayton TF9 4EU

t 01630 647237
w dorothyclivegarden.co.uk
e info@dorothyclivegarden.co.uk

522 Market Drayton

Wollerton Old Hall Garden

2 hrs Easter–Sep

Wollerton Old Hall Garden is a 4-acre plantsman's garden developed around a C16 house (not open) in rural Shropshire. The strong formal design has created many separate gardens, each with its own character, and there are numerous rare and unusual plants.

* Present garden developed from 1984
* Difficult-to-obtain perennials available in nursery

Location
Off A53, between Market Drayton & Shrewsbury

Opening
Good Fri–Sep Fri, Sun & Bank Hols 12noon–5pm

Admission
Adult £4.50, Child £1

Contact
Wollerton, Market Drayton TF9 3NA

t 01630 685760
w wollertonoldhallgarden.com
e info@wollertonoldhallgarden.com

523 Shifnal

The RAF Museum – Cosford

  3 hrs+  All year

Follow the story of man's flight – the successes and failures – through one of the largest aviation collections in the UK. More than 70 historic aircraft are displayed in three wartime hangars on an active airfield. The collection spans nearly 80 years of aviation history.

* New Cold War exhibition in 2007
* State-of-the-art flight simulator

Location
On A41, less than 1 mile from M54 junction 3

Opening
Daily: 10am–6pm (last admission 4pm)

Admission
Free. Charges for special events
Under-16s must be accompanied by an adult

Contact
Cosford, Shifnal TF11 8UP

t 01902 376200
w rafmuseum.org
e cosford@rafmuseum.com

524 Shifnal

Weston Park

  2 hrs+  Easter–Sep

The house was first mentioned in the *Domesday Book* in the C11, but Weston owes its unique character to the developments in the C17, under the direction of Lady Wilbraham. The beautiful landscaped gardens, the work of Capability Brown, were restored in 1991.

* Mary, daughter of George V, honeymooned here
* G8 Summit held here in 1998

Location
On A5, 3 miles off M54 junction 3

Opening
Dates vary, please phone for details
House 1pm–5pm
Park & Gardens 11am–6.30pm

Admission
House, Park & Gardens Adult £7, Child £4.50, Concs £6
Park & Gardens £4, £2.50, £3.50

Contact
Weston-under-Lizard, Shifnal TF11 8LE

t 01952 852100
w weston-park.com
e enquiries@weston-park.com

525 Shrewsbury

Attingham Park

  2 hrs+  All year

One of the great houses of the Midlands, this elegant mansion was built in 1785 for the first Lord Berwick (to the design of George Steuart) and has a picture gallery by John Nash. The Regency interiors contain collections of silver, Italian furniture and Grand Tour paintings.

* Park with walk by River Tern landscaped by Repton
* Family activity room opened in 2003

Location
On B4380, 4 miles SE of Shrewsbury

Opening
House Mar–Oct
Park All year
Please phone for details of opening times

Admission
Please phone for details

Contact
Shrewsbury SY4 4TP

t 01743 708162
w nationaltrust.org.uk
e attingham@nationaltrust.org.uk

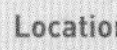

526 Shrewsbury

Hawkstone Park

  3 hrs  Jan–Oct

Created in the C18, Hawkstone became one of the greatest historic parklands in Europe. The park is spread around the Red Castle and the awe-inspiring Grotto Hill, and features intricate pathways, ravines, arches and bridges, towering cliffs and follies.

* Woodland full of ancient oaks
* Has won numerous awards

Location
Off A49, between Shrewsbury & Whitchurch

Opening
Please phone or visit the website for details

Admission
Adult £5.95, Child £3.95, Concs £4.95

Contact
Weston-under-Redcastle, Shrewsbury SY4 5UY

t 01939 200611
w hawkstone.co.uk
e info@hawkstone.co.uk

527 Shrewsbury

Wroxeter Roman City (Virconium)

  1 hr   All year

The largest excavated Romano-British city to have escaped development, Wroxeter was originally home to 6,000 people. The most impressive ruins are the C2 municipal baths and the remains of a huge dividing wall. Local finds are on display in the museum.

* Fourth-largest Roman settlement in Britain

Location
On B4380, 5 miles E of Shrewsbury

Opening
Apr–Sep daily 10am–6pm;
Oct daily 10am–5pm;
Nov–Mar Thu–Mon 10am–4pm

Admission
Adult £4, Child £2, Concs £3

Contact
Wroxeter, Shrewsbury SY5 6PH

t 01743 761330
w english-heritage.org.uk

528 Telford

Ironbridge Gorge Museums

  1–6 hrs  All year

There are 10 award-winning museums spread along what is often called 'the valley that changed the world'. That valley, beside the River Severn, is still spanned by the world's first iron bridge. See the machines that set industry on its way, and the products made by them.

* Blists Hill Victorian town, recreation of working community
* Enginuity – hands-on design & technology experiences

Location
5 miles S of Telford, signed from M54 junction 4

Opening
Daily: 10am–5pm; reduced opening in winter

Admission
Passport ticket to all 10 attractions
Adult £14, Child £9.50, Concs £12.50

Contact
Ironbridge, Telford TF8 7DQ

t 01952 884 391
w ironbridge.org.uk
e tic@ironbridge.org.uk

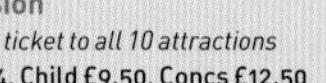

529 Alton

Alton Towers

6 hrs+ Mar–Oct

A famous, extensive theme park with a mix of rides and attractions to suit every member of the family. It includes 200 acres of landscaped gardens, rides, live entertainment and the historic Towers building. Come along and enjoy a fun-packed day out.

* New family spinning roller coaster
* 2 onsite hotels incorporating an indoor water-park

Location
Off B5030, near Uttoxeter (A50); take junction 15 or 16 from M6, or junction 23a or 28 from M1. Follow brown tourist signs

Opening
Daily: Mar–end Oct (gates open at 9am) 9.30am–5pm (later in summer)
Please phone or visit the website before visiting

Admission
Please phone for details

Contact
Alton, Stoke-on-Trent ST10 4DB

t 0870 4444455
w altontowers.com

530 Ashbourne

Sudbury Hall & Museum of Childhood

3 hrs Mar–Oct

This spectacular late C17 house has sumptuous interiors and a fine collection of portraits. The great staircase is one of the most elaborate of its kind in an English house. The C19 service wing is home to the Museum of Childhood with displays about children from the C18 onwards.

* Featured in BBC production of *Pride and Prejudice*
* 'Behind the Scenes' tours

Location
6 miles E of Uttoxeter at junction of A50 Derby–Stoke road & A515 Ashbourne road

Opening
Hall & Museum Mar–Oct Wed–Sun 1pm–5pm
Grounds Mar–Oct Wed–Sun 11am–6pm; open Bank Hols

Admission
Hall Adult £5.50, Child £2.50
Hall & Museum £10, £6
Garden £1, 50p

Contact
Sudbury, Ashbourne DE6 5HT

t 01283 585337/585305
w nationaltrust.org.uk
e sudburyhall@nationaltrust.org.uk

531 Burslem

Ceramica

 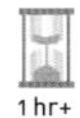 

1 hr+ All year

Ceramica is an interactive experience in the heart of the English Potteries, the centre of the ceramic industry. Learn how clay is transformed into china and the important part ceramics play in everyday life. Discover the past, present and future of ceramics in the displays.

* See a reconstruction of the inside of a bottle oven
* Josiah Wedgwood's kiln, discovered by Channel 4's *Time Team*

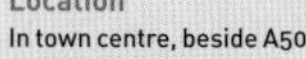

Location
In town centre, beside A50

Opening
Daily: Tue–Sat 9.30am–5pm, Sun 10.30am–4.30pm; Bank Hols & school hols please phone for details

Admission
Adult £4.10, Child & Concs £2.90

Contact
Market Place, Burslem, Stoke-on-Trent ST6 3DS

t 01782 832001
w ceramicauk.com
e info@ceramicauk.com

532 Burton upon Trent

Coors Visitor Centre

4 hrs · All year

Beer has been brewed in Burton upon Trent for centuries and the Museum of Brewing charts its history. It provides a blend of living heritage, historic galleries and family entertainment. The centre is home to two teams of shire horses and a vintage vehicle collection.

* See a working stationary steam engine
* Special events throughout the year

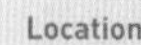

Location
A511 in centre of Burton upon Trent. Follow brown signs for visitor centre

Opening
Daily: 10am–5pm (last admission 4pm)

Admission
Adult £6, Child £3, Concs £4

Contact
Horninglow Street, Burton upon Trent DE14 1YQ

t 0845 600 0598
w coorsvisitorcentre.com
e enquiries@coorsbrewers.com

533 Halfpenny Green

Halfpenny Green Vineyards

1 hr · All year

Information boards describe many of the French, German and hybrid varieties of vine planted here and visitors to Halfpenny Green can follow the self-guided vineyard trail. After touring the vineyard, inspect the winery and taste the wines.

* Award-winning wines
* Vineyard trail & craft centre

Location
Off B4176, near Halfpenny Green Airfield

Opening
Daily: 10.30am–5pm

Admission
Free
Basic tour £2
Guided tour £9.95 (pre-booked)

Contact
Tom Lane, Halfpenny Green DY7 5EP

t 01384 221122
w halfpenny-green-vineyards.co.uk
e sales@halfpenny-green-vineyards.co.uk

534 Hanley

The Potteries Museum & Art Gallery

2 hrs · All year

At the home of the greatest collection of Staffordshire ceramics in the world you can see Reginald Mitchell's WWII Spitfire and all sorts of arts and crafts. The award-winning museum also hosts a lively programme of changing exhibitions with national touring shows and events.

* World's finest collection of Staffordshire ceramics
* Craft & activity centre for kids (Tue–Fri in school hols)

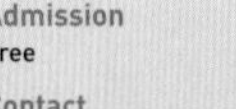

Location
A500 junction 15, signed from town centre

Opening
Daily: Mar–Oct Mon–Sat 10am–5pm, Sun 2pm–5pm;
Nov–Feb Mon–Sat 10am–4pm, Sun 1pm–4pm

Admission
Free

Contact
Bethesda Street, Hanley ST1 3DW

t 01782 232323
w stoke.gov.uk/museums
e museums@stoke.gov.uk

535 Lichfield

Erasmus Darwin's House

1 hr · All year

This elegant C18 house near Lichfield Cathedral, was home to Charles Darwin's grandfather, Erasmus, a renowned doctor, philosopher, inventor, scientist and poet. Period furnishings and audio-visual and interactive displays tell the story of this remarkable man.

* Conference facilities
* Licensed weddings

Location
In town centre, near cathedral

Opening
Please phone for details

Admission
Adult £2.50, Child £2

Contact
Beacon Street, Lichfield WS13 7AD

t 01543 306 260
w erasmusdarwin.org
e enquiries@erasmusdarwin.org

536 Lichfield

Lichfield Heritage Centre

 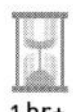 

1 hr+ Apr–Oct

The centre gives an account of Lichfield's varied history. It is home to the Staffordshire Millennium Embroideries, which are displayed in their own gallery, as well as fine examples of city, diocesan and regimental silver, ancient charters and archives.

* Audio-visual presentations
* Collection of photographs of Lichfield, old & new

Location
In town centre

Opening
Apr–May & Sep–Oct Wed–Sun 10am–5pm; Jun–Aug 10am–6pm

Admission
Adult £3, Child £1.50, Concs £2.30

Contact
Market Square, Lichfield WS13 6LG

t 01543 256611
w lichfieldheritage.org.uk
e info@lichfieldheritage.org.uk

537 Lichfield

Wall Roman Site (Letocetum)

1 hr Apr–Oct

Wall was an important staging post on the Roman military road to North Wales. It provided overnight accommodation and a change of horse for travelling Roman officials and imperial messengers. The foundations of a hotel and bath house can be seen.

* Many excavated finds displayed in museum
* Audio tour with Gallas the Roman soldier

Location
Off A5, near Lichfield

Opening
Apr–May & Sep–Oct Wed–Sun 10am–5pm; Jun–Aug daily 10am–6pm

Admission
Adult £3, Child £1.50, Concs £2.30

Contact
Watling Street, nr Lichfield WS14 0AW

t 01543 480768
w english-heritage.org.uk

538 Longton

Gladstone Pottery Museum

2 hrs+ All year

Gladstone is the only surviving complete Victorian pottery factory from the days when coal-burning ovens made the world's finest bone china. Demonstrations of traditional skills, and original workshops and huge bottle kilns make for a convincing and atmospheric time-warp.

* Try your hand at pottery crafts
* Flushed with Pride exhibition, a gallery devoted to the WC

Location
From M6 follow A500, then take A50 to Longton

Opening
Daily: 10am–5pm

Admission
Adult £4.95, Child £3.50, Concs £3.95

Contact
Uttoxeter Road, Longton, Stoke-on-Trent ST3 1PQ

t 01782 319232
w stoke.gov.uk/museums
e gladstone@stoke.gov.uk

539 Milford

Shugborough

3 hrs+ Mar–Oct

Shugborough is the UK's only complete working historic estate with C19 laundry, kitchens, dairy, mill and farm. Visitors can join in with the hands-on experience of mangling, baking and cheesemaking with costumed characters. There are also 900 acres of stunning parkland.

* Lucy the Train gives rides through the grounds
* Restored walled garden originally built in 1805

Location
6 miles from M6 junction 13

Opening
Daily: Mar–28 Oct 11am–5pm

Admission
Adult £10, Child £6, Concs £7

Contact
Shugborough, Milford ST17 0XB

t 01889 881388
w shugborough.org.uk
e shugborough.promotions@staffordshire.gov.uk

540 Stafford

Stafford Castle

3 hrs+ All year

Built by William the Conqueror to subdue rebellious locals, Stafford Castle has dominated the landscape throughout 900 years of turbulent history. Visitors today will find a more peaceful setting – follow the castle trail, explore the castle ruins and take in the panoramic view.

* Try on armour & chainmail
* Host of archaeological finds

Location
Off A518, 1 mile SW of Stafford

Opening
Apr–Oct Tue–Sun & Bank Hols 10am–5pm; Nov–Mar Sat–Sun 10am–4pm

Admission
Free

Contact
Castle Bank, Newport Road, Stafford ST16 1DJ

t 01785 257698
w staffordbc.gov.uk

541 Stoke-on-Trent

Biddulph Grange Garden

1 hr+ Easter–Dec

A rare survival of a high Victorian garden, restored by the National Trust. The garden is divided into a series of themed spaces, and includes a Chinese temple, Egyptian court, pinetum, dahlia walk, glen, avenues and many other settings.

* Inspiration of C19 horticulturist James Bateman
* Egyptian garden contains topiary obelisks of yew

    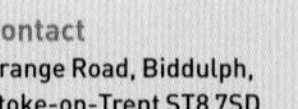

Location
Off A527, on N side of Biddulph

Opening
25 Mar–29 Oct Wed–Sun & Bank Hol Mon 11.30am–5.30pm; 4 Nov–17 Dec Sat–Sun only 11am–3pm

Admission
summer Adult £5.30, Child £2.60
winter £2, £1

Contact
Grange Road, Biddulph, Stoke-on-Trent ST8 7SD

t 01782 517999
w nationaltrust.org.uk
e biddulphgrange@nationaltrust.org.uk

542 Stoke-on-Trent

Spode Museum & Visitor Centre

 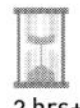 2 hrs+  All year

Visitors will see a fine collection of Spode ceramics, including teaware, dessertware and dinnerware, as well as beautiful ornamental pieces. The display includes items from the 1790s to 1833, illustrating the genius of two Josiah Spodes, I and II.

* Display includes designs for the royal family
* Fully guided factory tours available

Location
From M6 junction 15 take A500, turn left at 2nd roundabout, then follow signs

Opening
Daily: Mon–Sat 9am–5pm, Sun 10am–4pm, Bank Hols 9am–5pm

Admission
Free. Charges for factory tours

Contact
Church Street, Stoke-on-Trent ST4 1BX

t 01782 744011
w spode.co.uk
e spodemuseum@spode.co.uk
e visitorcentre@spode.co.uk

543 Tamworth

Middleton Hall

 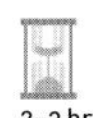 2–3 hrs  Apr–Sep 

The hall has an interesting architectural history, with its oldest buildings dating from 1300 and others dating from the C16 to the early C19. Attractions include the 11-bay Georgian west wing and the impressive C16 great hall, the restoration of which was completed in 1994.

* 24 embroideries on history of Sutton Coldfield
* Links with Lady Jane Grey, Elizabeth I & Jane Austen

Location
On A4091, 4 miles S of Tamworth, between Belfry & Drayton Manor Park

Opening
Apr–Sep Sun 2pm–5pm;
Bank Hols 11am–5pm

Admission
Adult £2.50, Child free, Concs £1.50
Bank Hols & special events £5, £1, £3

Contact
Middleton, Tamworth B78 2AE

t 01827 283095
w middletonhalltrust.co.uk
e middletonhalltrust@btconnect.com

544 Tamworth

The Snowdome

 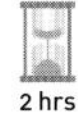 2 hrs  All year

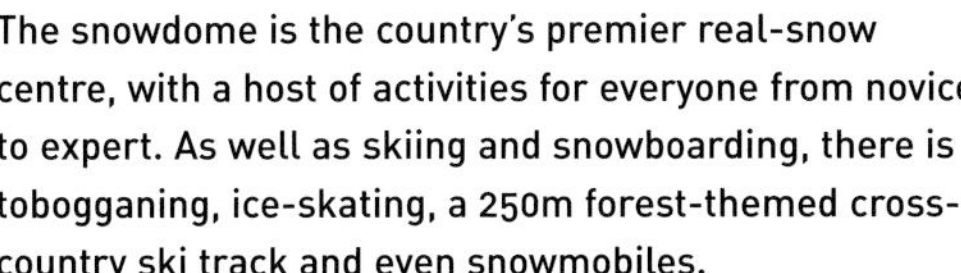

The snowdome is the country's premier real-snow centre, with a host of activities for everyone from novice to expert. As well as skiing and snowboarding, there is tobogganing, ice-skating, a 250m forest-themed cross-country ski track and even snowmobiles.

*Live music events
*Bar & restaurant facilities

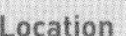

Location
5 min from junction 10 of M42. Only 1½ hours from N London, Bristol, Manchester & Leeds

Opening
Daily: 9am–11pm. Please phone for details of session times

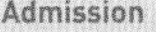

Admission
Please phone for details

Contact
Leisure Island, River Drive, Tamworth B79 7ND

t 08705 000011
w snowdome.co.uk
e info@snowdome.co.uk

545 Tamworth

Tamworth Castle

1 hr All year

This is a Norman shell-keep castle with intact apartments from the C12 to the C19. Fifteen period rooms are open to visitors, including the great hall, dungeon and haunted bedroom. There is also a permanent exhibition on Norman castles.

* The Tamworth Story is an interactive local history exhibit
* Living images, also known as 'talking heads'

Location
Take A51 & A453 through town centre, signed from A51

Opening
Tue–Sun 12noon–5.15pm;
Aug daily 12noon–5.15pm;
Autumn/winter times differ, please phone for details

Admission
Adult £4.95, Child £2.95, Concs £3.95

Contact
The Holloway, Ladybank,
Tamworth B79 7NA

t 01827 709629/709626
w tamworthcastle.gov.uk
e heritage@tamworth.gov.uk

546 Tutbury

Tutbury Castle

2 hr Easter–Sep

Built in the 1070s for one of William the Conqueror's barons, Tutbury Castle has been involved in some of the most dramatic events in English history. A bloody place of siege and battle, on four occasions it acted as a prison for Mary, Queen of Scots.

* Authentic Tudor privy garden & medieval herbery
* Secret staircase to the great hall recently uncovered

Location
Exit M1 junction 24a or M6 junction 15, near A50

Opening
Easter–17 Sep Wed–Sun 11am–5pm

Admission
Adult £4, Child & Concs £3.50

Contact
Tutbury, Burton-on-Trent DE13 9JF

t 01283 812129
w tutburycastle.com
e info@tutburycastle.com

547 Winkhill

Blackbrook Zoological Park

 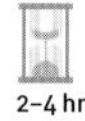  

2–4 hrs All year

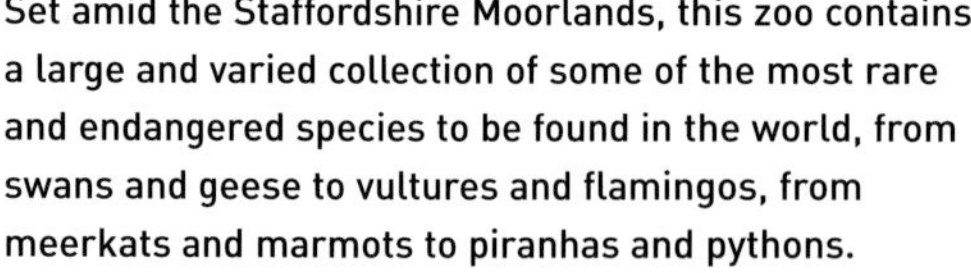

Set amid the Staffordshire Moorlands, this zoo contains a large and varied collection of some of the most rare and endangered species to be found in the world, from swans and geese to vultures and flamingos, from meerkats and marmots to piranhas and pythons.

* Largest collection of wildfowl in Britain
* Largest collection of cranes & storks in Britain

Location
From Leek take A523 & 1st right, signed to park, then 1st right again

Opening
Daily: 10.30am–5.30pm (earlier closing in winter)
Café Open in summer only

Admission
Adult £7.50, Child £5, Concs £5.95

Contact
Winkhill, nr Leek ST13 7QR

t 01538 308293
w blackbrookzoologicalpark.co.uk
e enquiries@blackbrookzoologicalpark.co.uk

548 Wolverhampton

Moseley Old Hall

2 hrs+ Mar–Dec

An Elizabethan house, famous for its associations with the fugitive Charles II who hid here in 1651. Faced with brick in the 1870s, it remains inside as Charles would have known it, with timber framing, oak panelling, period furniture and ingenious hiding places.

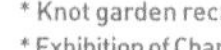

* Knot garden recreated in C17 style
* Exhibition of Charles II's escape after Battle of Worcester

Location
4 miles N of Wolverhampton, S of M54 between A449 & A460

Opening
17 Mar–31 Oct Wed &Sat–Sun 1pm–5pm;
4 Nov–18 Nov Sun 1pm–4pm; 28 Nov–16 Dec Sun 1pm–4pm (also special Christmas events)
All Bank Hol Mon 11pm–5pm and following Tues 1pm–5pm

Admission
Adult £5, Child £2.50

Contact
Moseley Old Hall Lane, Fordhouses,
Wolverhampton WV10 7HY

t 01902 782808
w nationaltrust.org.uk
e moseleyoldhall@nationaltrust.org.uk

549 Alcester

Coughton Court

  3 hrs  Mar–Oct

This beautiful Tudor house has been a family home since 1409. There is a fine collection of family portraits, furniture and a fascinating exhibition about the Gunpowder Plot. The gate house and courtyard are complemented by an Elizabethan knot garden.

* Stunning displays of roses & herbaceous plants
* 2 churches to visit

Location
On A435, 2 miles N of Alcester

Opening
Mar & Oct Sat–Sun 11–5pm;
Apr–Jun & Sep Wed–Sun 11am–5pm;
Jul–Aug Tue–Sun 11am–5pm

Admission
Adult £8.60, Child £4.30

Contact
nr Alcester B49 5JA

t 01789 400777
w nationaltrust.org.uk
e coughtoncourt@nationaltrust.org.uk

550 Alcester

Ragley Hall

  5 hrs   Apr–Sep

Ragley Hall is set in 27 acres of beautiful formal gardens. The home contains baroque plasterwork, the stunning C20 mural *The Temptation*, and a collection of paintings, china and furniture. In addition to the beautiful house, there are formal gardens and parkland.

* Ever-changing gardens
* Game fair & other events throughout the year

Location
Off Alcester bypass, signed at A46 junction

Opening
Please phone or visit the website for details

Admission
Adult £7, Child £4.50, Concs £6

Contact
Alcester B49 5NJ

t 01789 762090
w ragleyhall.com
e info@ragleyhall.com

©NTPL/Andreas von Einsiedel

551 Banbury

Farnborough Hall

  2 hrs+  Apr–Sep

A beautiful honey-coloured stone house, richly decorated in the mid-C18 and the home of the Holbech family for more than 300 years. The interior plasterwork is breathtaking and the charming grounds contain C18 temples, a terrace walk and an obelisk.

* Terrace walk open by prior appointment only

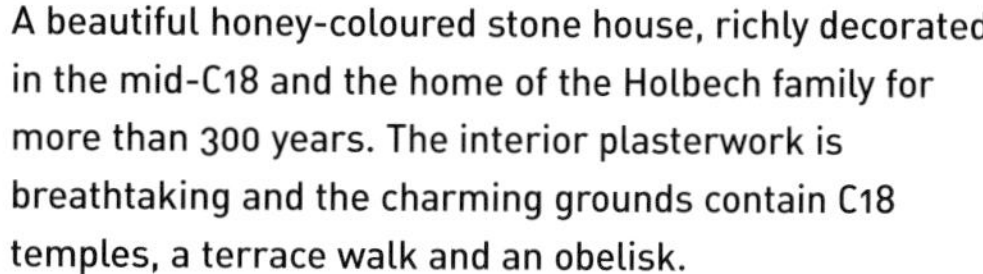

Location
6 miles N of Banbury, W of A423

Opening
1 Apr–30 Sep Wed & Sat 2pm–5.30pm;
30 Apr–1 May Mon & Sun 2pm–5.30pm

Admission
Adult £4.20, Child £2.10

Contact
Farnborough, Banbury OX17 1DU

t 01295 690002
w nationaltrust.org.uk
e farnboroughhall@nationaltrust.org.uk

552 Banbury

Upton House & Gardens

  1 hr+  Apr–Oct

Once owned by Walter Samuel, 2nd Viscount Bearsted and chairman of Shell 1921–46, Upton contains an outstanding collection of English and continental Old Master paintings, including works by Hogarth, Stubbs, Guardi, Canaletto, Brueghel and El Greco.

* Exhibition of Shell paintings & publicity posters
* More than 30 acres of glorious valley gardens

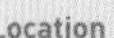

Location
Junction 12 of M40, on to A422, 7 miles NW of Banbury, 12 miles SE of Stratford-upon-Avon

Opening
House 2 Apr–Oct Mon–Wed & Sat–Sun 1pm–5pm
Gardens 2 Apr–Oct Mon–Wed 12noon–5pm, Sat–Sun 11am–5pm

Admission
House Adult £7, Child £3.70
Gardens £4.20, £2.10

Contact
nr Banbury OX15 6HT
t 01295 670266
w nationaltrust.org.uk
e uptonhouse@nationaltrust.org.uk

553 Coventry

Brandon Marsh Nature Centre

  1 hr+  All year

A visit to Brandon Marsh Nature Centre starts at the visitor centre, opened by Sir David Attenborough in 1998. This contains displays, hands-on activities and information about the nature reserve, which covers 220 acres and features many lakes and bird hides.

* Warwickshire Wildlife Trust Centre
* New tearoom & shop

Location
Off A45

Opening
Daily: Mon–Sat 9am–4.30pm, Sun 10am–4pm

Admission
Adult £2.50, Child & Concs £1.50

Contact
Brandon Lane, Coventry CV3 3GW
t 02476 308999
w warwickshire-wildlife-trust.org.uk
e enquiries@wkwt.org.uk

554 Gaydon

Heritage Motor Centre

  3 hrs   All year

The Heritage Motor Centre is home to the largest collection of classic, vintage and veteran British cars in the world. There are 200 vehicles on display, charting the history of the British car industry from the turn of the C20 to the present day.

* 1963 Morris Mini Cooper
* Regular programme of events

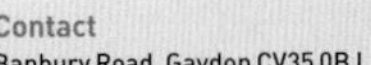

Location
2 min from M40 junction 12

Opening
Daily: 10am–5pm

Admission
Adult £8, Child £6, Concs £7

Contact
Banbury Road, Gaydon CV35 0BJ
t 01926 641188
w heritage-motor-centre.co.uk
e enquiries@heritage-motor-centre.co.uk

555 Henley-in-Arden

Henley-in-Arden Heritage & Visitor Centre

  1 hr  Easter–Oct

The history of a medieval market town, in a house dating from 1345. The displays start with the origins of the settlement in Norman times and trace the development of social and business life through the centuries, including the war years.

* Audio diaries of early memories
* Tales of industrial, social & sporting life in the town

Location
In town centre

Opening
Easter–Oct Tue–Fri 10.30am–4.30pm, Sat–Sun & Bank Hols 2.30pm–4.30pm

Admission
Free

Contact
Joseph Hardy House, 150 High Street, Henley-in-Arden B95 5BS
t 01564 795919
w heritagehenley.org.uk
e info@heritagehenley.org.uk

556 Kenilworth

Kenilworth Castle

2 hrs+ All year

One of the largest castle ruins in England, Kenilworth Castle is a powerful reminder of great leaders and historic events. A series of events are being staged throughout 2007 to celebrate 900 years of history at Kenilworth Castle.

* Walks to Old Kenilworth & ruined abbey
* Elizabethan festival & Shakespeare performances

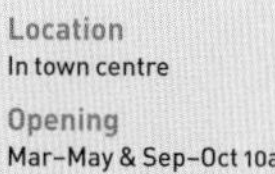

Location
In town centre

Opening
Mar–May & Sep–Oct 10am–5pm;
Jun–Aug 10am–6pm;
Nov–Feb 10am–4pm

Admission
Adult £5.90, Child £3, Concs £4.40

Contact
Castle Mews, Kenilworth CV8 1NE

t 01926 852078
w english-heritage.org.uk/kenilworthcastle

557 Kineton

Compton Verney Art Gallery

2 hrs+ Mar–Oct

An innovative art gallery, in an C18 mansion designed by Robert Adam and set in 120 acres of Capability Brown landscape. The Peter Moores collections include artefacts from Naples 1450–1800, and China 3000BC–AD1500, and a collection of British folk art.

* Major temporary exhibitions
* Projects for schools & groups

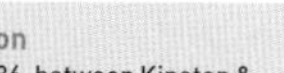

Location
Off B4086, between Kineton & Wellesbourne

Opening
Mar–Oct Tue–Sun 10am–5pm & Bank Hol Mon

Admission
Adult £6, Child £2, Concs £4

Contact
Compton Verney CV35 9HZ

t 01926 645500
w comptonverney.org.uk
e info@comptonverney.org.uk

558 Knowle

Baddesley Clinton

3 hrs+ Mar–Dec

This moated manor house dates from the C15 and little has changed here since 1634. During the Elizabethan era it was a haven for persecuted Catholics and there are three priest's holes. The garden includes stewponds, a lake and a nature walk.

* 80-seater restaurant
* Replica priest's hole, part of children's trail

Location
W of A4141, between Warwick & Birmingham, 7 miles NW of Warwick

Opening
House Mar–Nov Wed–Sun 1.30pm–5pm
Gardens Mar–Dec Wed–Sun 12noon–5.30pm

Admission
House Adult £6.80, Child £3.40
Gardens £3.40, £1.70

Contact
Rising Lane, Baddesley Clinton, Knowle, Solihull B93 0DQ
t 01564 783294
w nationaltrust.org.uk
e baddesleyclinton@nationaltrust.org.uk

559 Nuneaton

Bosworth Battlefield Visitor Centre & Country Park

2 hrs+ Jan–Oct

This is the site of one of the most famous battles in English history, between Richard III and Henry Tudor. The result gave England a new king and marked the beginning of the Tudor dynasty. Discover what it was like to be a soldier at the time and follow the battle trail.

* Walk down a medieval street
* Annual re-enactment of the battle

Location
2 miles S of Market Bosworth near Sutton Cheney

Opening
Visitor centre Mar Sat–Sun 11am–5pm; Apr–Oct daily 11am–5pm
Country Park Jan–Oct daily 7am onwards (closing times vary)

Admission
Adult £3.25, Concs £2.25

Contact
Sutton Cheney, Nuneaton CV13 0AD
t 01455 290429
w leics.gov.uk
e bosworth@leics.gov.uk

560 Royal Leamington Spa

Royal Pump Rooms

1 hr All year

The historic Royal Pump Rooms have been redeveloped and now include an art gallery and museum. Visitors can explore life in a Victorian spa town, relax in the magnificent Turkish Room and discover the water treatments used at the Royal Pump Rooms.

* Historic hammam room
* Temporary exhibition space & interactive gallery

Location
In town centre

Opening
Tue–Wed & Fri–Sat 10.30am–5pm, Thu 1.30–8pm, Sun 11am–4pm

Admission
Free

Contact
The Parade, Royal Leamington Spa CV32 4AA
t 01926 742700
w royal-pump-rooms.co.uk
e prooms@warwickdc.gov.uk

561 Rugby

Rugby Art Gallery

  1 hr+  All year

This gallery contains a collection of paintings, prints and drawings by well-known British artists such as Sir Stanley Spencer, L S Lowry, Percy Wyndham Lewis, Paula Rego, Barbara Hepworth, Bridget Riley and Lucian Freud.

* Rugby's collection of modern art
* Roman artefacts & local social history objects

Location
Signed from town centre

Opening
Tue & Thu 10am–8pm, Wed & Fri 10am–5pm, Sat 10am–4pm, Sun & Bank Hols 12noon–4pm

Admission
Free

Contact
Little Elbarow Street, Rugby CV21 3BZ

t 01788 533201
w rugbygalleryandmuseum.org.uk
e rugbyartgallery&museum@rugby.gov.uk

562 Stratford-upon-Avon

Anne Hathaway's Cottage

  1 hr  All year

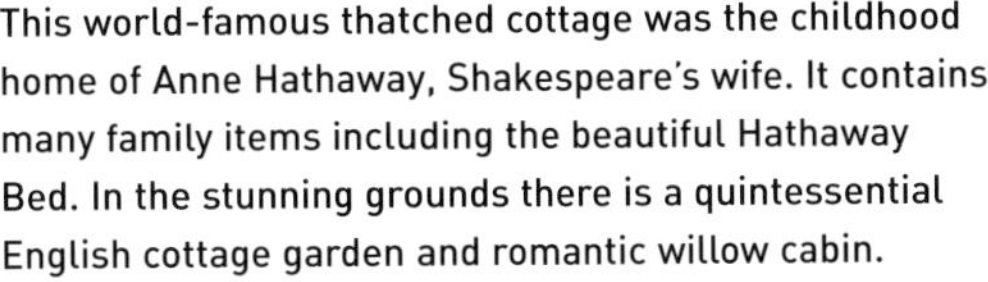

This world-famous thatched cottage was the childhood home of Anne Hathaway, Shakespeare's wife. It contains many family items including the beautiful Hathaway Bed. In the stunning grounds there is a quintessential English cottage garden and romantic willow cabin.

* Inhabited by the Hathaway family until the C19
* Shakespeare tree & sculpture garden, maze, orchard & brook

Location
1 mile from town centre

Opening
Apr–May & Sep–Oct Mon–Sat 9.30am–5pm, Sun 10am–5pm; Jun–Aug Mon–Sat 9am–5pm, Sun 9.30am–5pm; Nov–Mar daily 10am–4pm

Admission
Adult £5.50, Child £2, Concs £4.50

Contact
Cottage Lane, Shottery CV37 9HH

t 01789 292100
w shakespeare.org.uk
e info@shakespeare.org.uk

563 Stratford-upon-Avon

Hall's Croft

  1 hr  All year

The elegant C17 house that belonged to Shakespeare's eldest daughter Susanna and her husband, the physician John Hall. An impressive building with many exquisite furnishings and paintings of the period. This is reputed to be the most haunted of the Shakespeare houses.

* Exhibition of early medicine
* Exhibition of medical artefacts from the C16 & C17

Location
Near town centre

Opening
Daily: Apr–May & Sep–Oct 11am–5pm; Jun–Aug Mon–Sat 9.30am–5pm, Sun 10am–5pm; Nov–Mar 11am–4pm;

Admission
Adult £3.75, Child £1.75, Concs £3.00

Contact
Old Town, Stratford-upon-Avon CV37

t 01789 292107
w shakespeare.org.uk
e info@shakespeare.org.uk

564 Stratford-upon-Avon

Harvard House

  1 hr  May–Oct

This fine example of an Elizabethan town house and the former home of John Harvard, founder of Harvard University, is now home to the Museum of British Pewter. It also offers a children's activity area and interactive computer games.

* Many architectural features of interest

Location
In town centre

Opening
May–Oct Fri–Sun & Bank Hols 11am–4pm

Admission
Adult £2, Child free

Contact
High Street, Stratford-upon-Avon

t 01789 204507
w shakespeare.org.uk
e info@shakespeare.org.uk

565 Stratford-upon-Avon

Holy Trinity Church

  1 hr+  All year

Visit the graves of Shakespeare and his wife Anne Hathaway, their daughter Susanna and her husband Dr John Hall, and Thomas Nash, in the chancel of Holy Trinity Church. Also in the chancel are 26 fine C15 carved misericords.

* Beautiful church situated on banks of River Avon
* Church is approached along an avenue of lime trees

Location
Signed from town centre

Opening
Mar & Oct Mon–Sat 9am–5pm, Sun 12pm–5pm; Apr–Sep Mon–Sat 8.30am–6pm, Sun 12noon–5pm; Nov–Feb Mon–Sat 9am–4pm, Sun 12noon–5pm

Admission
Shakespeare's Grave Adult £1.50, Child & Concs 50p *Church* Free

Contact
Old Town, Stratford-upon-Avon CV37 6BG

t 01789 266316
w stratford-upon-avon.org.uk
e office@stratford-upon-avon.org.uk

566 Stratford-upon-Avon

Nash's House & New Place

  1 hr  All year

Nash's House was owned by Thomas Nash, husband of Shakespeare's granddaughter, and was the site of New Place, Shakespeare's large Stratford home where he died in 1616, now preserved as a picturesque garden space.

* Stratford's 1st Shakespeare festival staged here
* The Complete Works of William Shakespeare exhibition

Location
Signed from town centre

Opening
Daily: Apr–May & Sep–Oct 11am–5pm; Jun–Aug Mon–Sat 9.30am–5pm, Sun 10am–5pm; Nov–Mar 11am–4pm;

Admission
Adult £3.50, Child £1.70, Concs £3

Contact
Chapel Street, Stratford-upon-Avon CV37 6EP

t 01789 292325
w shakespeare.org.uk
e info@shakespeare.org.uk

567 Stratford-upon-Avon

Packwood House

  2 hrs  Mar–Nov

The original C16 house was restored between the world wars by Graham Baron Ash. The interior contains a fine collection of C16 textiles and furniture. The gardens have renowned herbaceous borders and a famous collection of yews.

* A curious feature is the large number of sundials
* Glorious gardens

Location
On A3400, 2 miles E of Hockley Heath

Opening
House 1 Mar–5 Nov Wed–Sun 12noon–4.30pm
Gardens 1 Mar–5 Nov Wed–Sun 11am–4.30pm

Admission
House & Gardens Adult £6.20, Child £3.10 *Gardens* £3.20, £1.60

Contact
Lapworth, Solihull B94 6AT

t 01564 783294
w nationaltrust.org.uk
e packwood@nationaltrust.org.uk

568 Stratford-upon-Avon

Shakespeare's Birthplace

1 hr All year

Home to the Shakespeare family and where William Shakespeare was born in 1564. The house contains both original artefacts and replicas depicting the house as Shakespeare would have known it as a child. An exhibition unfolds Shakespeare's life, work and times.

* Exhibitions tell the story of the house
* Exhibits of rare period items including *First Folio* (1623)

Location
Signed from town centre

Opening
Apr–May & Sep–Oct Mon–Sat 10am–5pm, Sun 10.30am–5pm; Jun–Aug, Mon–Sat 9am–5pm, Sun 9.30am–5pm; Nov–Mar Mon–Sat 10am–4pm, Sun 10.30am–4pm

Admission
Adult £7, Child £2.75, Concs £6

Contact
Henley Street, Stratford-upon-Avon CV37 6QW

t 01789 201823
w shakespeare.org.uk
e info@shakespeare.org.uk

569 Stratford-upon-Avon

The Shakespeare Countryside Museum & Mary Arden's House

  1 hr+  All year

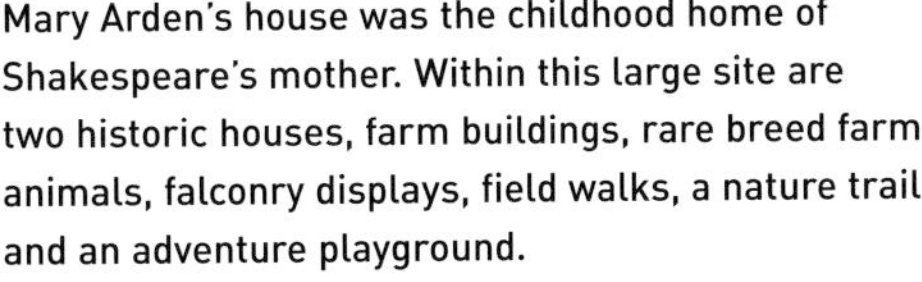

Mary Arden's house was the childhood home of Shakespeare's mother. Within this large site are two historic houses, farm buildings, rare breed farm animals, falconry displays, field walks, a nature trail and an adventure playground.

* Falconry displays
* Rare breeds farm

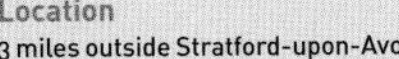   

Location
3 miles outside Stratford-upon-Avon

Opening
Apr–May Sep–Oct Mon–Sun 10am–5pm; Jun–Aug Mon–Sun 9.30am–5pm; Nov–Mar Mon–Sun 10am–4pm

Admission
Adult £6, Child £2.50, Concs £5

Contact
Station Road, Wilmcote CV37 9UN

t 01789 293455
w shakespeare.org.uk
e info@shakespeare.org.uk

570 Sutton Coldfield

Kingsbury Water Park

2 hrs+ All year

Warwickshire's premier waterside attraction, Kingsbury Water Park has 15 lakes in more than 600 acres of country park. Stroll along the surfaced paths, explore hidden corners, spot birds and wildlife, hire a cycle, or join in an event. There is also an adventure playground and a farm.

* Day-ticket fishing
* Miniature railway new in 2006

Location
Exit at junction 9 of the M42 & follow A4097 towards Kingsbury

Opening
Please phone for details

Admission
Car park £2.50

Contact
Bodymoor Heath, Sutton Coldfield B76 0DY

t 01827 872660
w warwickshire.gov.uk/countryside
e parks@warwickshire.gov.uk

571 Warwick

Lord Leycester Hospital

  1 hr  All year

This historic group of timber-framed buildings from the late C14 clusters round the Norman gateway into Warwick. For 150 years this was the home of Warwick's medieval guilds. Under Elizabeth I it became a retirement home for ex-servicemen and their wives and still is today.

* Museum of Queen's Own Hussars in Chaplain's Hall
* Brethren's kitchen, delicious food all day

Location
Near Tourist Information Centre

Opening
Tue–Sun & Bank Hols 10am–5pm

Admission
Adult £4.90, Child £3.90, Concs £4.40
Gardens £2

Contact
High Street, Warwick CV34 4BH

t 01926 491422
w lordleycester.com
e lordleycester@btinternet.com

572 Warwick

St John's House

  1 hr+  All year

A charming Jacobean house dating from about 1620, St John's became a branch of the Warwickshire Museum in 1961 and houses the social history collection. The galleries have themes such as costume, domestic life and school life, and are changed frequently.

* Museum of Royal Warwickshire Regiment
* Ever-changing display of costume

Location
Signed from town centre

Opening
Tue–Sat & Bank Hols 10am–5pm, Sun 2.30pm–5pm

Admission
Free

Contact
Warwick CV34 4NF

t 01926 412132
w warwickshire.gov.uk/museum
e museum@warwickshire.gov.uk

573 Warwick

Warwick Castle

 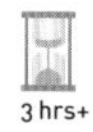 3 hrs+  All year

Built by William the Conqueror in 1068, this is a fine example of a medieval castle. Today visitors can see the mill and engine house where the power of the River Avon ground grain for 600 years. There's also a peacock garden, conservatory, and exquisite Victorian rose garden.

* Quality Assured Visitor Attraction
* Special events (detailed on website)

Location
2 miles from junction 15 of M40. Easily accessible by road or rail

Opening
Daily: Apr–Sep 10am–6pm; Oct–Mar 10am–5pm

Admission
Please phone for details

Contact
Warwick CV34 4QU

t 0870 442 2000
w warwick-castle.co.uk
e info@warwick-castle.com

574 Warwick

Warwickshire Museums

1 hr+ All year

The Warwickshire Museum Service is housed in the C17 market hall. This is one of the few buildings in central Warwick that survived a huge fire in the town in 1694. Displays of geology, biology and archaeology illustrate the natural history and heritage of the county.

* Famous Sheldon tapestry map of Warwickshire
* 180 million-year-old plesiosaur from Jurassic period

Location
In town centre

Opening
Apr–Sep Tue–Sat 10am–5pm, Sun & Bank Hols 11.30am–5pm; Oct–Apr Tue–Sat 10am–5pm

Admission
Free

Contact
Market Place, Warwick CV34 4SA

t 01926 412500
w warwickshire.gov.uk
e museums@warwickshire.gov.uk

576 Wellesbourne

Wellesbourne Watermill

2 hrs Easter–Sep

Visitors to this historic watermill can see the mill's machinery being driven by one of the country's largest wooden waterwheels. There are regular demonstrations showing how stoneground flour is milled. Coracles are used on the millpond, which is a tranquil haven for wildlife.

* Children's play area
* Animal farm park & maize maze

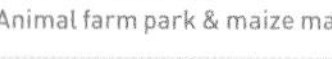   

Location
On B4086, between Wellesbourne & Kineton

Opening
Easter –Sep Thu–Sun & Bank Hols 10am–5pm; Jul–Sep Wed–Sun 10am–5pm

Admission
Adult £4.50, Child £3, Concs £3.50

Contact
Kineton Road, Wellesbourne CV35 9HG

t 01789 470237
w wellesbournemill.co.uk
e larahutsby@hotmail.com

575 Wellesbourne

Charlecote Park

2 hrs+ Mar–Dec

The mellow brickwork and great chimneys of Charlecote sum up the essence of Tudor England. There are associations with both Elizabeth I and Shakespeare – he knew the house well and is alleged to have been caught poaching the estate deer.

* Contains objects from Beckford's Fonthill Abbey
* Formal garden & Capability Brown deer park

Location
1 mile W of Wellesbourne, 5 miles E of Stratford, on N side of B4086

Opening
House Mar–Sep Fri–Tue 12noon–5pm; Oct Fri–Tue 12noon–4.30pm
Gardens Mar–Oct Fri–Tue 10.30am–6pm; Nov–Dec Sat–Sun 11am–4pm

Admission
House Adult £6.90, Child £3.50
Grounds £3.50, £1.85

Contact
Warwick CV35 9ER

t 01789 470277
w nationaltrust.org.uk
e charlecote.park@nationaltrust.org.uk

577 Baginton

Lunt Roman Fort

2 hrs Apr–Oct

This is a partial reconstruction of the fort established here in AD60. Visitors enter the fort by the reconstructed eastern gateway, which is built entirely of timber and based on depictions from Trajan's Column. There is also a museum of Roman military life with archaeological finds.

* Events & re-enactments with the XIII Legion
* Museum of Army Life

Location
In Baginton, near Coventry. Can be approached from A45 & A46

Opening
Apr–mid-Jul, mid-Sep–Oct Sat–Sun 10.30am–4.30pm; 16 Jul–18 Sep Wed–Sun 10.30am–4.30pm
Pre-booked parties at other times, please phone for details

Admission
Adult £2, Child & Concs £1

Contact
Coventry Road, Baginton CV8 3AJ
t 02476 832565/303567

578 Baginton

Midland Air Museum

2 hrs All year

Exhibits include the Avro Vulcan bomber, and more than 30 other historic aircraft (both civil and military), aero-engines and memorabilia. The Heritage Centre also houses a collection of material relating to Sir Frank Whittle.

* Giant 1959 Armstrong Whitworth Argosy freighter
* Meteor, Vulcan, Hunter, Starfighter & Phantom

Location
Off A45, between roundabout & Baginton

Opening
Daily: Apr–Oct Mon–Sat 10am–5pm, Sun & Bank Hols 10am–6pm; Nov–Mar 10.30am–5pm

Admission
Adult £4.50, Child £2.50, Concs £4

Contact
Coventry Airport, Baginton, Coventry CV8 3AZ
t 02476 301033
w midlandairmuseum.co.uk
e midlandairmuseum@aol.com

579 Birmingham

Birmingham Museum & Art Gallery

2 hrs All year

This magnificent building houses one of the world's finest collections of Pre-Raphaelite art, as well as displays of silver, sculpture, ceramics, archaeology and social history. British watercolours and Arts & Crafts movement work is also on show.

* Waterhall gallery of modern arts
* Gas Hall exhibition space

Location
Adjacent to Council House, signed from end of New Street railway station

Opening
Daily: Mon–Thu & Sat 10am–5pm, Fri 10.30am–5pm, Sun 12.30pm–5pm

Admission
Free

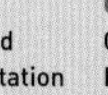

Contact
Chamberlain Square, Birmingham B3 3DH
t 0121 303 2834
w bmag.org.uk
e bmag_enquiries@birmingham.gov.uk

580 Birmingham

Ikon Gallery

1 hr All year

One of Europe's leading contemporary art galleries, Ikon shows the best in international and British art in a changing programme of exhibitions and events. A variety of media are represented, including sound, video, mixed media, photography, painting, sculpture and installation.

* Exhibitions in Ikon's events room & tower room
* Situated in a converted neo-Gothic school building

Location
15 min from city centre, signed from Victoria Square

Opening
Tue–Sun & Bank Hols 11am–6pm

Admission
Free

Contact
1 Oozells Square, Brindleyplace, Birmingham B1 2HS
t 0121 248 0708
w ikon-gallery.co.uk
e marketing@ikon-gallery.co.uk

581 Birmingham

Museum of the Jewellery Quarter

 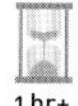  

1 hr+ All year

Visit a real jewellery factory that has changed little since the early part of the last century. The museum tells the story of jewellery making in Birmingham from its origins in the Middle Ages to the present day, and includes an explanation of jewellery-making techniques.

* Free entry includes a guided tour of the factory
* Workshops & exhibitions throughout the year

Location
Adjacent to Jewellery Quarter Clock & Jewellery Quarter Station

Opening
Nov–Easter Tue–Sat 11.30am–4pm;
Easter–Oct Tue–Sun 11.30am–4pm

Admission
Free

Contact
75–79 Vyse Street, Birmingham B18 6HA

t 0121 554 3598
w bmag.org.uk
e bmag.enquiries@birmingham.gov.uk

582 Birmingham

National Sea Life Centre

3 hrs All year

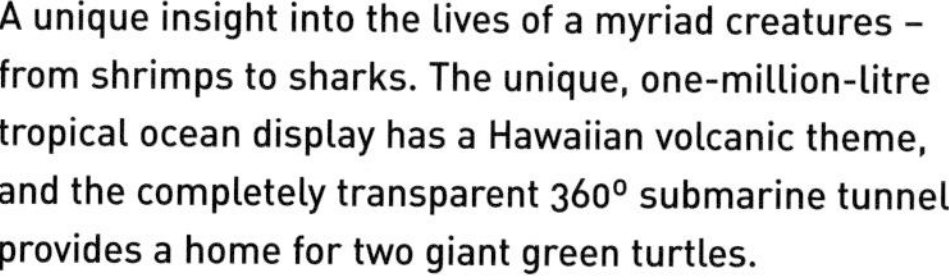

A unique insight into the lives of a myriad creatures – from shrimps to sharks. The unique, one-million-litre tropical ocean display has a Hawaiian volcanic theme, and the completely transparent 360° submarine tunnel provides a home for two giant green turtles.

* Programme of talks & feeding demonstrations
* Totally tropical centre

Location
Between National Indoor Arena & International Convention Centre

Opening
summer daily 10am–5pm
winter Mon–Fri 10am–4pm, Sat–Sun 10am–5pm

Admission
Adult £12.50, Child £8.50, Concs £9

Contact
The Waters Edge, Brindleyplace, Birmingham B1 2HL

t 0121 643 6777 / 633 4700
w sealifeeurope.com
e slcbirmingham@merlinentertainments.biz

583 Birmingham

Royal Birmingham Society of Artists Gallery

2 hrs All year

One of the oldest art societies in the UK, the Royal Birmingham Society of Artists was given royal status in 1868 by Queen Victoria, and played an important part in the Pre-Raphaelite movement. The gallery exhibits the work of members and local designers.

* Regularly changing programme of exhibitions
* Craft gallery, including ceramics, jewellery & more

Location
Follow New Hall Street to Brook Street

Opening
Mon–Wed & Fri 10.30am–5.30pm,
Thu 10.30am–7pm, Sat 10.30am–5pm

Admission
Free

Contact
4 Brook Street, St Paul's Square, Birmingham B3 1SA

t 0121 236 4353
w rbsa.org.uk
e secretary@rbsa.org.uk

584 Birmingham

ThinkTank

4 hrs   All year

Thinktank is Birmingham's science museum, a wonderful modern attraction offering 10 galleries of historical artefacts, modern interactives and futuristic facts. Visitors can explore everything from aircraft and steam engines to intestines and tastebuds!

* Planetarium new in Dec 2005
* 3 exhibits exploring the theme of space

Location
Follow blue banners. 15 min walk from New Street railway station

Opening
Daily: 10am–5pm

Admission
Adult £6.95, Child £4.95, Concs £5

Contact
Curzon Street, Birmingham B4 7XG

t 0121 202 2222
w thinktank.ac
e findout@thinktank.ac

585 Birmingham

Tolkien's Birmingham

2 hrs   Apr–Sep

J R R Tolkien garnered inspiration from childhood haunts in Birmingham. The imagery he skilfully created can be attributed to various places and buildings in the city. See for yourself where Tolkien dreamed up *The Hobbit* and *Lord of the Rings* or choose a guided tour.

* Indepth knowledge from specialist tour guide for groups only
* Please wear appropriate footwear

Location
Various areas of Birmingham

Opening
Apr–Sep by appointment
Please phone for details of guided tours

Admission
Adult £5, Child £2.50

Contact
59 Springfield Road,
Kings Heath,
Birmingham B14 7DU

t 0121 444 4046
w birminghamheritage.org.uk
e bobblaackham@btinternet.com

586 Bournville

Cadbury World

3 hrs   Feb–Dec

Discover the fascinating history of chocolate, from its Aztec origins to its manufacture in Victorian England. Learn about the Cadbury family and their early struggles to develop the business. Follow the journey of chocolate from its origins as cocoa to liquid chocolate in the factory.

* Purple Planet – see yourself moulded in chocolate
* Essence – produce your own Cadbury product

Location
Signed from M42

Opening
Feb–Dec; times vary, please phone for details

Admission
Adult £12.50, Child £9.50, Concs £9.95
Pre-booking recommended

Contact
Linden Road, Bournville,
Birmingham B30 2LU

t 0845 4503599
w cadburyworld.co.uk
e cadbury.world@csplc.com

587 Bournville

Selly Manor

2 hrs

All year

Dating back to 1327, Selly Manor is a medieval timber-framed manor house with Tudor extensions. By the late C19 it was due for demolition but it was saved by George Cadbury, who had it moved piece by piece and rebuilt in the village of Bournville.

* In the unique village of Bournville near Cadbury World
* Events & activities throughout the year

Location
3 miles S of city centre on Maple Road next to Bournville village green

Opening
Jan–Dec Tue–Fri 10am–5pm;
Apr–Sep Tue–Fri 10am–5pm, Sat–Sun & Bank Hols 2pm–5pm;

Admission
Adult £3, Child £1, Concs £2

Contact
Bournville, Birmingham B30 1UB

t 0121 472 0199
w bvt.org.uk/sellymanor
e sellymanor@bvt.org.uk

588 Castle Bromwich

Castle Bromwich Hall Gardens

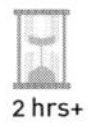
2 hrs+

Apr–Sep

This unique example of an English baroque garden is being restored to how it was during the period 1680–1740. The 10-acre walled garden contains rare and interesting period plants, vegetables and herbs. Classical patterned parterres can be seen at the end of the Holly Walk.

* C19 holly maze, plant & gift shop
* Restored summer house & greenhouse

Location
Signed from M6 junction 5

Opening
Apr–Sep Wed–Fri 1.30pm–4.30pm,
Sat, Sun & Bank Hols 1.30pm–5.30pm

Admission
Adult £3.50, Child 50p, Concs £3

Contact
Chester Road, Castle Bromwich, Birmingham B36 9BT

t 0121 749 4100
w cbhgt.org.uk
e admin@cbhgt.org.uk

589 Coventry

Coventry Cathedral

1 hr+ All year

Coventry Cathedral was bombed and destroyed in 1940, during WWII. The striking new cathedral, designed by Basil Spence, was consecrated in 1962, and stands alongside the old ruins. It is filled with work from leading artists of the time.

* Stunning tower views & Blitz exhibition
* Bookshop & gift shops open daily

Location
In central Coventry

Opening
Daily: 9am–5pm (services permitting)

Admission
Free, donations welcome

Contact
1 Hilltop, Coventry CV1 5AB

t 02476 521200
w coventrycathedral.org.uk
e information@coventrycathedral.org.uk

590 Coventry

Herbert Art Gallery & Museum

1 hr All year

The Herbert is currently undergoing a major redevelopment. Although most of the galleries are closed until late 2007, a programme of exhibitions and events will be taking place throughout the year, including activities for families with children.

* Ongoing events throughout the year

Location
Central Coventry, near cathedral, next to Tourist Information Centre

Opening
Daily: Mon–Sat 10am–5.30pm, Sun 12noon–5pm

Admission
Free

Contact
Jordan Well, Coventry CV1 5QP

t 0247 6832386
w theherbert.org
e info@theherbert.org

591 Dudley

Black Country Living Museum

3 hrs+ All year

Set amid 26 acres, the museum occupies an urban heritage park. Historic buildings from around the Black Country have been moved and rebuilt to create a tribute to the traditional skills and enterprise of the people who lived in the heart of industrial Britain.

* Tramcars & trolleybuses transport visitors
* Costumed demonstrators & working craftsmen

Location
On A4037, 3 miles from M5 junction 2

Opening
Mar–Oct daily 10am–5pm;
Nov–Feb Wed–Sun 10am–4pm

Admission
Adult £11, Child £6, Concs £9

Contact
Tipton Road, Dudley DY1 4SQ

t 0121 557 9643
w bclm.co.uk
e info@bclm.co.uk

592 Dudley

Dudley Canal Trust

1 hr

Feb–Nov

Explore Dudley's subterranean world of limestone mines and canal systems. Visitors can admire the mining and engineering feats of men of the C18 and modern tunnelling techniques of today. Computer displays show scenes from the past 200 years of mining.

* Learn about the geological history of the area
* Special events throughout the year

Location
Follow signs to Dudley past Black Country Living Museum to traffic lights, turn left & attraction is on the left

Opening
Mar–Oct 10am–5pm;
Feb & Nov 10am–4pm

Admission
Adult £4.25, Child £3.55, Concs £3.90

Contact
The Ticket Office, Birmingham New Road, Dudley DY1 4SB

t 01384 236275
w dudleytunneltrust.org.uk
e dcttrips@btclick.com

593 Dudley

Dudley Museum & Art Gallery

1 hr+

All year

This museum contains a collection of C17, C18 and C19 British and European paintings, furniture and ceramics, together with Oriental ceramics, Japanese netsuke and inro, Bilston enamels, commemorative medals, and Greek, Roman and Egyptian pottery.

* Geological collection of fossils, rocks & minerals
* Greek exhibition – Theatre style

Location
Off Priory Street, near bus station

Opening
Mon–Sat 10am–4pm

Admission
Free

Contact
St James' Road, Dudley DY1 1HU

t 01384 815575
w dudley.gov.uk
e dudley.museums@dudley.gov.uk

594 Edgbaston

Birmingham Botanical Gardens & Glasshouses

2 hrs+ All year

The gardens originally opened in 1832 and today tropical, subtropical, Mediterranean and desert glasshouses stand in 15 acres of beautiful gardens. This fine collection of plants includes more than 200 trees and the National Bonsai Collection.

* Designed by J C Loudon, a leading garden planner
* Sculpture trail, waterfowl & exotic birds

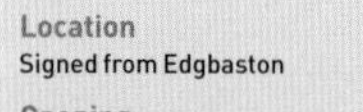

Location
Signed from Edgbaston

Opening
Apr–Sep Mon–Sat 9am–7pm, Sun 10am–7pm; Oct–Mar Mon–Sat 9am–5pm, Sun 10am–5pm (or dusk)

Admission
Adult £6.10, Child & Concs £3.60

Contact
Westbourne Road, Edgbaston, Birmingham B15 3TR

t 0121 454 1860
w birminghambotanicalgardens.org.uk
e admin@birminghambotanicalgardens.org.uk

595 Kingswinford

Broadfield House Glass Museum

2 hrs All year

The museum has a collection of British glass, much of which was made locally, from C18 tableware to Victorian cameo vases to modern sculptural pieces. Permanent displays and temporary exhibitions celebrate the art of glassmaking. There is also a glassmaking studio.

* Watch & wonder at the glassblowers' skills
* The Glass Dance windows made by David Prytherch

Location
Off A491, between Stourbridge & Wolverhampton

Opening
Tue–Sun & Bank Hols 12noon–4pm

Admission
Free

Contact
Compton Drive, Kingswinford DY6 9NS

t 01384 812745
w glassmuseum.org.uk
e glass.museum@dudley.gov.uk

596 Solihull

National Motorcycle Museum

3 hrs All year

Internationally renowned, it is the largest motorcycle museum in the world. The exhibits cover 60 years of British motorcycling with more than 650 machines all lovingly restored to the manufacturer's original specifications.

* Extensive book department
* Regular rallies and events

Location
Just off M42, junction 6

Opening
Daily: 10am–6pm

Admission
Adult £6.95, Child & Concs £4.95

Contact
Coventry Road, Bickenhill, Solihull B92 0EJ

t 01675 443311
w nationalmotorcyclemuseum.co.uk
e admin@nationalmotorcyclemuseum.co.uk

597 Stourbridge

Red House Glass Cone

 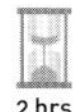 

2 hrs All year

The glass cone has a history spanning 400 years. Explore underground passages and tunnels and climb the spiral staircase within the 100ft cone to a viewing platform. An audio-guide and exhibition galleries explain the history and process of glassmaking.

* Demonstrations of glassmaking
* Stuart Crystal gift centre

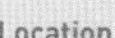

Location
10 miles from M5 junction 2 (Oldbury) or junction 4 (Stourbridge). Situated near Stourbridge town centre on A491 Stourbridge to Wolverhampton road

Opening
Daily: Apr–Oct Mon–Sat 10am–5pm, Sun 10am–4pm; Nov–Mar 10am–4pm

Admission
Free.
Audio Guides £1.50

Contact
High Street, Wordsley, Stourbridge DY8 4AZ

t 01384 812750
w dudley.gov.uk/redhousecone

598 Walsall

New Art Gallery

2 hrs All year

This Arts Lottery-funded gallery opened in 2000 and is said to be one of the most exciting art galleries to be built in the UK in the past 20 years. Traditional art is showcased in the Garman Ryan Collection, donated by Lady Kathleen Garman, widow of sculptor Sir Jacob Epstein.

* Building designed by Caruso St John Architects
* Exhibitions dedicated to best of contemporary art

Location
Follow A454 (Wolverhampton Street) into town centre

Opening
Tue–Sat & Bank Hols 10am–5pm, Sun 12noon–5pm

Admission
Free

Contact
Gallery Square, Walsall WS2 8LG

t 01922 654400
w artatwalsall.org.uk
e info@artatwalsall.org.uk

599 Walsall

Walsall Leather Museum

2 hrs All year

Located at the heart of Britain's saddlery and leather goods trade, this fascinating museum tells the story of Walsall's leather workers, past and present. Regular demonstrations of traditional leather crafts take place in historic workshops.

* Collection of contemporary designer leatherwork
* Regular exhibitions & special events

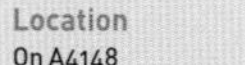

Location
On A4148

Opening
Mar–Oct Tue–Sat 10am–5pm, Sun 12noon–5pm;
Nov–Apr Tue–Sat 10am–4pm, Sun 12noon–4pm

Admission
Free

Contact
Littleton Street West, Walsall WS2 8EQ

t 01922 721153
w walsall.gov.uk/leathermuseum
e leathermuseum@walsall.gov.uk

600 Wolverhampton

Bantock House & Park

  1 hr+  All year

This Grade II-listed family home was built in 1788. The ground floor has recently been restored to its Edwardian splendour, while the upstairs features superb displays of enamels, Japanned ware and steel jewellery, and includes lots of hands-on activities for all ages.

* Host of attractions throughout the year
* Live music at 1940s weekends

    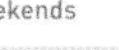

Location
Signed from Wolverhampton ring road

Opening
Apr–Oct Tue–Sun 11am–5pm; Nov–Mar Tue–Sun 12noon–4pm; open Bank Hol Mons

Admission
Free

Contact
Finchfield Road, Wolverhampton WV3 9LQ

t 01902 552195
w wolverhampton.gov.uk
e bantockhouse@dial.pipex.com

601 Wolverhampton

Wightwick Manor

  2 hrs  Mar–Dec

This is a fine example of a house built and furnished in the Arts & Crafts movement style. It features many original William Morris wallpapers and fabrics, Pre-Raphaelite paintings, Kempe glass and tiles by William de Morgan.

* Beautiful garden designed by Thomas Mawson
* Talks & tours bring the house to life

Location
Off A454, beside Mermaid Inn, 3 miles W of Wolverhampton

Opening
Mar–24 Dec Thu & Sat 12.30pm–5pm

Admission
Adult £6.50, Child £3.30
Timed ticket Please phone for details

Contact
Wightwick Bank, Wolverhampton WV6 8EE

t 01902 761400
w nationaltrust.org.uk
e wightwickmanor@nationaltrust.org.uk

602 Wolverhampton

Wolverhampton Art Gallery

  1 hr+  All year

The gallery has an innovative programme of temporary exhibitions, alongside a series of workshops and special events. The collection includes British and American Pop Art as well as traditional C18 and C19 paintings by Gainsborough, Turner and Landseer.

* Contemporary art collection is the finest in the region
* Sensing Sculpture, a tactile sculpture court

Location
Next to St Peter's Church

Opening
Mon–Sat 10am–5pm; closed Bank Hols

Admission
Free

Contact
Lichfield Street, Wolverhampton WV1 1DU

t 01902 552055
w wolverhamptonart.org.uk
e info@wolverhamptonart.org.uk

603 Bewdley

Arley Arboretum

 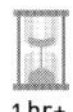 

1 hr+ Mar–Oct

One of the oldest arboretums in Britain, Arley boasts more than 300 species of trees set in formal and informal plantings and gardens. The collection has been built up over 200 years and contains many spectacular and rare domestic and exotic trees.

* Crimean pines tallest in the UK
* Beautiful Italian gardens

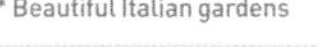

Location
Between Kidderminster & Bridgnorth on A442, just over a mile from hamlet of Shatterford, brown signed from this road.

Opening
Mid-Mar–Oct, Wed–Sun & Bank Hol Mon 11am–5pm

Admission
Adult £4, Child £1

Contact
Arley Estate Office, Arley, Bewdley DY12 1XG

t 01299 861368
w arley-arboretum.org.uk
e info@arley_arboretum.org.uk

604 Bewdley

West Midland Safari & Leisure Park

3 hrs+ Feb–Nov

This 4-mile drive-through safari covers an area of more than 150 acres and is home to a variety of exotic and unusual animals including rare and beautiful white tigers, elephants, rhinos, giraffes, lions, wallabies, emus, camels, zebras, bison, wolves and llamas.

* Safari bus tours
* Discovery trail

Location
On A456 between Kidderminster & Bewdley

Opening
Daily: Feb–Nov Mon–Fri 10am–4pm, Sat–Sun 10am–5pm

Admission
Please phone for details

Contact
Spring Grove, Bewdley DY12 1LF

t 01299 402114
w wmsp.co.uk
e info@wmsp.co.uk

605 Broadway

Broadway Tower & Country Park

1 hr+ All year

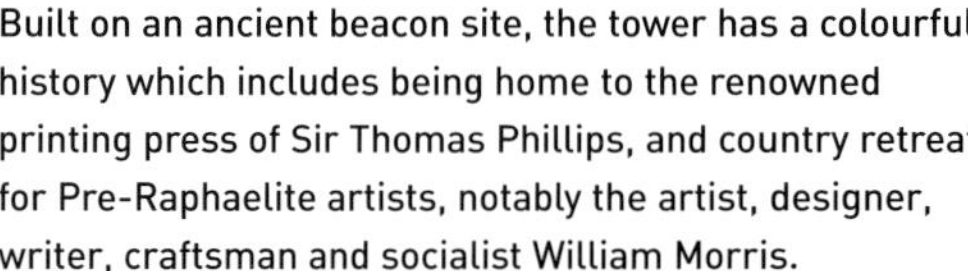

Built on an ancient beacon site, the tower has a colourful history which includes being home to the renowned printing press of Sir Thomas Phillips, and country retreat for Pre-Raphaelite artists, notably the artist, designer, writer, craftsman and socialist William Morris.

* Today houses exhibition connected with its past
* Said to be one of England's outstanding viewpoints

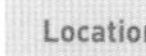

Location
Off A44 1 mile SE of Broadway

Opening
Apr–Oct daily 10.30am–5pm; Nov–Mar Sat–Sun 10.30am–4pm

Admission
Adult £3.80, Child £2.30, Concs £3

Contact
Middle Hill, Broadway WR12 7LB

t 01386 852390
w broadway-cotswolds.co.uk
e broadwaytower1@aol.com

606 Broadway

Snowshill Manor

1 hr Apr–Oct

A Cotswold manor house containing Charles Paget Wade's extraordinary display of craftsmanship and design, including clocks, toys and Japanese armour. The garden is a lively mix of architectural features, bright colour and delightful scents.

* Cottage & organic garden also on display

Location
Turn from A44 Broadway bypass into Broadway, then by village green turn right uphill to Snowshill

Opening
25 March–29 Oct Wed–Sun & Bank Hols
House 12noon–5pm
Garden 11am–5.30pm

Admission
House & Gardens Adult £7.30, Child £3.65 *Gardens* Adult £4, Child £2

Contact
Snowshill, nr Broadway WR12 7JU

t 01386 852410
w nationaltrust.org.uk
e snowshillmanor@nationaltrust.org.uk

607 Bromsgrove

Avoncroft Museum of Historic Buildings

3 hrs Mar–Nov

Avoncroft is a fascinating world of historic buildings spanning seven centuries, rescued and rebuilt on a beautiful 15-acre open-air site. You can see craftsmen working in a C19 nailshop, furnished historic houses and a Danzey Green windmill, one of the few still working in UK.

* See a variety of craft demonstrations
* See a church, gaol & working windmill

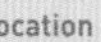    

Location
2 miles S of Bromsgrove off A38

Opening
Mar Tue–Thur & Sat–Sun 10.30am–4pm; Apr–Jun, Sep & Oct Tue–Fri 10.30am–4.30pm, Sat–Sun 10.30am–5pm; Jul–Aug daily 10.30am–5pm; Nov Sat–Sun 10.30am–4.30pm

Admission
Adult £6, Child £3, Concs £5

Contact
Stoke Heath, Bromsgrove B60 4JR

t 01527 831363
w avoncroft.org.uk
e admin@avoncroft.org.uk

©NTPL/Nick Meers

608 Droitwich

Hanbury Hall

2 hrs+ Mar–Oct

Completed in 1701, this homely William and Mary-style house is famed for its beautiful painted ceilings and staircase, and has other fascinating features including an orangery, ice house, pavilions and working mushroom house, as well as beautiful parkland walks.

* Tercentenary exhibition opened in 2001
* Garden surrounded by 160 acres of parkland

Location
Near junction 5 of M5, 5 miles W of Droitwich

Opening
Mid Mar–Oct Sat–Wed 1pm–5pm
Please phone for details of other times

Admission
Please phone for details

Contact
School Road, Droitwich WR9 7EA

t 01527 821214
w nationaltrust.org.uk
e hanburyhall@nationaltrust.org.uk

609 Kidderminster

Bodenham Arboretum

 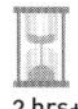 2 hrs+  All year

Bodenham Arboretum is a collection of more than 2,700 trees set in 156 acres, with 11 pools, 5 miles of footpaths and a working farm with a herd of pedigree Herefords. In addition there is an award-winning visitor centre set in the hillside overlooking the Big Pool.

* Christmas Nativity trail
* Laburnum Tunnel is a highlight in late May/Jun

Location
Signed from Wolverley

Opening
Jan–Feb Sat–Sun 11am–5pm;
Mar–Dec Wed–Sun 11am–5pm;
Oct daily 11am–5pm

Admission
Adult £5, Child £2

Contact
Wolverley, Kidderminster DY11 5SY

t 01562 852444
w bodenham-arboretum.co.uk

610 Kidderminster

Harvington Hall

  2 hrs  Mar–Oct

A moated medieval and Elizabethan manor house where many of the rooms still have their original Elizabethan wall paintings, discovered under whitewash in 1936. The hall also contains the finest series of priest's holes anywhere in the country.

* Georgian chapel in garden
* Moat broadens into a small lake, home to waterfowl

Location
3 miles SE of Kidderminster just off A450 Birmingham–Worcester road

Opening
Mar & Oct Sat–Sun 11.30am–4.30pm;
Apr–Sep Wed–Sun 11.30am–4.30pm

Admission
Adult £5, Child £3.50, Concs £4.50

Contact
Harvington, Kidderminster DY10 4LR

t 01562 777846
w harvingtonhall.com
e harvingtonhall@btconnect.com

611 Malvern

Great Malvern Priory

  1 hr  All year

Malvern Priory is one of the greatest parish churches in the country. It was founded in 1085 and has some of the finest examples of stained glass in the UK, plus carved misericords from the C15 and C16 and the best preserved collection of medieval floor and wall tiles in the country.

* Venue for many concerts
* Restored organ, millennium windows by Tom Denny

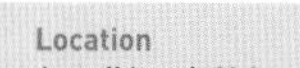

Location
Just off A449 in Malvern

Opening
Daily: Apr–Sep 9am–5pm;
Oct–Mar 9am–4.30pm

Admission
Free, donations welcomed

Contact
Church Street, Malvern WR14 2AY

t 01684 561020
w greatmalvernpriory.org.uk
e office@greatmalvernpriory.org.uk

612 Pershore

Croome Park

  2 hrs  Mar–Dec

Capability Brown's first complete landscape design, Croome is being restored to its C18 splendour with generous support from the Heritage Lottery Fund. Admire the beauty, enjoy relaxing walks or take part in one of our many activities.

* 1st phase of 10-year restoration project is complete
* Restoration of park buildings also in progress

Location
8 miles S of Worcester & E of A38

Opening
Mar–Apr & Sep–Oct Wed–Sun 10am–5.30pm; Mar–Aug daily 10am–5.30pm; Bank Hols 10am–5.30pm; Nov–Dec Wed–Sun 10am–4pm

Admission
Adult £3.90, Child £1.90

Contact
NT Estate Office, The Builders' Yard, High Green, Severn Stoke WR8 9JS

t 01905 371006
w nationaltrust.org.uk
e croomepark@nationaltrust.org.uk

613 Stourbridge

Hagley Hall

  1 hr   Jan–Feb

Commissioned in 1756 and designed by Sanderson Miller, this was the last of the great Palladian houses to be built. Van Dyck paintings, Chippendale furniture and exquisite rococo plasterwork are displayed throughout the house.

* Surrounded by 350 acres of landscaped deer park
* See where two of the Gunpowder Plot conspirators hid

Location
E of Kidderminster, junction 4 of M5, signed from junction of A456 and A491

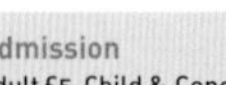

Opening
Jan–Feb Sun–Fri 2pm–5pm; Please phone or visit the website for details of Bank Hols opening times

Admission
Adult £5, Child & Concs £2.50

Contact
Hagley DY9 9LG

t 01562 882408
w hagleyhall.info
e hagleyhall@compuserve.com

614 Worcester

The Commandery

  1 hr+  Easter–Dec

This remarkable building was originally founded around 1,000 years ago and over the centuries it has been adapted for different users while retaining the fabric of its history. Brand new for 2007 are hands-on activities and an audio tour.

* Medieval great hall
* Exploring 1,000 years of history

Location
Just outside city walls at Sidbury Gate

Opening
Easter–Dec please phone for details

Admission
Please phone for details

Contact
Sidbury, Worcester WR1 2HU

t 01905 361821
w worcestercitymuseums.org.uk
e thecommandery@cityofworcester.gov.uk

615 Worcester

Leigh Court Barn

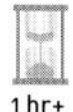

1 hr+ Apr–Sep

This is a striking example of medieval architecture. At 130 feet long and 36 feet wide (40m x 11m), the barn is the largest cruck structure in the UK. Once part of Leigh Court Manor, the barn has 10 bays and two porches.

* Originally built for the monks of Pershore Abbey

Location
5 miles W of Worcester on an unclassified road off A4103

Opening
Apr–Sep Thu–Sun & Bank Hols 10am–6pm

Admission
Free

Contact
Leigh, Worcester WR6 5LB

t 0121 625 6820
w english-heritage.org.uk

616 Worcester

Royal Worcester Porcelain Works

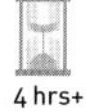

4 hrs+ All year

The works were established in 1751 along the banks of the River Severn. Our Royal Worcester shops offer an extensive range of quality bone china, porcelain and giftware with great savings and special offers all year. You can also paint your own design on a plate.

* One of the world's leading ceramics museums
* Huge variety of porcelain, bone china & earthenware

Location
3 miles from junction 7 of M5, follow signs to city centre – near cathedral

Opening
Daily: Mon–Sat 9am–5.30pm, Sun 11am–5pm

Admission
Prices vary, please phone or visit the website for details

Contact
Severn Street, Worcester WR1 2NE

t 01905 746000
w factoryshopsroyal-worcester.co.uk
e siteshops@royal-worcester.co.uk

617 Worcester

Sir Edward Elgar Birthplace Museum

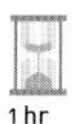

1 hr Feb–Dec

The cottage and the Elgar Centre together tell the story of Sir Edward Elgar, composer of much of England's best-known classical music. Visit the study containing his gramophone, and see family photographs and countless mementos including his books and golf clubs.

* Celebrate 150th anniversary of Elgar's birth
* Watch historic film of his final years

Location
3 miles from Worcester on A44 towards Leominster

Opening
Daily: 11am–5pm; (closed 22 Dec–1 Feb)

Admission
Adult £5, Child £2, Concs £4.50

Contact
Crown East Lane, Lower Broadheath WR2 6RH

t 01905 333224
w elgarmuseum.org
e birthplace@elgarmuseum.org

618 Worcester

Upton Heritage Centre

1 hr+

Apr–Sep

Located in the oldest surviving building in Upton-upon-Severn, the Pepperpot bell tower, are displays illustrating the growth and development of the town and its involvement in the Civil War of 1651. There are also other exhibits on local history.

* Battle of Upton display

Location
On B4211 from Great Malvern & A38 & A4104 from Worcester

Opening
Daily: Apr–Sep 1.30pm–4.30pm; Open some mornings, please phone for details

Admission
Free

Contact
Tourist Information Centre, 4 High Street, Worcester WR8 0HB

t 01684 594200

619 Worcester

Witley Court

2 hrs

All year

An early Jacobean manor house, Witley Court was converted in the C19 into a vast Italianate mansion with porticos by John Nash. The spectacular ruins of this once-great house are surrounded by magnificent landscaped gardens.

* Huge stone fountains that once shot 120 feet upwards
* Recent £1m garden renovation

Location
10 miles NW of Worcester on A443

Opening
Mar–Apr & Sep–Oct daily 10am–5pm; Jun–Aug daily 10am–6pm; Nov–Feb Thu–Mon 10am–4pm

Admission
Adult £5.20, Child £2.60, Concs £3.90

Contact
Great Witley WR6 6JT

t 01299 896636
w english-heritage.org.uk
e mark.badger@english-heritage.org.uk

620 Worcester

Worcester Cathedral

1 hr

All year

Worcester Cathedral has been a place of prayer and worship since AD680. The present building was begun in 1084. Its many attractions include King John's tomb, Prince Arthur's chantry, the early C12 Chapter House and St Wulstan's crypt.

* Tower open 10.30am–4.30pm Sat & summer hols
* Magnificent Victorian stained-glass windows

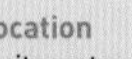

Location
In city centre, off College Street

Opening
Daily: 7.30am–6pm, services 3 times daily

Admission
Free, donations welcomed

Contact
10a College Green, Worcester WR1 2LH

t 01905 28854
w worcestercathedral.org.uk
e info@worcestercathedral.org.uk

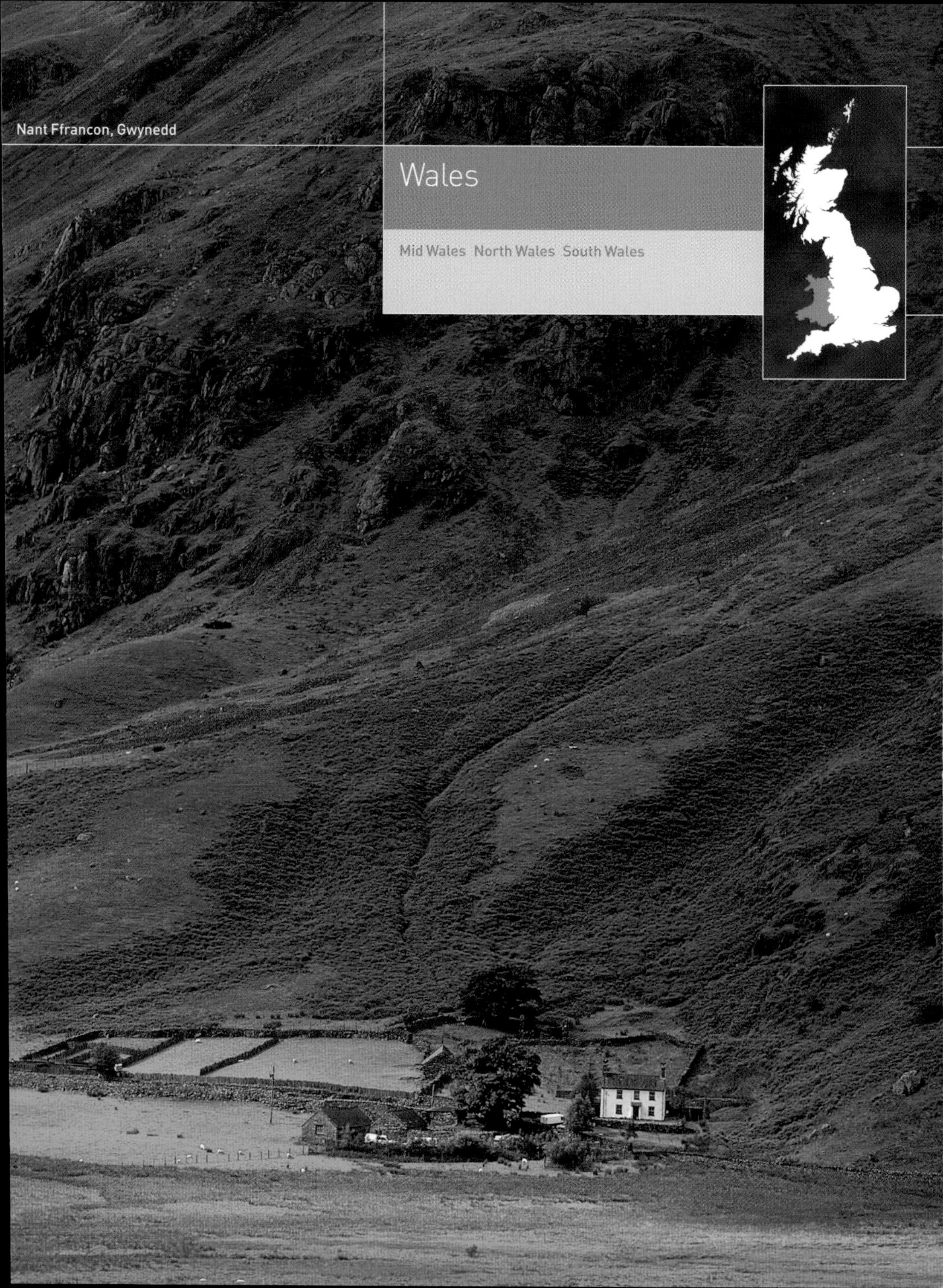

Nant Ffrancon, Gwynedd

Wales

Mid Wales North Wales South Wales

Carmel Head
Amlwch
Crosby
Bootle
Wallasey
Birkenhead
839-853
835-837
838
759
Ellesmere Port
746
738-739
Great Ormes Head
Anglesey
Holyhead
ISLE OF ANGLESEY
Holy Island
Llangefni
Beaumaris
Menai Bridge
Bangor
Llandudno
Conwy
Colwyn Bay
641
Rhyl
Prestatyn
Abergele
Llanfairfechan
Holywell
St Asaph
Flint
Queensferry
635-636
642
638-639
Bethesda
Caernarfon
Denbigh
FLINTSHIRE
Mold
CONWY
Llanrwst
643
Llanberis
Ruthin
Betws-y-coed
DENBIGHSHIRE
Wrexham
Blaenau Ffestiniog
Ruabon
637
Ffestiniog
644-645
Llangollen
Lleyn Peninsula
Porthmadog
Criccieth
647
646
Pwllheli
Bala
640
Ellesmere
Oswestry
Abersoch
Bardsey Island
628
Barmouth
Dolgellau
Mallwyd
Shrewsbury
Welshpool
629-631
Tywyn
Machynlleth
634
Aberdyfi
Montgomery
Newtown
Cambrian Mountains
Bishop's Castle
Llanidloes
Aberystwyth
Llangurig
621-622
POWYS
Knighton
Rhayader
632
Presteigne
633
Aberaeron
Llandrindod Wells
625
New Quay
Tregaron
Kington
506
WALES
CEREDIGION
624
Lampeter
Builth Wells
Strumble Head
Cardigan
654-655
627
Hay-on-Wye
Newcastle Emlyn
Fishguard
Llandovery
659
499
PEMBROKESHIRE
CARMARTHENSHIRE
Brecon
623
626
Brecon Beacons
660
Carmarthen
Llandeilo
Crickhowell
Haverfordwest
Narberth
656
658
Abergavenny
St Clears
Ammanford
Ebbw Vale
Brynmawr
Milford Haven
Merthyr Tydfil
Blaenavon
662
Neyland
Kidwelly
Rhymney
648
666-667
Pembroke Dock
Llanelli
Burry Port
Aberdare
Pontypool
Tenby
663
669
Mountain Ash
Pembroke
M4
Swansea
Neath
Glyncorrwg
668
Bargoed
Cwmbran
Caldey Island
SWANSEA
664-665
Maesteg
Risca
St Govan's Head
Port Einon
Port Talbot
Pontypridd
649
Caerphilly
Newport
Mumbles Head
650-653
Porthcawl
Bridgend
CARDIFF
VALE OF GLAMORGAN
Cowbridge
Clevedon

621 Aberystwyth

Animalarium

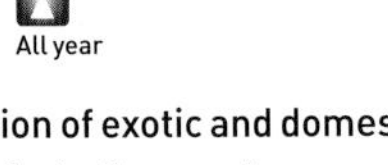

3 hrs | All year

Meet a wide selection of exotic and domestic animals, birds and reptiles – including monkeys, marmosets, lemurs and wallabies. Pony rides run twice daily from Easter to September. There is an animal-petting area, a fruit bat cave and a daily snake-handling demonstration.

* Welsh Tourist Board seal of approval
* Crocodile-feeding twice a week

Location
At Borth, between Aberystwyth & Machynlleth

Opening
Daily: *summer* 10am–6pm
winter 11am–4pm

Admission
Please phone for details

Contact
Borth, Ceredigion SY25 6RA

t 01970 871224
w animalarium.co.uk

622 Aberystwyth

Vale of Rheidol Railway

3 hrs+ | Easter–Oct

Take a ride on a steam train for the 11 miles between Aberystwyth and Devil's Bridge. During the hour-long journey you'll have spectacular views of the wooded Rheidol Valley. From Devil's Bridge there are walks to Mynach Falls, Devil's Punchbowl and Jacob's Ladder.

* One of the Great Little Trains of Wales
* Last steam railway owned by British Rail

Location
Trains depart from Aberystwyth centre, beside main railway station

Opening
Please phone for details

Admission
Return fare Adult £12.50, Child from £3, Concs £11

Contact
Park Avenue, Aberystwyth, Cardiganshire SY23 1PG

t 01970 625819
w rheidolrailway.co.uk
e info@rheidolrailway.co.uk

623 Brecon

Brecon Beacons National Park Visitor Centre

1 hr+ | All year

The attractions of the Brecon Beacons National Park range from lush, green, open countryside to historical and cultural heritage. There are attractions to suit all the family including museums, theatres and family activity centres, plus beautiful walks and rides.

* Centre of internationally renowned festivals
* Selection of guided walks available

Location
National Park Mountain Centre is 5½ miles SW of Brecon

Opening
Daily: Mar–Apr & Sep–Oct 9.30am–5pm; May–Jun 9.30am–5.30pm; Jul–Aug 9.30am–6pm; Nov–Feb 9.30am–4.30pm

Admission
Free. Car park charges vary

Contact
NPVC, Libanus, Brecon, Powys LD3 8ER

t 01874 623366
w breconbeacons.org
e mountain.centre@breconbeacons.org

624 Cardigan

Felinwynt Rainforest & Butterfly Centre

1 hr+ | Easter–Oct

This tropical rainforest in the heart of Wales is home to exotic and unusual plants, birds, insects and butterflies from all over the world. You'll see the scarlet swallowtail and the giant atlas moth free-flying in natural surroundings.

* Welsh Tourist Board Star Attraction
* Video room

Location
Off A487, 6 miles N of Cardigan. Follow brown tourist signs

Opening
Daily: Easter–Oct 10.30am–5pm

Admission
Adult £3.95, Child £1.95, Concs £3.75

Contact
Felinwynt, Cardigan, Ceredigion SA43 1RT

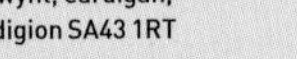

t 01239 810882/810250
w butterflycentre.co.uk
e dandldevereux@btinternet.com

625 Llandrindod Wells

The National Cycle Collection

1 hr+ All year

How big is a penny-farthing's wheel? And just how uncomfortable were those early cycles compared with today's high-tech versions? See more than 250 bicycles from 1819, such as the hobby-horse, boneshakers and penny-farthings up to the most modern cycles of today.

* The Dunlop story
* Displays about past racing stars

Location
Just off Temple Street in town centre. Llandrindod Wells is on A483

Opening
Mar–Oct daily 10am–4pm;
Nov–Feb Tue, Thu & Sun 10am–4pm

Admission
Adult £3, Child £1, Concs £2

Contact
The Automobile Palace, Temple Street, Llandrindod Wells, Powys LD1 5DL

t 01597 825531
w cyclemuseum.org.uk
e cycle.museum@care4free.net

626 Llangorse

Llangorse Rope & Riding Centre

4 hrs+ All year

The centre offers a range of indoor and outdoor climbing and riding activities, from scaling rock surfaces and crossing rope bridges to trekking and hacking. There are qualified instructors on hand and onsite accommodation is available.

* Largest indoor climbing & riding centre in Wales
* WTB's Best New Business in Wales Award 2006

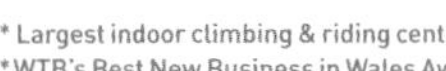       

Location
On B4560, off A40
Brecon–Abergavenny road

Opening
Climb Daily: Mon–Sat 9am–10pm, Sun 9am–5pm
Ride Daily: 10am–4.30pm

Admission
Please phone or visit the website for details

Contact
Gilfach Farm, Llangorse, Brecon Beacons, Powys LD3 7UH

t 01874 658272
w activityuk.com
e info@activity.uk.com

627 Llanwrda

Dolaucothi Gold Mines

  2 hrs+  Easter–Oct

These unique gold mines are set amid wooded hillsides overlooking the beautiful Cothi Valley. The Romans, who exploited the site almost 2,000 years ago, left behind a complex of pits, channels, adits and tanks. Mining resumed in the C19 and peaked in 1938.

* Historical tours
* Opportunity to pan for gold

Location
Between Lampeter & Llanwrda on A482

Opening
Daily: Easter–Oct 10am–5pm

Admission
Adult £3.40, Child £1.70

Contact
Pumsaint, Llanwrda SA19 8US

t 01558 650177
w nationaltrust.org.uk
e dolaucothi@nationaltrust.org.uk

628 Llanwyddyn

Lake Vyrnwy Nature Reserve

  2 hrs+  All year

This man-made lake was completed in 1888. In dry weather, if the water level drops far enough, the ruins of the submerged village of Llanwyddyn reappear. With various hides, vantage points and nature trails, it is a spectacular place for bird-watching.

* Moorland, woodland & water habitats
* Craft shops & café

Location
10 miles W of Llanfyllin

Opening
Apr–Dec daily 10.30am–5.30pm;
Jan–Mar Sat–Sun 10.30am–4.30pm

Admission
Free

Contact
Brynawel, Llanwyddyn,
Powys SY10 0LZ

t 01691 870278
w rspb.org.uk
e vyrnwy@rspb.org.uk

629 Machnylleth

Centre for Alternative Technology

3 hrs+ All year

This is a 40-acre haven of biodiversity. It has examples of wind, water and solar power, energy conservation, environmentally sound buildings, self-builds, organic agriculture and alternative sewage systems. In summer entry is via a unique water-balanced cliff railway.

* Largest public display centre of its kind in Europe
* Interactive games & gadgetry in redevoloped visitor centre

Location
3 miles N of Machynlleth on A487 to Dolgellau. Clearly signed

Opening
Daily: Apr–mid Jul 10.30am–5.30pm; mid Jul–Aug 9.30am–6pm; Sep–Oct 10am–5.30pm; Nov–Mar 10am–dusk

Admission
Adult £8, Child £4, Concs £7

Contact
Machynlleth, Powys SY20 9AZ

t 01654 705950
w cat.org.uk
e info@cat.org.uk

630 Machynlleth

Corris Craft Centre

2 hrs+ Apr–Nov

Corris Craft Centre is home to 10 craft workshops in which visitors are invited to see the skills of the craftworkers and to buy from the displays of wooden toymaking, pottery, jewellery, leatherwork, handcarved candles, glassware, wood-turning and card-designing.

* Patchwork quilting & rustic furniture for sale

Location
On A487 between Machynlleth & Dolgellau

Opening
Daily: Apr–Nov 10am–5.30pm
Please phone for details of winter opening times

Admission
Free

Contact
Corris, Machynlleth, Powys SY20 9RF

t 01654 761584
w kingarthurslabyrinth.com
e king.arthurs.labyrinth@corris-wales.co.uk

631 Machynlleth

King Arthur's Labyrinth

2 hrs+ Apr–Nov

Glide in a boat through an underground waterfall and deep into the spectacular caverns under the mountains where tales of King Arthur are told with stunning sound and light effects. Back above ground, join the Bard's Quest to search for legends lost in the Maze of Time.

* Large fully operational craft centre
* Shop sells items on the Arthurian theme

Location
On A487 between Machynlleth & Dolgellau

Opening
Daily: Apr–5 Nov 10am–5pm (last tour 5pm)

Admission
Adult £5.50, Child £3.90, Concs £4.95

Contact
Corris, Machynlleth, Powys SY20 9RF

t 01654 761584
w kingarthurslabyrinth.com
e king.arthurs.labyrinth@corris-wales.co.uk

632 Rhayader

Gigrin Farm

1 hr+ All year

A family-run upland sheep farm with wonderful views of the Wye and Elan valleys. It has breeding ewes along with ponies, assorted ducks and a number of pea fowl. In 1994 it became the Official Kite Country, Red Kite Feeding Station – a big draw for bird-watchers.

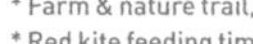

* Farm & nature trail, new wetland project
* Red kite feeding times 2pm summer & 3pm winter

Location
On A470, ½ mile S of Rhayader

Opening
Daily: 1pm–5pm

Admission
Adult £3, Child £1, Concs £2.50

Contact
South Street, Rhayader, Powys LD6 5BL

t 01597 810243
w gigrin.co.uk
e redkites@gigrin.co.uk

633 Presteigne

The Judge's Lodging

1 hr+ Mar–Dec

Explore the gas-lit world of the Victorian judges and their servants and felonious guests at this national award-winning, historic house. It is totally hands-on, with an eavesdropping audio tour. Grim cells and a vast courtroom echo to the trial of a local duck thief.

* Family-friendly with kids' activity boxes
* Local history exhibition

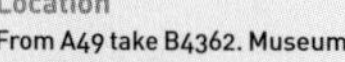

Location
From A49 take B4362. Museum is in town centre

Opening
Mar–Oct daily 10am–5pm; Nov–Dec Wed–Sun 10am–4pm (closed 22 Dec–1 Mar)

Admission
Adult £4.95, Child £3.95, Concs £4.50

Contact
Broad Street, Presteigne, Powys, Mid Wales LD8 2AD

t 01544 260650
w judgeslodging.org.uk
e info@judgeslodging.org.uk

634 Welshpool

Powis Castle & Garden

3 hrs Mar–Oct

This world-famous garden, overhung with enormous clipped yews, shelters rare and tender plants, and includes statues, an orangery and an aviary on the terraces. The medieval castle contains one of the finest collections of paintings and furniture in Wales.

* Collection of Indian treasures at the Clive Museum
* Beautiful interiors dating from 1600 to 1904

 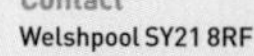

Location
1 mile S of Welshpool; signed from A483

Opening
Please phone for details

Admission
Adult £9.60, Child £4.80
Garden £6.60, £3.30

Contact
Welshpool SY21 8RF

t 01938 551944
w nationaltrust.org.uk
e powiscastle@nationaltrust.org.uk

635 Anglesey

Anglesey Sea Zoo

2 hrs+ Feb–Oct

This is Wales's largest marine aquarium, nestling on the shores of the Menai Strait. With more than 50 displays, the Sea Zoo has recreated the habitats of the fauna and flora that can be found around Anglesey and the North Wales coastline.

* Major seahorse conservation project
* Lobster hatchery & gift & pearl shop

Location
On A55 cross Britannia Bridge on to Anglesey & follow brown lobster signs to Brynsiencyn. Nearest railway station is Bangor

Opening
Daily: Feb–Mar 11am–3pm; Easter–Oct 10am–6pm

Admission
High season Adult £6.95, Child £5.95, Concs £6.50 *Low season* Adult £5.95, Child £4.95, Concs £5.50

Contact
Brynsiencyn, Isle of Anglesey LL61 6TQ

t 01248 430411
w angleseyseazoo.co.uk
e info@angleseyseazoo.co.uk

636 Anglesey

Plas Newydd

3 hrs

Apr–Oct

This C18 house built by James Wyatt is a fine mixture of classical and Gothic. Restyled in the 1930s, the house is famous for its association with Whistler, whose work is exhibited here. There is also a museum for the 1st Marquess of Anglesey who led the cavalry at the Battle of Waterloo.

* Marine walk on the Menai Strait
* Fine spring garden with Australasian arboretum

Location
Junctions 7 & 8 off A55

Opening
Apr–Oct Sat–Wed
House 12noon–5pm
Gardens 11am–5.30pm

Admission
Adult £6, Child £3

Contact
Llanfairpwll, Anglesey LL61 6DQ

t 01248 715272/714795
w nationaltrust.org.uk
e plasnewydd@nationaltrust.org.uk

637 Blaenau Ffestiniog

Llechwedd Slate Caverns

2 hrs

All year

Take two underground train rides – The Miner's Tramway takes passengers into the mountain, past early Victorian mining remains and spectacular caverns; the Deep Mine descends on Britain's steepest passenger railway, with a gradient of 1:1.8.

* Explore 10 chambers on foot
* Experience life in the Victorian village

Location
On A470 between Blaenau Ffestiniog & Dolwyddelan

Opening
Daily: Apr–Sep 10am–5.15pm;
Oct–Mar 10am–4.15pm

Admission
One tour Adult £8.25, Child £6.75, Concs £7.50
Combined tours £13.50, £9.50, £12

Contact
Blaenau Ffestiniog LL41 3NB

t 01766 830306
w llechwedd-slate-caverns.co.uk
e quarrytours@aol.com

638 Caernarfon

Caernarfon Castle

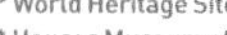

1 hr+

All year

Designed to replicate the walls of Constantinople, with its unique polygonal towers, intimidating battlements and colour-banded masonry, the castle dominates the town. In 1969 it was the setting for the investiture of Prince Charles as Prince of Wales.

* World Heritage Site
* Houses Museum of the Royal Welsh Fusiliers

Location
In town centre on A55. Nearest railway station is Bangor

Opening
Daily: Apr–May & Oct 9.30am–5pm;
Jun–Sep 9.30am–6pm;
Nov–Mar Mon–Sat 9.30am–4pm,
Sun 11am–4pm

Admission
Adult £4.90, Child & Concs £4.50

Contact
Castle Ditch, Caernarfon, Gwynedd LL55 2AY

t 01286 677617
w cadw.wales.gov.uk

639 Caernarfon

Welsh Highland Railway (Caernarfon)

  3 hrs  All year

Take a 12-mile ride, from the coast to the slopes of Snowdon, on North Wales's newest railway. Enjoy the spectacular scenery of lakes, mountains and forest en route to the heart of Snowdonia itself.

* Charge of £2.50 for dogs

Location
Main railway station on St Helens Road in Caernarfon, signed from A487

Opening
Daily: Mar–Oct; limited winter service, please phone for details

Admission
Adult £16.50, Child £8.25, Concs £13.20 (Adult price includes 1 child)

Contact
Harbour Station, Porthmadog, Gwynedd LL49 9NF

t 01766 516024
w festrail.co.uk
e enquiries@festrail.co.uk

640 Chirk

Chirk Castle

  2 hrs  Easter–Oct

A magnificent Marcher fortress, completed in 1310. The austere exterior belies the comfortable and elegant state rooms inside, with elaborate plasterwork, superb Adam-style furniture, tapestries and portraits. There is also a formal garden of clipped yew, roses and climbers.

* Renovated laundry room
* Terrace with stunning views & a classical pavilion

Location
1 mile off A5, 2 miles W of Chirk

Opening
Easter–Oct Wed–Sun 12noon–5pm

Admission
Adult £7, Child £3.50

Contact
Chirk, Wrexham LL14 5AF

t 01691 777701
w nationaltrust.org.uk
e chirkcastle@nationaltrust.org.uk

641 Colwyn Bay

The Welsh Mountain Zoo

4 hrs+

All year

The beautiful gardens which are home to this caring conservation zoo are set high above the breathtaking Colwyn Bay. Visit the New Sealions Rock! and watch the daily shows including Penguins' Playtime, Chimp Encounter, Sealion Feeding and Birds of Prey Display.

* Shows weather permitting, during summer
* Children's farm & Jungle Adventureland

Location
3 min from A55 (Rhos-on-Sea exit). Follow signs

Opening
Daily: *summer* 9.30am–6pm
winter 9.30am–5pm

Admission
Adult £7.75, Child £5.50, Concs £6.60

Contact
Old Highway, Colwyn Bay, North Wales LL28 5UY

t 01492 532938
w welshmountainzoo.org

©NTPL

642 Gwynedd

Greenwood Forest Park

4 hrs+

Mar–Nov

Enjoy family adventure and fun at Greenwood Forest Park with its exciting Green Dragon family roller coaster. Ride the Great Green Run, the longest sledge slide in Wales. Have a Jungle Boat Adventure, shoot traditional longbows, build dens or enjoy a Forest Theatre show.

* World's only people-powered roller coaster
* Crocodile maze & treetop tower

Location
Take A4144, leading to B4366 between Bangor & Caernarfon, near Bethel off B4366

Opening
Daily: Mar–Sep 10am–5.30pm; school summer hols 10am–6pm; Oct–Nov 11am–5pm

Admission
Please phone or visit the website for details

Contact
Y Felinheli, Gwynedd, North Wales LL56 4QN

t 01248 670076
w greenwoodforestpark.co.uk
e info@greenwoodforestpark.co.uk

643 Llanberis

Snowdon Mountain Railway

2 hrs+ Mar–Nov

This tremendously ambitious feat of engineering is unique in Britain. The rack-and-pinion railway, which rises to within 66 feet of the summit of the highest mountain in England and Wales (3,560ft), was built and opened in 1896.

* Owing to renovations during 2007, trains will travel only as far as Clogwyn

Location
Llanberis railway station on A4086, 7½ miles from Caernarfon. 15 min drive from A55/A5 junction at Bangor. Nearest railway station is Bangor

Opening
Daily: mid March–Nov
Please phone for details

Admission
Please phone for details

Contact
Llanberis, Gwynedd LL55 4TY

t 0870 4580033
w snowdonrailway.co.uk
e info@snowdonrailway.co.uk

644 Llangollen

Llangollen Wharf

1 hr+ Easter–Oct

Take a horse-drawn boat trip or a motorised aqueduct cruise along the beautiful Llangollen Canal. Longer horse-drawn trips can be arranged for large groups, and a self-steer day-hire boat for groups of up to 10 people is also available.

* Lunches & cream teas can be pre-ordered

Location
Off A5 Shrewsbury road & near A483 to Chester

Opening
Daily: Easter–Oct 10am–5pm

Admission
Horse-drawn boats Adult £4.50, Child £2.50
Aqueduct cruise £9, £7

Contact
Welsh Canal Holiday Craft Ltd
The Wharf, Llangollen LL20 8TA

t 01978 860702

© www.proadventure.co.uk, proadventure ltd

645 Llangollen

ProAdventure

4 hrs+ All year

Try a wide variety of outdoor adventure activities from gentle open canoeing to adrenaline-filled white-water rafting. Other activities include gorge walking, kayaking, rock climbing, abseiling and mountain biking.

* Activity weekends & family days available
* Pre-booking essential

WC

Location
Situated in E of N Wales roughly 8 miles from Wrexham & 18 miles from Chester. Manchester, Liverpool & Birmingham are 1½ hours or less away

Opening
Please phone for details

Admission
Please phone for details

Contact
23 Castle Street,
Llangollen LL20 8NY

t 01978 861912
w proadventure.co.uk
e sales@proadventure.co.uk

646 Minffordd

Portmeirion

  4 hrs+  All year

This unique village is set on a private peninsula on the southern shores of Snowdonia. It was created by the Welsh architect Clough Williams-Ellis (1883–1978) in order to demonstrate how a naturally beautiful place could be developed without its being spoiled.

* Used as a location for cult TV series *The Prisoner*
* Cottages in the village let by Portmeirion Hotel

Location
Signed off A487 at Minffordd between Penrhyndeudraeth & Porthmadog

Opening
Daily: 9.30am–5.30pm

Admission
Adult £6.50, Child £3.50, Concs £5

Contact
Gwynedd LL48 6ET

t 01766 770000
w portmeirion-village.com
e info@portmeirion-village.com

647 Porthmadog

The Ffestiniog Railway

  3 hrs+  All year

Take a 13-mile ride on this historical railway. For 140 years steam-hauled trains have run from the harbour at Porthmadog to the mountains at Blaenau Ffestiniog, passing farmland and forest, mountains and moors, lakes and waterfalls.

* Regular special events
* Refurbished café/bar at Harbour railway station

Location
Next to harbour in Porthmadog on A487

Opening
Daily: Mar-Nov; limited winter service
Please phone for details

Admission
Adult £16.50, Child £8.25, Concs £13.20
(Adult price includes 1 child)

Contact
Harbour Station, Porthmadog, Gwynedd LL49 9NF

t 01766 516000
w festrail.co.uk
e info@festrail.co.uk

648 Blaenafon

Big Pit National Mining Museum

 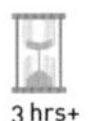 

3 hrs+ Feb-Nov

This is a real colliery. Kitted out in helmet, cap-lamp and battery pack, you descend 300 feet (90 metres) to another world – of shafts, coalfaces and levels, of underground roadways, air doors and stables. It now features new interactive exhibitions.

* Enjoy simulated mining
* Winding engine house & blacksmith's workshop

Location
Leave M4 at junction 25a/26, then follow signs from A465

Opening
Daily: Feb–Nov 9.30am–5pm
Underground tours run 10am–3.30pm

Admission
Free

Contact
Blaenafon, Torfaen NP4 9XP

t 01495 790311
w nmgw.ac.uk
e bigpit@nmgw.ac.uk

649 Caerphilly

Caerphilly Castle

1 hr+ All year

Caerphilly Castle is one of the most impressive examples of medieval castle building in Britain. Spread over some 30 acres of land, it is the second-largest castle in Britain after Windsor. In the words of the poet Tennyson, 'It isn't a castle – it's a town in ruins.'

* The Big Cheese weekend 27 Jul, nonstop entertainment
* Many summer demonstrations & events

Location
Exit M4 at junction 32, then take A470 or A469 for Caerphilly

Opening
Daily: 31 Mar–31 May & 28 Sep–25 Oct 9.30am–5pm; 1 Jun–27 Sep 9.30am–6pm; 26 Oct–3. Mar Mon–Sat 9.30am–4.30pm, Sun 11am–4pm

Admission
Adult £3.50, Child & Concs £3

Contact
Bridge Street, Caerphilly, Wales CF83 1JD

t 02920 883143
w cadw.wales.gov.uk
e caerphilly.castle@cadw.co.uk

650 Cardiff

Cardiff Castle

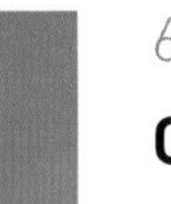    

2 hrs+ All year

Cardiff Castle is one of Wales's leading tourist attractions. Situated in the very heart of the capital, alongside city-centre shopping and the magnificent Bute Park, the castle's enchanting fairytale towers are matched by an elaborate and splendid interior.

* Guided tours of lavish & opulent interiors
* Set in beautiful grounds

    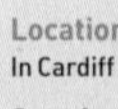

Location
In Cardiff city centre

Opening
Daily: Mar–Oct 9.30am–6pm; Nov–Feb 9.30am–5pm

Admission
Adult £6.95, Child £4.30, Concs £5.40

Contact
Castle Street, Cardiff CF10 3RB

t 02920 878100
w cardiffcastle.com
e cardiffcastle@cardiff.gov.uk

651 Cardiff

Millennium Stadium Tours

  1 hr  All year

Experience the moments before a match when Wales charge down the players' tunnel cheered on by tens of thousands of rugby or football fans. Feel the pre-match tension and the joy of victory in the changing rooms before celebrating in the Cardiff Arms Suite.

* Sit in the Royal Box & lift a trophy
* One of the proposed venues for the 2012 Olympics

Location
In Cardiff city centre

Opening
Daily: 9.30am–5.30pm

Admission
Adult £5.50, Child £3, Concs £3.50

Contact
Millennium Stadium Shop, Gate 3, Westgate Street, Cardiff CF10 1JE

t 02920 822040
w millenniumstadium.co.uk

652 Cardiff

St Fagans National History Museum

  3 hrs+  All year

Standing in the grounds of the magnificent St Fagans Castle, this museum shows how the people of Wales have lived, worked and spent their leisure time over the past 500 years. More than 30 buildings have been moved from various parts of Wales and reassembled here.

* Exhibitions of costume, daily life & farming tools

Location
4 miles W of Cardiff city centre. Exit M4 at junction 33

Opening
Daily: 10am–5pm

Admission
Free. Car park £2.50

Contact
St Fagans, Cardiff CF5 6XB

t 02920 573500
w museumwales.ac.uk
e welshlife@museumwales.ac.uk

653 Cardiff

Techniquest

  2 hrs+  All year

This science discovery centre in Cardiff Bay has more than 150 hands-on exhibits that bring science and technology to life. Among the amazing activities, visitors can fire a rocket, launch a hot-air balloon, play a giant keyboard and much more. Musiquest was new in autumn 2005.

* Explore the universe in the planetarium
* Enjoy a fascinating interactive Science Theatre show

Location
Exit M4 at junction 33, then follow signs on A4232

Opening
Daily: Mon–Fri 9.30am–4.30pm
Sat–Sun & Bank Hols 10.30am–5pm

Admission
Adult £6.90, Child & Concs £4.80

Contact
Stuart Street, Cardiff CF10 5BW
t 02920 475475
w techniquest.org
e info@techniquest.org

654 Cardigan

Cardigan Heritage Centre

  1 hr  Mar–Oct

Set in a converted C18 warehouse on Teifi Wharf, the centre has permanent exhibits tracing the history of Cardigan from the days before the coming of the Normans right up to the present day. There are also static displays and regularly changing exhibitions.

* Guided tours by appointment
* Arts activities & quizzes for children

Location
Take A487 to Cardigan. Centre is on bank of River Teifi, next to Cardigan Bridge

Opening
mid Mar–Oct Sun–Fri 10am–5pm

Admission
Adult £2, Child £1, Concs £1.50

Contact
Teifi Wharf, Cardigan, Wales
t 01239 614404

655 Cardigan

Cardigan Island Coastal Farm Park

  3 hrs+   Mar–Oct

This park is located on a stunning headland overlooking the marine reserve of Cardigan Island, home to thousands of nesting seabirds. On the cliffs below there is a colony of Atlantic grey seals, and dolphins are frequently sighted. For young visitors there are plenty of farm animals to see.

* Beautiful cliff-top walks
* Restaurant and giftshop

Location
M4 from Cardiff or Swansea to Camarthen. Then A484 to Cardigan. Follow B4548 signs to Gwbert. A487 from Aberystwyth. A478 from Tenby

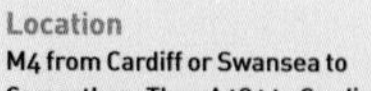

Opening
Daily: Mar–Oct 10am–6pm

Admission
Adult 3.50, Child £2.50, Concs £3.20

Contact
Gwbert, Cardigan SA43 1PR
t 01239 612196
w cardiganisland.com

656 Carmarthen

National Botanic Garden of Wales

  2 hrs+ All year

The first new national botanic garden in the UK for more than 200 years, this centre is dedicated to conservation, science, education, leisure and the arts. In the former C18 park of Middleton Hall, this 568-acre estate has a pollution-free environment, spectacular views and a rich heritage.

* Apiary gardens
* Regular calendar of special events

Location
On A48 near Carmarthen, signed from M4 & A40

Opening
Daily: Easter–Oct 10am–6pm;
Oct–Mar 10am–4.30pm

Admission
Adult £7.50, Child £3.50, Concs £5.50

Contact
Garden of Wales, Llanarthne, Carmarthenshire SA32 8HG
t 01558 668768
w gardenofwales.org.uk
e info@gardenofwales.org.uk

657 Chepstow

Tintern Abbey

  1 hr  All year

This Cistercian abbey is one of the greatest monastic ruins in Wales, and since the early C20 every effort has been made to maintain what is one of the finest and most complete abbey churches in the country. A favourite of many artists and the poet Wordsworth.

* Site exhibition
* Audio tour & Braille plan

Location
Off A466 4 miles N of Chepstow

Opening
Daily: 31 Mar–31 May 9.30am–5pm;
1 Jun–27 Sep 9.30am–6pm;
28 Sep–25 Oct 9.30am–5pm;
26 Oct–30 Mar Mon–Sat 9.30am–4pm,
Sun 11am–4pm

Admission
Adult £3.50, Child & Concs £3

Contact
Plas Carew, Units 5–7 Cefn Coed, Nantgarw, Cardiff CF15 7QQ

t 01291 689251
w cadw.wales.gov.uk
e brite.winterborn.cadw@wales.gsi.gov.uk

658 Dan-yr-Ogof

National Showcaves Centre for Wales

  2 hrs+  Apr–Oct

Descend below ground to explore a wonderland of stalactites, waterfalls and natural cave formations extending over 10 kilometres. The tour of the showcaves is self-guided but commentaries play at selected points so you can enjoy a visit at your own speed.

* Top Wales visitor attraction
* One of 10 attractions on site

Location
On A4067 between Swansea & Brecon. Signed from junction 45 of M4

Opening
Daily: Apr–Oct 10am–5pm (last admission to caves 3pm)

Admission
Adult £10, Child £6

Contact
Dan-yr-Ogof, nr Abercraf, Upper Swansea Valley, Powys SA9 1GJ

t 01639 730801
w showcaves.co.uk
e james@showcaves.co.uk

659 Llanboidy

Welsh Chocolate Farm

  2 hrs  Apr–Oct

Engage all of your senses learning all about chocolate at this award-winning centre. Stroll through the model village and see the chocolate being crafted into a variety of delicious products. At the cinema learn about its history and cultivation.

* 2 chocolate shops & guided tours throughout the day
* Hands-on chocolate decorating

Location
Leave A40 at St Clares then follow signs

Opening
Apr–Oct Mon–Sat 10am–5pm

Admission
Adult 3.25, Child £2.85

Contact
Llanboidy SA34 0EX

t 01994 448800
w welshchocolatefarm.com
e chocolate.farm@btopenworld.com

660 Llandeilo

Floating Sensations

3 hrs+ May–Sep

Take a tranquil flight with breathtaking views over the beautiful Carmarthenshire countryside. Flying in small balloons for only six people, our passengers get a truly personal experience and feel part of our friendly team.

* Pre-booking essential
* Highly weather-dependent

Location
Take A476 towards Llandeilo. Turn left at cross road towards village of Golden Grove. Take first right after Towy bridge & turn right after 2nd bridge & then 1st right again. Birdshill Farm is 3rd driveway on the left

Opening
Please phone for details

Admission
Please phone for details

Contact
Birds Hill, Llandeilo SA19 6SG

t 01558 823983
w floatingoverwales.com
e enquiries@floatingoverwales.com

661 Monmouth

Caldicot Castle & Country Park

2 hrs+ Apr–Sep

This castle, set in 55 acres of beautiful parkland, was founded by the Normans, developed in royal hands as a stronghold in the Middle Ages and restored as a Victorian family home. Explore the medieval towers and enjoy breathtaking views from the battlements.

* Audio tours for adults & children

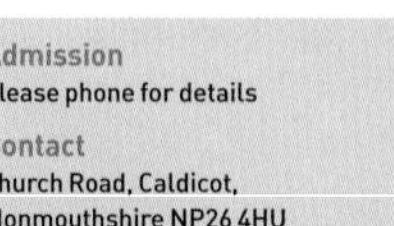

Location
From M4 take junction 23 & B4245. From M48 take junction 2 on to B4245. Signed from B4245

Opening
Daily: Apr–Sep 11am–5pm

Admission
Please phone for details

Contact
Church Road, Caldicot, Monmouthshire NP26 4HU

t 01291 420241
w caldicotcastle.co.uk
e caldicot@monmouthshire.gov.uk

©NTPL/Andrew Butler

662 Narberth

Colby Woodland Garden

3 hrs Apr–Oct

This attractive woodland garden has a fine collection of rhododendrons and azaleas. Follow the pathways through secluded valleys and woodland. The house is not open to the public but there is access to the walled garden.

* Regular guided walks with garden staff

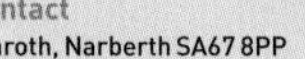

Location
1 mile inland from Amroth, follow signs from A477 (Tenby/Carmarthen)

Opening
Daily: Apr–Oct 10am–5pm

Admission
Adult £4, Child £2

Contact
Amroth, Narberth SA67 8PP

t 01834 811885
w nationaltrust.org.uk

663 Neath

Aberdulais Falls

1 hr+ Mar–Dec

For more than 400 years this famous waterfall provided the energy to drive the wheels of industry, from that of copper to tinplate. A unique hydro-electricity scheme makes Aberdulais Falls energy self-sufficient, producing power using a giant waterwheel.

* Waterwheel is the largest used in Europe
* Visitor & Tourist Information Centre new for 2007

Location
On A4109, 3 miles NE of Neath, 4 miles from junction 43 of M4

Opening
Please phone for details

Admission
Please phone for details

Contact
Aberdulais, nr Neath SA10 8EU

t 01639 636674
w nationaltrust.org.uk

664 Swansea

Craig-y-nos Country Park

2 hrs All year

An ideal place for a stroll through trees, alongside water and in grassy meadows. There are no rides, amusements, playgrounds or machines, just 40 acres of historic gardens to enjoy. The centre has a 'go-wild' zone for kids where they can listen to bats and climb inside a hollow tree.

* New eco-trail
* Events throughout the year

Location
Midway between Brecon & Swansea on A4067

Opening
Please phone for details

Admission
Free. Car park fee

Contact
Brecon Road, Pen-y-cae, Swansea Valley SA9 1GL

t 01639 730395
w breconbeacons.org
e cyncp@breconbeacons.org

665 Swansea

National Waterfront Museum

2 hrs+ All year

This stunning museum combining a former dockside warehouse with new exhibition galleries explores the industrialisation of Wales in a series of interactive displays. See how industry has shaped everything in Wales from landscape and lifestyles to health and religion.

* Regular events & special exhibitions throughout the year

Location
On Marina next to old Leisure Centre building opposite Princess Way

Opening
Daily: 10am–5pm

Admission
Free

Contact
Oystermouth Road, Maritime Quarter, Swansea SA1 3RD

t 01792 638950
w waterfrontmuseum.co.uk
e waterfront@museumwales.ac.uk

666 Tenby

Heatherton Country Sports Park

4 hrs All year

This leisure park offers a wide range of activities including clay-pigeon shooting, coarse fishing, archery, pitch and putt, indoor bowls, baseball, go-karting, paintball, adventure golf, horse-riding, bumper boats, a driving range and a maze.

* Play Robot Wars
* Suitable for groups & birthday parties

Location
2 miles outside Tenby on B4318 Tenby–Pembroke road

Opening
Daily: Jun–Sep 10am–10pm; Oct–May 10am–6pm

Admission
Free. Pay-as-you-go activities

Contact
St Florence, Tenby, Pembrokeshire SA69 9EE

t 01646 651025
w heatherton.co.uk

667 Tenby

Manor House Wild Animal Park

4 hrs Easter-Sep

Set in wooded grounds and floral gardens beside an C18 manor house, the zoo has a close-encounters unit where visitors can feed and pet animals, including snakes. There are regular falconry displays and informative talks.

* Visitors may be allowed to hold certain birds of prey

Location
3 miles outside Tenby on B4318

Opening
Daily: Easter–Sep 10am–6pm

Admission
Adult £6, Child & Concs £5

Contact
St Florence, Tenby,
Pembrokeshire SA70 8RJ

t 01646 651201
w manorhousewildanimalpark.co.uk
e mail@manorhousewildanimalpark.co.uk

668 Treharris

Llancaiach Fawr Manor

1 hr+ All year

This splendid semi-fortified Tudor manor house has been refurbished to its C17 state. Step back in time to the year 1645 where the servants of the household will tell you tales of their lives during the Civil War years.

* Listen to the gossip of the day – from more than 350 years ago
* Stroll in the formal gardens

Location
On B4254 between Nelson & Gelligaer, 2½ miles from A470

Opening
Mar–Oct daily 10am–5pm;
Nov–Feb Tue–Sun 10am–5pm

Admission
Adult £4.95, Child £3.50, Concs £3.75

Contact
Nelson, Treharris CF46 6ER

t 01443 412248
w caerphilly.gov.uk/visiting

669 Trelewis

Welsh International Climbing & Activity Centre

4 hrs+ All year

In addition to climbing, the centre offers a wealth of indoor and outdoor activities for all abilities, including abseiling, caving, gorge walking, kayaking, mountain walking and expeditions. It also has a fitness suite and family and bunkhouse accommodation.

* One of the biggest indoor climbing walls in Europe
* High-ropes assault course

Location
From B4255 follow signs to Bedlinog, then ½ mile from Trelewis

Opening
Daily: Mon–Fri 9am–10pm,
Sat–Sun 9am–7pm

Admission
Prices vary according to activity

Contact
Taff Bargoed Centre, Trelewis,
Merthyr Tydfil CF46 6RD

t 01443 710749
w indoorclimbingwalls.co.uk
e enquiries@indoorclimbingwalls.co.uk

Arndale, Yorkshire Dales

Yorkshire

East Riding North Yorkshire
South Yorkshire West Yorkshire

©MAPS IN MINUTES™ 2006. ©Crown Copyright, Ordnance Survey 20
Appleby-in-Westmorland
856-857
Newton Aycliffe
Stockton-on-Tees
871
Middlesbrough
Darlington
861-862
Guisborough
688
Brough
TEESSIDE
Whitby
Stokesley
Scotch Corner
Richmond
North York Moors
M6
Catterick
Sedbergh
Hawes
686
Leyburn
Northallerton
Scalby
Scarborough
694-695
Thirsk
Pickering
Kirkby Lonsdale
NORTH YORKSHIRE
683
684
Filey
680
687
Ripon
Easingwold
Malton
Flamborough Head
ENGLAND
691-693
Bridlington
690
A1(M)
670-673
Settle
Knaresborough
Driffield
681-682
Harrogate
685
Skipton
York
689
Pocklington
LANCASHIRE
696-697
Ilkley
Wetherby
698-710
Market Weighton
Keighley
Yeadon
LEEDS & BRADFORD
674
Clitheroe
Colne
Bingley
Tadcaster
EAST RIDING OF YORKSHIRE
815
Nelson
Shipley
LEEDS
Beverley
805-806
Burnley
BRADFORD
Garforth
Selby
HULL
M621
791
Accrington
719-721
722-727
M62
Hessle
Halifax
Castleford
675-679
Withernsea
Blackburn
Rawtenstall
Todmorden
Batley
Goole
792-793
Brighouse
M62
Pontefract
Barton-upon-Humber
728-730
Wakefield
Chorley
W. YORKSHIRE
M18
454
Rochdale
Hemsworth
821
M66
M62
Huddersfield
Thorne
Immingham
798-804
Scunthorpe
Grimsby
Spurn Head
Bury
M1
M180
M181
M180
Standish
Bolton
Middleton
Barnsley
453
Cleethorpes
Wigan
810
M60
Brigg
448
Oldham
Doncaster
822
823-834
Penistone
SOUTH YORKSHIRE
Caistor
Salford
MANCHESTER
711
St Helens
Stocksbridge
M62
753-754
Glossop
A1(M)
Bawtry
Rotherham
The Wolds
Sale
M60
M60
Stockport
SHEFFIELD
Gainsborough
712
731
Cheadle
713
449
Warrington
Altrincham
714-717
Louth
M56
MANCHESTER
SHEFFIELD CITY
Market Rasen
758
Peak
419-421
Wilmslow
Whaley Bridge
M1
Worksop
Retford
Knutsford
Dronfield
District
740
446
718
491-493
Staveley
741-744
Buxton
422-423
Northwich
Lincoln
Chesterfield
747-749
Macclesfield
M6
Middlewich
478
487-488
Horncastle
Washingborough
429
417
Bakewell
416
Ollerton
DERBYSHIRE
Congleton
Mansfield
752
Clay Cross
LINCOLNSHIRE
460
751
479
Biddulph
455
Sutton in Ashfield
NOTTINGHAMSHIRE
737
Matlock
480
Crewe
Leek
461
Coningsby
430-431
Kidsgrove
Kirkby in Ashfield
Alfreton
414
531
Newark-on-Trent
Wirksworth
424
489-490
541-542
547
Ripley
STOKE-ON-TRENT
447
432
Belper
745
Hucknall
Newcastle-under-Lyme
425
477
Sleaford
Boston
529
Ashbourne
481-486
534
538
Ilkeston
NOTTINGHAM
Nantwich
DERBY
Stapleford
Beeston
Grantham
Uttoxeter
Stone
426-428
Long Eaton
450-452
Market Drayton
STAFFORDSHIRE
530
546
418
Holbeach
Spalding
EAST MIDLANDS
Burton upon Trent
Melton Mowbray
Stafford
M1
Loughborough
Bourne
457-458
540
M6
Newport
539
Rugeley
532
415
442
434
The Fens
433
Ashby-de-la-Zouch
Coalville
RUTLAND
445
459
535-537
497-498
Stamford
Cannock
Lichfield
435-436
Oakham
Telford
512
528
M42
438-441
Wisbech
LEICESTERSHIRE
M54
548
Brownhills
Tamworth
494
516
523-524
LEICESTER
437
Uppingham
495
543-545
559
Oadby
WOLVERHAMPTON
600-602
Walsall
496
Peterborough
Sutton Coldfield
570
Hinckley
598-599
351-353
Bridgnorth
West Bromwich
M6
Blaby
March
M69
475
513-515
533
588
Nuneaton
Dudley
579-585
M1
Oundle
Market Harborough
444
595
591-593
BIRMINGHAM
Bedworth
Corby
A1(M)
Halesowen
468
BIRMINGHAM
596
Rothwell
464-465
Sawtry
355
Chatteris
603-604
Stourbridge
586-587
594
589-590
M6
Kidderminster
577-578
443
473
597
M5
Solihull
CAMBRIDGESHIRE
COVENTRY
469
Kettering
609-610
M42
347-
613
WEST MIDLANDS
553
Rugby
561
466
Huntingdon
Stourport-on-Severn
Bromsgrove
556
NORTHAMPTONSHIRE
M42
558
St Ives
607
M40
M45
463
Brampton
Redditch
Leamington
Wellingborough
Rushden
Waterbeach

LEEDS CI

670 Bridlington

Bempton Cliffs Nature Reserve

2 hrs | All year

One of the best places in Britain to see seabirds. More than 200,000 birds nest on the cliffs, including gannets, puffins, guillemots, razorbills and kittiwakes. Five safe viewing areas are situated along 3 miles of chalk cliffs. The first mile is suitable for wheelchairs.

* Gannets first colonised the cliffs in the 1920s
* Puffins can be seen in spring & summer

Location
On cliff road from Bempton, on B1229 from Flamborough to Filey

Opening
Visitor centre
Daily: Jan–Feb & Nov 9.30am–4pm; Mar–Oct 10am–5pm; Dec please phone for details

Admission
£3.50 car park fee for non-members

Contact
11 Cliff Lane, Bempton, Bridlington YO15 1JD

t 01262 851179
w rspb.org.uk

671 Bridlington

Bridlington Leisure World

 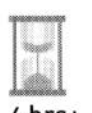 

4 hrs+ | All year

The complex includes three swimming pools, one with waves, slides, storm effects and water features, a 25m training pool and a learner pool. There is also a multi-purpose hall for indoor bowling and family activities plus a fitness studio.

* Small theatre & bar
* One of the East Riding's premier leisure attractions

Location
Off A165 (off the M62)

Opening
Please phone for details

Admission
Activities individually priced

Contact
The Promenade, Bridlington, Yorkshire YO15 2QQ

t 01262 606715
w bridlingtonleisure.co.uk
e adam.mainprize@eastriding.gov.uk

672 Bridlington

Park Rose Owl & Bird of Prey Centre

 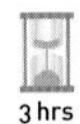  

3 hrs | Mar–Oct

Set in 3½ acres of woodland, the centre has 40 aviaries displaying many owls and birds of prey. There are daily guided information tours, and koi carp and aquatic plants to admire.

* Flying displays throughout summer, weather permitting
* Gift shop & tours by arrangement

Location
On A165/A166, 2 miles S of Bridlington

Opening
Daily: Mar–Oct 10am–5pm

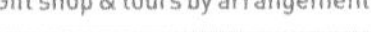

Admission
Adult £2, Child & Concs £1.50

Contact
Carnaby Covert Lane, Bridlington YO15 3QF

t 01262 606800

673 Bridlington

Sewerby Hall & Gardens

3 hrs | Apr–Oct

Set in 50 acres of early C19 parkland in a dramatic clifftop position overlooking Bridlington Bay, the hall contains a magnificent orangery, period rooms and art and photographic galleries. Attractions also include a beautiful walled garden and a pitch and putt golf course.

* Display of Amy Johnson's awards & trophies
* Children's zoo includes monkeys & penguins

Location
From Bridlington follow signs for Flamborough & then Sewerby

Opening
Hall Daily: Apr–Oct 10am–5pm
Gardens All year dawn–dusk

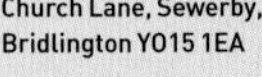

Admission
Adult £3.50, Child £1.50, Concs £2.80
Grounds Free

Contact
Church Lane, Sewerby, Bridlington YO15 1EA

t 01262 673769
w sewerby-hall.co.uk
e sewerby.hall@eastriding.gov.uk

674 Hornsea

Hornsea Museum

1 hr+ Easter–Sep

This award-winning museum shows how village life has changed in North Holderness from the pre-industrial age of the early C17 through to post WWII. Sited in an C18 farm house, the museum has a Victorian kitchen and other domestic rooms plus rural craft workshops.

* Local industrial display & photographic exhibition
* Extensive display of Hornsea pottery

Location
In town centre, off B1242

Opening
Easter–Sep Tue–Sat, Bank Hol Mon & autumn half-term 11am–5pm, Sun 2pm–5pm

Admission
Adult £2.50, Child & Concs £2

Contact
Burns Farm, 11 Newbegin, Hornsea HU18 1AB

t 01964 533443
w hornseamuseum.com
e contact@hornseamuseum.com

675 Hull

The Deep

2–3 hrs All year

Experience marine life close-up in this museum shaped like a ship. Take the world's only underwater lift, walk through subaqua tunnels, watch sharks galore swim overhead, then explore exhibitions about corals, Arctic sea life and the Big Bang.

* 10m -deep tank containing 2.5 million litres of water
* Lots of hands-on and interactive activities

Location
Within walking distance of town centre on banks of Humber

Opening
Daily: 10am–6pm

Admission
Adult £8, Child £6, Concs £6.50

Contact
Hull HU1 4DP

t 01482 381000
w thedeep.co.uk
e info@thedeep.co.uk

676 Hull

Ferens Art Gallery

1 hr+ All year

Opened in 1927, the award-winning Ferens Art Gallery combines internationally renowned permanent collections with exhibitions and live art. The first-class permanent collection of paintings and sculpture spans centuries, from the medieval period to the present day.

* Innovative Children's Gallery new in autumn 2005
* Masterpieces by Canaletto, Spencer & Hockney

Location
In city centre

Opening
Daily: Mon–Sat 10am–5pm, Sun 1.30pm–4.30pm

Admission
Free

Contact
Queen Victoria Square, Kingston upon Hull HU1 3RA

t 01482 613902
w hullcc.gov.uk/museums/ferens
e museums@hull.gov.uk

677 Hull

Fort Paull

2 hrs+ Mar–Dec

Fort Paull has more than 1,000 years of history, dating back to Viking landings. It has played a part in Britain's sea defences for almost 500 years – from its time as a fortress built by Henry VIII to the anti-aircraft defence visited by Sir Winston Churchill.

* The only surviving Blackburn Beverley aircraft
* Explore the underground labyrinths

Location
Village of Paull is S of Hull in direction of Hedon

Opening
Daily: Apr–Oct 10am–6pm; Nov–Dec & Mar 11am–4pm

Admission
Adults £4.50, Child & Concs £3

Contact
Battery Road, Paull, Hull HU12 8FP

t 01482 896236
w fortpaull.com
e fortpaull@aol.com

678 Hull

Hull Arena

2 hrs+ All year

An Olympic-size ice rink that is home to the Hull Stingrays, who play in the British National Ice Hockey Elite league. The rink is open to the public every day, for a variety of family sessions and discos. Times for these vary so it is best to phone in advance.

* One of the North's leading music venues
* See ice hockey played at the highest level

Location
Just off A63 in centre of Kingston upon Hull

Opening
Public skating Mon–Fri 12.15pm–3.30pm; Sat–Sun 10am–12noon & 2.15pm–4.15pm
Please phone to confirm disco sessions

Admission
All skating £3.20 + £1 skate hire
Evening disco £3.70

Contact
Kingston Street, Kingston upon Hull HU1 2DZ

t 01482 325252
w hullcc.gov.uk/leisure
e hullarena@hullcc.gov.uk

679 Hull

Streetlife Museum of Transport

2 hrs+ All year

Visit this award-winning attraction and experience a first-class collection of transport exhibits, including a motor car gallery, a major extension of the popular carriage gallery, a larger street scene with several shops and a hands-on interactive exhibition area.

* Supported by Heritage Lottery Funding
* Animated horses & simulated carriage rides

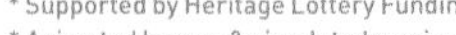

Location
In high street near Wilberforce House

Opening
Daily: Mon–Sat 10am–5pm, Sun 1.30pm–4.30pm

Admission
Free

Contact
High Street, Hull HU1 1PS

t 01482 613902
w hullcc.gov.uk/museums/streetlife
e museums@hull.gov.uk

680 Clapham

Ingleborough Cave

2 hrs+ All year

Ingleborough Cave is a wonderland of sculpted passages and beautiful caves, part of the enormous 17km Gaping Gill cave system. An expert guide will lead you more than half a kilometre into the mountain to see the stunning calcite flows, stalagmites and stalactites.

* Nature trail near entrance
* Santa's Grotto at Christmas

Location
Just off B1249 between Driffield & Beeford

Opening
Mar–mid Oct-daily 10am–5pm; mid-Oct–Feb Sat–Sun 10am–4pm

Admission
Adult £6, Child £3, Concs £4.50

Contact
Clapham LA2 8EE

t 01524 251242
w ingleboroughcave.co.uk
e info@ingleboroughcave.co.uk

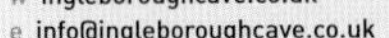

681 Harrogate

RHS Garden Harlow Carr

2 hrs All year

One of Yorkshire's most relaxing yet inspiring locations. Highlights include the spectacular Gardens Through Time, streamside, alpine, scented and kitchen gardens, contemporary herbaceous borders and woodland and wildflower meadows.

* Extensive plant centre & Betty's café
* All-year colour & interest

Location
Off B6162, 1½ miles from Harrogate town centre

Opening
Daily: Mar–Oct 9.30am–6pm; Nov–Feb 9.30am–4pm (last admission 1 hr before close)

Admission
Adult £6, Child £1.60
RHS members free

Contact
Crag Lane, Harrogate HG3 1QB

t 01423 565418
w rhs.org.uk/harlowcarr
e admin-harlowcarr@rhs.org.uk

682 Harrogate

Royal Pump Room Museum

1 hr+ All year

Visit the strongest sulphur wells in Europe, once a draw for more than 15,000 people every summer. You can find out what Harrogate's link is with Russian royalty and also see a display of old-fashioned shops. Don't forget to taste the water – it is something you will not forget.

* See historical spa treatments
* Combine a visit with Knaresborough Castle

Location
Within easy walking distance from any town centre car park. Follow signs

Opening
Apr–Oct Mon–Sat 10am–5pm, Sun 2pm–5pm; Nov–Mar Mon–Sat 10am–4pm, Sun 2pm–4pm

Admission
Adult £2.80, Child £1.50, Concs £1.70

Contact
Crown Place, Harrogate HG1 2RY

t 01423 556188
w harrogate.gov.uk/museum
e museum@harrogate.gov.uk

683 Helmsley

Duncombe Park

3 hrs May–Oct

Used as a girls' school for 60 years, Duncombe Park has been restored as a grand, 200-room family home, housing a fine collection of English and continental furniture. Its naturally landscaped gardens have fine views over valley and moors.

* 450 acres of parkland is National Nature Reserve
* Way-marked walks through woods & river valley

Location
1 mile from town centre

Opening
May–Oct Sun–Thu 11am–5.30pm
House tours 12.30pm–3.30pm hourly

Admission
Adult £7.25, Child £3.25, Concs £5.50

Contact
Helmsley YO62 5EB

t 01439 772625
w duncombepark.com
e info@duncombepark.com

684 Kirby Misperton

Flamingo Land Theme Park & Zoo

6 hrs+ Apr–Nov

The zoo is home to more than 1,000 animals, including tigers, zebras, monkeys, sealions and meerkats, and the largest flock of pink flamingos in the country. The bird walk has birds of all sizes from finches to ostriches and the park has eight roller coaster rides.

* Lost Kingdom display
* New Kumsli roller coaster

Location
Off A64 Scarborough–York road on A169 Malton–Pickering road

Opening
Daily: Apr–Nov 10am–5pm or 6pm
Please phone for details

Admission
Please phone for details

Contact
Kirby Misperton,
Malton YO17 6UX

t 01653 668287
w flamingoland.co.uk
e info@flamingoland.co.uk

685 Knaresborough

Mother Shipton's Cave & Petrifying Well

1 hr+ Mar–Oct

Mother Shipton is perhaps England's most famous prophetess, foretelling the Spanish Armada and the Great Fire of London. She lived 500 years ago during the reigns of Henry VIII and Elizabeth I. Visit the cave, petrifying well, museum and 12 acres of historic woodland park.

* Oldest tourist attractions in Britain
* Includes free all-day parking

Location
Signed from A1 on A59

Opening
Mar Sat–Sun 10am–5.30pm;
Apr–Oct daily 10am–5.30pm

Admission
Adult £5.50, Child £3.75, Concs £4.50

Contact
Prophecy House,
Knaresborough HG5 8DD

t 01423 864600
w mothershipton.co.uk
e adrian@mothershipton.co.uk

686 Leyburn

Bolton Castle

1 hr+ All year

This spectacular medieval fortress in the heart of the Yorkshire Dales was completed in 1399. Today visitors can explore five floors of displays depicting castle life in the C15 and see where Mary, Queen of Scots was once imprisoned in the C16.

* Film location for *Ivanhoe, Elizabeth & Heartbeat*

Location
6 miles W of Leyburn, just off A684.
Signed from Wensley

Opening
Daily: Mar–Nov 10am–5pm;
Dec–Feb 10am–4pm
Please phone for details

Admission
Adults £5, Child & Concs £3.50

Contact
Leyburn DL8 4ET

t 01969 623981
w boltoncastle.co.uk

687 Malton

Eden Camp Modern History Museum

4 hrs All year

In this unique military museum, historical scenes are reconstructed using movement, lighting, sound, smells and smoke machines. Attractions include an original prisoner of war camp built in 1942. It is the only museum of its kind in the world.

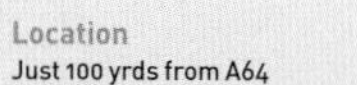

* Covers complete C20 British military history
* Multiple award-winning attraction

Location
Just 100 yrds from A64
(York–Scarborough) & A169
(Malton–Pickering) interchange

Opening
Daily: 10am–5pm

Admission
Adult £4.50, Child & Concs £3.50

Contact
Malton YO17 6RT

t 01653 697777
w edencamp.co.uk
e admin@edencamp.co.uk

688 Ormesby

Ormesby Hall

 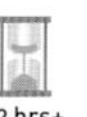 2 hrs+  Apr–Oct

Set in 270 acres of parkland, this C18 Palladian mansion, now owned by the National Trust, is notable for its fine plasterwork and carved wood decoration. Visit the Victorian laundry, kitchen, game larder and stable block. There is also an attractive garden and holly walk.

* National Trust property
* Large model railway

Location
3 miles SE of Middlesbrough. Take A174 then A172 & follow signs

Opening
Apr–Oct Sat–Sun & Bank Hols 1.30pm–4.30pm

Admission
Adult £4, Child £2.50

Contact
Ormesby Hall, Ormesby TS7 9AS

t 01642 324188
w nationaltrust.org.uk
e ormesbyhall@nationaltrust.org.uk

689 Pocklington

Burnby Hall Gardens

  3 hrs   Easter–Oct

Burnby Hall Gardens are world-famous for the National Collection of waterlilies, which contains more varieties than any other collection in Europe. There is also an extensive range of ornamental trees, plants and shrubs, and numerous fish and birds.

* Winner of Yorkshire in Bloom 2004
* 2 large lakes in 10 acres of beautiful gardens

Location
20 min E of York off A1079

Opening
Daily: Easter–Oct 10am–6pm

Admission
Adult £3.50, Child £1.60, Concs £2.75
Gardens free in winter

Contact
33 The Ball, Pocklington YO42 2QF

t 01759 307125
w burnbyhallgardens.com
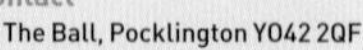
e brian@brianpetrie.plus.com

690 Ripley

Ripley Castle & Gardens

  2 hrs+  All year

Home to the Ingilby family for more than 700 years, the castle is famous as the place where Jane Ingilby held Oliver Cromwell at gunpoint. There is an impressive collection of arms and armour from the English Civil War and extensive hot houses in the gardens and grounds.

* Guided tours leave front door every hour
* Home to the National Hyacinth Collection

Location
3 miles N of Harrogate on A61

Opening
Daily: Jul–Aug 10.30am–3.30pm; Sep–Jun Tue, Thu, Sat–Sun & Bank Hols, please phone for details as they may vary

Admission
Adult £6.50, Child £4, Concs £5.50

Contact
The Ripley Castle Estate, Harrogate HG3 3AY

t 01423 770152
w ripleycastle.co.uk
e enquiries@ripleycastle.co.uk

691 Ripon

Fountains Abbey & Studley Royal Estate

 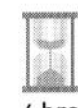 4 hrs  All year

The spectacular ruins of this C12 Cistercian abbey stand alongside a deer park, a Victorian church and an elegant C18 landscape garden with water features and follies. On some evenings the abbey is floodlit.

* Best surviving example of a monastic mill
* Declared a World Heritage Site in 1987

Location
4 miles W of Ripon on B6265

Opening
Daily: Nov–Feb 10am–4pm;
Mar–Oct 10am–5pm;
Nov–Jan closed Fri

Admission
Adult £6.50, Child £3.50

Contact
Ripon HG4 3DY

t 01765 608 888
w nationaltrust.org.uk
e info@fountainsabbey.org.uk

692 Ripon

Newby Hall & Gardens

  4 hrs   Easter–Sep

One of England's renowned Adam houses, this is an exceptional example of C18 interior decoration, recently restored to its original beauty. Contents include the Gobelins Tapestry Room, a famous gallery of classical statues and some of Chippendale's finest furniture.

* 25 acres of award-winning gardens & kids' adventure garden
* Miniature railway, woodland walk & special events

Location
Off B6265 between Boroughbridge & Ripon

Opening
Jul–Aug daily 11am–5.30pm;
Apr–Jun, Sep & Bank Hols Tue–Sun 11am–5.30pm

Admission
Adult £9.20, Child £6.40, Concs £8.20

Contact
Ripon HG4 5AE

t 0845 4504068
w newbyhall.com
e info@newbyhall.com

693 Ripon

Theakston Brewery & Visitor Centre

 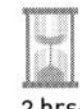 2 hrs+  All year

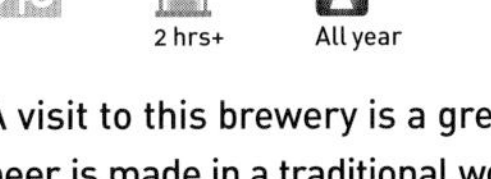

A visit to this brewery is a great opportunity to see how beer is made in a traditional working brewery. Tours follow the entire brewing process from blending the ingredients to filling the casks. Finish your visit in the visitor centre bar for a complimentary sample of the legendary ales.

* Home of the legendary Old Peculier
* Full-time working craft cooper & cooperage

Location
Masham is on A1608 N of Ripon

Opening
Daily: Nov–Mar 10.30am–3pm;
Apr–Jun & Sep–Oct 10.30am–4pm;
Jul–Aug 10.30am–5pm
Tours 11am–3.30pm hourly

Admission
Adult £4.75, Child £2.50, Concs £4

Contact
Masham, Ripon HG4 4DX

t 01765 680000
w theakstons.co.uk
e bookings@theakstons.co.uk

694 Scarborough

Scarborough Castle

 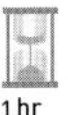 1 hr  All year

Dominating the headland, this impressive castle was built in the early C13 and later enhanced by King John and Henry III. It suffered naval bombardment in 1914 and during WWII it was home to a secret listening post. It offers wonderful views of the Yorkshire coastline.

* Vast C13 fortress
* Site of an Iron Age settlement

Location
In Castle Road, E of town centre

Opening
Apr–Sep daily 10am–6pm;
Oct–Mar Thu–Mon 10am–4pm

Admission
Adult £3.50, Child £1.80, Concs £2.60

Contact
Castle Road, Scarborough

t 01723 372451
w english-heritage.org.uk/yorkshire

695 Scarborough

Wykeham Lakes

1 hr+ All year

The ideal place to enjoy a range of watersports, including sailing, windsurfing, boating, scuba-diving and canoeing.Tuition is available. If you prefer fishing, choose from two trout lakes, three coarse-fishing lakes and pike fishing all year round.

* A full range of ticket options, including day, part day, sporting & season tickets are available

Location
6 miles W of Scarborough off A170 between West Ayton & Wykeham

Opening
Boating & watersports lake Daily: 7am–dusk *Fishing* All year *Bird watching* By arrangement with Wykeham Estate

Admission
Prices vary according to activity/ duration, please phone for details

Contact
Charm Park, Wykeham, Scarborough

t *fishing* 07946 534001
sailing 0845 4560164
w wykehamwatersports.co.uk

696 Skipton

Bolton Abbey

2 hrs+ All year

This estate covers 30,000 acres of beautiful countryside in the Yorkshire Dales. There are medieval buildings – C12 priory ruins to explore – and 80 miles of moorland, woodland and riverside footpaths. A guide book and walks leaflets are available. There is also a gift shop.

* Landscape was inspiration for Wordsworth & Turner
* Grounds include a 6-mile stretch of River Wharfe

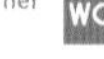    

Location
Between Harrogate & Skipton, off A59 on B6160

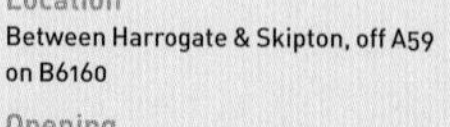

Opening
Daily: 9am–dusk

Admission
Vehicle pass £5 (occupants free), £3.50 for disabled badge holders

Contact
Skipton BD23 6EX

t 01756 718009
w boltonabbey.com
e tourism@boltonabbey.com

697 Skipton

Skipton Castle

1 hr+ All year

More than 900 years old, the castle is one of England's best-preserved and most complete medieval castles, surviving a three-year siege during the Civil War. Climb from the depths of the dungeons to the very top of the watch tower, and visit the excellent book shop.

* View the banqueting hall, kitchen & bedchambers
* Comprehensive tour sheets in 9 languages

Location
In town centre

Opening
Mar–Sep Mon–Sat 10am–6pm, Sun 12noon–6pm; Oct–Feb 10am–4pm, Sun 12noon–4pm

Admission
Adult £5.40, Child £2.90, Concs £4.80

Contact
Skipton BD23 1AW

t 01756 792442
w skiptoncastle.co.uk
e info@skiptoncastle.co.uk

698 York

The Bar Convent

1 hr+ All year

The oldest working convent in England, established in 1686. The founder of the order, Mary Ward, was a pioneer of education for women and its members ran a school for 299 years. The Bar Convent Museum tells the early history of Christianity in the North of England.

* C18 neoclassical chapel still used for weekly service
* Conference facilities & B&B available

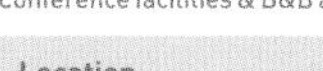

Location
2 min walk from railway station

Opening
Mon–Fri 10am–4pm
Tours By request
(closed for religious holidays)

Admission
Adult £1.50, Child free

Contact
17 Blossom Street,
York YO24 1AQ

t 01904 643 238
w bar-convent.org.uk
e info@bar-convent.org.uk

699 York

Castle Howard

2 hrs+ Mar–Oct

One of Britain's finest stately homes, located in the beautiful Howardian Hills. The magnificent house is distinguished by its famous dome and inside there are enormous collections of important art treasures. Spectacular gardens form part of a 10,000 acre estate.

* Adventure playground, boat trips & farm shop
* Outdoor guided tours & historical characters

Location
15 miles NE of York

Opening
Daily: Mar–Oct 10am–4pm

Admission
Adult £9.50, Child £6.50, Concs £8.50

Contact
Castle Howard, York YO60 7DA

t 01653 648333
w castlehoward.co.uk
e house@castlehoward.co.uk

700 York

Clifford's Tower

1 hr All year

Clifford's Tower is all that remains of York Castle. The original wooden tower was burned down during anti-Jewish riots in 1190. The height of the motte was increased and the tower was rebuilt in stone. Today the tower is just a shell, but you can climb to the top for a good view of York.

* Used as a prison after the Civil War
* Castle continued to be used for executions until 1896

Location
Opposite York Castle Museum

Opening
Daily: Apr–Sep 10am–6pm; Oct 10am–5pm;
Nov–Mar 10am–4pm

Admission
Adult £3, Child £1.50, Concs £2.30

Contact
Tower Street, York YO1 9SA

t 01904 646940
w english-heritage.org.uk/yorkshire
e cliffords.tower@english-heritage.org.uk

701 York

Jorvik

1 hr All year

Discover what life was like more than 1,000 years ago. See more than 800 locally found Viking items and journey through a reconstruction of actual Viking streets, complete with sounds and smells. Witness the skills of Viking craftsmen in an interactive exhibition.

* Jorvik is the name given to York by Vikings in AD975
* Wheelchair users please phone 01904 543402

Location
Take A64 to York & follow brown tourist signs

Opening
Daily: Apr–Oct 10am–5pm;
Nov–Mar 10am–4pm

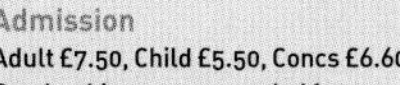

Admission
Adult £7.50, Child £5.50, Concs £6.60
Pre-booking recommended for individual tours

Contact
Jorvik, Coppergate, York YO1 9WT

t 01904 543403/643211
w vikingjorvik.com
e jorvik@yorkarchaeology.co.uk

702 York

National Railway Museum

  3 hrs+  All year

The collection includes 103 locomotives and 177 items of rolling stock from the *Rocket* to the *Eurostar*. Permanent displays include Palaces on Wheels with pre-Victorian royal saloons, a Japanese bullet train and a railway-themed children's play area.

* Home of *Flying Scotsman*
* Literally millions of photographs & artefacts

Location
200 yrds from railway station, signed from town centre

Opening
Daily: 10am–6pm

Admission
Free, except for special events

Contact
Leeman Road, York YO26 4XJ

t 01904 621261
w nrm.org.uk
e nrm@nmsi.ac.uk

703 York

Norwich Union Wheel of Yorkshire

  4 hrs+  All year

The wheel, climbing 54 metres into the sky, has 42 enclosed air-conditioned pods each accommodating eight people. From your vantage point high above York enjoy panoramic views over the city's historic centre including the Minster and the River Ouse.

* Luxury VIP pod with leather interior
* Evening tickets available

Location
200 yrds from railway station, signed from town centre

Opening
Daily: 10am–6pm (last admission 5.15pm) please phone for details of evening tickets

Admission
Adult £6, Child £4

Contact
Leeman Road, York YO26 4XJ

t 01904 686282
w nrm.org.uk

704 York

Rievaulx Abbey

  1 hr   All year

Founded by St Bernard of Clairvaux in the C12, this Cistercian abbey was once home to some 150 monks and 500 lay brethren. Although much of what was built by the monks is in ruins, recent digs reveal the monks ate strawberries and ran a flourishing iron industry.

* Towering medieval architecture
* Exhibition of the Works of God

Location
In Rievaulx, 2¼ miles W of Helmsley on a minor road off B1257

Opening
Apr–Sep daily 10am–6pm; Oct Mon & Thu–Sun 10am–5pm; Nov–Mar Mon & Thu–Sun 10am–4pm

Admission
Adult £4.20, Child £2.10, Concs £3.20

Contact
Rievaulx, York YO62 5LB

t 01439 798228
w english-heritage.co.uk/yorkshire

705 York

York Art Gallery

  1 hr+  All year

See some of Europe's finest art, with examples of oil and canvas, watercolours and ceramics. The gallery traces 600 years of British and European art, from the time of the Wars of the Roses right up to the present day.

* Outstanding collection of Pioneer Studio pottery
* Full programme of temporary exhibitions

Location
Opposite Tourist Information Centre, 3 min walk from York Minster

Opening
Daily: 10am–5pm

Admission
Free

Contact
Exhibition Square, York YO1 7EW

t 01904 697687
w york.artgallery.org.uk
e art.gallery@ymt.org.uk

706 York

York Castle Museum

2 hrs All year

Experience life as a Victorian. Walk down cobbled streets and peer through windows of shops long gone. Take a journey through 400 years of life in Britain, from parlours to prisons, marriages to the mill house, and see the toys that children used to treasure.

* Stumble into the underworld of the highwayman
* Victorian Street Kirkgate has had a massive makeover

Location
In city centre

Opening
Daily: 9.30am–5pm

Admission
Adult £6.50, Child £3.50, Concs £5

Contact
Eye of York, York YO1 9RY

t 01904 687687
w york.castlemuseum.org.uk
e castle.museum@ymt.org.uk

707 York

York Dungeons

1 hr+ All year

Deep in the heart of historic York, buried beneath its paving stones, lies the North's most chilling horror attraction. The York Dungeons bring more than 2,000 years of gruesomely authentic history vividly back to life ... and death.

* See how torture was part of everyday life until the C19
* Labyrinth of the Lost

Location
In city centre

Opening
Daily: Apr–Sep 10am–5pm;
Oct–Mar 10.30am–4.30pm

Admission
Adult £10.95, Child £7.95, Concs £8.95

Contact
The York Dungeons,
12 Clifford Street, York YO1 9RD

t 01904 632599
w thedungeons.com
e yorkdungeons@merlinentertainments.biz

708 York

York Minster

 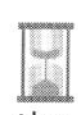 

1 hr+ All year

Savour the peaceful atmosphere of the largest Gothic cathedral in Northern Europe, a place of worship for more than 1,000 years, and a treasure house of stained glass. Take an audio tour of the undercroft, or a guided tour of the Minster.

* Climb the tower for an amazing view
* Visited by 2 million people every year

Location
In city centre

Opening
Daily: Mon–Sat 9.30am–5pm,
Sun 12.30pm–3.45pm
Tower Please visit the website for details

Admission
Adult £5, Child free, Concs £4

Contact
Deangate, York YO1 7HH

t 01904 557216
w yorkminster.org
e visitors@yorkminster.org

709 York

Yorkshire Air Museum

3 hrs All year

Admire displays such as the restored control tower, Air Gunners Museum, airborne forces display and Squadron Memorial Rooms. See Yorkshire's pioneering Cayley glider, the Wright Flyer, Halifax bomber, and modern jets like the Harrier GR3 and Tornado GR4.

* See the only restored Halifax bomber
* Historical aircraft from the earliest days of flight

Location
Take B1228 off A63/A1079 roundabout

Opening
Daily: *summer* (Apr–Sep) 10am–5pm
winter (Oct–Mar) 10am–3.30pm

Admission
Adult £5, Child £3, Concs £4

Contact
Halifax Way, Elvington York, YO41 4AU

t 01904 608595
w yorkshireairmuseum.co.uk
e museum@yorkshireairmuseum.co.uk

710 York

Yorkshire Museum & Gardens

2 hrs All year

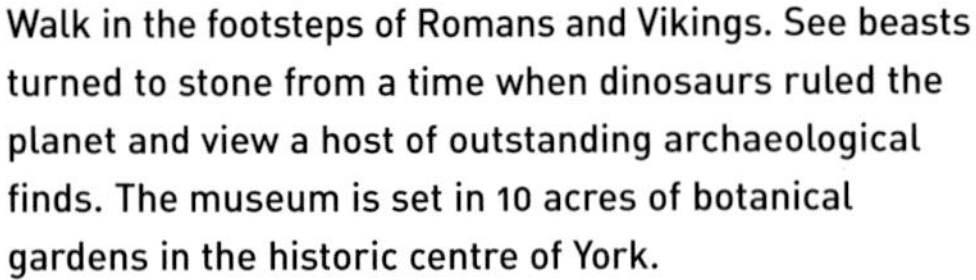

Walk in the footsteps of Romans and Vikings. See beasts turned to stone from a time when dinosaurs ruled the planet and view a host of outstanding archaeological finds. The museum is set in 10 acres of botanical gardens in the historic centre of York.

* Ruins of St Mary's Abbey in grounds
* Events & exhibitions throughout the year

   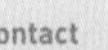 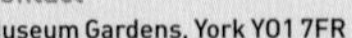 

Location
5–10 min walk from railway station

Opening
Daily: 10am–5pm

Admission
Adult £4, Child £2.50, Concs £3

Contact
Museum Gardens, York YO1 7FR

t 01904 687687
w yorkshire.museum.org.uk
e yorkshire.museum@ymt.org.uk

711 Conisbrough

Conisbrough Castle

2 hrs+ All year

The white circular keep of this C12 castle is a spectacular structure made of magnesian limestone, the oldest of its kind in England. Recently restored, with two new floors and a roof, it is an outstanding example of medieval architecture.

* Inspiration for Sir Walter Scott's classic novel *Ivanhoe*
* Closed for private functions some Sats during summer

Location
NE of town centre on A630

Opening
Daily: Apr–Sep 10am–5pm;
Oct–Mar 10am–4pm

Admission
Adult £4, Child £2.15, Concs £2.75

Contact
Castle Hill, Conisbrough DN12 3BU

t 01709 863329
w conisbroughcastle.org.uk
e info@conisbroughcastle.org.uk

712 Maltby

Roche Abbey

1 hr Apr–Sep

Founded in 1147, the fine early Gothic transepts of this Cistercian monastery still survive to their original height. In the C18 Capability Brown transformed the already beautiful valley, incorporating the ruins. Excavation has revealed the complete layout of the abbey.

* Visit the website for full programme of special events

Location
1½ miles S of Maltby off A634

Opening
Apr–Sep Thu–Mon 10am–5pm;
Jul–Aug daily 10am–5pm

Admission
Adult £3, Child £1.50, Concs £2.30

Contact
The Abbey Lodge, Maltby, nr Rotherham S66 8NW

t 01709 812739
w english-heritage.org.uk/yorkshire

713 Rotherham

Magna Science Adventure Centre

3 hrs+ All year

Set within a vast former steelworks, Magna is a hands-on visitor attraction that explores the powerful themes of earth, air, fire and water. Operate a real JCB, fire a water cannon or explode a rock face. Visit the UK's largest outdoor water park.

* Feel the force of a tornado in the Air Pavilion
* Test your bravery as a virtual fireball races towards you

Location
Just off M1, 1 mile along A6178 from Meadowhall shopping centre

Opening
Daily: 10am–5pm (closed some Mons in off-peak time, please phone for details)

Admission
Adult £9.95, Child & Concs £7.95

Contact
Sheffield Road, Templeborough, Rotherham S60 1DX

t 01709 720002
w visitmagna.co.uk
e info@magnatrust.co.uk

714 Sheffield

The Graves Art Gallery

1 hr+ All year

Admire Sheffield's collections of C19 and C20 British and European art. The paintings encapsulate the story of the development of modern art, the main trends traced through works by many well-known artists including Bonnard, Picasso and Spencer.

* Exciting programme of temporary exhibitions
* Sheffield's latest contemporary acquisition *Kiss* by Marc Quinn

WC

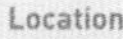

Location
In city centre above Central Library

Opening
Mon–Sat 10am–5pm

Admission
Free

Contact
Surrey Street, Sheffield S1 1XZ

t 0114 278 2600
w sheffieldgalleries.org.uk
e info@sheffieldgalleries.org.uk

715 Sheffield

Millennium Galleries

2 hrs+ All year

With four individual galleries under one roof, there is something for everybody to enjoy here. Admire treasures from the past and masterpieces from Britain's national collections, and discover new creations by contemporary artists and designers.

* Material regularly borrowed from the Tate & V&A
* Metalwork gallery

   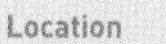

Location
In city centre near Winter Garden

Opening
Mon–Sat 10am–5pm,
Sun 11am–5pm

Admission
Free. Exhibitions may charge

Contact
Arundel Gate, Sheffield S1 2PP

t 0114 278 2600
w sheffieldgalleries.org.uk
e info@sheffieldgalleries.org.uk

716 Sheffield

Renishaw Hall Gardens

4 hrs+ Mar–Sep

The hall was home to the Sitwell family for more than 350 years, and the beautiful Italianate garden, park and lake were created by the eccentric Sir George Sitwell. Today visitors can enjoy lakeside walks, various galleries and gardens.

* Hall open by special arrangement only
* Regular calendar of events

Location
Just 2 miles from junction 30 of M1, between Ecrington & Renishaw on A6135

Opening
Mar–Sep Thu–Sun & Bank Hol Mon 10.30am–4.30pm. Please phone for details of special events

Admission
Adult £5, Child free, Concs £4.25

Contact
Renishaw Hall, nr Sheffield S21 3WB

t 01246 432310
w sitwell.co.uk
e info2@renishaw-hall.co.uk

717 Sheffield

Sheffield Ski Village

3 hrs+ All year

This all-season dry-slope ski resort offers skiing, snowboarding and toboggan rides for all ages and abilities, with lessons available at all levels and equipment for hire. Afterwards relax in the authentic village inn pub. It is ideal for groups and parties.

* More than 1 mile of piste
* Thunder Valley Toboggan Run

Location
5 min from city centre, off A61 Penistone Road

Opening
Daily: *summer* Mon–Fri 4pm–10pm, Sat–Sun 10am–8pm, Bank Hols 10am–10pm *winter* Mon–Fri 10am–10pm, Sat–Sun, Bank Hols & 26 Dec–2 Jan 9am–10pm

Admission
Please phone for details

Contact
Vale Road, Sheffield S3 9SJ

t 0114 276 9459
w sheffieldskivillage.co.uk
e info@sheffieldskivillage.co.uk

718 Sheffield

Tropical Butterfly House & Wildlife Centre

3 hrs+ All year

Come and enjoy the host of exotic wildlife at this centre. Explore the tropical house with its 35 species of butterfly, plus toads, iguanas and even two marmoset monkeys. There's a reptile and insect room, a birds of prey centre and 3½ acres of nature trail.

* Falconry & parrot displays
* Pets' corner & indoor play area

Location
Take junction 31 of M1, onto A57 to Worksop. At 2nd lights turn left to Dinnington. Turn right before The Cutler pub

Opening
Apr–Sep Mon–Fri 10am–4.30pm, Sat–Sun 10am–5.30pm; Oct–Mar Mon–Fri 11am–4.30pm, Sat–Sun 10am–5pm

Admission
Adult £5.99, Child £4.99, Concs £5.25

Contact
Hungerhill Farm, Woodsetts Road, North Anston, nr Sheffield S25 4EQ

t 01909 569416
w butterflyhouse.co.uk
e info@butterflyhouse.co.uk

719 Bradford

National Museum of Photography, Film & Television

3 hrs All year

This is one of the most visited national museums outside London, located in Bradford in recognition of the city's historic contribution to the development of cinema and filmmaking in the UK. The museum's archive includes the first negative and the earliest television footage.

* First moving pictures – 1888 film of Leeds Bridge
* More than 3 million historical items

Location
In city centre off Little Horton Lane

Opening
Tue–Sun & Bank & Public Hols
10am–6pm

Admission
Free, except for cinemas

Contact
Bradford BD1 1NQ

t 0870 701 0200
w nmpft.org.uk
e talk.nmpft@nmsi.ac.uk

720 Halifax

Manor Heath Park & Jungle Experience

3 hrs All year

This 19-acre park is set in the former gardens of John Crossley's Victorian mansion. There are many different areas, from the exotic Jungle Experience with magnificent orchids and ferns and the Savage Garden with carnivorous plants to the more practical walled garden.

Location
In Manor Heath Road off Skircoat Moor Road in Savile Park area S of town centre

Opening
Daily: *summer* 10am–4.30pm
winter 10am–4pm (last admission 20 min before close)

Admission
Free

Contact
Manor Heath Road, Savile Park, Halifax HX3 0EB

t 01422 365631
w calderdale.gov.uk/manorheath
w parks@calderdale.gov.uk

721 Halifax

Shibden Hall

 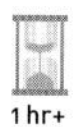 

1 hr+ All year

Built in 1420, the hall was home to the Lister family for more than 300 years and contains furnishings from several different centuries. The barn houses a collection of horse-drawn vehicles and the Folk Museum is a reconstruction of an early C19 village.

* See coopers, wheelwrights, apothecaries, a Crispin inn & an old ale brewery

Location
Signed from Halifax & M62

Opening
Daily: Mar–Nov Mon–Sat 10am–5pm, Sun 12noon–5pm;
Dec–Feb Mon–Sat 10am–4pm, Sun 12noon–4pm
(last admission 30 min before close)

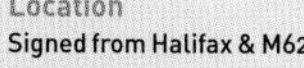

Admission
Adult £3.50, Child & Concs £2.50

Contact
Lister's Road, Halifax HX3 6XG

t 01422 352246
w calderdale.gov.uk/tourism
e shibden.hall@calderdale.gov.uk

722 Leeds

Harewood House & Bird Gardens

3–4 hrs Mar–Nov

This is one of the country's premier avian collections. More than 100 species of threatened and exotic birds are housed in sympathetic environments with the aim of promoting conservation and education. The Capability Brown gardens also provide many attractions.

* Boat trips across the lake & adventure playground
* Extensive collections of art & furniture in the house

Location
On A61, 7 miles from Leeds & Harrogate

Opening
Daily: Mar–Nov 10am–5pm

Admission
All attractions Mon–Fri Adult £11.30, Child £8.50, Concs £10
Sat–Sun £13.50, £8.50, £12.20
Grounds Mon–Fri Adult £8.80, Child £5.90, Concs £7.95
Sat–Sun £10.90, £7.25, £10

Contact
Harewood House Estate Trust Ltd, Harewood, Leeds LS17 9LG

t 0113 218 1010
w harewood.org
e info@harewood.org

723 Leeds

Leeds City Art Gallery

2 hr All year

There is something for everyone at Leeds City Art Gallery, from traditional prints, watercolours, paintings and sculptures to contemporary works. The exhibitions are ever-changing, displaying some of the most outstanding works of British art outside London.

* Designated as a collection of national importance
* Renovation work due for completion Apr 2007

   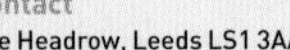

Location
In city centre, next to Central Library

Opening
Daily: Mon–Sat 10am–5pm, Wed 10am–8pm, Sun 1pm–5pm (closed Bank Hols)

Admission
Free

Contact
The Headrow, Leeds LS1 3AA

t 0113 247 8248
w leeds.gov.uk/artgallery
e city.art.gallery@leeds.gov.uk

724 Leeds

Royal Armouries Museum

 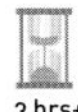 

3 hrs+ All year

The Royal Armouries Museum in Leeds was opened in 1996 as the new home for the National Collection of arms and armour. Five themed galleries cover war, tournaments, self-defence, hunting, and the arms and armour of the Orient.

* See Henry VIII's tournament armour
* Live action events & interactive technology

Location
S of city centre, near junction 4 of M621

Opening
Daily: 10am–5pm

Admission
Free. Car park fee

Contact
Armouries Drive, Leeds LS10 1LT

t 08700 344344
w royalarmouries.org.uk
e enquiries@armouries.org.uk

725 Leeds

Temple Newsam House & Farm

2 hrs All year

This magnificent country house contains one of the most important collections of decorative arts in Britain, including splendid Chippendale furniture and silver. The 1,500 acres of parkland, woodland, farmland and gardens include a rare breeds centre with more than 400 animals.

* One of the largest rare breeds centres in the country
* Grounds ideal for picnics

Location
On Temple Newsam Road, off Selby Road, 4 miles from city centre, off A63

Opening
Nov–Mar Tue–Sun 10.30am–4pm;
Apr–Oct Tue–Sun 10am–5pm
(last admission 45 min before close)

Admission
House or Farm Adult £3.50, Child £2.50
House & Farm £5.50, £3.50

Contact
Temple Newsam Road, Leeds LS15 0AE
t 0113 264 7321
w leeds.gov.uk/templenewsam
e temple.newsam@leeds.gov.uk

726 Leeds

Thackray Museum

3 hrs All year

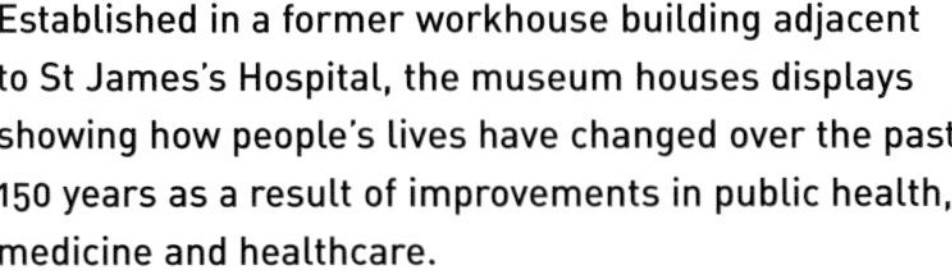

Established in a former workhouse building adjacent to St James's Hospital, the museum houses displays showing how people's lives have changed over the past 150 years as a result of improvements in public health, medicine and healthcare.

* Step inside the human body in the Life Zone
* Experience life as a Victorian character & decide their fate

Location
Follow signs for St James's Hospital. Museum is 100m past main entrance

Opening
Daily: 10am–5pm (last admission 3pm)

Admission
Adult £5.50, Child £4, Concs £4.50
Car park £1

Contact
Beckett Street, Leeds LS9 7LN

t 0113 244 4343
w thackraymuseum.org
e info@thackraymuseum.org

727 Leeds

Tropical World

2 hrs All year

Explore the tropics in the butterfly house, home to 30–40 species, and the Coronation house, filled with unusual plants. The Amazon is recreated in the South American house and is home to whistling ducks and macaws. The Nocturnal Zone has bush babies and fruit bats.

* Largest collection of tropical plants outside Kew
* Insect zone & desert house

Location
Off A58 at Oakwood, 3 miles N of city centre

Opening
Daily: 10am–6pm
(last admission 5.30pm)

Admission
Adult £3, Child (8–15) £2

Contact
Canal Gardens, Roundhay Park, Leeds LS8 2ER

t 0113 266 1850

728 Wakefield

National Coalmining Museum

  3 hrs+  All year

Tours take visitors 140 metres underground and trace mining techniques and conditions from the C19, when women and children worked underground, to the use of pit ponies, and on to the introduction of mechanical systems.

* Exhibition of modern mining methods
* Each guide is a former local miner

Location
On A642 between Wakefield & Huddersfield

Opening
Daily: 10am–5pm

Admission
Free

Contact
Caphouse Colliery, New Road, Overton, Wakefield WF4 4RH

t 01924 848806
w ncm.org.uk
e info@ncm.org.uk

729 Wakefield

Sandal Castle

  1 hr+  All year

Originally a motte and bailey castle dating from the C12, the stone castle overlooking the River Calder was demolished on the orders of Parliament after being besieged during the Civil War in 1645. It was restored to its present state in the 1970s and 1980s.

* Overlooks the site of 1460 Battle of Wakefield
* Spectacular views

Location
On A61, 2 miles from city centre in the direction of Barnsley

Opening
Castle Daily: dawn–dusk
Visitor centre Easter–Oct half-term daily 11am–4.30pm, otherwise Sat–Sun only
Please phone for details

Admission
Free

Contact
Manygates Lane, Sandal, Wakefield WF2 7DG

t 01924 249779

730 Wakefield

Yorkshire Sculpture Park

  2 hrs+  All year

One of Europe's leading open-air galleries showing modern and contemporary work by leading UK and international artists. A changing programme of exhibitions, displays and projects is held throughout the 500 acres of C18 landscaped grounds.

* 4 indoor galleries including underground gallery
* Visitor centre & craft & gift shop

Location
1 mile from M1 junction 38 on A637

Opening
Daily: *summer* 10am–6pm
winter 10am–5pm

Admission
Free. Car park £3

Contact
West Bretton, Wakefield WF4 4LG

t 01924 832631
w ysp.co.uk
e info@ysp.co.uk

Saint Rows, Chester
North West
Cheshire Cumbria Lancashire
Manchester Merseyside

Dalbeattie
Brampton
763
Hexham
Gateshead
Jarrow
890
891
898-899
Washington
Carlisle
896
Consett
Stanley
764-766
858
903-904
Wigton
Chester-le-Street
Alston
M6
872
Durham
Brandon
863-868
870
CUMBRIA
DURHAM
Maryport
Spennymoor
Cockermouth
Penrith
A1(M)
Workington
767-768
Bishop Auckland
780-783
859-860
Appleby-in-Westmorland
869
Newton Aycliffe
Stockton-on-Tees
871
Keswick
776-777
856-857
Whitehaven
Brough
Darlington
861-862
Egremont
TEESSIDE
Lake District
771
Ambleside
Scotch Corner
Richmond
760
Windermere
Coniston
M6
789-790
Catterick
Kendal
Sedbergh
769
772
Hawes
686
Leyburn
Northallerton
773-775
778-779
Thirsk
Millom
Ulverston
Kirkby Lonsdale
NORTH YORKSHIRE
Grange-over-Sands
784-788
680
Ripon
770
ENGLAND
Barrow-in-Furness
Carnforth
691-693
761-762
814
807
690
Morecambe
A1(M)
Isle of Walney
Settle
Heysham
Lancaster
Knaresborough
811-813
681-682
Harrogate
685
Skipton
Fleetwood
Ilkley
LANCASHIRE
696-697
Wetherby
809
Garstang
Keighley
Yeadon
LEEDS & BRADFORD
Clitheroe
Bingley
794-797
815
Colne
Shipley
Nelson
Blackpool
LEEDS
M55
817-820
805-806
BRADFORD
Garforth
Kirkham
Preston
Burnley
M621
Accrington
Lytham St Anne's
Warton
791
Halifax
719-721
722-727
Blackburn
Rawtenstall
Todmorden
Castleford
792-793
Brighouse
Batley
Leyland
M62
728-730
Southport
M6
Chorley
Rochdale
W. YORKSHIRE
Wakefield
816
821
M62
Huddersfield
808
M61
798-804
M66
855
Ormskirk
Standish
Bury
Bolton
M1
Formby
Middleton
Barnsley
Wigan
810
M60
MERSEYSIDE
Oldham
M58
822
823-834
Penistone
Crosby
Kirkby
Salford
MANCHESTER
Bootle
Skelmersdale
St Helens
Stocksbridge
M62
753-754
Glossop
Wallasey
LIVERPOOL
854
Rotherham
Sale
M60
M60
Stockport
SHEFFIELD
Birkenhead
839-853
Warrington
731
Cheadle
714-717
713
Prestatyn
Altrincham
SHEFFIELD CITY
835-837
838
Widnes
757
MANCHESTER
Colwyn Bay
Rhyl
LIVERPOOL
758
M56
Peak
641
Runcorn
Wilmslow
Whaley Bridge
419-421
Dronfield
759
Knutsford
Ellesmere Port
750
District
Holywell
740
Staveley
746
Frodsham
741-744
Buxton
Abergele
M56
St Asaph
Flint
738-739
Northwich
422-423
Chesterfield
Queensferry
Macclesfield
747-749
Denbigh
Chester
Middlewich
M6
Bakewell
429
FLINTSHIRE
416
DERBYSHIRE
CONWY
Mold
Winsford
752
Congleton
732-736
Clay Cross
CHESHIRE
751
Sutton in Ashfield
Matlock
Betws-y-coed
755-756
737
Biddulph
Ruthin
Crewe
Leek
430-431
Alfreton
414
Kidsgrove
531
Wirksworth
424
Ripley
DENBIGHSHIRE
Nantwich
541-542
547
432
Wrexham
Belper
745
STOKE-ON-TRENT
Newcastle-under-Lyme
425
Ruabon
529
Ashbourne
644-645
534
538
WREXHAM
Llangollen
Whitchurch
Ilkeston

CHESHIRE

CUMBRIA

LANCASHIRE

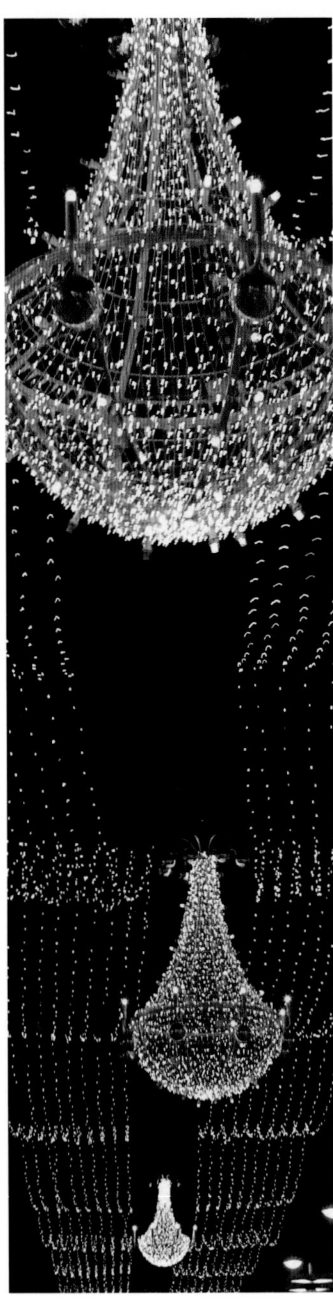

731 Altrincham

Dunham Massey

3 hrs Mar–Oct

This early Georgian house was extensively renovated in the early C20. The result is one of Britain's most sumptuous Edwardian interiors housing collections of C18 walnut furniture, paintings and Huguenot silver. You can also visit the extensive servants' quarters.

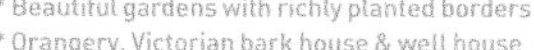

* Beautiful gardens with richly planted borders
* Orangery, Victorian bark house & well house

Location
3 miles SW of Altrincham, M6 junction 19, M56 junction 7

Opening
House & Garden Mar–Oct Sat–Wed 12noon–5pm, *Garden* All Year daily 11am–5.30pm

Admission
House & Gardens Adult £6.50, Child £3.25
Gardens £4.50, £2.25

Contact
Altrincham WA14 4SJ

t 0161 941 1025
w nationaltrust.org.uk
e dunhammassey@nationaltrust.org.uk

732 Chester

Bithell Boats (Show Boats of Chester)

1 hr+ All year

Discover a delightful range of cruises on the River Dee, including a 30-minute city cruise past the suspension bridge, following the sweep of the meadows; or the two-hour cruise up river to Ironbridge, past the Eccleston ferry and the beautiful scenery of the Eaton Estate.

* Bus & boat trip tickets available
* Evening floodlight cruises & ghost tours

Location
All cruises depart from the Groves close to centre of Chester

Opening
Apr–Oct daily 11am–4.30pm; Nov–Mar Sat–Sun 11am–4pm

Admission
Adults £6, Child £2, Concs £4.50

Contact
River Cruise, Boating Station, Souters Lane, Chester CH1 1SD

t 01244 325394
w showboatsofchester.co.uk
e showboatschester@aol.com

733 Chester

Cheshire Military Museum

1 hr+ All year

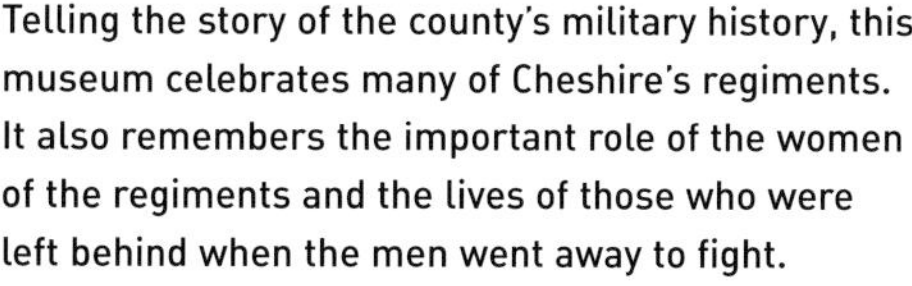

Telling the story of the county's military history, this museum celebrates many of Cheshire's regiments. It also remembers the important role of the women of the regiments and the lives of those who were left behind when the men went away to fight.

* Interactive computer displays
* Hands-on exhibits

Location
Close to city centre

Opening
Daily: 10am–5pm (last admission 4pm)

Admission
Adult £2, Child & Concs £1

Contact
The Castle, Chester CH1 2DN

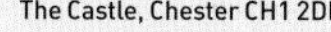

t 01244 403933
w chester.ac.uk/militarymuseum
e museum@chester.ac.uk

734 Chester

Chester Cathedral

1 hr All year

This is the most complete medieval monastic complex standing in the UK. Records show a church has existed on this site since the early C10, and the foundation of a Benedictine monastery in 1092. In 1541 it became the Cathedral Church of Christ and the Blessed Virgin Mary.

* Restoration in latter part of C19 by Sir Gilbert Scott
* Stunning stained glass, fabrics & sculptures

Location
In city centre

Opening
Daily: Mon–Sat 9am–5pm, Sun 1pm–5pm

Admission
Adult £4, Child £1.50, Concs £3

Contact
12 Abbey Square, Chester CH1 2HU

t 01244 324756
w chestercathedral.com
e fry@chestercathedral.com

735 Chester

Chester Zoo

5 hrs+ All year

Founded in 1934 and covering more than 100 acres, Chester Zoo is one of the largest zoos in the UK and receives more than a million visitors each year. It is home to more than 7,000 animals, representing around 400 different species, and a spectacular plant collection.

* Elephant centre now open, secret world of the Okapi
* Internationally renowned for innovative enclosures

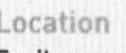

Location
Easily accessible from M53 & M56
Follow brown tourist signs

Opening
Daily: from 10am (closing times vary, please phone for details)

Admission
Prices vary, please phone or visit the website for details

Contact
Upton-by-Chester,
Chester CH2 1LH

t 01244 380280
w chesterzoo.org
e reception@chesterzoo.co.uk

© Chester Zoo

736 Chester

Grosvenor Museum

1 hr+ All year

Hear the story of Chester from the Roman fortress of Deva to the present day. Learn about its Roman people, army and buildings, visit a Roman graveyard with tombstones of the legion's soldiers and enjoy artists' views of the city's past.

* Discover the natural history of Cheshire
* Georgian house with recreated period rooms

Location
In city centre

Opening
Daily: Mon–Sat 10.30am–5pm,
Sun 1pm–4pm

Admission
Free

Contact
27 Grosvenor Street, Chester CH1 2DD

t 01244 402008
w grosvenormuseum.co.uk
e srodrigrez@chestercc.gov.uk

737 Congleton

Little Moreton Hall

2 hrs Mar–Dec

This moated house, with its irregular half-timbered façades opening on to a cobbled courtyard, was built in the mid-C15. The house was extended between 1570 and 1580 when the Long Gallery was added, giving the hall its curious top-heavy look.

* A warren of rooms, some no larger than cupboards
* *Moll Flanders* & *Lady Jane* filmed here

Location
4 miles S of Congleton on A34, 10 min from junctions 16 & 17 of M6

Opening
Mar–Oct Wed–Sun 11.30am–5pm;
Nov–Dec Sat–Sun 11.30am–4pm

Admission
Adult £5.50, Child £2.80, Family ticket (2 Adult & 2 Child £13)

Contact
Congleton CW12 4SD

t 01260 272018
w nationaltrust.org.uk
e littlemoretonhall@nationaltrust.org.uk

738 Ellesmere Port

Blue Planet Aquarium

 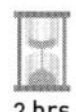 2 hrs  All year

The aquarium features one of the world's largest underwater viewing tunnels. Visitors can get up close to huge sharks, graceful rays and hundreds of other fish. Exhibits span the Scottish Highlands, the mighty Amazon, the depths of Lake Malawi and mangroves.

* Shark-inhabited Caribbean reef
* Touchpools with anemones, rays & octopus play park

Location
Nr junction 10 of M53, adjacent to Cheshire Oaks designer outlet village

Opening
Daily: from 10am (closing times vary, please phone for details)

Admission
Adult £9.95, Child & Concs £7.50

Contact
Cheshire Oaks, Ellesmere Port CH65 9LF

t 0151 357 8800
w blueplanetaquarium.com
e info@blueplanetaquarium.com

739 Ellesmere Port

The Boat Museum

  4 hrs+  All year

Board some of the boats from the world's largest floating collection of traditional canal craft. Discover how people lived in homes no larger than the hallway of a modern house, and tour the Georgian and Victorian buildings full of fascinating exhibitions.

* Visit Pump House & Power Hall
* Experience domestic life in dock workers' cottages

Location
Junction 9 of M53 and follow signs

Opening
Apr–Oct daily 10am–5pm;
Nov–Mar Sat–Wed 11am–4pm

Admission
Adult £7.10, Child £5.25, Concs £5.80, Family ticket £20.65

Contact
South Pier Road, Ellesmere Port CH65 4FW

t 0151 355 5017
w boatmuseum.org.uk
e bookings@thewaterwaystrust.org

740 Knutsford

Tatton Park

  4 hrs+  All year

An impressive estate with more than 1,000 acres of stunning parkland that is home to herds of red and fallow deer. Its major attractions include a Tudor hall, a neoclassical mansion, a working farm and award-winning gardens.

* Picnic concerts, classic car & RHS flower shows
* Victorian kitchens & servants' quarters

Location
Signed from junction 19 of M6, & junction 7 of M56

Opening
Park Daily
summer 10am–7pm (last entry 6pm)
winter 11am–5pm (last entry 4pm)
Times for individual attractions vary. Please phone for details.

Admission
Car park £4
Per attraction Adult £3.50, Child £2

Contact
Knutsford WA16 6QN

t 01625 534400
w tattonpark.org.uk
e tatton@cheshire.gov.uk

© Joe Wainwright

741 Macclesfield

Capesthorne Hall

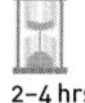
2–4 hrs

Apr–Oct

A turreted, redbrick C18 Jacobean-style building, Capesthorne Hall has collections including fine art, marble sculptures and tapestries, plus Regency, Jacobean and rococo antiques. Enjoy the treasured collections of Americana and children's toys.

* Guided tours by arrangement
* Grounds include a chapel, gardens & lakes

Location
Off A34 between Manchester & Stoke-on-Trent, 3 miles S of Alderly Edge, junction 6 of M56

Opening
Apr–Oct Sun, Mon & Bank Hols 12noon–5pm

Admission
Adult £6.50, Child £3, Concs £5.50
Mondays £10 per car for 4 people

Contact
Siddington, Macclesfield SK11 9JY

t 01625 861221
w capesthorne.com
e info@capesthorne.com

742 Macclesfield

Gawsworth Hall

1 hr+

Apr–Sep

An ancient manor house that includes the Fitton family chapel, licensed in 1365. The original Norman house was rebuilt in 1480 and remodelled in 1701. A famous duel took place in 1712 between Lord Mohun and the Duke of Hamilton in which both duellists were killed.

* Samuel Johnson, the last professional jester, lived here
* Open-air theatre season Jun–Aug

Location
On A536 between Macclesfield & Congleton

Opening
Daily: Apr–Sep 2pm–5pm. Times may vary, please phone for details

Admission
Adult £6, Child £3

Contact
Church Lane, Macclesfield SK11 9RN

t 01260 223456
w gawsworthhall.com
e enquiries@gawsworthhall.com

743 Macclesfield

Jodrell Bank Science Centre & Arboretum

2 hrs+ Mar–Oct

This is the visitor centre for the Lovell radio telescope. There is an observational pathway around the base of the telescope, a small exhibition area and a 3D theatre as well as the Space Café and shop.

* 35-acre arboretum is a tree lover's paradise
* Environmental discovery centre

Location
Between Holmes Chapel & Chelford, on A535, 8 miles W of Macclesfield

Opening
Daily: Mar–Oct 10.30am–5.30pm

Admission
Adult £1.50, Child £1

Contact
Lower Withington, Macclesfield SK11 9DL

t 01477 571339
w jb.man.ac.uk/scicen
e visitorcentre@jb.man.ac.uk

744 Macclesfield

Macclesfield Silk Industry Museum

2 hrs All year

This building was once the Macclesfield School of Art, built in 1877 to train designers for the silk industry. It now houses exhibitions exploring the properties of silk, design education, Macclesfield's diverse textile industries, workers' lives and historic machinery.

* Temporary exhibits
* Try your hand at weaving & designing (various days)

Location
5 min from town centre

Opening
Mon–Sat 11am–5pm;
Bank Hols 1pm–5pm

Admission
Adult £4.10, Child free, Concs £3.45

Contact
Park Lane, Macclesfield SK11 6TJ

t 01625 612045
w macclesfield.silk.museum
e info@macclesfield.silk.museum

745 Nantwich

Hack Green Secret Nuclear Bunker

1 hr+ Jan–Nov

One of the nation's most secret defence sites, Hack Green has played a central role in the defence of Britain for almost 60 years. Once through the blast doors, visitors are transported into the chilling world of the Cold War to learn what living conditions were like here.

* Sounds & smells of a civil defence HQ
* Soviet Spy Mouse Trail for children

Location
Off A530 Whitchurch road, outside Nantwich, 30 min from Chester

Opening
Mar–Oct 10.30am–5.30pm;
Jan–Feb & Nov Sat–Sun 11am–4.30pm

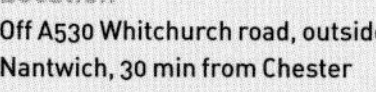

Admission
Adult £6.30, Child £4, Concs £5.90

Contact
PO Box 127, Nantwich CW5 8AQ

t 01270 623353
w hackgreen.co.uk
e coldwar@hackgreen.co.uk

746 Neston

Ness Botanic Gardens

1 hr+ All year

When a Liverpool cotton merchant began to create a garden in 1898, he laid the foundations of one of the major botanic gardens in the UK. Now internationally renowned, the collection includes breathtaking rhododendrons and azaleas.

* Adopt a tree scheme
* Heather, herb & water gardens

Location
6 miles from exit of M53, 5 miles from western end of M56, off A540 Chester–Hoylake road

Opening
Daily: Mar–Oct 9.30am–5pm;
Nov–Feb 9.30am–4pm

Admission
Adult £5, Child free, Concs £4.50

Contact
Ness, Neston CH64 4AY

t 0151 353 0123
w nessgardens.org.uk
e nessgdns@liv.ac.uk

747 Northwich

Anderton Boat Lift

1 hr+ Mar–Oct

Reopened in 2002 after a £7 million restoration, the Anderton Boat Lift is one of the greatest monuments to Britain's last canal age and is known as the 'Cathedral of the Canals'. Built in 1875, it was the world's first, and is currently England's only, boat lift.

* New operations centre open
* Quality Assured Visitor Attraction

Location
Follow A556 & then A559 to Northwich town centre, then follow signs

Opening
Daily: Mar–Oct 10am–5pm
Please phone or visit the website for boat & lift times

Admission
Please phone or visit the website for details

Contact
Lift Lane, Anderton, Northwich CW9 6FW

t 01606 786777
w andertonboatlift.co.uk
e info@andertonboatlift.co.uk

748 Northwich

Arley Hall & Gardens

2 hrs Apr–Oct

These charming English gardens feature a double herbaceous border laid out in 1846, a pleached lime avenue, giant cylinders of *Quercus ilex*, topiary and collections of roses, rhododendrons and azaleas. The hall reveals fine panelling and plasterwork.

* Voted one of the top 50 gardens in Europe
* Gardens include rose & fallen timber gardens

Location
Junction 19 or 20 of M6, or junction 9 or 10 of M56

Opening
Hall Apr–Oct Tue, Sun & Bank Hols 12noon–5pm
Gardens Apr–Sep Tue–Sun & Bank Hols 11am–5pm; Oct Sat–Sun 11am–5pm

Admission
House Adult £2.50, Child £1, Concs £2
House & Gardens £5, £2, £4.50

Contact
Arley, Northwich CW9 6NA

t 01565 777353
w arleyhallandgardens.com
e enquiries@arleyhallandgardens.com

749 Northwich

Lion Salt Works

1 hr All year

The Lion Salt Works is a unique survival of the traditional inland salt works that once produced this essential commodity. The site illustrates the whole process of salt production and dates from the late C19/C20. It is the only surviving salt site in Cheshire.

* Cheshire once produced 86% of the nation's salt
* Building renovation in progress

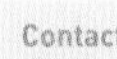 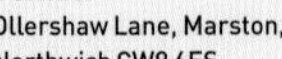

Location
Junction 19 from M6 via A556.
Junction 10 from M56 via A559

Opening
Sun–Thu 1.30pm–4.30pm

Admission
Adult £1, Child 50p

Contact
Ollershaw Lane, Marston, Northwich CW9 6ES

t 01606 41823
w lionsaltworkstrust.co.uk
e afielding@lionsalt.demon.co.uk

750 Runcorn

Norton Priory Museum

3 hrs+ All year

This 38-acre site includes a museum, a magnificent 800-year-old vaulted storage range, a historic priory, remains excavated by archaeologists, and the unique St Christopher statue. The woodland gardens are the setting for a collection of contemporary sculptures.

* Four North West in Bloom awards
* BBC2 programme *Hidden Gardens* filmed here

Location
From junction 11 of M56 take turn for Warrington & follow signs

Opening
Nov–Mar daily 12noon–4pm; Apr–Oct Mon–Fri 12noon–5pm, Sat–Sun 12noon–6pm

Admission
Adult £4.75, Child & Concs £3.45, Family ticket (2 Adult & 3 Child) £12.50

Contact
Tudor Road, Manor Park, Runcorn WA7 1SX

t 01928 569895
w nortonpriory.org
e info@nortonpriory.org

751 Sandbach

Sandbach Crosses

½ hr All year

Rare Saxon stone crosses, carved with animals and biblical scenes, stand in the cobbled market square of Sandbach. The crosses are believed to date from the C9. Close inspection reveals the ancient carvings.

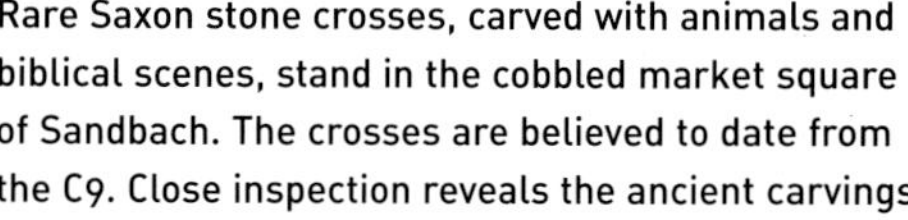

* One of the most photographed sights in Cheshire
* Restored in 1816 after destruction by iconoclasts

Location
Market Square, Sandbach

Opening
Daily: All reasonable times

Admission
Free

Contact
English Heritage, Canada House, 3 Chepstow Street, Manchester M1 5FW

t 0161 242 1400
w english-heritage.org.uk
e northwest@english-heritage.org.uk

752 Scholar Green

Rode Hall

2 hrs+ Apr–Sep

The house was constructed in two stages, the earlier two-storey wing and stable block around 1705 and the main building in 1752. The house contains examples of furniture by Gillow of Lancaster, a collection of portraits and an important collection of English porcelain.

* Rode Hall stands in a Repton landscape
* Garden renowned for its snowdrops & kitchen garden

Location
5 miles SW of Congleton between A34 & A50

Opening
House Apr–Sep Wed & Bank Hols 2pm–5pm;
Garden Apr–Sep Tue–Thu 2pm–5pm

Admission
House & Gardens Adult £5, Concs £4
Gardens Adult £3, Concs £2.50

Contact
Scholar Green, Cheshire ST7 3QP

t 01270 873237
w rodehall.co.uk
e enquiries@rodehall.co.uk

753 Stockport

Bramall Hall

  2 hrs  All year

This is a grand black-and-white timber-framed Tudor building. The hall was built in the traditional local style with an oak framework, joined using mortice and tenon joints and held in place with oak pegs. Wattle and daub or lath and plaster were used to fill the spaces in the timbers.

* Guided tours available on request
* Open woodland

Location
Junction 1 or 27 of M60

Opening
Apr–Sep Sun–Thu 1pm–5pm, Fri & Sat 1pm–4pm, Bank Hols 11am–5pm; Oct–Jan Tue–Sun 1pm–4pm, Bank Hols 11am–4pm; 2 Jan–Mar Sat–Sun only 1pm–4pm, Bank Hols 11am–4pm

Admission
Adult £3.95, Child & Concs £3

Contact
Bramall Park, Stockport SK7 3NX

t 0845 833 0974
w bramallhall.org.uk
e bramall.hall@stockport.gov.uk

754 Stockport

Lyme Park

  2 hrs+  Mar–Oct

Originally a Tudor house, Lyme was transformed by the Venetian architect Leoni into an Italianate palace. Some of the Elizabethan interiors survive and contrast dramatically with later rooms. The state rooms are adorned with Mortlake tapestries.

* Pemberley in BBC adaptation of *Pride & Prejudice*
* Important collection of English clocks

Location
On A6, 12 miles S of city centre. Follow signs

Opening
Daily: late Mar–Oct
Please phone for details

Admission
House Adult £5, Child £2.50
Gardens £3.50, £2
House & Gardens £6.50, £3.30

Contact
Disley, Stockport SK12 2NX

t 01663 762023/766492
w nationaltrust.org.uk
e lymepark@nationaltrust.org.uk

755 Tarporley

Beeston Castle

  1 hr+  All year

Standing majestically on sheer, rocky crags, Beeston has stunning views. Its history stretches back more than 4,000 years, to when it was a Bronze Age hill fort. Building of the castle began in 1226, and it soon became a royal stronghold, falling centuries later in the English Civil War.

* Exhibition outlines the history of this strategic site
* Panoramic views of the Cheshire Plain

Location
11 miles SE of Chester on a minor road off A49

Opening
Daily: Apr–Sep 10am–6pm; Oct–Mar Thu–Mon 10am–4pm

Admission
Adult £4, Child £2, Concs £3

Contact
Tarporley CW6 9TX

t 01829 260464
w english-heritage.org.uk

756 Tarporley

Oulton Park Race Circuit

All day Apr–Oct

Set in 320 acres of glorious Cheshire countryside, Oulton Park offers spectacular car and motorcycle racing, with British superbikes, touring cars and Formula 3, and family-fun days. Experience the thrill yourself with racing, rally and young-drive activities.

* Full racing programme
* Driving experiences throughout the year.

Location
Take junction 18 of M6 & follow A54 to Chester for 12 miles. Turn left on to A49 to Whitchurch & follow signs

Opening
Please phone for details

Admission
Please phone for details

Contact
Motorsport Vision, Little Budworth, Tarporley, Cheshire CW6 9BW

t 01829 760301
w oultonpark.co.uk

757 Warrington

Warrington Museum & Art Gallery

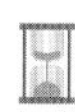

1 hr+ All year

This museum houses exhibitions on Warrington and the surrounding area, together with exhibitions by renowned artists. Shows have included etchings by Picasso and fashions by the Warrington-born designer Ozzie Clark. There is also a gallery with a fossil-handling section.

* Temporary exhibition programme
* Education department for schools

Location
In town centre

Opening
Mon–Fri 9am–5pm, Sat 9am–4pm (closed Sun & Bank Hols)

Admission
Free

Contact
Museum Street, Warrington WA1 1JB

t 01925 442733
w warrington.gov.uk/museum
e museum@warrington.gov.uk

758 Widnes

Catalyst Science Discovery Centre

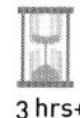

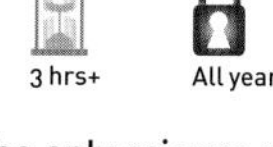

3 hrs+ All year

This is the only science centre in the UK devoted solely to chemistry and how the products of chemistry are used in everyday life – from medicines to Meccano. The centre aims to inform visitors about chemistry and its role in our lives – past, present and future.

* 3 interactive galleries with 100+ exhibits
* Virtual-reality theatre & discovery lab

Location
Junction 12 of M56 & junction 7 of M62

Opening
Tue–Fri & Bank Hols 10am–5pm, Sat–Sun 11am–5pm

Admission
Adult £4.95, Child & Concs £3.95
Family ticket £15.90

Contact
Mersey Road, Widnes WA8 0DF

t 0151 420 1121
w catalyst.org.uk
e info@catalyst.org.uk

759 Wirral

Sunlight Vision

4 hrs+ All year

A picturesque C19 village founded by William Hesketh Lever for his soap factory workers and named after his famous Sunlight soap. The Heritage Centre explores the history of the village and community. The Lady Lever Art Gallery houses rich and varied collections.

* C18 furniture & Wedgwood china
* Gift shop & garden centre

Location
20 min from Liverpool. From junction 5 of M53 take A41 to Birkenhead. Follow signs

Opening
Daily: 10am–4pm

Admission
Adult £1, Child 60p, Concs 80p

Contact
95 Greendale Road, Port Sunlight, Wirral CH62 4XE

t 0151 644 6466
w portsunlightvillage.com

760 Ambleside

Hill Top

 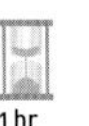 

1 hr Apr–Oct

This delightful C17 house was home to Beatrix Potter when she wrote many of her famous stories. It remains as she left it and every room contains something that appears in her books. The pretty cottage garden contains a mix of flowers and vegetables, just as Beatrix would have had it.

* Timed entry to avoid overcrowding
* Shop specialising in Beatrix Potter gifts

Location
2 miles S of Hawkshead, near Sawrey, 3 miles from Bowness via ferry

Opening
Apr–May & Sep–Oct Sat–Wed 10.30am–4.30pm; Jun–Aug Sat–Thu 10.30am–4.30pm
Garden Apr–Oct daily 10.30am–5pm

Admission
Adult £5.40, Child £2.70

Contact
Nr Sawrey, Hawkshead, Ambleside LA22 0LF

t 01539 436269
w nationaltrust.org.uk
e hilltop@nationaltrust.org.uk

761 Barrow-in-Furness

Dock Museum

3 hrs All year

A spectacular modern museum built over an original Victorian graving dock. Displays explore the history of Barrow-in-Furness and how it grew from a tiny C19 hamlet to become the biggest iron and steel centre in the world and a major shipbuilding force in just 40 years.

* Attractions include film shows & model ships

Location
Follow signs in Barrow-in-Furness

Opening
Easter–Oct Tue–Fri 10am–5pm, Sat–Sun 11am–5pm;
Nov–Easter Wed–Fri 10.30am–4pm, Sat–Sun 11am–4.30pm
(last admission 45 min before close)

Admission
Free

Contact
North Road, Barrow-in-Furness LA14 2PW

t 01229 894444
w dockmuseum.org.uk
e dockmuseum@barrowbc.gov.uk

762 Barrow-in-Furness

Furness Abbey

1 hr All year

St Mary of Furness was founded in 1123 by Stephen, later king of England. It originally belonged to the small Order of Savigny but it passed to the Cistercians in 1147, becoming one of the richest monasteries in England – second only to Fountains Abbey in Yorkshire.

* Romantic building, often visited by Wordsworth
* Visitor centre with exhibition about the abbey

Location
½ mile NE of Barrow-in-Furness

Opening
Apr–Sep daily 10am–5pm;
Oct–Mar Thu–Mon 10am–4pm

Admission
Adult £3.40, Child £1.70, Concs £2.60

Contact
Abbey Approach, Barrow-in-Furness, Cumbria LA13 0PJ

t 01229 823420
w english-heritage.org.uk
e furness.abbey@english-heritage.org.uk

763 Brampton

Lanercost Priory

 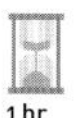 

1 hr · Easter–Oct

Situated near the Scottish border in Cumbria are the impressive remains of this C12 Augustinian priory. It boasts a rich history, from the tranquillity of life as a monastic house to its involvement in the turbulent Anglo-Scottish wars of the C14, to its eventual dissolution.

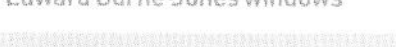

* Dacre Hall is open to view C16 wall-paintings
* Edward Burne-Jones windows

Location
Off a minor road S of Lanercost, 2 miles NE of Brampton

Opening
Daily: 10am–5pm

Admission
Adult £2.70, Child £1.40, Concs £2

Contact
Lanercost, Brampton CA8 2HQ

t 01697 73030
w english-heritage.org.uk
e northwest@english-heritage.org.uk

764 Carlisle

Carlisle Castle

1 hr+ · All year

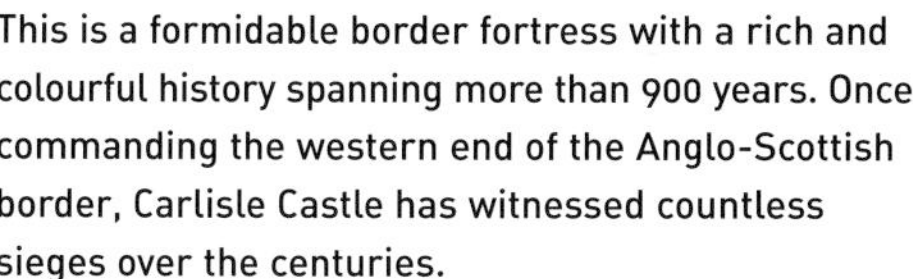

This is a formidable border fortress with a rich and colourful history spanning more than 900 years. Once commanding the western end of the Anglo-Scottish border, Carlisle Castle has witnessed countless sieges over the centuries.

* Admission includes entrance to Roman exhibition
* See the legendary 'licking stones'

Location
On N side of city, beyond cathedral

Opening
Daily: Apr–Sep 9.30am–5pm; Oct–Mar 10am–4pm

Admission
Adult £4.10, Child £2.10, Concs £3.10

Contact
Carlisle CA3 8UR

t 01228 591922
w english-heritage.org.uk
e northwest@english-heritage.org.uk

765 Carlisle

Carlisle Cathedral

2 hrs · All year

Founded in 1122 and battered by centuries of border warfare, the cathedral retains many items of interest, notably the east window with its fine tracery containing C14 stained glass. Other items include the magnificent C16 Brougham triptych and stunning medieval painted panels.

* Beautifully painted ceiling in the choir
* Display of cathedral & diocesan silver in the treasury

Location
In city centre

Opening
Daily: Mon–Sat 7.30am–6.15pm, Sun 7.30am–5pm. Bank Hols *summer* 10am–6.15pm *winter* 10am–4pm

Admission
Free, donations welcomed (£4 recommended)

Contact
7 The Abbey, Castle Street, Carlisle CA3 8TZ

t 01228 535169
w carlislecathedral.org.uk
e office@carlislecathedral.org.uk

766 Carlisle

Tullie House

  2 hrs  All year

Tullie House museum and art gallery offers visitors a multifaceted experience, combining the features of a historic house with a modern museum. It has a superb collection of Roman artefacts and the displays include many hands-on exhibits that appeal to all ages.

* Major new exhibition Freshwater Life
* Displays of key artworks by Pre-Raphaelites

Location
Signed from junctions 42, 43 & 44 of M6

Opening
Daily: Apr–Jun & Sep–Oct Mon–Sat 10am–5pm, Sun 12noon–5pm ; Jul–Aug Mon–Sat 10am–5pm, Sun 11am–5pm; Nov–Mar Mon–Sat 10am–4pm, Sun 12noon–4pm

Admission
Adult £5.20, Child £2.60, Concs £3.60

Contact
Castle Street, Carlisle CA3 8TP

t 01228 534781
w tulliehouse.co.uk
e enquiries@tullie-house.co.uk

767 Cockermouth

Lakeland Sheep & Wool Centre

  2 hrs  All year

This centre offers visitors the opportunity to meet Cumbria's most famous residents – 19 different breeds of sheep! Discover interesting facts about each breed and be amazed by the remarkable skills of the sheepdogs handling a flock.

* Show theatre holds up to 170 people
* Extensive retail outlet for wool & sheepie gifts

Location
On A66 at A5086 roundabout

Opening
Daily: 9.30–5pm
Sheepdog shows Mar–Oct Sun–Thu 10.30am, 12noon, 2pm & 3.30pm

Admission
Show Adult £4.50, Child £3.50

Contact
Egremount Road, Cockermouth CA13 0QX

t 01900 822673
w sheep-woolcentre.co.uk

768 Cockermouth

Wordsworth House

2 hrs Mar–Oct

Meet members of the Wordsworth household and find out what life was like for the maid, manservant and clerk. Enjoy the sights and sounds of a working C18 kitchen. There is also a wonderful garden overlooking the banks of the River Derwent.

* William Wordsworth's childhood home
* Events & hands-on activities

Location
Just off A66, in town centre

Opening
Late Mar–Oct Tue–Sat 11am–4.30pm; Jul–Aug Mon–Sat 11am–4.30pm

Admission
Adult £4.70, Child £2.60

Contact
Main Street, Cockermouth CA13 9RX

t 01900 820884
w nationaltrust.org.uk
e wordsworthhouse@nationaltrust.org.uk

769 Coniston

Brantwood

3 hrs All year

As the home of John Ruskin, Brantwood became a great literary and artistic centre. The house is filled with Ruskin's work as well as his original furniture, books and personal items. Brantwood's attraction is increased by 250 acres of woodland and lakeside meadows.

* Vibrant exhibition & events programme
* Well-marked nature trail winds through the estate

Location
E shore of Coniston Water on B5285

Opening
Mid-Mar–mid-Nov daily 11am–5.30pm; mid-Nov–mid-Mar Wed–Sun 11am–4.30pm

Admission
Adult £5.50, Child £1

Contact
Coniston LA21 8AD

t 01539 441396
w brantwood.org.uk
e enquiries@brantwood.org.uk

770 Dalton-in-Furness

South Lakes Wild Animal Park

3 hrs+ All year

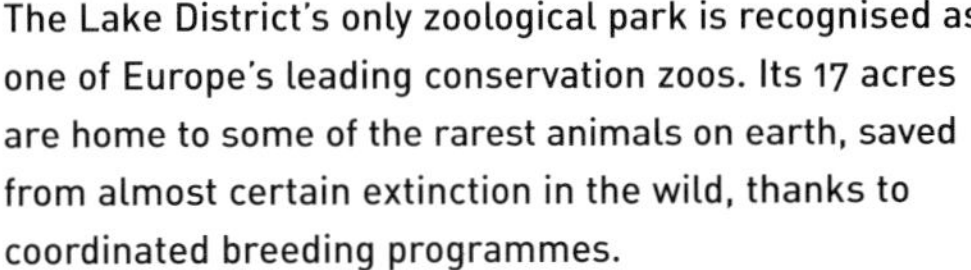

The Lake District's only zoological park is recognised as one of Europe's leading conservation zoos. Its 17 acres are home to some of the rarest animals on earth, saved from almost certain extinction in the wild, thanks to coordinated breeding programmes.

* Rhinos, giraffes & tigers as close as you can safely get
* Hand-feed lemurs, kangaroos & giraffes

Location
Follow signs from junction 36 of M6

Opening
summer 10am–5pm;
winter 10am–4.30pm

Admission
Adult £10.50, Child & Concs £7

Contact
South Lakes Wild Animal Park, Dalton-in-Furness LA15 8JR

t 01229 466086
w wildanimalpark.co.uk
e office@wildanimalpark.co.uk

771 Grasmere

Dove Cottage & Wordsworth Museum

1 hr All year

The home of William Wordsworth from December 1799 to May 1808, the years of his best work as a poet. The cottage remains much as it was during that time. The garden was a passion for Wordsworth and he spent many hours developing his 'domestic slip of mountainside'.

* Perhaps the country's best Lake District landscaped art collection
* Also shows period images of Grasmere

Location
S of Grasmere on A591 Kendal–Keswick road

Opening
Daily: 5 Feb–9 Jan 2008
9.30am–5.30pm

Admission
Adult £6.20, Child £3.90, Concs £5.60

Contact
Grasmere LA22 9SH

t 01539 435544
w wordsworth.org.uk
e enquiries@wordsworth.org.uk

772 Hawkshead

Beatrix Potter Gallery

  ½ hr  Apr–Oct

This gallery houses annually changing exhibitions of original sketches and watercolours painted by Beatrix Potter for her children's stories. The C17 building was once the office of Beatrix's husband, William Heelis.

* Interior remains substantially unaltered
* 2007 exhibit The Tale of Tom Kitten

Location
In town centre

Opening
Apr–Oct Sat–Wed 10.30am–4pm

Admission
Adult £3.60, Child £1.80, Family ticket £9

Contact
Main Street, Hawkshead LA22 0NS

t 01539 436355
w nationaltrust.org.uk
e beatrixpottergallery@nationaltrust.org.uk

773 Kendal

Kendal Museum

  1 hr+  Feb–Dec

Founded in 1796, Kendal Museum houses one of the country's oldest collections of local archaeology, history and geology. There is also an international natural history collection, including lakeland flora and fauna from prehistory to the C20.

* Wildlife garden simulates local habitats
* Changing programme of temporary exhibitions

Location
10 min from junction 36 of M6

Opening
Apr–Oct Mon–Sat 10.30am–5pm; Feb–Mar & Nov–Dec Mon–Sat 10.30am–4pm

Admission
Adult £2.70, Child free, Concs £2.10

Contact
Station Road, Kendal LA9 6BT

t 01539 721374
w kendalmuseum.org.uk
e info@kendalmuseum.org.uk

774 Kendal

Levens Hall

  2 hrs  Apr–Oct

The world-famous C17 topiary garden was designed by Guillaume Beaumont, who also laid out the gardens at Hampton Court. The original designs have remained largely unchanged for 300 years. The house has lots of beautiful Elizabethan rooms with many notable paintings.

* Dining room has embossed leather wall-coverings

Location
5 miles S of Kendal on A6

Opening
Mid-Apr–mid-Oct Sun–Thu
House 12noon–5pm
Gardens from 10am

Admission
Adult £9, Child £4

Contact
Kendal, Cumbria LA8 0PD

t 01539 560321
w levenshall.co.uk
e houseopening@levenshall.co.uk

775 Kendal

Museum of Lakeland Life

  1 hr  All year

In 1973 the museum was the first winner of the coveted Museum of the Year Award. The permanent collections include displays linked to the Arts & Crafts Movement, *Swallows and Amazons* author Arthur Ransome and the Victorian period.

* Temporary displays largely from costume collection
* Large shop selling local crafts & toys

Location
Next to Abbots Hall Gallery, junction 36 of M6

Opening
Apr–Oct Mon–Sat 10.30am–5pm; 20 Jan–Mar & Nov–Dec Mon–Sat 10.30am–4pm

Admission
Adult £3.75, Child £2.75

Contact
Kendal, Cumbria LA9 5AL

t 01539 722464
w lakelandmuseum.org.uk
e info@lakelandmuseum.org.uk

776 Keswick

Derwent Water Marina

  1 hr +  All year

This centre specialises in watersports with RYA sailing courses, windsurfing courses, and canoe, kayak and dinghy hire available. Other activities include ghyll scrambling, abseiling, climbing and walking. A great experience for families, friends and groups.

* Self-catering apartments available
* Boats for sale

Location
From Keswick take A66 & follow signs for Portinscale

Opening
Daily: 9am–5.30pm (closed 20 Dec–12 Jan)

Admission
Activities priced individually. Please phone or visit the website for details

Contact
Portinscale, Keswick, Cumbria CA12 5RF
t 01768 772912
w derwentwatermarina.co.uk
e info@derwentwatermarina.co.uk

777 Keswick

Keswick Climbing Wall

  1 hr+   All year

With more than 400 metres of climbing wall ranging from flat panels to 25 fixed ropes, a 22m-long bouldering wall and 12m abseiling tower, we cater for everyone from novice to expert. Additionally, we organise a host of outdoor activities from ghyll scrambling to raft building.

* New bungy trampoline
* Full range of courses for all abilities

Location
Leave M6 at junction 40 (Penrith) & follow A66 W towards Keswick. Take 1st exit left at roundabout on to Crossthwaite Road then turn left at T-junction. Take 1st left turn & follow brown & white tourist signs

Opening
Please phone for details

Admission
Please phone for details

Contact
Southey Hill, Keswick CA12 5NR
t 01768 772000
w keswickclimbingwall.co.uk
e info@keswickclimbingwall.co.uk

778 Newby Bridge

Aquarium of the Lakes

 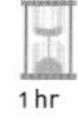 1 hr  All year

Explore a range of naturally themed Lake District habitats featuring the UK's largest collection of freshwater fish. See otters, British sharks and a variety of British mammals. Discover our underwater tunnel featuring giant carp and diving ducks.

* Large number of nocturnal creatures

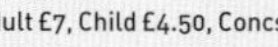

Location
15 min from junction 36 of M6. Take A590 to Newby Bridge & follow signs

Opening
Daily: Apr–Oct 9am–6pm; Nov–Mar 9am–5pm (last admission 1 hr before close)

Admission
Adult £7, Child £4.50, Concs £6

Contact
Lakeside, Newby Bridge LA12 8AS
t 01539 530153
w aquariumofthelakes.co.uk
e aquariumofthelakes@reallive.co.uk

779 Newby Bridge

Scott Park Bobbin Mill

1 hr Apr–Oct

This gem of the Industrial Revolution has remained largely unchanged since it was built by John Harrison in 1835. Scott Park created the wooden bobbins vital to the spinning and weaving industries of Lancashire.

* Mill worked continuously until 1971
* Steam days (Mon, Tue, Wed & Thu) show engines working

Location
2 miles N of Newby Bridge, off A590

Opening
Daily: Apr–Sep 10am–5pm;
Oct Tue–Sat 10am–5pm

Admission
Adult £4.10, Child £2.10, Concs £3.10, Family ticket £10.30

Contact
Finsthwaite, nr Newby Bridge, Ulverston LA12 8AX

t 01539 531087
w english-heritage.org.uk
e northwest@english-heritage.org.uk

780 Penrith

Acorn Bank Garden & Watermill

2 hrs Easter–Oct

Ancient oaks and the high enclosing walls keep out the extremes of the Cumbrian climate, resulting in a spectacular display of shrubs, roses and herbaceous borders. Sheltered orchards contain a variety of traditional fruit trees.

* Famed herb garden has huge collection of plants
* Watermill remains open to public during restoration

Location
N of Temple Sowerby, 6 miles E of Penrith on A66

Opening
Mar Sat–Sun 11am–4pm;
Apr–Oct Wed–Sun & Bank Hols 10am–5pm

Admission
Adult £3.20, Child £1.60

Contact
Temple Sowerby, nr Penrith CA10 1SP

t 01768 361893
w nationaltrust.org.uk
e acornbank@nationaltrust.org.uk

781 Penrith

Brougham Castle

1 hr Apr–Oct

Brougham Castle was built by Robert de Vieuxpont in the early C13 near the site of a Roman fort. His great keep largely survives. Reinforced by an impressive double gate house, and other C14 additions, this castle made a formidable barrier to Scots invaders.

* Once home to Lady Anne Clifford
* Introductory exhibition includes Roman carved stone

Location
½ mile SE of Penrith off A66

Opening
Apr–Sep daily 10am–5pm;
Oct Thu–Mon 10am–4pm

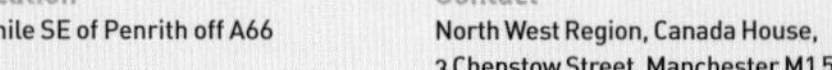

Admission
Adult £2.70, Child £1.40, Concs £2

Contact
North West Region, Canada House, 3 Chepstow Street, Manchester M1 5FW

t 01768 862488
w english-heritage.org.uk
e northwest@english-heritage.org.uk

782 Penrith

Dalemain Historic House & Gardens

 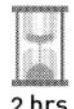 

2 hrs Easter–Oct

A medieval, Tudor and early Georgian house that has been home to the Hasell family since 1679. The Tudor legacy is a series of winding passageways, unexpected rooms and oak panelling. A good example of the Georgian period is the breathtaking Chinese room.

* C15 medieval hall
* Estate includes many famous valleys & fells

Location
On A592 Penrith–Ullswater road

Opening
House Sun–Thu 11am–4pm
Gardens & Tearoom 10.30am–5pm
Please phone for details

Admission
Adult £6.50, Child free

Contact
Penrith CA11 0HB

t 01768 486450
w dalemain.com
e admin@dalemain.com

783 Penrith

Wetheriggs Pottery

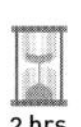  

2 hrs All year

The country's only remaining steam-powered pottery, Wetheriggs still produces traditional and contemporary earthenware and stoneware, handmade as it has been for the past 140 years. Visitors can still see potters at work, the old workings and a restored steam engine.

* Pottery & craft shops
* Tearoom

Location
Only 4 miles S of Penrith. Follow brown signs from M6 (junction 40) or A6 roundabouts

Opening
Easter–Oct 10am–5.30pm;
Nov–Easter 10am–4.30pm

Admission
Free

Contact
Clifton Dykes, Penrith, Cumbria CA10 2DH

t 01768 892733
w wetheriggs-pottery.co.uk
e info@wetheriggs-pottery.co.uk

784 Ulverston

Conishead Priory & Buddhist Temple

1 hr Easter–Oct

A stunning example of early Georgian Gothic architecture, dominated by two 100ft (30m) octagonal towers. Other special features include decorative ceilings and a vaulted great hall with fine stained glass. The Buddhist Kadampa Temple was established at the priory in 1997.

* Anyone welcome to visit the temple by appointment
* Prayers for world peace every Sun morning

Location
On A5087, 2 miles S of Ulverston

Opening
Please phone for details

Admission
Free

Contact
Priory Road, Ulverston LA12 9QQ

t 01229 584029
w manjushri.org
e info@manjushri.org

785 Ulverston

Gleaston Water Mill

2 hrs All year

This imposing watermill has been part of the local landscape for more than 400 years. Located close to the ruins of Gleaston Castle, the present building dates from 1774. Visitors can see the 18ft (5.5m) waterwheel and machinery operating most days.

* Thousands of piggy collectables, observation apiary site
* Try our homemade food, all cooked in our tearooms

Location
Follow signs from A5087 Ulverston–Barrow-in-Furness coast road

Opening
Tue–Sun & Bank Hols 10.30am–5pm

Admission
Adult £2.50, Child £1.50

Contact
Gleaston, nr Ulverston LA12 0QH

t 01229 869244
w watermill.co.uk

786 Ulverston

Holker Hall & Gardens

3 hrs

Mar–Oct

Only a short distance from the sea, Holker Hall is situated on the magnificent wooded slopes of the Cartmel Peninsula. The house exhibits all the grandeur and prosperity of the late Victorian era and is set in immaculate gardens.

* Gift shop & food hall
* Holker Festival 1–3 Jun 2007

Location
Follow signs from A590 from Barrow-in-Furness or M6 junction 36

Opening
House & Gardens 25 Mar–28 Oct Sun-Fri 10am–5.30pm
Museum Mar–Dec daily
Please phone or visit the website

Admission
House & Gardens Adult £10.50, Child £5.70, Concs £9.75

Contact
Cark-in-Cartmel, Cumbria LA11 7PL
t 01539558328
w holker-hall.co.uk
e publicopening@holker.co.uk

787 Ulverston

Lakeland Motor Museum

3 hrs

Mar–Dec

This unique collection includes more than 30,000 motoring exhibits. There are die-cast scale models of historical transport, rally cars and tractors, as well as classic, comical and curious cars, superb scooters, magnificent motorcycles and much more.

* More than 100 years of motoring history

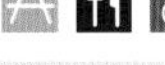

Location
At Holker Hall signed from junction 36 M6 via A590

Opening
Daily: Mar–17 Dec from 10.30am

Admission
Adult £6, Child £3.50, Concs £5.50

Contact
Cark-in-Cartmel LA11 7PL
t 01539 558509
w lakelandmotormuseum.co.uk
e info@lakelandmotormuseum.co.uk

788 Ulverston

Laurel & Hardy Museum

1 hr

Feb–Dec

Visit the world-famous museum devoted to Laurel and Hardy in Ulverston, the town where Stan was born on 16 June 1890. Everything you ever wanted to know about them is here. The collection includes letters, photographs, personal items and furniture.

* Small cinema shows films & documentaries all day

Location
In town centre

Opening
Daily: Feb–Dec 10am–4.30pm

Admission
Adult £3, Child & Concs £2

Contact
4c Upper Brook Street, Ulverston LA12 7BH
t 01229 582292
w laurel-and-hardy-museum.co.uk

789 Windermere

Lake District National Park

4 hrs

All year

Enjoy some of England's most dramatic mountain and lake scenery in one of the finest of Britain's national parks. Gain a better understanding of the area at the visitor centre at Brockhole on Lake Windermere.

* Exhibition, displays & gardens down to the lake
* Gardens designed by Mawson

Location
Visitor centre on A591 between Windermere & Ambleside

Opening
Visitor centre Daily: Mar–Oct 10am–5pm
Gardens & Grounds All year daily

Admission
Free. Car park pay & display

Contact
The Lake District Visitor Centre, Brockhole, Windermere LA23 1LJ
t 01539 446601
w lake-district.gov.uk

790 Windermere

Windermere Lake Cruises

1½ hrs

All year

Steamers and launches sail daily between Ambleside, Bowness and Lakeside with main-season connections for the Lakeside & Haverthwaite Steam Railway, Wray Castle and the Lake District National Park (Brockhole). Or sail to the aquarium and the World of Beatrix Potter.

* 24-hour Freedom tickets for unlimited travel
* Other links to lake's attractions – visit the website

Location
Take junction 36 of M6. Follow brown tourist signs along A590 to Lakeside or A591 to Windermere for Bowness & Ambleside

Opening
Daily: *summer* open during daylight hours *winter* 9.45am–4.30pm

Admission
Adult from £5.50, Child from £2.75

Contact
Lakeside, Newby Bridge, Ulverston LA12 8AS

t 01539 531188
w windermere-lakecruises.co.uk
e mail@windermere-lakecruises.co.uk

791 Accrington

Haworth Art Gallery

2 hrs

All year

This Edwardian house, set in parkland, houses the finest public collection of Tiffany art glass outside the USA. There is also an excellent collection of oil paintings from the C19.

* Regularly changing exhibitions
* Tearoom open weekends only

Location
Leave M65 at junction 7

Opening
Wed–Fri 2pm–5pm, Sat–Sun 12noon–4.30pm; Bank Hol Mon 2pm–5pm

Admission
Free

Contact
Haworth Park, Manchester Road, Accrington BB5 2JS

t 01254 233782
w hyndburnbc.gov.uk

792 Blackburn

Blackburn Museum & Art Gallery

2 hrs

All year

The museum is housed in a fine Arts & Crafts-style building that opened in 1872 as a museum and a library. Highlights include the Hart Collection of more than 10,000 rare coins, 500 books and illuminated manuscripts, and a superb collection of Victorian oils and watercolours.

* Lewis Collection of more than 1,000 Japanese prints
* Award-winning South Asian Gallery & Egyptian Room

Location
In town centre

Opening
Tue–Sat 10am–4.45pm

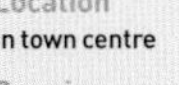

Admission
Free

Contact
Museum Street, Blackburn BB1 7AJ

t 01254 667130
w council.blackburn/services/museum
e paul.flintoff@blackburn.gov.uk

793 Blackburn

Whalley Abbey Gatehouse

1 hr All year

Situated beside the River Calder, this is the outer gate house of the nearby Cistercian abbey. There was originally a chapel on the first floor. The adjacent parish church has further remains including three pre-Norman Conquest cross shafts. The abbey has an exhibition centre.

* Vast display of remains

Location
In Whalley, 6 miles NE of Blackburn on a minor road off A59

Opening
Daily: All reasonable times

Admission
Free

Contact
Whalley, Clitheroe BB7 9SS

t 01793 414910
w english-heritage.org.uk

795 Blackpool

Blackpool Lifeboat Station & Visitor Centre

1 hr Easter–Nov

This lifeboat station accommodates an Atlantic 75 B-class and two D-class lifeboats, launching vehicles and ancillary equipment. The visitor centre incorporates current and historic displays and sea-safety information. There is an accessible public viewing area.

* Station was established by the RNLI in 1864
* Nelson's flagship *Foudroyant* wrecked in a gale near here in 1897

Location
Central Promenade

Opening
Daily: Easter–Nov 10am–4pm

Admission
Free

Contact
Central Promenade, Blackpool FY1 5JA

t 01253 620424/290816
w rnli.org.uk
e blackpool@rnli.org.uk

794 Blackpool

Blackpool Illuminations

2 hrs Aug–Nov

Experience Blackpool's annual spectacular event. Six miles of lights electrify this well-loved resort's promenade as the world-famous illuminations shine every night for 66 nights. Enjoy a grandstand seat aboard a cleverly disguised tram.

* View the giant clifftop tableaux
* Festival of Light throughout the town

Location
Promenades

Opening
Nightly: 31 Aug–4 Nov

Admission
Free

Contact
Blackpool Tourism, 1 Clifton Street FY1 1LY

t 01253 478222
w visitblackpool.com
e tourism@blackpool.gov.uk

796 Blackpool

The Blackpool Piers

4 hrs+ Easter–Nov

Blackpool's Piers are a fantastic place for all the family to be entertained, day and night throughout the season. Ride the roller coaster, big wheel and dodgems. Visit one of our many Family Fun Bars for tempting food and drink and free entertainment.

* Children's entertainer (all piers)
* Fairground rides (South & Central Piers)

Location
North Pier on North Promenade, South Pier on South Promenade, Central Pier on Central Promenade

Opening
Daily: Easter–Nov from 10am (subject to weather conditions)

Admission
Free, except North Pier (50p toll) Charges for individual rides

Contact
6 Piers Ltd, Saga House, Ecclestone, Churley, Lancs PR7 5PH

t 01253 292029
w blackpoollive.com

797 Blackpool

Blackpool Tower & Circus

5 hrs+ Easter–Nov

Inside the tower visitors will find an award-winning circus and a world-famous ballroom. Explore the Charlie Cairoli exhibition, Under Sea World, the Hornpipe Gallery, the Tower Top ride and the Walk of Faith.

* Please phone for details of venue for evening entertainment
* Indoor adventure play area

Location
Take M55 for Blackpool & follow signs

Opening
Daily: Easter–May 10am–6pm; Jun–Nov 10am–11pm

Admission
Tower Adult £12.95, Child £8.95, Concs £7.95

Contact
Leisure Park Ltd, 97 Church Street, Blackpool FY1 4BJ

t 01253 622242 /01253 292029
w blackpooltower.co.uk
e website@leisure-parcs.co.uk

798 Bolton

Animal World & Butterfly House

1 hr All year

Animal World provides a caring environment for a variety of animals and birds, from farm animals to chipmunks, from wildfowl to tropical birds. Butterfly House features free-flying butterflies and moths in a tropical environment, as well as insects and reptiles.

* Collection of tropical plants. See our giant rabbits
* Tree frogs & lizards from all over the world.

Location
In Bolton. Take A58 to Moss Bank Way

Opening
Daily: Apr–Sep 10am–4.30pm; Oct–Mar Sat–Thu 10am–3.30pm, Fri 10am–2.30pm

Admission
Free

Contact
Moss Bank Park, Moss Bank Way, Bolton BL1 6NQ

t 01204 334050
w visit-bolton.com
e animal.world@bolton.gov.uk

799 Bolton

Bolton Aquarium

2 hrs All year

If you're curious about catfish, partial to piranhas or want to be knowledgeable about knifefish, visit Bolton Aquarium. Fish from around the world can be seen in an environment designed to offer an insight into their hidden lives. The aquarium is one of the oldest in the country.

* Notable collection of piranha fish
* Predatory giant green knifefish from Venezuela

Location
In town centre

Opening
Mon–Sat 9am–5pm (closed Bank Hols)

Admission
Free

Contact
Le Mans Crescent, Bolton BL1 1SE

t 01204 332200
w boltonmuseums.org.uk
e aquarium@bolton.gov.uk

800 Bolton

Bolton Museum & Art Gallery

2 hrs All year

Bolton Museum and Art Gallery has something for the whole family, from the Ancient Egypt Gallery, to galleries on themes as diverse as Costume, Local History and the Story of Bolton to Natural History and Wildlife on Your Doorstep. There are also activities, talks and workshops.

* Varied programme of events & exhibitions
* Educational play area & organised workshops

Location
In town centre

Opening
Mon–Sat 9am–5pm (closed Bank Hols)

Admission
Free

Contact
Le Mans Crescent, Bolton BL1 1SE
t 01204 332211
w boltonmuseums.org.uk
e museums@bolton.gov.uk

801 Bolton

Bolton Wanderers Football Club

2 hrs All year

Look behind the scenes at the Reebok Stadium, home of Bolton Wanderers. Begin at the interactive museum where the history of the club is brought to life. Visit the players' dressing and warm-up rooms, the officials' changing rooms and the manager's dugout.

* All stadium tours must be pre-booked

Location
Junction 6 of M61

Opening
Daily: Mon–Fri 9.30am–5pm, Sat 9am–5pm, Sun 11am–5pm

Admission
Adult £2.50, Child & Concs £1.50

Contact
Reebok Stadium, Burnden Way, Bolton BL6 6JW
t 01204 673650
w bwfc.premiumtv.co.uk
e sparker@bwfc.co.uk

802 Bolton

Hall i' th' Wood Museum

1 hr All year

This half-timbered hall, built in the C15, was owned by wealthy yeomen and merchants. After 1697, it was rented out to various tenants and a young Samuel Crompton lived here with his parents. He later invented the spinning mule, which revolutionised the cotton industry.

* Activities ongoing all year
* Experience life in Tudor & Stuart times by dressing in period costumes

Location
2 miles N of town centre

Opening
Easter–Oct Wed–Sun 11am–5pm; Nov–Mar Sat–Sun 11am–5pm

Admission
Adult £2, Child & Concs £1

Contact
Green Way, Bolton BL1 8UA
t 01204 332370
w boltonmuseums.org.uk
e hallithwood@bolton.gov.uk

803 Bolton

Smithills Hall

1 hr All year

This is one of the earliest examples of a Lancashire manor house and has recently had additional rooms restored to their full splendour. It has been developed by generations of owners, and mirrors changes in fashion and living conditions from the late C14 to the C19.

* Gift shop & various events throughtout the year
* Stained-glass windows in the chapel

Location
Take M62 for Bolton

Opening
Easter–Sep Mon–Fri 11am–5pm, Sun 1pm–5pm; Oct–Easter Sun–Fri 12noon–4pm (last tour 1 hour before close)

Admission
Adult £3, Child & Concs £1.75

Contact
Smithills Dean Road, Bolton BL1 7NP

t 01204 332377
w boltonmuseums.org.uk
e museums@bolton.gov.uk

804 Bolton

Turton Tower

2 hrs Mar–Oct

Turton Tower was originally built by the Orrell family to defend their land, and later became a luxurious home. The house was lavishly furnished and extended in the Tudor and early Stuart periods. Today Turton displays a rich, extensive collection of paintings and furniture.

* Experience the relaxing woodland gardens
* Victorian follies & tennis court

Location
Take A66 & A676 & follow signs

Opening
Mar–Apr & Oct Sat–Wed 12noon–4pm; May–Sep Sat–Thu 12noon–5pm

Admission
Adult £4, Child free, Concs £3

Contact
Chapeltown Road, Turton, Bolton BL7 0HG

t 01204 852203
w lancsmuseums.gov.uk
e turton.tower@mus.lancscc.gov.uk

805 Burnley

Gawthorpe Hall

2 hrs Easter–Oct

An Elizabethan gem, Gawthorpe resembles the great Hardwick Hall and is probably by the same architect, Robert Smythson. In the mid-C19 Sir Charles Barry was commissioned to restore the house. Charlotte Brontë was a frequent visitor.

* Many notable paintings & C17–C19 furniture
* Unparalleled collection of British C19–C20 needlework

Location
On E outskirts of Padiham, N of A671

Opening
Easter–Oct Tue–Thu & Sat–Sun 1pm–5pm

Admission
Adult £4, Child free, Concs £3

Contact
Padiham, Burnley BB12 8UA

t 01282 771004
w lancsmuseum.gov.uk
e gawthorpe.hall@mus.lancscc.gov.uk

806 Burnley

Queen Street Mill

1 hr Mar–Nov

A unique survivor of the textile industry, Queen Street Mill was the last commercial steam-powered textile mill in Europe. The actual mill closed in 1982 but it is preserved as a museum that recreates the days when steam ran the world.

* Smell the oil, see the steam & breathe the atmosphere
* 300 Lancashire looms

Location
Corner of Queen Street & Harrison Street, Harle Syke

Opening
Mar & Nov Tue–Thu 12noon–4pm; Apr & Oct Tue–Fri 12noon–5pm; May–Sep Tue–Sat 12noon–5pm

Admission
Adult £3, Child free, Concs £2

Contact
Harle Syke, Burnley BB10 2HX

t 01282 412555
w lancsmuseums.gov.uk
e queenstreet.mill@mus.lancscc.gov.uk

807 Carnforth

Leighton Hall

2 hrs May–Sep

Leighton Hall is the home of the famous Gillow furniture-making dynasty. Learn about the past of this ancient Lancashire family, wander through the grounds and pretty gardens and witness flying displays by trained birds of prey.

* C19 walled garden, landscaped parkland & woodland
* Entertaining guides reveal the family's history

Location
Take junction 35A of M6, to North Carnforth & follow brown tourist signs

Opening
May–July & Sep Tue–Fri & Sun 2pm–5pm, Bank Hols 2pm–5pm; Aug Tue–Fri & Sun 12noon–5pm, Aug Bank Hol 12.30pm–5pm

Admission
Adult £5.50, Child £4, Concs £5

Contact
Carnforth LA5 9ST

t 01524 734474
w leightonhall.co.uk
e info@leightonhall.co.uk

808 Chorley

Astley Hall Museum & Art Gallery

1 hr Easter–Sep

This hall dates back to Elizabethan times but changes have been made over the centuries. The collections range from C18 creamware and glass to the first Rugby League Cup and C16 shovelboard table.

* Programme of special exhibitions, events & activities
* C17 plaster ceilings

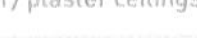

Location
W of Chorley town centre off A581 Chorley-Southport road

Opening
Easter–Sep Sat–Sun & Bank Hols 12noon–5pm

Admission
Free

Contact
Astley Park, Chorley PR7 1NP

t 01257 515927
w chorley.gov.uk/astleyhall
e astley.hall@churley.gov.uk

809 Fleetwood

Fleetwood Museum

1 hr Apr–Nov

Built in 1838 and occupying the old Customs House designed by architect Decimus Burton, this fascinating museum brings the story of Fleetwood and the surrounding coast to life. Trace Fleetwood's past – its cargo trade and famous fishing industry.

* Understand a fisherman's life & the harsh working conditions
* See the *Harriet*, the last surviving fishing smack in the North West

Location
Follow M55 to Fleetwood, then A585

Opening
Daily: Mon–Sat 10am–4pm, Sun 1pm–4pm

Admission
Adult £3, Child free, Concs £2

Contact
Queen's Terrace, Fleetwood FY7 6BT

t 01253 876621
w nettingthebay.org.uk
e fleetwood@muslancscc.gov.uk

810 Horwich

Horwich Heritage Centre

  2 hrs  All year

This centre aims to preserve and present the rich history and heritage of Horwich by featuring specific aspects of Horwich life over the centuries, using videos, displays, artefacts and exhibits. There is a new shop and an archive facility.

* Exhibition of local historic works
* Full range of publications on Horwich available

Location
Junction 6 of M61 & A673

Opening
Tue & Fri 10am–12noon & 2pm–4pm, Wed 2pm–4pm, Sat 10am–1pm

Admission
Free

Contact
Longworth Road, Horwich BL6 7BG

t 01204 847797
w horwichheritage.co.uk

811 Lancaster

Judges' Lodgings

  1 hr  Easter–Oct

This is Lancaster's oldest town house, home to Thomas Cavell, keeper of the castle during Lancashire's witch trials of 1612. Later used as a residence for judges visiting Lancaster Castle, it is now a museum displaying a wealth of furniture, porcelain, silver and paintings.

* Collection of Gillow furniture in period rooms
* Collection of dolls, toys & games from the C18 to the present day

Location
Near railway station, on cobbled roads just down from castle

Opening
Easter–Jun & Oct Mon–Fri 1pm–4pm, Sat–Sun 12noon–4pm;
Jul–Sep Mon–Fri 10am–4pm, Sat–Sun 12noon–4pm

Admission
Adult £3, Child free, Concs £2

Contact
Church Street, Lancaster LA1 1YS

t 01524 32808
w lancsmuseums.gov.uk
e judges.lodgings@mus.lancscc.gov.uk

812 Lancaster

Lancaster Castle

  1 hr+  All year

One of the best-preserved and hardest-working castles in the country, still used today as a court and prison. Visitors can see where the Lancashire Witches were tried and condemned to death, the Hanging Corner where prisoners were hanged, the dungeons and the Drop Room.

* Display of heraldic shields in the Shire Hall
* Beautiful Gillow furniture in grand jury room

Location
Off Meetinghouse Lane, turn right into Castle Hill

Opening
Daily: 10am–5pm
Admission by guided tour only

Admission
Adult £5, Child & Concs £4

Contact
Castle Parade, Lancaster LA1 1YJ

t 01524 64998
w lancastercastle.com
e christine.goodier@mus.lancscc.gov.uk

813 Lancaster

Lancaster Maritime Museum

  2 hrs  All year

Lancaster Maritime Museum occupies two historic buildings on St George's Quay, the main C18 harbour. The former Customs House of 1764, designed by Richard Gillow, contains displays on the history of the port of Lancaster and the local fishing industry.

* Lancaster Canal & Morecambe Bay ecology displays
* *Sir William Priestley* & *Coronation Rose* ships

Location
St George's Quay

Opening
Easter–Oct 11am–5pm;
Nov–Easter 12.30pm–4pm

Admission
Adult £3, Child free, Concs £2

Contact
St George's Quay, Lancaster LA1 1RB

t 01524 382264
w lancsmuseums.gov.uk
e sarah.riddle@mus.lancscc.gov.uk

814 Morecambe

Eric Morecambe statue

  1 hr  All year

Unveiled by the Queen in 1999, this larger-than-life statue depicts Eric Morecambe in a characteristic pose with a pair of binoculars around his neck (he was a keen ornithologist). The statue is set against the backdrop of Morecambe Bay and the Lake District hills.

* People queue to have their photograph taken here

Location
Leave M6 at junction 34 or 35 & follow signs for Morecambe. Statue is in Central Promenade area

Opening
Daily; All reasonable times

Admission
Free

Contact
Central Promenade, Morecambe, or Tourist Information Centre

t 01524 582808
w citypostcountryside.co.uk

815 Nelson

British in India Museum

  1 hr   All year

The museum was opened in 1972 and has now moved to Nelson. On display are Indian regimental ties, paintings, photographs of military and civilian subjects, model soldiers, medals, coins, picture postcards, postage stamps, toys and examples of Indian dress.

* Learn about the people behind the Raj

Location
Take A56–A6068 between Burnley & Keighley

Opening
Mon–Fri 10am–4pm

Admission
Adult £3.50, Child 50p

Contact
Hendon Mill, Hallam Road, Nelson BB9 8AD

t 01282 613129

816 Ormskirk

Rufford Old Hall

  2 hrs+  Mar–Oct

This is a fine C16 building famed for its great hall, which has an intricately carved 'moveable' wooden screen and hammerbeam roof. It is rumoured that Shakespeare performed in this hall for the owner, Sir Thomas Hesketh.

* Fine collections of C16–C17 oak furniture
* Arms, armour & tapestries

Location
7 miles N of Ormskirk in Rufford village on E side of A59

Opening
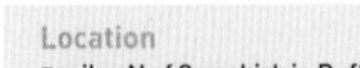
17 Mar–Oct Sat–Wed 1pm–5pm

Admission
House & Gardens Adult £4.90, Child £2.50
Gardens £2.80, £1.30

Contact
Rufford, Ormskirk L40 1SG

t 01704 821254
w nationaltrust.org.uk
e ruffordoldhall@nationaltrust.org.uk

817 Preston

British Commercial Vehicle Museum

  2 hrs  Apr–Oct

This is one of Britain's most important heritage collections. It contains a unique line-up of historic commercial vehicles and buses representing a century of truck and bus building. It is located in the heart of Leyland.

* Sound & Light show on WWI
* Popemobile

Location
Junction 28 of M6. Follow signs

Opening
Apr–Sep Sun, Tue–Thu & Bank Hol Mon 10am–5pm; Oct Sun only

Admission
Adult £4, Child £2

Contact
King Street, Leyland, Preston PR25 2LE

t 01772 451011
w bccm.co.uk

818 Preston

Harris Museum & Art Gallery

2 hrs All year

Discover the best of Preston's heritage in a beautiful Grade I-listed building. The Harris has large collections of paintings, sculpture, textiles, costume, glass and ceramics, as well as the Story of Preston Gallery that brings the history of the city to life.

* Exciting programme of exhibitions
* National reputation for contemporary art shows

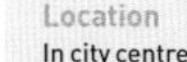 

Location
In city centre

Opening
Daily: Mon & Wed–Sat 10am–5pm, Tue 11am–5pm, Sun 11am–4pm

Admission
Free

Contact
Market Square, Preston PR1 2PP

t 01772 258248
e harris.museum@preston.gov.uk

819 Preston

Museum of Lancashire

2 hrs All year

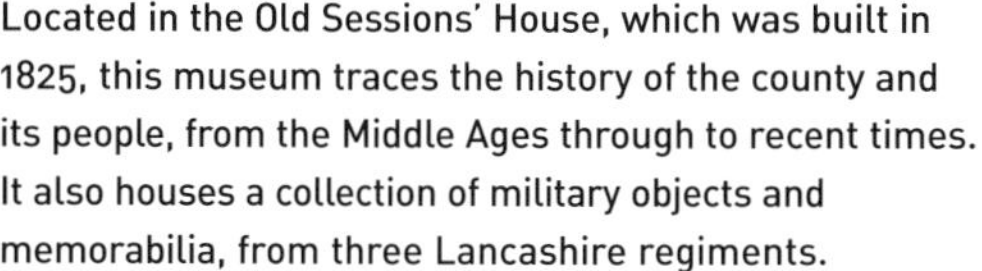

Located in the Old Sessions' House, which was built in 1825, this museum traces the history of the county and its people, from the Middle Ages through to recent times. It also houses a collection of military objects and memorabilia, from three Lancashire regiments.

* Colourful uniforms & splendid swords displayed
* Reconstruction of a WWI trench, programme of family events

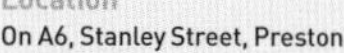

Location
On A6, Stanley Street, Preston

Opening
Mon–Wed, Fri & Sat 10.30am–5pm

Admission
Adult £3, Child free, Concs £2

Contact
Stanley Street, Preston PR1 4YP

t 01772 534075
w lancsmuseums.gov.uk
e museums.enquiries@mus.lancscc.gov.uk

820 Preston

National Football Museum

2 hrs All year

Embark on a journey through football's history. Learn how the game was invented, how it has developed over the past 150 years, and what the future may hold for players and supporters. Learn about the individuals and teams who have helped to shape the game we know today.

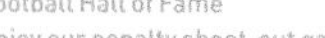 

* Football Hall of Fame
* Enjoy our penalty shoot-out game

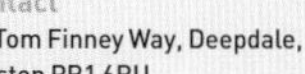

Location
2 miles from junction 31, 31A or 32 of M6. Follow signs

Opening
Tue–Sat 10am–5pm, Sun 11am–5pm

Admission
Free

Contact
Sir Tom Finney Way, Deepdale, Preston PR1 6RU

t 01772 908403/442
w nationalfootballmuseum.com
e enquiries@nationalfootballmuseum.com

821 Rivington

Lever Park

3 hrs+ All year

Sited on the West Pennine moors, this park has good facilities for fishing, walking and refreshments as well as an arboretum and pinetum. Other interesting features include the remains of Lord Leverhulme's gardens and two cruck barns.

* Ruined replica of Liverpool Castle & Rivington Pike
* Reservoir

Location
Off A673 north of Horwich. On Rivington Lane

Opening
Wed–Sun & Bank Hols 10.30am–4.30pm

Admission
Free

Contact
Great House Information Centre, Rivington Lane, Horwich BL6 7SB

t 01204 691549
w unitedutilities.com

822 Wigan

Haigh Country Park

5 hrs+ All year

This park includes an arts and crafts gallery with exhibitions of pottery, embroidery and paintings. The model village features a railway, helipad, pub and castle. The walled garden originally supplied the hall with fruit and vegetables and now provides a peaceful retreat.

* Miniature railway, crazy golf & children's play area
* 9-&-18 hole golf complex

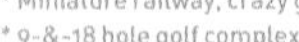    

Location
Near B5238 & B5239

Opening
Park Daily: dawn–dusk
Visitor centre Daily. Times vary, please phone for details

Admission
Free

Contact
Haigh, Wigan WN2 1PE

t 01942 832895
w haighhall.net
e hhgen@wlct.org

823 Manchester

Chinese Arts Centre

1 hr All year

This modern building offers changing contemporary art exhibitions, workshops, education programmes and information about Chinese art and culture, with a particular emphasis on supporting Sino-British artistic expression.

* State-of-the-art education suite
* Traditional Chinese tearooms

Location
In Market Buildings, Thomas Street, city centre

Opening
Mon–Sat 10am–6pm, Sun 11am–5pm

Admission
Free

Contact
Thomas Street, Manchester M4 1 EU

t 0161 832 7271
w chinese-arts-centre.org
e info@chinese-arts-centre.org

824 Manchester

Heaton Hall & Park

2 hrs Easter–Sep

Heaton Hall has beautifully restored interiors housing a collection of furniture and musical instruments. In the park there is a range of facilities for all tastes including cafés, an Animal Centre, a Tram Museum, bowling greens, a golf course, horse-riding and a boating lake.

* Architect James Wyatt remodelled the house in 1772
* One of the finest neoclassical houses in the country

Location
In middle of Heaton Park off Middleton Road in East Manchester

Opening
Easter–Sep Wed–Sun & Bank Hols 10am–5.30pm
Park Daily: All reasonable times

Admission
Free

Contact
Heaton Park, Prestwich, Manchester M25 5SW

t 0161 235 8888
w manchestergalleries.org

825 Manchester

Imperial War Museum North

  1 hr+  All year

The museum, situated on the banks of the Manchester Ship Canal, offers people of all ages thought-provoking displays and direct access to its evocative collections. It gives valuable insights into the enormous impact of war in the C20 and C21.

* Highlights of WWII art
* The Animals' War (open summer 2007)

Location
Junction 9 of M60, then follow signs to quays

Opening
Daily: Mar–Oct 10am–6pm; Nov–Feb 10am–5pm

Admission
Free

Contact
Trafford Wharf Road, The Quays, Trafford Park M17 ITZ

t 0161 836 4000
w iwm.org.uk
e iwmnorth@iwm.org.uk

826 Manchester

Jewish Museum of Manchester

 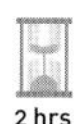 2 hrs  All year

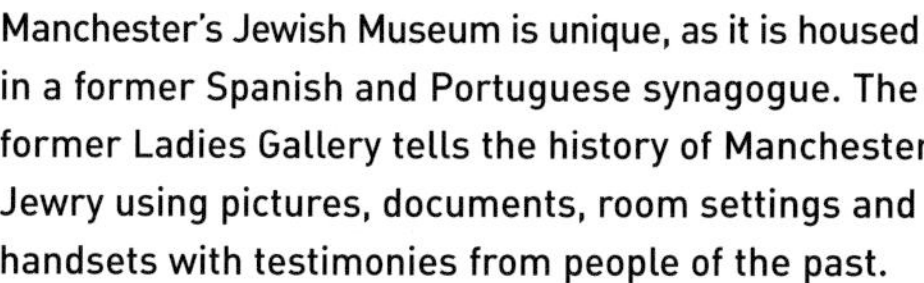

Manchester's Jewish Museum is unique, as it is housed in a former Spanish and Portuguese synagogue. The former Ladies Gallery tells the history of Manchester Jewry using pictures, documents, room settings and handsets with testimonies from people of the past.

* Lavish Moorish decor & stained glass
* Events & exhibitions throughout the year

Location
On A665, 1 mile from city centre

Opening
Mon–Thu 10.30am–4pm,
Sun 10.30am–5pm
(closed Sat & Jewish hols)

Admission
Adult £3.95, Child & Concs £2.95

Contact
190 Cheetham Hill Road, Manchester M8 8LW

t 0161 834 9879
w manchesterjewishmuseum.com
e don@manchesterjewishmuseum. com

827 Manchester

Manchester Art Gallery

4 hrs+ All year

Manchester Art Gallery houses one of the country's finest art collections in spectacular surroundings. Highlights include outstanding Pre-Raphaelite paintings, craft and design and early C20 British art. It also has a lively new space with hands-on activities for families.

* Collection spans 6 centuries of fine & decorative art
* Exceptional collection of C19 British paintings

Location
In city centre

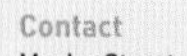

Opening
Tue–Sun 10am–5pm
(closed Mon except Bank Hols)

Admission
Free

Contact
Mosley Street, Manchester M2 3JL

t 0161 235 8888
w manchestergalleries.org

828 Manchester

Manchester Museum

4 hrs+ All year

This museum, with its displays and exhibitions in 15 galleries, houses collections from all over the world. Visit the famous Egyptology galleries, the Prehistoric Life Gallery featuring 'Stan', a full-size T. Rex, and the Zoology Gallery containing mammals and birds.

* Ethnology collections from South America
* Vivarium, housing live reptiles & amphibians

Location
In Oxford Road to S of city centre

Opening
Daily: Tue–Sat 10am–5pm,
Sun–Mon & Bank Hols 11am–4pm

Admission
Free. Special events may charge

Contact
University of Manchester,
Oxford Road,
Manchester M13 9PL

t 0161 275 2634
w manchester.ac.uk/museum
e museum@manchester.ac.uk

829 Manchester

Museum of Science & Industry in Manchester

4 hrs+ | All year

Situated in the oldest-surviving passenger railway buildings in the world, the museum tells the story of Manchester, the world's first industrial city – its industry and the science behind it. Stimulate the senses in Xperiment, an interactive science gallery.

* Demonstrators operate thunderous cotton machinery
* Exciting events & exhibitions throughout the year

Location
On Liverpool Road in Castlefield, signed from city centre

Opening
Daily: 10am–5pm

Admission
Free. Exhibitions may charge

Contact
Liverpool Road, Castlefield, Manchester M3 4FP

t 0161 832 2244
w msim.org.uk
e marketing@msim.org.uk

830 Manchester

Museum of Transport

 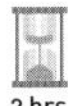 

2 hrs | All year

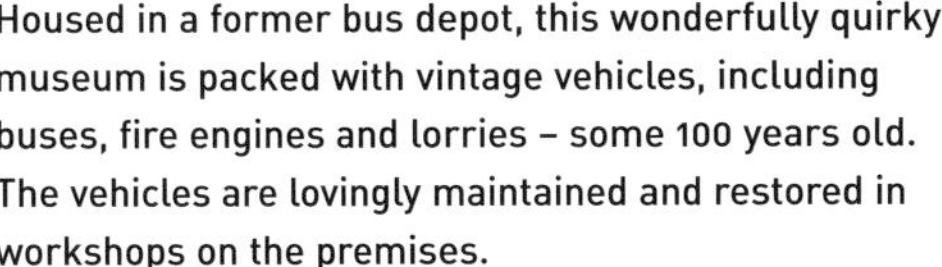

Housed in a former bus depot, this wonderfully quirky museum is packed with vintage vehicles, including buses, fire engines and lorries – some 100 years old. The vehicles are lovingly maintained and restored in workshops on the premises.

* Biggest collection of vintage buses in the UK

Location
1 mile N of city centre at N end of Boyle Street, next to Queen's Road bus garage

Opening
Mar–Oct Wed, Sat–Sun & Bank Hols 10am–5pm; Nov–Feb 10am–4pm

Admission
Adult £4, Child & Concs £2

Contact
Boyle Street, Cheetham, Manchester M8 8UW

t 0161 205 2122
w gmts.co.uk
e busmuseum@btconnect.com

831 Manchester

Old Trafford Museum & Tour

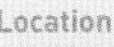

2 hrs | All year

Britain's first purpose-built football museum covers the history of Manchester United from 1878 to the present day. There are frequently updated exhibits and guided tours of the stadium. Picture yourself with the players, using the latest digital imaging technology.

* Record your own commentary on United games
* Multi-award winner

Location
From Chester Road (A56) turn into Sir Matt Busby Way, or use Old Trafford Metrolink station

Opening
Museum Daily: 9.30am–5pm
Tour Daily: 9.40am–4.30pm
Pre-booking recommended

Admission
Museum & Tour Adult £9.50, Child & Concs £6.50

Contact
Sir Matt Busby Way, Old Trafford, Manchester M16 0RA

t 0870 442 1994
w manutd.com
e tours@manutd.co.uk

832 Manchester

Trafford Ecology Park

2 hrs+ All year

Once an industrial wasteland, Trafford Ecology Park has been transformed into a thriving activity centre and haven for wildlife. Visitors can see the displays, take part in the events, or simply discover the wealth of wild flowers, trees, birds and animals that flourish here.

* Spread around on a reclaimed boating lake
* Based in what was Europe's largest industrial estate

Location
From M602 take A576. From M60 junction 9 take A5081

Opening
Mon–Fri 9am–5pm
(closed Sat–Sun & Bank Hols)

Admission
Free

Contact
Lake Road, Trafford Park, Manchester M17 1TU

t 0161 873 7182
w trafford.gov.uk
e ecology.reception@groundworks.org.uk

833 Manchester

Urbis

2 hrs All year

Urbis explores urban culture and the cities of today and tomorrow. Make your own ID cards; keep one and stick one on the wall for all to see. Select your crime, choose your city and receive your sentence from the world's only automatic law dispenser.

* A visit begins with a sky glide in the glass elevator
* Combination of audio, visual & tactile environments

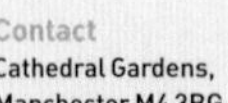

Location
In city centre

Opening
Sun–Wed 10am–6pm, Thu–Sat 10am–8pm

Admission
Free. Charge may apply to Level 1 gallery

Contact
Cathedral Gardens, Manchester M4 3BG

t 0161 605 8200
w urbis.org.uk
e info@urbis.org.uk

834 Manchester

The Whitworth Art Gallery

1 hr All year

This gallery houses an impressive range of watercolours, prints, drawings, modern art and sculpture, as well as the largest collection of textiles and wallpapers outside London. The Whitworth uses its collections to create changing exhibitions exploring different themes.

* Programme of innovative touring exhibitions
* Specialist centre for works on paper & textiles

Location
Follow Oxford Road to S of Manchester city centre & to S of University of Manchester campus

Opening
Mon–Sat 10am–5pm, Sun 2pm–5pm
Sat afternoon free eye-opener tour at 2pm. Please phone to confirm

Admission
Free

Contact
University of Manchester, Oxford Road, Manchester M15 6ER

t 0161 275 7450
w manchester.ac.uk/whitworth
e whitworth@manchester.ac.uk

835 Birkenhead

Birkenhead Priory & St Mary's Tower

 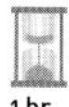 1 hr  All year

This Benedictine monastery, established around 1150, is the oldest standing building on Merseyside. There is a memorial to those who lost their lives aboard the submarine *Thetis*. Enjoy the magnificent views up, down and across the River Mersey to Liverpool.

* Views of Birkenhead, Oxton Ridge, Bidston & the Wirral
* Concerts on Sun in Aug

Location
M53 on to A41, then follow signs to Birkenhead

Opening
Easter–Oct Wed–Fri 1pm–5pm, Sat–Sun 10am–5pm;
Nov–Easter Wed–Fri 12noon–4pm, Sat–Sun 10am–4pm

Admission
Free

Contact
Priory Street, Birkenhead CH41 5JH
t 0151 666 1249
w wirral.gov.uk
e comments@wirral.gov.uk

836 Birkenhead

Birkenhead Tramway & Wirral Transport Museum

  1 hr  All year

Birkenhead is the home of the first street tramway in Europe. Take the tramway from Woodside visitor centre to the Old Colonial pub at the Taylor Street terminus. From there visit the Wirral Transport Museum, which houses restored and part-restored local buses and trams.

* Open-topped 1901 Birkenhead tram 20
* Day-to-day service operated by 2 Hong Kong trams

Location
Signed to Taylor Street from Woodside ferry terminal

Opening
Weekends & Bank Hols 1pm–5pm; school hols, Easter, spring half-term & summer Wed–Sun 1pm–5pm

Admission
Adult £1, Child 50p

Contact
1 Taylor Street, Birkenhead CH41 1BG
t 0151 647 6780
w wirraltransportmuseums.org

837 Birkenhead

Williamson Art Gallery & Museum

 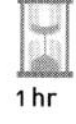 1 hr   All year

The Williamson houses a superb art collection, with Cammell Laird's and other ship models illustrating local and maritime history. On display are Victorian oil paintings, Della Robbia pottery and Liverpool porcelain, tapestries by Arthur Lee & Sons and British watercolours.

* Part of Merseyside embroidery trail
* Varied programme of temporary exhibitions

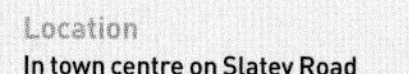

Location
In town centre on Slatey Road

Opening
Tue–Sun &Bank Hols 10am–5pm

Admission
Free

Contact
Slatey Road, Birkenhead CH43 4UE
t 0151 652 4177
w wirral.gov.uk
e williamsonartgallery@wirral.gov.uk

838 Knowsley

National Wildflower Centre

  2 hrs  Apr–Sep

The National Wildflower Centre is set in a Victorian park within 35 acres of parkland. It has an innovative visitor centre where visitors can learn all about wild flowers. It places an emphasis on creative conservation and preserving and reintroducing wild flowers in Britain.

* Seasonal wildflower demonstration areas
* Working garden nursery & shop

Location
In Knowsley's Court Hey Park, off junction 5 of M62

Opening
Daily: Apr–Sep 10am–5pm

Admission
Adult £3, Child free, Concs £1.50

Contact
Court Hey Park, Knowsley L16 3NA
t 0151 738 1913/722 8292
w nwc.org.uk
e info@nwc.org.uk

839 Liverpool

Aintree Racecourse & Visitor Centre

2 hrs+

June–Sept

Discover the history of a race once believed to be suitable only for scoundrels. There is a museum and picture gallery plus the chance to explore the weighing room, stables and parade ring before browsing through the memorabilia and papers in the Reading Room.

* Venue for the Grand National

Location
5 miles from Liverpool city centre, well signed

Opening
Group visits only, please phone for details

Admission
Adult £7, Child & Concs £4

Contact
Ormskirk Road, Aintree, Liverpool L9 5AS

t 0151 523 2600
w aintree.co.uk

840 Liverpool

Albert Dock

4 hrs+

All year

The Albert Dock is an architectural triumph. Opened in 1846, it became a treasure house of precious cargoes from all over the world. Today redevelopment has transformed it into a busy and cosmopolitan centre as well as a top heritage attraction.

* Converted C19 warehouse buildings
* Visit albertdock.com for a webcam view of the attraction

Location
On Liverpool's waterfront, adjacent to Pier Head

Opening
Daily from 10am

Admission
Free

Contact
Edward Pavilion, Albert Dock, Liverpool L3 4AF

t 0151 708 7334
w albertdock.com
e enquiries@albertdock.com

841 Liverpool

Beatles Story

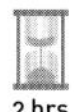

2 hrs All year

Imagine reliving the greatest story the pop world has ever known – in the city where it all began! Take a nostalgic trip through the multi-award-winning Beatles Story experience, on Liverpool's historic Albert Dock.

* Living history audio tour
* Personal insights from those who really knew the Fab Four

Location
Follow signposts to Albert Dock

Opening
Daily: 10am–6pm (last admission 5pm)

Admission
Adult £8.99, Child £4.99, Concs £5.99

Contact
Albert Dock, Britannia Vaults, Liverpool L3 4AD

t 0151 709 1963
w beatlesstory.com
e info@beatlesstory.com

842 Liverpool

Cains Brewery

1 hr+ All year

Cains has always been renowned for producing award-winning cask ales. Incorporating the Brewery Tap, now one of Liverpool's drinking landmarks, Robert Cains's original Mersey brewery stands today as a fine example of Victorian brewhouse architecture.

* Tours include buffet & 2 pints in the Brewery Tap pub

Location
In West Parliament Street, near Albert Dock

Opening
Tours: Mon–Fri at 6.30pm

Admission
Adult (over-18s only) £3.75
Pre-booking essential

Contact
Stanhope Street, Liverpool L8 5XJ

t 0151 709 8734
w cains.co.uk
e brewerytour@cainsbeers.com

843 Liverpool

The Cavern Club

4 hrs+ All year

Visit this world-famous nightclub and learn all there is to know about the Cavern Club, from its early days as a jazz club in the cellar of a fruit warehouse, to the live music venue of today. This is a carbon copy of the original club where the Beatles found fame.

* Paul McCartney played his last gig of the century here
* Wall of Fame

Location
In city centre

Opening
Mon–Wed 11am–6pm, Thu 11am-2am, Fri–Sat 11am–2.45am, Sun 12noon–12.30am

Admission
Free. Sat Adult £2

Contact
Mathew Street, Liverpool L2 6RE

t 0151 236 1965
w caverncitytours.com
e office@thecavernliverpool.com

844 Liverpool

Conservation Centre

1 hr All year

This Conservation Centre is housed in the former Midland Railway goods depot, which was built in the 1870s. The centre cares for all the National Museums of Liverpool collections. There are more than a million objects, ranging from tiny natural history specimens to space rockets.

* Conservation science section
* Many world-famous masterpieces cared for here

Location
Near Queen's Square bus station

Opening
Please phone for details

Admission
Free

Contact
Whitechapel, Liverpool L1 6HZ

t 0151 478 4999
w liverpoolmuseums.org
e conservation@liverpoolmuseums.org.uk

845 Liverpool

Everton Football Club

1¼ hrs All year

A tour of Goodison Park will include a behind-the-scenes look at what it's like to play for the Toffees. Walk down the tunnel and imagine the roar of 40,000 fans, explore the dressing room and see where the players relax and celebrate – or commiserate – after a game.

WC

Location
3 miles N of city centre

Opening
Tours Mon, Wed, Fri & Sun 11am & 1pm

Admission
Adult £8.50, Child & Concs £5
Pre-booking essential

Contact
Goodison Park, Liverpool L4 4EL

t 0870 442 1878
w evertonfc.com
e stadiumtours@evertonfc.com

846 Liverpool

Liverpool Cathedral

2 hrs All year

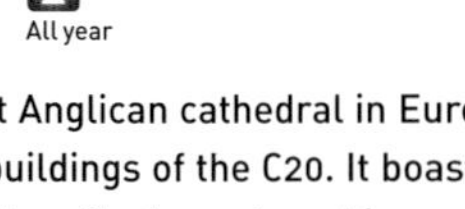

This is the largest Anglican cathedral in Europe and one of the great buildings of the C20. It boasts the highest Gothic arches, the largest working organ and the heaviest ring of bells in the world and throughout the year hosts exhibitions, concerts and recitals.

* Visitor centre opened autumn 2006
* The grand organ has 9,765 pipes

WC

Location
Half a mile from city centre

Opening
8am–6pm (subject to services)

Admission
Free, donations welcomed
Tower Adults £4.25, Child & Concs £2.50

Contact
St James' Mount, Liverpool L1 7AZ

t 0151 709 6271
w liverpoolcathedral.org.uk
e info@liverpoolcathedral.org.uk

847 Liverpool

Liverpool Football Club Museum & Tour Centre

1 hr All year

A tour of Anfield includes a walk down the players' tunnel and the opportunity to touch the famous sign that proclaims 'This is Anfield'. Experience the dressing room where the manager delivers his team talks. The museum is packed with things to do, see and listen to.

* Film takes visitors through the life of the club
* Hillsborough memorial tribute to 96 fans who died in 1989

   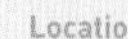

Location
3 miles from city centre, 4 miles from M62, 7 miles from end of M57 & M58

Opening
Daily: 10am–5pm
(last admission 4pm; closes 1 hr before kick-off)

Admission
Adult £9, Child & Concs £5.50

Contact
Anfield Road, Liverpool L4 0TH
t 0151 260 6677
w liverpoolfc.tv
e events@liverpoolfc.tv

848 Liverpool

Merseyside Maritime Museum

4 hrs+ All year

The museum tells the history of this great port and the vessels which used it, from slavers to luxury liners and submarine hunters to passenger ferries. During the summer you can walk the quayside and even climb aboard a pilot boat, the *Edmund Gardner*.

* 3-masted schooner in dry dock
* Maritime archive & library

Location
Short walk from city centre

Opening
Daily: 10am–5pm

Admission
Free

Contact
Albert Dock, Liverpool L3 4AQ
t 0151 478 4499
w liverpoolmuseums.org.uk/maritime

849 Liverpool

Sefton Park Palm House

1 hr All year

Sefton Park Palm House is a Grade II-listed Victorian glasshouse. It is an octagonal three-tiered structure, showcasing the Liverpool Botanical Collection that was created from specimens brought to the city from all over the world during its maritime heyday.

* One of the largest municipal collections in the country
* 4 sculptures by Leon-Joseph Chavailiaud

Location
Take M62 on to A5058 towards Queen's Drive & Alliton Road

Opening
Nov–Mar 10.30am–4pm;
Apr–Oct 10.30am–5pm
Restricted opening during events, please phone for details

Admission
Free

Contact
Sefton Park, Liverpool L17 1AP
t 0151 726 2415
w palmhouse.org.uk
e info@palmhouse.org.uk

850 Liverpool

Mendips & 20 Forthlin Road

  2 hrs  Mar–Oct

This is a joint tour of Mendips, the childhood home of John Lennon, and Forthlin Road, the home of the McCartney family, where the Beatles met, rehearsed and wrote many of their earliest songs. Displays include contemporary photographs and Beatles memorabilia.

* Audio tour features Sir Paul McCartney
* Evocative photographs of life at 20 Forthlin Road

Location
Morning tours leave from Conservation Centre in city centre. Afternoon tours leave from Speke Hall

Opening
Morning tours depart 10.30am & 11.20am from Conservation Centre; Afternoon tours depart 2.15pm & 3.55pm from Speke Hall

Admission
Adult £12, Child £1

Contact
20 Forthlin Road, Allerton, Liverpool L24 1YP

t 0151 233 2457 – am tours
0151 427 7231 – pm tours
w nationaltrust.org.uk
e spekehall@nationaltrust.org.uk

851 Liverpool

Speke Hall, Garden & Estate

  2 hrs  Mar–Dec

Behind the black-and-white half-timbered façade of this hall are interiors that represent many centuries. The great hall and priest's holes evoke Tudor times, while the oak parlour and smaller rooms show the Victorian desire for privacy and comfort.

* Fine Jacobean plasterwork & carved furniture
* Fully-equipped Victorian kitchen & servants' hall

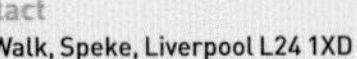

Location
8 miles SE of central Liverpool, next to Liverpool Airport, signed

Opening
Mar–Oct Wed–Sun 1pm–5.30pm; Nov–Dec Sat–Sun 1pm–4.30pm

Admission
Adult £6.50, Child £3.50

Contact
The Walk, Speke, Liverpool L24 1XD

t 0151 427 7231
w nationaltrust.org.uk
e mendips@nationaltrust.org.uk

852 Liverpool

Tate Liverpool

2 hrs

All year

Tate Liverpool is one of the largest galleries of modern art outside London and displays special exhibitions that bring together artworks from around the world. The exhibitions show art from 1900 to the present day and include photography, video and installation.

* Photography, printmaking, painting & sculpture
* Free daily talks, shops & café

Location
Walking distance from Liverpool Lime Street railway station, signed from city centre

Opening
Jan–May, Sep–Dec Tue–Sun 10am–5.50pm; Jun–Aug daily 10am–5.50pm

Admission
Tate Liverpool Free
Exhibition Adult £4, Child free, Concs £3

Contact
Tate Liverpool, Albert Dock, Liverpool L3 4BB

t 0151 702 7400
w tate.org.uk/liverpool
e visitliverpool@tate.org.uk

853 Liverpool

The Walker

1 hr

All year

The Walker holds one of the finest collections of fine and decorative art in Europe. The gallery has recently undergone a major £4.3 million refurbishment programme. The improvements include special exhibition galleries for important touring shows.

* Children's gallery
* Craft & design gallery of decorative arts

Location
Opposite entrance to Birkenhead tunnel, 5 min from Tourist Information Centre

Opening
Daily: 10am–5pm

Admission
Free

Contact
William Brown Street, Liverpool L3 8EL

t 0151 478 4199
w thewalker.org.uk
e thewalker@liverpoolmuseums.org.uk

854 Prescot

Knowsley Safari Park

3 hrs+

All year

During the 5-mile-long drive visitors can see a wide range of wild animals, including camels, buffalo, white rhinos, emus, wallabies and lions. A separate reptile house is home to snakes, iguanas, lizards, scorpions and stick insects.

* 500 acres of rolling countryside
* Elephants, giraffes, otters & meerkats in walkaround attraction

Location
Leave M62 at junction 6 & then M57 at junction 2, & follow signs

Opening
Daily: Mar–Oct 10am–4pm; Nov–Feb 10.30am–3pm

Admission
Adult £10, Child & Concs £7
Family ticket (2 Adult & 2 Child) £30

Contact
Prescot, Merseyside L34 4AN

t 0151 430 9009
w knowsley.com
e safari.park@knowsley.com

855 Southport

Formby

2 hrs

All year

This nature reserve is home to one of Britain's last thriving colonies of red squirrels. These can be seen in the pine trees, while the shoreline attracts waders such as oystercatchers and sanderlings. As well as the beautiful beach, there are miles of walks across the sand dunes.

* Programme of events throughout the year
* Country walks

Location
15 miles N of Liverpool, 2 miles W of Formby, 2 miles off A565 & 6 miles S of Southport

Opening
Daily: dawn–dusk

Admission
Free. Car park £3.30

Contact
Blundell Avenue, Formby L37 1PH

t 01704 878591
w nationaltrust.org.uk
e formby@nationaltrust.org.uk

Angel of the North, Gateshead

North East

Durham Northumberland Tyne & Wear

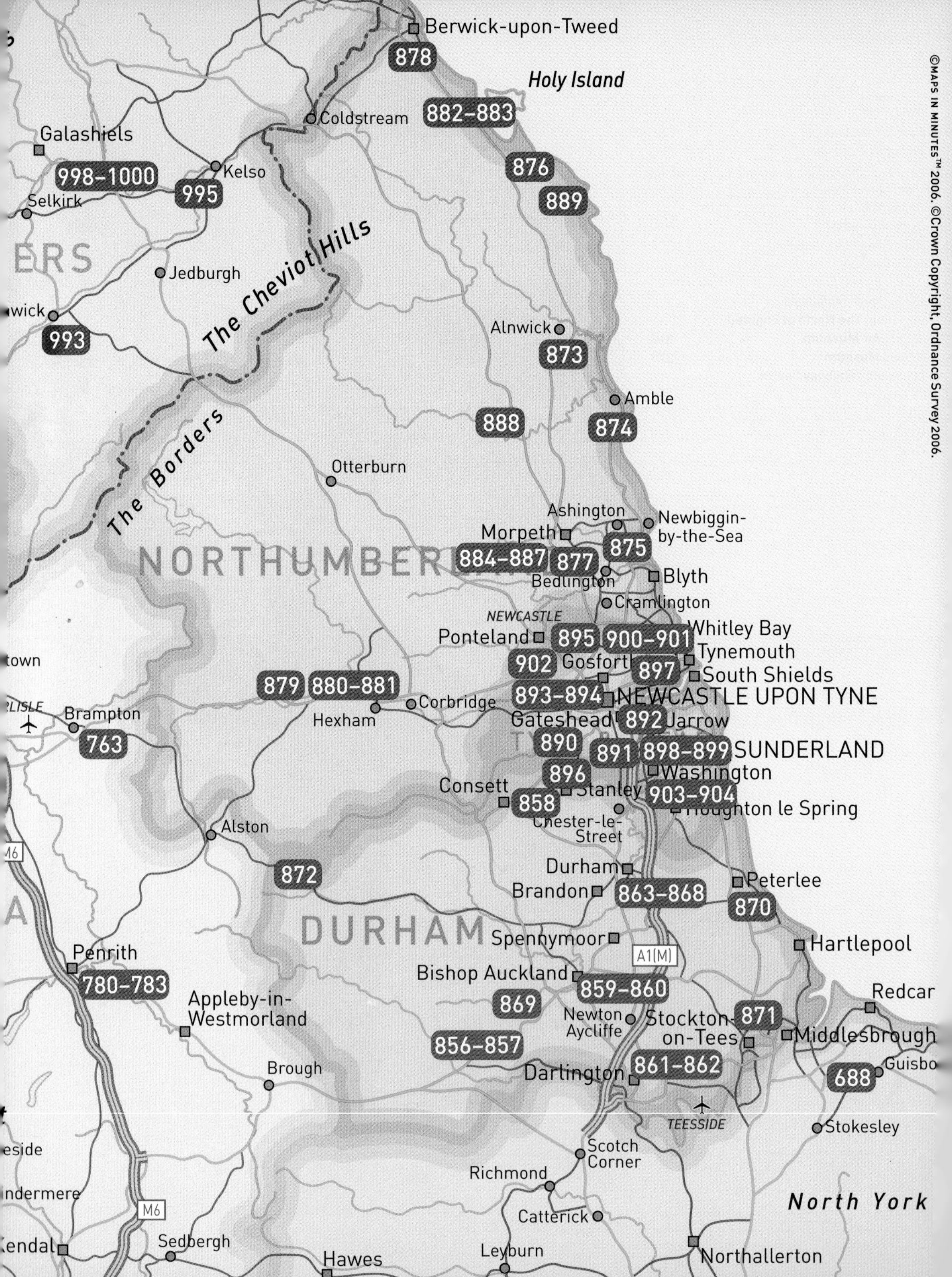
Berwick-upon-Tweed
878
Holy Island
Coldstream
882–883
Galashiels
Kelso
998–1000
995
876
889
Selkirk
ERS
Jedburgh
The Cheviot Hills
wick
993
Alnwick
873
Amble
888
874
The Borders
Otterburn
Ashington
Newbiggin-by-the-Sea
Morpeth
875
NORTHUMBERLAND
884–887
877
Blyth
Bedlington
Cramlington
NEWCASTLE
Whitley Bay
Ponteland
895
900–901
Tynemouth
902
Gosforth
897
South Shields
town
879
880–881
893–894
NEWCASTLE UPON TYNE
Corbridge
Brampton
Hexham
Gateshead
892
Jarrow
763
890
891
898–899
SUNDERLAND
896
Washington
Consett
Stanley
903–904
858
Houghton le Spring
Chester-le-Street
Alston
M6
872
Durham
Peterlee
Brandon
863–868
870
DURHAM
Spennymoor
Hartlepool
A1(M)
Penrith
Bishop Auckland
780–783
859–860
Redcar
Appleby-in-Westmorland
869
Newton Aycliffe
Stockton-on-Tees
871
Middlesbrough
856–857
Brough
Darlington
861–862
Guisbo
688
TEESSIDE
Stokesley
eside
Scotch Corner
Richmond
ndermere
North York
M6
Catterick
Kendal
Sedbergh
Leyburn
Northallerton
Hawes

DURHAM

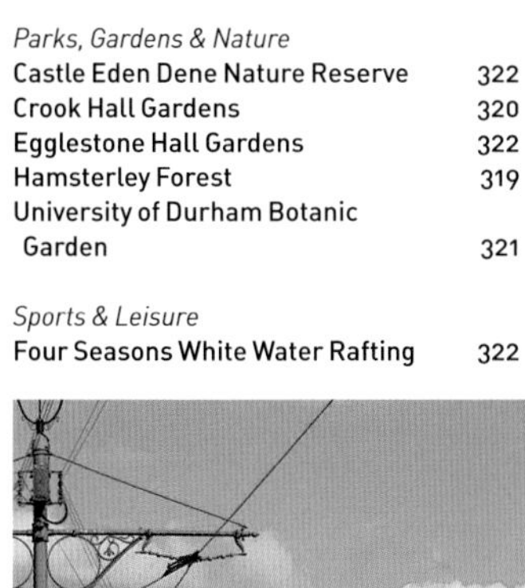

NORTHUMBERLAND

TYNE & WEAR

856 Barnard Castle

Barnard Castle

  1 hr+  All year

This imposing English Heritage property sits high above the River Tees. The C12 stone castle was once one of the largest in northern England, the principal residence of the Baliol family, and a major power base in the many conflicts between England and Scotland.

* Beautiful views of River Tees
* Home to Richard III & Henry VII

Location
In Barnard Castle town, off Galgate on A688

Opening
Daily: Apr–Sep 10am–6pm; Oct 10am–4pm; Nov–Mar Thu–Mon 10am–4pm

Admission
Adult £3.40, Child £1.70, Concs £2.60

Contact
Barnard Castle, County Durham DL12 8PR

t 01833 638212
w english-heritage.org.uk

857 Barnard Castle

Bowes Museum

  3 hrs   All year

Founded by local businessman John Bowes and his French wife, Josephine, this magnificent museum, which opened in 1892, houses one of Britain's finest collections of paintings, ceramics, furniture and textiles. There are special outdoor events and family fun days.

* Set in 23 acres of parkland, with parterre garden
* Outstanding temporary art exhibition programme

Location
Just off A66, 20 min from Scotch Corner (A1)

Opening
Daily: 11am–5pm

Admission
Adult £7, Child free, Concs £6

Contact
Barnard Castle DL12 8NP

t 01833 690606
w thebowesmuseum.org.uk
e info@thebowesmuseum.org.uk

858 Beamish

Beamish, The North of England Open-Air Museum

  4 hrs+  All year

Beamish is a unique living, working experience of life as it was in the north of England in the early C19 and C20. It shows how the region was transformed in that time from its thinly populated rural roots to being a site of heavy industrialisation.

* Costumed guides explain each attraction
* Former European Museum of the Year

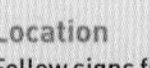    

Location
Follow signs from junction 63 of A1(M)

Opening
Apr–Oct daily 10am–5pm;
Nov–Mar Tue–Thu & Sat–Sun 10am–4pm

Admission
Adult £16, Child £10, Concs £12.50
Nov–Mar £6 per person

Contact
Beamish DH9 0RG

t 0191 370 4000
w beamish.org.uk
e museum@beamish.org.uk

859 Bishop Auckland

Hamsterley Forest

2–4 hrs · All year

Covering some 2,000 hectares, Hamsterley Forest has something for everyone – play and picnic areas, several walks, and cycle routes ranging from a 1½-mile easy-access footpath to a 7-mile black cycle route and downhill descent course for the more adventurous.

* Largest forest in County Durham

Location
From A68 at Witton-le-Wear follow brown tourist signs

Opening
Forest Daily: 7.30am–sunset
Visitor centre Apr–Oct Mon–Fri 10am–4pm, Sat–Sun 11am–5pm
Please phone for details of Nov–Mar

Admission
Free. Toll for forest drive & car park fee (£2 per car)

Contact
Redford, Bishop Auckland DL13 3NL
t 01388 488312
w forestry.gov.uk

860 Bishop Auckland

Harperley POW Camp

2 hrs+ · All year

Harperley was one of the few purpose-built POW camps in Britain. It housed low-risk prisoners, first from Italy and then from Germany; at its height it held 1,500 prisoners. In addition to the museum, there is a garden centre and a farm shop.

* Children's outdoor play area & 1940s house
* Featured in BBC programme *Restoration*

Location
Approximately 250m from junction of A68 & A689 near village of Crook

Opening
Daily: 10am–5pm

Admission
Free

Contact
Firtree, Crook, County Durham DL15 8DX
t 01388 767098
w powcamp.com
e info@powcamp.com

861 Darlington

Darlington Railway Centre & Museum

 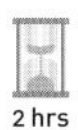 

2 hrs · All year

The museum celebrates nearly 180 years of railway history in the town and in the North East. Of greatest significance is George Stephenson's locomotive, which hauled the inaugural multicarriage train on the Stockton and Darlington Railway.

* Including an 1840s Darlington-built locomotive
* Museum is in 1842 railway station

Location
1 mile from town centre on A167

Opening
Daily: 10am–5pm

Admission
Adult £2.50, Child & Concs £1.50
Extra charge on special event days

Contact
North Road Station, Darlington DL3 6ST
t 01325 460532
w drcm.org.uk
e museum@darlington.gov.uk

862 Darlington

Raby Castle

3 hrs+ Easter–Sep

Built in the C14, Raby Castle is one of the largest and most impressive of English medieval castles, with towers, turrets, interiors and artworks from the medieval, Regency and Victorian periods. Enjoy walled gardens, a deer park and a children's adventure playground.

* Great kitchen little altered in 600 years
* Paintings by Reynolds & other Old Masters

Location
1 mile N of Staindrop on A688

Opening
Castle, Park & Gardens May–Jun & Sep 1pm–5pm; July–Aug Sun–Fri 1pm–5pm; Easter weekend & all other Bank Hols Sat–Mon 1pm–5pm;
Park & Garden May–Sep & Bank Hols Sun– Fri 11am–5.30pm

Admission
Castle, Park & Gardens Adult £9, Child £4, Concs £8 *Park & Gardens* £4, 2.50, £3.50

Contact
PO Box 50, Staindrop, Darlington DL2 3AH
t 01833 660202
w rabycastle.com
e admin@rabycastle.com

863 Durham

Durham Castle

1 hr Mar–Sep

Dating from 1072, this is one of the largest Norman castles and one of the grandest Romanesque palaces to survive in England. It was the seat of the Prince Bishops until 1832 and is now a residential college for the University of Durham.

* World Heritage Site
* Entrance by guided tour only

WC

Location
In city centre. Uphill walk or No. 40 bus to Palace Green

Opening
Daily: mid-Mar–mid-Apr & Jul–Sep 10am–12.30pm & 2pm–4.30pm. Other times usually Mon, Wed, Sat–Sun afternoons but please phone to confirm

Admission
Adult £5, Child & Concs £3.50

Contact
Durham DH1 3RW
t 0191 334 3800
w durhamcastle.com
e university-college.www@durham.ac.uk

864 Durham

Crook Hall Gardens

1 hr+ Easter–Sep

On the banks of the River Wear with views of Durham cathedral and castle, Crook Hall is a Grade I-listed medieval manor house with C13 hall. There are various beautiful gardens with traditional and modern planting schemes and an established maze.

* Fruit trees wreathed in rambling roses
* 'A tapestry of colourful blooms' according to Alan Titchmarsh

WC  

Location
Short walk from Durham's Millburngate shopping centre, opposite Gala Theatre

Opening
Easter weekend 11am–5pm; May Sun & Bank Hol Mon 11am–5pm; 26 May–8 Sep, Wed–Sun 11am–5pm; Halloween weekend 3pm–dusk; Dec please phone for details

Admission
Adult £4.50, Concs £4

Contact
Frankland Lane, Sidegate, Durham DH1 5SZ
t 0191 384 8028
w crookhallgardens.co.uk
e info@kbacrookhall.co.uk

865 Durham

Old Fulling Museum of Archaeology

  1 hr  All year

This former mill has become one of the most photographed buildings in the North East. It now houses the Museum of Archaeology, among whose striking exhibits is a major collection of Roman inscriptions from the north of England and an outstanding collection of Samianware.

* Artefacts from ancient Greece & Rome
* Medieval finds from Durham city centre

Location
Between Cathedral and Castle in city centre

Opening
Apr–Oct 11am–4pm;
Nov–Mar Fri–Mon 11.30am–3.30pm

Admission
Adult £1, Child & Concs 50p

Contact
The Banks, Durham DH1 3EB

t 0191 334 1823
e fulling.mill@dur.ac.uk
w dur.ac.uk/fulling.mill

866 Durham

Oriental Museum

 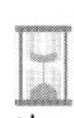 1 hr  All year

The only museum of its kind in the UK, entirely devoted to art and archaeology from cultures throughout the Orient. The collections range from prehistoric Egypt and China to the work of living artists. The museum is part of the University of Durham.

* Used as a resource by researchers from around the world
* Students of higher education enter free

Location
S side of Durham, signed from A177

Opening
Daily: Mon–Fri 10am–5pm,
Sat–Sun 12noon–5pm

Admission
Adult £1.50, Concs 75p

Contact
Elvet Hill, off South Road, Durham DH1 3TH

t 0191 334 5694
w dur.ac.uk/oriental.museum
e oriental.museum@durham.ac.uk

867 Durham

Prince Bishop River Cruiser

  1 hr  All year

The 150-seater cruiser sails regularly from Durham city centre. The one-hour trip offers spectacular views of the cathedral, the castle and other tourist attractions. There is wheelchair access to the open-air upper deck and saloons.

* Sun deck & onboard barbecue
* 1-hour Santa cruises in Dec

Location
Cruiser is found below Prince Bishop shopping centre in Durham

Opening
Please phone for details

Admission
Adult £4.50, Child £2, Concs £4

Contact
The Boathouse, Elvet Bridge, Durham DH1 3AH

t 0191 386 9525

868 Durham

University of Durham Botanic Garden

  2 hrs  All year

The garden features a large glasshouse that is split between the tropical house and the cactus house. Outside there are more than 20 collections featuring plants from around the world, including a mutant bed highlighting some of nature's weirder creations.

* Exhibitions of local art
* Different trails for children to follow

Location
Signed from city centre

Opening
Daily: Mar–Oct 10am–5pm;
Nov–Feb 10am–4pm

Admission
Adult £2, Child £1, Concs £1.50

Contact
Hollingside Lane, South Road, Durham DH1 3TN

t 0191 334 5521
w dur.ac.uk/botanic.garden
e botanic.garden@durham.ac.uk

869 Egglestone

Egglestone Hall Gardens

2 hrs All year

Discover a secret walled garden, informally laid out in 4 acres with winding paths and lawns. Enjoy the rare plants and shrubs growing with organic vegetables, borders, and fell views. The 'Garden of Tranquillity' is next to the ruins of a C17 church.

* Cafe, bistro, gift shop & delicatessen

Location
S of Egglestone. 5 miles NW of Barnard Castle off B6278

Opening
Daily: 10am–5pm

Admission
Adult £1, Child free

Contact
Egglestone, Barnard Castle, County Durham DL12 0AG

t 01833 650115
w egglestonehallgardens.co.uk
e mbhock@btinternet.com

870 Peterlee

Castle Eden Dene Nature Reserve

 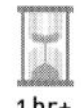 

1 hr+ All year

A wooded ravine, cut deep into limestone, forms the largest area of semi-natural woodland in north-east England, renowned for its yew trees. The tangled landscape is a survivor of the wildwood that once covered most of Britain. Access is by marked paths only.

* 12 miles of footpaths within its 500 acres
* More than 450 species of plants recorded in wood

Location
On A19, follow signs

Opening
Daily: dawn–dusk

Admission
Free

Contact
Oakerside Dene Lodge, Stanhope Chase, Peterlee SR8 1NJ

t 0191 586 0004
w englishnature.org.uk

871 Stockton-on-Tees

Four Seasons White Water Rafting

2 hrs All year

A nationally recognised centre for canoeing, kayaking and white-water rafting. The tidal River Tees guarantees white water all year, with fast-flowing rapids carrying you down the course on an exhilarating and adrenaline-fuelled trip. Equipment can be hired.

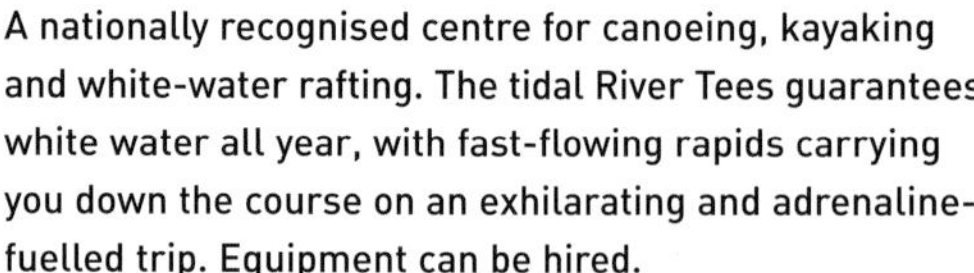

* Customisable difficulty for beginners & experts
* Training for all levels

Location
On N bank of River Tees near Tees Barrage Bridge, Stockton-on-Tees

Opening
All year – booking advised
Please phone for details

Admission
From £15 according to activities

Contact
Tees Barrage, Stockton-on-Tees TS18 2QW

t 01642 678000
w 4seasons.co.uk
e kanu@4seasons.co.uk

872 Upper Weardale

Killhope Lead Mining Museum

 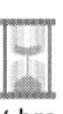 

4 hrs Easter–Oct

This fully restored lead mine explores the lives of Victorian mining families. Guided tours take visitors along the original tunnels (wellingtons, hard hat and cap-lamp provided). A woodland walk gives access to further reminders of lead mining.

* Warm clothes required even during summer
* Winner of Family Friendly Museum 2004

Location
Off A689 between Stanhope & Alston

Opening
Daily: Easter–Oct 10.30am–5pm

Admission
Adult £6, Child £3, Concs £5.50
No under-4s allowed in mine

Contact
The North of England Lead Mining Museum, nr Cowshill, Upper Weardale DL13 1AR

t 01388 537505
w durham.gov.uk/killhope
e killhope@durham.gov.uk

873 Alnwick

Alnwick Castle

  3 hrs+  Apr–Oct

Visit a medieval castle with wonderful Renaissance furnishings inside its walls. The Regiment Museum of the Royal Northumberland Fusiliers is housed in the Abbott's Tower, along with the museum of local archaeology and the Percy Tenantry volunteers.

* Home to Percy family for 700 years
* Award-winning garden

Location
Alnwick, 35 miles N of Newcastle upon Tyne, 1 mile from A1

Opening
Daily: Apr–Oct 10am–6pm

Admission
Adult £8.50, Child £3.50, Concs £7.50
Family ticket (2 Adult & 4 Child) £22

Contact
Alnwick NE66 1NQ

t 01665 510777
w alnwickcastle.com
e enquiries@alnwickcastle.com

874 Amble

Warkworth Castle

  1 hr+  All year

The magnificent eight-towered keep stands high on a hill overlooking the River Coquet. It was once home to the Percy family, who at times wielded more power in the north than the king. Sir Henry Percy (Harry Hotspur) was immortalised in Shakespeare's *Henry IV*.

* Opening scenes of *Henry IV* set in Warkworth
* Duke's Rooms first opened in 2003

Location
8 miles SE of Alnwick, on A1068

Opening
Daily: Apr–Sep 10am–5pm;
Oct 10am–4pm; Nov–Mar Sat–Mon 10am–4pm

Admission
Adult £3.40, Child £1.70, Concs £2.60

Contact
nr Amble, Morpeth NE65 0UJ

t 01665 711423
w english-heritage.org.uk

875 Ashington

Wansbeck Riverside Park

  2–5 hrs  All year

Stretching along the banks of the River Wansbeck, the park provides miles of pleasant walks and trails right down to the sea at Sandy Bay. There are picnic areas for families and play facilities for children. The river can be used for fishing for a small fee.

* Caravan park & cafeteria
* 4-mile riverside walk

Location
Take A1068. Park is located between Ashington & Bedlington

Opening
Daily: 8am–dusk

Admission
Free

Contact
Green Lane, Ashington NE63 8TX

t 01670 843444
w wansbeck.gov.uk
e i.graham@wansbeck.gov.uk

876 Bamburgh

Bamburgh Castle

  2 hrs  Mar–Oct

One of the finest castles in England. Perched on a basalt outcrop extending into the North Sea, it was restored in 1750 and again extensively by the C19 industrialist Lord Armstrong. Tour the magnificent King's Hall, Cross Hall, reception rooms and armoury.

* Still home to the Armstrong family
* Exhibits include fine furniture, tapestries & arms

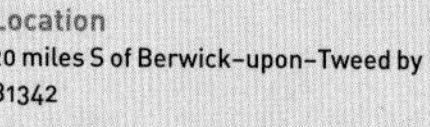

Location
20 miles S of Berwick-upon-Tweed by B1342

Opening
Daily: mid-Mar–Oct 11am–4.30pm

Admission
Adult £6, Child £2.50, Concs £5

Contact
Bamburgh NE69 7DF

t 01668 214515
w bamburghcastle.com
e bamburghcastle@aol.com

877 Bedlington

Bedlington Country Park

  3 hrs  All year

This country park covers 5 miles of horse and nature trails and woodland walks on the banks of the River Blythe. It is teeming with wildlife such as otters, kingfishers, woodpeckers and red squirrels, as well as native trees, shrubs and rare flora.

* Unique wild orchid only found growing here

Location
Between A189 & A1068, S of Bedlington

Opening
Daily: dawn–dusk

Admission
Free

Contact
Wansbeck District Council, Council Offices, Front Street, Bedlington NE22 5TU

t 01670 843444
w wansbeck.gov.uk
e i.graham@wansbeck.gov.uk

878 Berwick-upon-Tweed

Berwick Barracks Museum & Art Gallery

  1 hr+   All year

The barracks are home to a number of attractions, including 'By Beat of Drum', showing what life was like for British infantry soldiers until Queen Victoria's reign. The regimental museum also tells the history of the King's Own Scottish Borderers.

* One of the first purpose-built barracks
* Walk on ramparts affords great views of River Tweed

Location
Off Church Street in town centre

Opening
Daily: Easter–Sep 10am–5pm (4pm in Oct);
Nov–Mar please phone for details

Admission
Adult £3.30, Child £1.70, Concs £2.50

Contact
The Parade,
Berwick-upon-Tweed PD15 1DF

t 01289 304493
w english-heritage.org.uk

879 Carlisle–Newcastle

Hadrian's Wall

  1 hr+  All year

One of the most important monuments built by the Romans in Britain. It is the best-known frontier in the entire Roman Empire and is a designated World Heritage site. Various attractions along the wall include Roman forts and several museums.

* Museum brings Roman history to life
* 84-mile coast-to-coast walk along Wall

Location
A69 between Newcastle & Carlisle runs parallel to Hadrian's Wall (approximately 2–5 miles S)

Opening
Times vary, please phone for details

Admission
Prices vary, please phone for details

Contact
Hadrian's Wall Heritage Ltd, 14b Gilesgate, Hexham NE46 3NJ

t 01434 322002
w hadrians-wall.org
e info@hadrians-wall.org

880 Hexham

Cherryburn

1 hr

Mar–Oct

This C19 farmhouse was the birthplace of Thomas Bewick, who pioneered wood-engraving. Bewick was an outstanding artist and naturalist and drew on his passion to produce beautiful engravings of wildlife. The cottage contains an exhibition on his life and works.

* Occasional demonstrations of printing
* 'Folk in the Farmyard' every Sunday afternoon

Location
Take A695 to Mickley Square & follow signs, 11 miles from Hexham

Opening
18 Mar–29 Oct Thu–Tue 11am–5pm (last admission 4.30pm)

Admission
Adult £3.75, Child £1.75

Contact
Station Bank, Mickley, nr Stocksfield NE43 7DD

t 01661 843276
w nationaltrust.org.uk
e cherryburn@nationaltrust.org.uk

881 Hexham

Vindolanda

2 hrs+

Feb–Nov

A fascinating Roman fort and settlement lying just to the south of Hadrian's Wall. On the site itself stands a full-size replica of a section of Hadrian's Wall in both stone and timber, giving the visitor a true idea of the impressive might of the monument.

* Ongoing excavations Apr–Aug 2007
* Rare & fascinating personal documents to be read

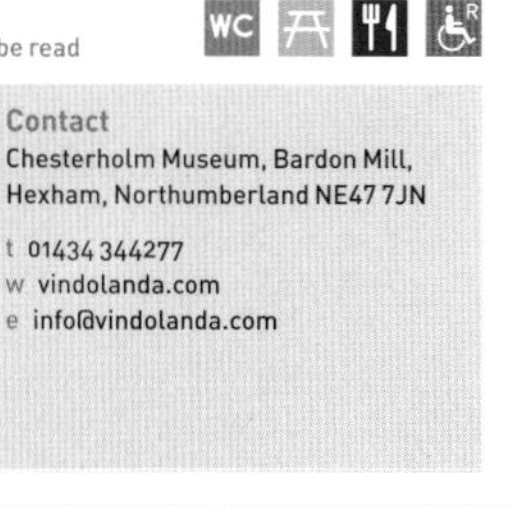

Location
Take A69 & B6318 near Bardon Mill, then follow signs

Opening
Apr–Sep 10am–6pm;
Feb–Mar & Oct–Nov 10am–5pm

Admission
Adult £4.95, Child £3, Concs £4.10

Contact
Chesterholm Museum, Bardon Mill, Hexham, Northumberland NE47 7JN

t 01434 344277
w vindolanda.com
e info@vindolanda.com

882 Holy Island–Lindisfarne

Lindisfarne Castle

1 hr

Feb–Oct

Imposing atop a rocky crag and accessible only across a causeway at low tide, Lindisfarne Castle, originally a Tudor fort, was converted into a private house in 1903 by the young Edwin Lutyens. The small rooms are full of intimate decoration and design.

* Charming walled garden planned by Gertrude Jekyll
* Check crossing times before making a long journey

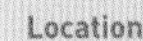

Location
Holy Island, 6 miles E of A1, across causeway

Opening
Daily: mid-Feb–end Feb please phone for details; mid-Mar–Oct Tue–Sun times vary depending on tides, usually 10.30am–3pm or 12noon–4pm

Admission
Adult £5.20, Child £2.60, Family ticket £13

Contact
Holy Island,
Berwick-upon-Tweed TD15 2SH

t 01289 389244
w nationaltrust.org.uk
e lindisfarne@nationaltrust.org.uk

883 Holy Island–Lindisfarne

Lindisfarne Priory

1 hr+

All year

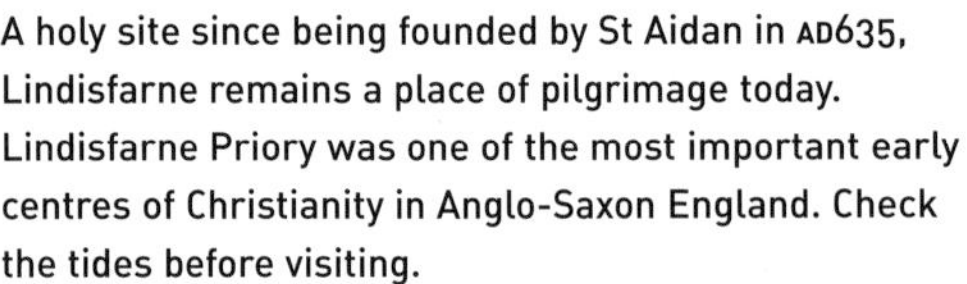

A holy site since being founded by St Aidan in AD635, Lindisfarne remains a place of pilgrimage today. Lindisfarne Priory was one of the most important early centres of Christianity in Anglo-Saxon England. Check the tides before visiting.

* Anglo-Saxon carvings in museum
* Refurbished museum

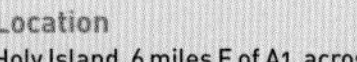

Location
Holy Island, 6 miles E of A1, across causeway

Opening
Daily: Apr–Sep 9.30am–5pm; Oct 9.30am–4pm; Nov–Jan Sat–Mon 10am–2pm; Feb–Mar 10am–4pm
Times vary depending on tides

Admission
Adult £3.70, Child £1.90, Concs £2.80

Contact
Holy Island, Berwick-upon-Tweed TD15 2RX

t 01289 389200
w english-heritage.org.uk

884 Morpeth

Belsay Hall, Castle & Gardens

3 hrs

All year

A dramatic, well-preserved medieval tower house, to which a Jacobean manor house was added in 1614. Belsay Hall (1807), designed by Sir Charles Monck in Greek Revival style after the Temple of Theseus in Athens, has great architectural importance within Europe.

* 2 acres of rhododendrons at their best May–Jun
* Formal terraces & winter garden, original planting

Location
In Belsay, 14 miles NW of Newcastle upon Tyne on A696

Opening
Apr–Oct daily 10am–5pm;
Nov–Mar Thu–Mon 10am–4pm

Admission
Adult £5.50, Child £2.80, Concs £4.10

Contact
Belsay NE20 0DX

t 01661 881636
w english-heritage.org.uk

885 Morpeth

Carlisle Park

  1–3 hrs  All year

In the heart of historic Morpeth lies Carlisle Park with ancient woodland walks, a C12 castle and an C11 motte. The formal gardens display immaculate annual and carpet bedding, and link to the William Turner Garden, a modern version of a Tudor knot and physic garden.

* Quality Assured Visitor Attraction
* Boating, bowls, paddling pool, walks & beautiful gardens

Location
Follow signs to Morpeth town centre. Carlisle Park is within walking distance of many car parks, as well as bus station & railway station

Opening
Daily: All reasonable times
Turner Garden Daily: 7.30am–dusk
Sporting facilities Apr–Oct 10am–9pm

Admission
Free

Contact
Castle Morpeth Borough Council, Coopies Lane Depot, Coopies Lane Industrial Estate, Morpeth NE61 6JT
t 01670 500777
w castlemorpeth.gov.uk
e firstcall@castlemorpeth.gov.uk

886 Morpeth

Cragside Estate

  3 hrs+  Apr–Dec

Cragside was the innovative home of Lord Armstrong, Victorian inventor and landscape genius. Surrounding the house is one of the largest handmade rock gardens in Europe. In the pinetum below, England's tallest Douglas fir soars above other woodland giants.

* House was at cutting edge of technology when built in 1880s

Location
1 mile N of Rothbury on B6341

Opening
Estate Apr–Oct Tue–Sun & Bank Hol Mon 10.30am–7pm (last admission 5pm); Nov–16 Dec 11am–4pm (last admission 3pm)

Admission
Please phone for details

Contact
Rothbury, Morpeth NE65 7PX
t 01669 620333
w nationaltrust.org.uk
e cragside@nationaltrust.org.uk

887 Morpeth

Wallington

  3 hrs+  Easter–Oct

Wallington House reopened in 2004 after extensive renovation. The Wallington estate was laid out in the C18 by Sir Walter Blackett. The original formality underlies the natural landscape, with walks offering a variety of lawns, shrubberies, lakeland and woodland.

* Stone griffin heads on the lawn's play area
* Set in evocative Northumberland moorland

Location
12 miles W of Morpeth on B6343

Opening
House, Garden & Grounds Easter–Oct Wed–Mon 1pm–5.30pm
Grounds All year: daily 10am–dusk

Admission
House, Gardens & Grounds Adult £8, Child £4 *Gardens & Grounds* £5.50, £2.75

Contact
Cambo, Morpeth NE61 4AR
t 01670 773600
w nationaltrust.org.uk
e wallington@nationaltrust.org.uk

888 Rothbury

Brinkburn Priory

  1 hr  Apr–Sep

Founded in 1135 as a house for the Augustinian canons, the church is the only complete surviving building of the monastery. In the summer season a number of choral events can be attended at this functioning church.

* Adjacent manor house has open ground floor
* Lovely setting beside River Coquet

Location
4½ miles SE of Rothbury off B6344

Opening
Apr–Sep Thu–Mon 10am–5pm

Admission
Adult £2.70, Child £1.40, Concs £2

Contact
Longframlinton, Morpeth NE65 8AR
t 01665 570628
w english-heritage.org.uk

©NTPL/Joe Cornish

889 Seahouses

Farne Islands

  2½ hrs  Varies

Lying 2–3 miles off the Northumberland coast, the islands are home to a large colony of Atlantic or grey seals and the most famous seabird sanctuary in Britain. Visitors can see 20 different species, including puffins, eider ducks and tern.

* Views of Bamburgh Castle
* Regular ferry services for a small charge

WC

Location
Islands are 2–3 miles off N Northumberland coast. Take B1340, then a boat from Seahouses harbour

Opening
Please phone for details

Admission
May–Jul Adult £5.20, Child £2.60
All other times £4.20, £2.10

Contact
The Sheiling, 8 St Adams, Seahouses NE68 7SR

t 01665 721099
w nationaltrust.org.uk

890 Dunston

Whickham Thorns Outdoor Activity Centre

  1 hr+  All year

This centre offers a wide range of activities, including climbing, skiing, snowboarding, mountain biking, orienteering and archery. There are snowboarding and skiing courses for beginners, activity days and mountain bikes for hire.

* High-ropes aerial assault course
* First boulder park in the North East

Location
Off A1 on opposite side of motorway from MetroCentre

Opening
Apr–Sep daily Mon–Fri 9am–8pm, Sat 11am–6pm, Sun 12noon–3pm;
Oct–Mar please phone for details
Closed Bank Hols

Admission
Free. Please phone for activity prices

Contact
Market Lane, Dunston, Gateshead NE11 9NX

t 0191 433 5767
w gateshead.gov.uk

891 Gateshead

BALTIC

  1 hr+  All year

A major new international centre for contemporary art, situated on the south bank of the River Tyne. Housed in a 1950s grain warehouse (part of the former Baltic Flour Mills), BALTIC is a site for the production, presentation and experience of contemporary art.

* Constantly changing programme of exhibitions
* Displays of work by artists in residence

Location
Gateshead Quayside, 10 min walk from town centre

Opening
Times vary, please phone or visit website for details

Admission
Free

Contact
Gateshead Quays, South Shore Road, Gateshead NE8 3BA

t 0191 478 1810
w balticmill.com
e info@balticmill.com

892 Jarrow

Bede's World & St Paul's Church

3 hrs | All year

The extraordinary life of the Venerable Bede (AD 673–735) left a rich legacy that is celebrated today at Bede's World, the site where Bede lived and worked 1,300 years ago. Visitors can explore the site of the Anglo-Saxon monastery of St Paul and medieval monastic ruins.

* Herb garden based on Anglo-Saxon & medieval plants
* Anglo-Saxon demo farm, complete with animals

Location
Near S end of Tyne Tunnel, off A185

Opening
Apr–Oct Mon–Sat 10am–5.30pm, Sun 12noon–5.30pm;
Nov–Mar Mon–Sat 10am–4.30pm, Sun 12noon–4.30pm;
Church closed during services

Admission
Adult £4.50, Child & Concs £3

Contact
Church Bank NE32 3DY

t 0191 489 2106
w bedesworld.co.uk
e visitorinfo@bedesworld.co.uk

893 Newcastle upon Tyne

Centre for Life

3 hrs+ | All year

Discover amazing facts about life and understand how DNA spells out instructions for every species. Explore where life comes from and how it works. Meet your 4-billion-year-old family, find out what makes you unique and test your brainpower.

* Open-air ice rink in winter (separate charge)
* Enjoy the thrill of the motion simulator

Location
Near Newcastle Central station

Opening
Daily: Mon–Sat 10am–6pm, Sun 11am–6pm

Admission
Adult £6.95, Child £4.50, Concs £5.50

Contact
Times Square,
Newcastle upon Tyne NE1 4EP

t 0191 243 8210
w life.org.uk
e info@life.org.uk

894 Newcastle upon Tyne

Discovery Museum

3 hrs | All year

Discovery is the region's biggest free museum and the gateway to fun and facts about life on Tyneside. Explore Newcastle's past from Roman times to the present day, Tyneside's world-changing inventions, and a fun approach to science. Take a walk through fashion, too.

* See Roman, Norman & medieval Newcastle upon Tyne
* Find out about life along the River Tyne

Location
Short walk from Newcastle Central station

Opening
Daily: Mon–Sat 10am–5pm, Sun 2pm–5pm

Admission
Free

Contact
Blandford Square,
Newcastle upon Tyne NE1 4JA

t 0191 232 6789
w twmuseums.org.uk/discovery
e discovery@twmuseums.org.uk

895 North Shields

Stephenson Railway Museum

1 hr | May–Oct

Relive the glorious days of the steam railway at the Stephenson Railway Museum. The museum is home to George Stephenson's *Billy* (a forerunner to the world-famous *Rocket*) and many other engines from the age of steam.

* Many activities throughtout the year
* Gift shop selling souvenirs, etc

Location
Well signed from junction of A19/A1058

Opening
May–Oct Sat–Sun 11am–4pm
School hols daily 11am–4pm

Admission
Free

Contact
Middle Engine Lane,
North Shields NE29 8DX

t 0191 200 7146
w twmuseums.org.uk/stephenson
e stephenson@twmuseums.org.uk

896 Rowlands Gill

Gibside

 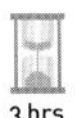 

3 hrs All year

One of the North's finest landscapes, much of which is a Site of Special Scientific Interest. A forest garden is currently under restoration, embracing many miles of riverside and forest walks. Deer, kingfishers, herons, red kites and even badgers may be spotted.

* Outstanding buildings, including a Palladian chapel
* Greenhouse & stables

Location
6 miles SW of Gateshead on B6314

Opening
summer Daily: 10am–6pm
(last admission 4.30pm)
winter Daily: 10am–4pm
(last admission 3.30pm)

Admission
Adult £5, Child £3

Contact
nr Rowlands Gill, Burnopfield
NE16 6BG

t 01207 541820
w nationaltrust.org.uk
e gibside@nationaltrust.org.uk

897 South Shields

Arbeia Roman Fort

2 hrs All year

Arbeia was once an essential part of a mighty frontier system. Built in approximately AD160, it guarded the entrance to the River Tyne. See excavated remains, stunning reconstructions of original buildings and displays of finds discovered at the site.

* 3 reconstructed buildings on their original sites
* Time Quest archaeological dig

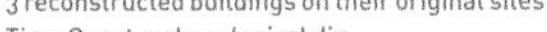

Location
10 min walk from South Shields Metro & bus station; signed from Ocean Road

Opening
Easter–Sep Mon–Sat 10am–5.30pm, Sun 1pm–5pm; Oct–Easter Mon–Sat 10am–3.30pm

Admission
Free

Contact
Baring Street,
South Shields NE33 2BB

t 0191 456 1369
w twmuseums.org.uk
e info@twmuseums.org.uk

898 Sunderland

Souter Lighthouse

1 hr+ Apr–Oct

When it first shone its light in 1871, Souter was the most advanced lighthouse in the world, and the first purpose-built lighthouse to utilise electricity. Explore the compass room, Victorian keeper's cottage, engine room and huge optic, and enjoy the stunning views.

* When operational, light could be seen for 26 miles
* See engine room & cramped living quarters

Location
2½ miles S of South Shields on A183

Opening
31 Mar–Oct Sat–Thu 11am–5pm
(last admission 4.30pm)

Admission
Adult £4, Child £2.50

Contact
Coast Road, Whitburn,
Sunderland SR6 7NH

t 0191 529 3161
w nationaltrust.org.uk
e souter@nationaltrust.org.uk

899 Sunderland

Sunderland Museum & Winter Gardens

 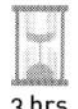 

3 hrs All year

Hands-on exhibits and interactive displays tell the story of Sunderland from its prehistoric past through to the present day. The art gallery features paintings by L S Lowry alongside Victorian masterpieces. The Winter Gardens contain more than 1,500 flowers and plants.

* Good facilities for disabled visitors
* Many educational exhibits & audio guides in Winter Gardens

Location
In city centre on Burdon Road

Opening
Daily: Mon–Sat 10am–5pm, Sun 2pm–5pm

Admission
Free

Contact
Burdon Road,
Sunderland SR1 1PP

t 0191 553 2323
w twmuseums.org.uk/sunderland
e sunderland@twmuseums.org.uk

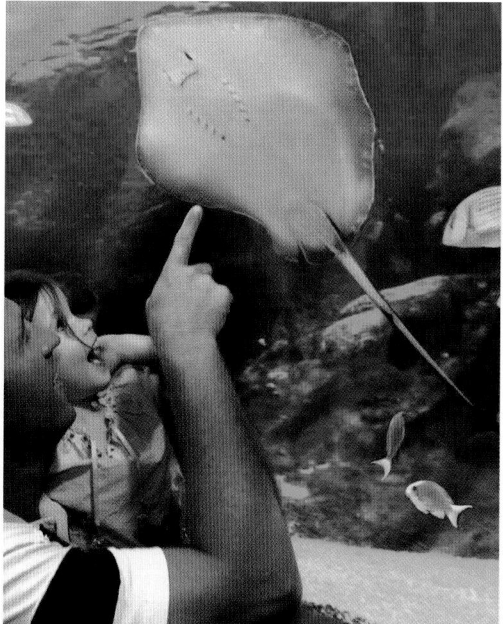

900 Tynemouth

Blue Reef Aquarium

 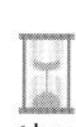 

1 hr+ All year

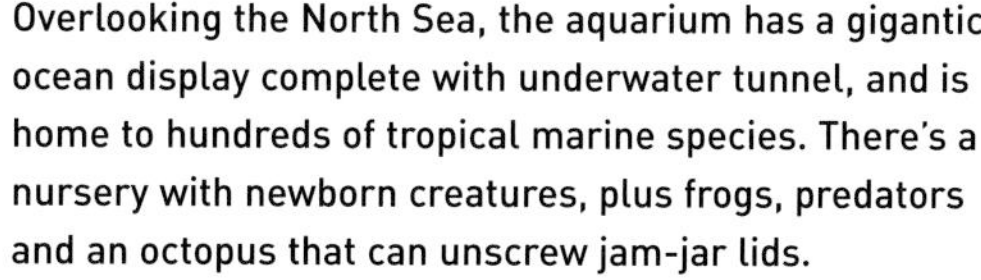

Overlooking the North Sea, the aquarium has a gigantic ocean display complete with underwater tunnel, and is home to hundreds of tropical marine species. There's a nursery with newborn creatures, plus frogs, predators and an octopus that can unscrew jam-jar lids.

* See Asian short-clawed otters
* Giant Pacific octopus

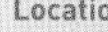

Location
From A19 take A1058 to town centre & follow brown tourist signs

Opening
Daily: Mar–Oct 10am–5pm; Nov–Feb 10am–4pm

Admission
Adult £5.99, Child £3.99, Concs £4.99
Family ticket (2 Adult & 2 Child) £17.50

Contact
Grand Parade, Tynemouth NE30 4JF

t 0191 258 1031
w bluereefaquarium.co.uk
e tynemouth@bluereefaquarium.co.uk

901 Tynemouth

Tynemouth Priory & Castle

 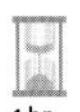 1 hr  All year

A burial place of saints and kings, this commanding castle has provided defence against the Vikings, medieval Scots, Napoleon and C20 Germany. The Benedictine priory was founded in 1090 on the site of an ancient Anglian monastery.

* Restored magazines of a coastal defence gun battery on view at weekends

Location
In Tynemouth, near North Pier

Opening
Apr–Sep daily 10am–5pm;
Oct–Mar Thu–Mon 10am–4pm

Admission
Adult £3.40, Child £1.70, Concs £2.60

Contact
Tynemouth NE30 4BZ

t 0191 257 1090
w english-heritage.org.uk

902 Wallsend

Segedunum Roman Fort, Baths & Museum

  2 hrs+  All year

For almost 300 years Segedunum, which means 'strong fort', was home to 600 Roman soldiers and was the last outpost of Hadrian's Wall. Today the complex combines the excavated remains with reconstructions and hands-on museum displays of life in Roman Britain.

* The most extensively excavated site in Britain
* 100ft-high viewing tower plus audio guide

Location
1 min walk from Wallsend Metro & bus station

Opening
Daily: Apr–Oct 10am–5pm;
Nov–Mar 10am–3pm

Admission
Adult £3.95, Child free, Concs £2.25

Contact
Buddle Street, Wallsend NE28 6HR

t 0191 236 9347
w twmuseums.org.uk

903 Washington

Washington Old Hall

  2 hrs   Apr–Oct

From 1183 this house was the family home of George Washington's direct ancestors, who took their surname from the village of Washington. The manor remained in the family until 1613. Mementoes of the American connection and the War of Independence are on display.

* Fine collection of blue & white Delftware
* Heavily carved oak furniture, Jacobean-style garden

Location
5 miles W of Sunderland, A1231.
Well signed

Opening
Apr–Oct Sun–Wed 11am–5pm;
also Good Fri (last admission 4.30pm)

Admission
Adult £4, Child £2.50

Contact
The Avenue,
Washington Village NE38 7LE

t 0191 416 6879
w nationaltrust.org

904 Washington

Wildfowl & Wetlands Trust Washington

 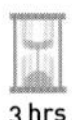 3 hrs  All year

Ideally placed to provide a stopover and wintering habitat for migratory wildfowl after their passage over the North Sea, this recreated wetland provides large flocks of curlew and redshank with a safe place to roost and herons with a place to breed.

* Nuthatch sighted in 2003 for the first time in 10 years
* See waders, kingfishers, snipe, shovelers & flamingoes

Location
E of Washington, 4 miles from A1(M)

Opening
Daily: *summer* 9.30am–5.30pm;
winter 9.30am–4pm

Admission
Adult £5.95, Child £3.95, Concs £4.95,
Family ticket £15.50

Contact
Pattinson, Washington NE38 8LE

t 0191 416 5454
w wwt.org.uk
e info.washington@wwt.org.uk

Rannoch Moor, Perthshire
Scotland
Central Scotland Grampian
Highlands and Islands Southern Scotland

SCOTLAND
Inner Hebrides
Grampian Mountains
North
Southern Uplands
Lammermuir Hills
The Cheviot Hills
The Borders
Bagh a Chaisteil (Castlebay)
Rum
Eigg
Muck
Coll
Tiree
Ulva
Isle of Mull
Iona
Luing
Scarba
Colonsay
Oronsay
Jura
Islay
Coul Point
Rhinns Point
Gigha
Kintyre
Mull of Kintyre
Arran
Holy I.
Fife Ness
St Abb's Head
Holy Island
Burrow Head
ARGYLL AND BUTE
PERTH AND KINROSS
ANGUS
STIRLING
FIFE
FALKIRK
NORTH AYRSHIRE
EAST AYRSHIRE
SOUTH AYRSHIRE
S. LANARKSHIRE
DUMFRIES AND GALLOWAY
BORDERS
MIDLOTHIAN
E. LOTHIAN
NORTHUMBERLAND
CUMBRIA
DURHAM
Mallaig
Invergarry
Newtonmore
Laggan
Spean Bridge
Dalwhinnie
Braemar
Ballater
Banchory
Stonehaven
Fort William
Glencoe
Ballachulish
Portnacroish
Tobermory
Lochaline
Craignure
Connel
Oban
Fionnphort
Inveraray
Strachur
Lochgilphead
Ardlussa
Port Askaig
Port Ellen
Tarbert
Kennacraig
Tayinloan
Campbeltown
Tighnabruaich
Dunoon
Rothesay
Millport
Largs
Kilbirnie
Brodick
Ardrossan
Irvine
Kilwinning
Kilmarnock
Troon
Prestwick
Ayr
Maybole
Dalmellington
Girvan
Cairnryan
Stranraer
Portpatrick
Drummore
Newton Stewart
Whithorn
New Galloway
Castle Douglas
Dalbeattie
Kirkcudbright
Dumfries
Lochmaben
Lockerbie
Moffat
Annan
Gretna
Langholm
Longtown
Carlisle
Brampton
Wigton
Maryport
Cockermouth
Workington
Keswick
Penrith
Appleby-in-Westmorland
Alston
Hexham
Corbridge
Ponteland
Consett
Bishop Auckland
Spennymoor
Brandon
Durham
Gateshead
Morpeth
Ashington
Bedlington
Otterburn
Alnwick
Berwick-upon-Tweed
Coldstream
Kelso
Jedburgh
Hawick
Selkirk
Galashiels
Peebles
Eyemouth
Dunbar
North Berwick
Haddington
Musselburgh
Dalkeith
Bonnyrigg
Penicuik
EDINBURGH
South Queensferry
Inverkeithing
Livingston
Bathgate
Linlithgow
Bo'ness
Grangemouth
Armadale
Airdrie
Shotts
Motherwell
Hamilton
Carluke
Lanark
Biggar
Abington
Lesmahagow
Strathaven
East Kilbride
GLASGOW
Paisley
Johnstone
Port Glasgow
Greenock
Gourock
Helensburgh
Dumbarton
Alexandria
Clydebank
Kirkintilloch
Cumbernauld
Kilsyth
Denny
Falkirk
Stirling
Alloa
Dunblane
Bridge of Allan
Callander
Tarbet
Crianlarich
Lochearnhead
Killin
Crieff
Auchterarder
Dunfermline
Cowdenbeath
Kirkcaldy
Glenrothes
Kinross
Falkland
Auchtermuchty
Ladybank
Cupar
Buckhaven
Elie
St Andrews
Tayport
Newport-on-Tay
Dundee
Monifieth
Carnoustie
Arbroath
Montrose
Brechin
Forfar
Kirriemuir
Coupar Angus
Blairgowrie
Dunkeld
Aberfeldy
Pitlochry
Perth
Bridge of Earn
Mauchline
Cumnock
New Cumnock
M6
M8
M9
M73
M74
M80
M90
A74(M)

Outer Hebrides
Isle of Lewis
Rudha Rhobhanais (Butt of Lewis)
Port Nis (Port of Ness)
Cellar Head
974
Gallan Head
Steornabhagh (Stornoway)
975
Eye Peninsula
WESTERN ISLES
Hushinish Point
Taransay
Shiant Islands
Tairbeart (Tarbert)
Harris
Scalpay
Pabbay
Berneray
Loch nam Madadh (Lochmaddy)
Ronay
Rudha Hallagro
Uig
978
Dunvegan
Portree
Rona
Raasay
Cape Wrath
Durness
Whiten Head
Tongue
Bettyhill
Strathy Point
Melvich
Scrabster
Thurso
Dunnet Head
Castletown
Island of Stroma
Duncansby Head
John O'Groats
Noss Head
Wick
Mainland
Kirkwall
Orkney Islands
Unapool
Altnaharra
Kinbrace
Latheron
Lochinver
Helmsdale
Highlands
Lairg
Greenstone Point
Ullapool
Rudha Reidh
Bonar Bridge
Dornoch
Tarbat Ness
Tain
985
Gairloch
Alness
Invergordon
Cromarty
Kinlochewe
Torridon
Achnasheen
Garve
Dingwall
Nairn
Forres
963
Lossiemouth
Elgin
Cullen
Buckie
Banff
Macduff
Fraserburgh
964
MORAY
981
968
Inverness
Keith
Turriff
Aberlour
962
Dufftown
Huntly
Peterhead
965
Lochcarron
Stromeferry
969
Cannich

CENTRAL SCOTLAND

905 Aberfeldy

Highland Adventure Safaris

2 hrs

All year

An exciting way to experience the exhilaration and freedom of this beautiful part of the Highlands. Visitors can immerse themselves in the great outdoors by trying out Land Rovers on Ecotours, wildlife-watching trips or an exciting off-road driving experience.

* 4-star visitor attraction with shop, café & deer park
* Skills courses available (also try gold-panning)

Location
From A827 at Aberfeldy follow B846 for 2 miles past Castle Menzies until you see the signs

Opening
Daily: *summer* 9am–5pm
winter please phone for details

Admission
Prices vary, please phone for details

Contact
Drumdewan, Aberfeldy, Perthshire PH15 2JQ
t 01887 820071
w highlandadventuresafaris.co.uk
e info@highlandadventuresafaris.co.uk

906 Aberfoyle

Forest Hills Watersports

4 hrs+

All year

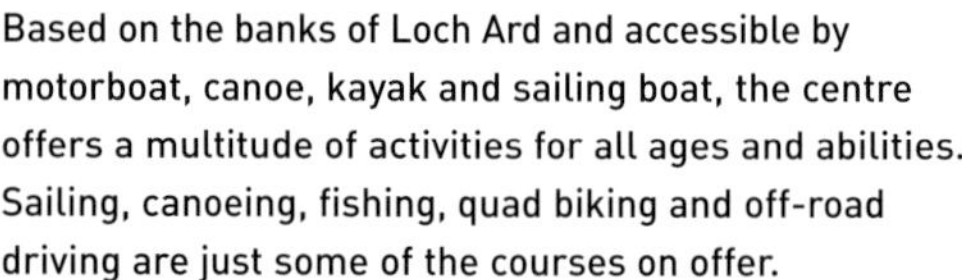

Based on the banks of Loch Ard and accessible by motorboat, canoe, kayak and sailing boat, the centre offers a multitude of activities for all ages and abilities. Sailing, canoeing, fishing, quad biking and off-road driving are just some of the courses on offer.

* Equipment available for hire
* Courses taught by qualified instructors

Location
Off junction 10 of M9 & junction 16 of M8. Follow signs for Aberfoyle, then to Forest Hills Watersports, 4 miles along B829

Opening
Daily: *summer* 9.30am–7pm
winter 10.30am–5pm

Admission
Activities priced individually

Contact
Kinlochard, Aberfoyle, Stirlingshire FK8 3TL
t 01877 387775
w goforth.co.uk
e info@goforth.co.uk

907 Arbroath

Arbroath Abbey

2 hrs+

All year

This was the site of the signing of the Declaration of Arbroath in 1320, when Scotland's nobles affirmed their allegiance to Robert the Bruce as their king. The recent addition of a visitor centre has reinforced its reputation as one of Scotland's most important historical places.

* Displays on abbey life, audio visual facilities
* Full colour guide book just published

Location
On A92, in town centre

Opening
Daily: Apr–Sep 9.30am–6.30pm; Oct–Mar 9.30am–4.30pm

Admission
Adult £4, Child £1.60, Concs £3

Contact
Arbroath, Angus DD11 1EG
t 01241 878756
w historic-scotland.gov.uk
e hs.explorer@scotland.gsi.gov.uk

908 Crieff

Auchingarrich Wildlife Centre

2 hrs+ All year

This award-winning centre features the Highland Cattle Centre. You can see these majestic beasts, stroke them and feed them. Other animals include wallabies, raccoons, otters, chipmunks, porcupines and Scotland's largest collection of waterfowl and ornamental birds.

* More than 150 species of animals & birds
* Hatchings every day Easter–Oct

Location
On B827, 2 miles N of Comrie

Opening
Daily: 10am–5pm

Admission
Adult £5.50, Child & Concs £4

Contact
Glascorrie Road, Crieff, Perthshire PH6 2JS

t 01764 679469
w auchingarrich.co.uk
e gillianscarter@tiscali.co.uk

909 Crieff

Drummond Castle Gardens

1 hr May–Oct

Drummond Castle Gardens are considered Scotland's most important formal gardens and are certainly among the finest in Europe. The magnificent Italianate parterre was first laid in the C17 by John Drummond and it was renewed in the 1950s.

* Charles I's sundial
* Gardens featured in the film *Rob Roy*

Location
Off A822, 2 miles S of Crieff

Opening
Daily: May–Oct 1pm–6pm (last admission 5pm)
Also open at Easter

Admission
Adult £4, Child £1.50, Concs £3

Contact
Drummond Castle, nr Crieff, Perthshire PH5 4HZ

t 01764 681433
w drummondcastlegardens.co.uk
e the gardens@drummondcastle.sol.co.uk

910 Crieff

The Famous Grouse Experience at Glenturret Distillery

1 hr+ All year

A stunning audio-visual tour of Scotland takes you on an airborne journey with The Famous Grouse. Swoop over numerous famous Scottish landmarks – from Loch Ness to Edinburgh Castle – and afterwards stroll along a nature trail or enjoy a picnic in the grounds.

* Audio-visual presentation
* Award-winning famous restaurant

Location
Off A85, 1 mile from Crieff

Opening
Daily: 10am–6pm (last tour 4.30pm)

Admission
1-hour tour Adult £7.50, Child (over 10) & Concs £5, Child (under 10) free
½-hour tour please phone for details

Contact
Glenturret Distillery, The Hosh, Crieff, Perthshire PH7 4HA

t 01764 656565
w famousgrouse.com
e enquiries@famousgrouse.com

© The Famous Grouse Experience. Glenturret Distillery

911 Crieff

Stuart and Waterford Crystal Factory Shop

½ hr

All year

Be tempted by a large display of Stuart Crystal, Waterford Crystal and Wedgwood china, with factory seconds. There is also an engraving service for that personalised special gift or memento.

* Souvenir gift shop
* Chip repair service

Location
Signed from town centre

Opening
Jun–Sep daily 10am–6pm;
Oct–May Mon–Sat 10am–5pm,
Sun 11am–5pm

Admission
Free

Contact
Muthill Road, Crieff,
Perthshire PH7 4HQ

t 01764 654004

912 Cupar

Hill of Tarvit Mansion House & Garden

2 hrs

Easter–Sep

This fascinating mansion house, built in 1906, reflects the period 1870–1920, when Scotland was the industrial workshop of the world. It is a showcase for Flemish tapestries, Chinese porcelain and bronzes, French and English furniture and paintings by many eminent artists.

* Edwardian-style interior
* Set in beautiful gardens

Location
Off A916, 2 miles S of Cupar

Opening
Easter–May Thu–Mon 1pm–5pm;
Jun–Sep daily 1pm–5pm

Admission
Please phone for details

Contact
Cupar, Fife KY15 5PB

t 01334 653127
w nts.org.uk
e hilloftarvit@nts.org.uk

913 Dundee

Atholl Country Life Museum

1 hr

May–Sep

This museum of local life has exhibitions on rural trades and agricultural and domestic life. Displays cover a wide variety of subjects – road, rail and postal services, the kirk and school, and photographs of the local way of life.

* Gamekeeper's corner
* Display of stuffed wild animals

Location
Turn off A9 for Blair Atholl,
7 miles N of Pitlochry

Opening
Daily: Easter & May–Sep
1.30pm–5pm; Jul–Aug Mon–Fri from 10am

Admission
Adult £3, Child £1, Concs £2.50

Contact
Blair Atholl, Pitlochry,
Perthshire PH18 5SP

t 01796 481232
w blairatholl.org.uk
e john.museum@virgin.net

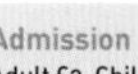
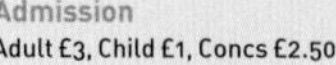

914 Dundee

Discovery Point

1 hr +

All year

Climb aboard Captain Scott's royal research ship, *Discovery*, which was originally built in Dundee to sail to the Antarctic and is now berthed on the River Tay and open to visitors. The ship represents the city's shipbuilders' greatest achievement.

* State-of-the-art multimedia exhibitions
* Scottish Family Attraction of the Year 2004

Location
In city centre, opposite railway station

Opening
Daily: Apr–Oct Mon–Sat 10am–6pm,
Sun 11am–6pm;
Nov–Mar Mon–Sat 10am–5pm,
Sun 11am–5pm

Admission
Adult £6.45, Child £3.85, Concs £4.90

Contact
Discovery Quay, Dundee DD1 4XA

t 01382 201245
w rrsdiscovery.com
e info@dundeeheritage.co.uk

915 Dunfermline

Dunfermline Abbey & Palace

1 hr · All year

The elegant ruins of Dunfermline Abbey are what is left of a great Benedictine abbey founded by Queen Margaret in the C11. Robert the Bruce was buried in the choir, and the royal palace next door, also partially ruined, was the birthplace of Charles I.

* Substantial parts of the abbey nave remain
* Next to the ruin of the royal palace

Location
Off M90, in town centre

Opening
Apr–Sep daily 9.30am–6.30pm; Oct–Mar Mon–Wed & Sat 9.30am–4.30pm, Sun 2pm–4.30pm (last admission ½ hr before close)

Admission
Adult £3, Child £1.30, Concs £2.30

Contact
St Margaret Street, Dunfermline, Fife KY12 7PE

t 01383 739026
w historic-scotland.gov.uk

916 Dunfermline

Knockhill Racing Circuit

3 hrs · All year

Scotland's national motorsport centre features major international and national motorsport events for cars and motorcycles. It is a key venue for corporate entertainment, as visitors can drive, race and rally cars, go off-road on a 4 × 4 course and do many other activities.

* Hands-on driving experiences
* Relaxing hospitality at race events

Location
Signed from M90 junction 4

Opening
Daily: 9am–6pm

Admission
Prices vary depending on event, please phone for details

Contact
Dunfermline, Fife KY12 9TF

t 01383 723337
w knockhill.co.uk
e enquiries@knockhill.co.uk

917 East Fortune

Museum of Flight

2 hrs+ All year

Man's fascination with flight is celebrated at this protected WWI and WWII airfield. Experience the highs and lows of the supersonic Concorde, and explore more than 40 other aircraft, from the earliest designs to the supersonic fighter.

* Britten-Norman Islander on display, an aircraft described as the most versatile in the world

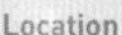

Location
Off A1, 20 miles E of Edinburgh

Opening
Apr–Jun & Sep–Oct daily 10am–5pm; Jul–Aug daily 10am–6pm; Nov–Mar Sat–Sun 10am–4pm

Admission
Museum Adult £5, Child free, Concs £4

Concorde booking pass extra: Adult £3, Child & Concs £2. Pass must be booked in advance.
Booking line 0870 421 4299

Contact
East Fortune Airfield,
East Lothian EH39 5LF

t 01620 897240
w nms.ac.uk
e info@nms.ac.uk

918 Edinburgh

Edinburgh Castle

1 hr+ All year

A majestic landmark that dominates the city's skyline, Edinburgh Castle is the top visitor attraction in Scotland. Perched on an extinct volcano and offering stunning views, this fortress is a powerful national symbol and part of Edinburgh's World Heritage site.

* Guided & audio tours
* Scottish Crown Jewels & Stone of Destiny

Location
In city centre, at top of Royal Mile

Opening
Daily: Apr–Sep 9.30am–6pm; Oct–Mar 9.30am–5pm

Admission
Adult £10.30, Child £4.50, Concs £8.50

Contact
Castle Hill, Edinburgh EH1 2NG

t 0131 225 9846
w historic-scotland.gov.uk

919 Edinburgh

Edinburgh Dungeon

1 hr All year

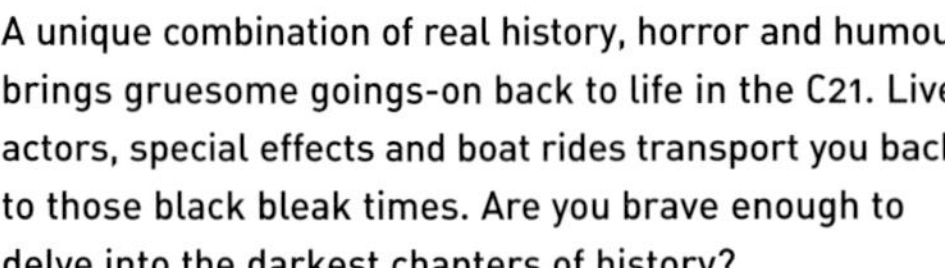

A unique combination of real history, horror and humour brings gruesome goings-on back to life in the C21. Live actors, special effects and boat rides transport you back to those black bleak times. Are you brave enough to delve into the darkest chapters of history?

* Haunted Labyrinth opened in 2005
* Great Fire of Edinburgh 'Inferno', new attraction

Location
In city centre

Opening
Daily: 10 Mar–29 Jun 10am–5pm; 30 Jun–29 Jul 10am–6pm; 30 Jul–3 Sep 10am–7pm; 4 Sep–31 Oct 10am–5pm; 1 Nov–9 Mar Fri–Mon 11am–4pm, weekends 10am–4pm

Admission
Adult £11.95, Child £7.95, Concs £9.95

Contact
31 Market Street, Edinburgh EH1 1QB

t 0131 240 1000
w thedungeons.com
e edinburghdungeon@merlinentertainments.biz

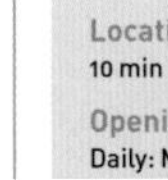

920 Edinburgh

Edinburgh Zoo

4 hrs All year

This is Scotland's most popular wildlife attraction, with more than 1,000 animals, including meerkats, koala bears, tigers, a red panda and blue poison arrow frogs. Set in beautiful parkland, it has the world's biggest penguin pool, home to Europe's largest colony of penguins.

* African Plains Experience & Magic Forest
* Hilltop safari, tour & maze & animal handling

Location
10 min from city centre

Opening
Daily: Mar & Oct 9am–5pm; Apr–Sep 9am–6pm; Nov–Feb 9am–4.30pm

Admission
Adult £10, Child* £7, Concs £7.50

Contact
134 Corstorphine Road, Edinburgh EH12 6TS

t 0131 334 9171
w edinburghzoo.org.uk
e info@edinburghzoo.org.uk

*Adult (over 17) must accompany children under 14 at all times

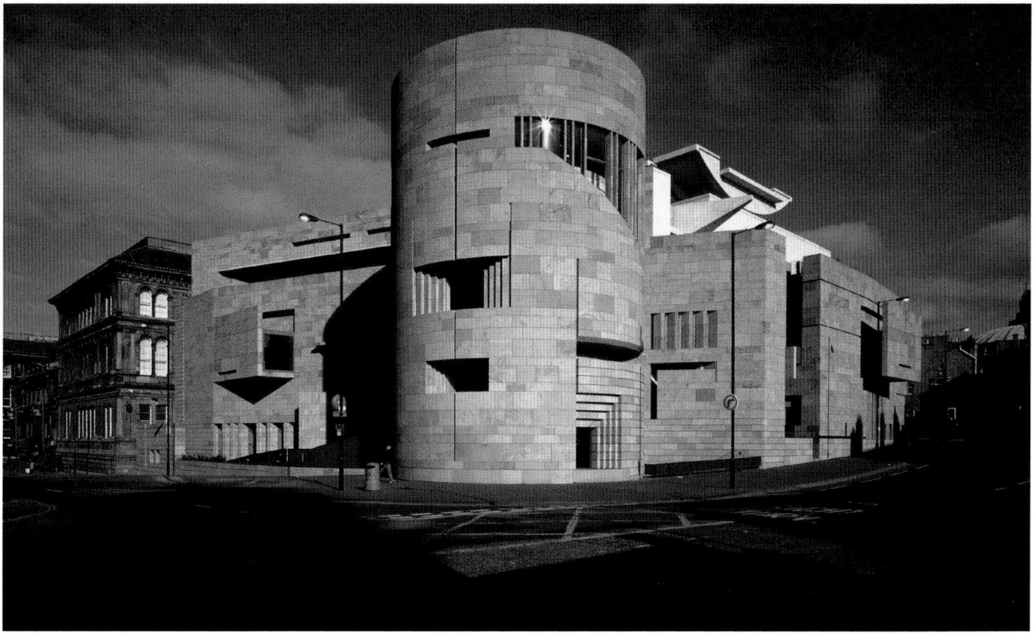

921 Edinburgh

Museum of Scotland

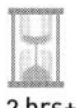
2 hrs+

All year

This museum presents, for the first time, the history of Scotland – its land, its people and their achievements – through the rich national collections. The stunning series of galleries takes you through time from Scotland's geological beginnings right up to the C20.

* More than 10,000 artefacts
* Same site as Royal Museum

WC

Location
Off A7 South Bridge, in city centre

Opening
Daily: 10am–5pm

Admission
Free

Contact
Chambers Street, Edinburgh EH1 1JF

t 0131 247 4422
w nms.ac.uk
e info@nms.ac.uk

922 Edinburgh

National Gallery of Scotland

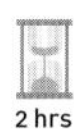
2 hrs

All year

The gallery is home to Scotland's greatest collection of European paintings and sculpture, ranging from the Renaissance to Post-Impressionism. One of Edinburgh's major attractions, it is also one of the finest galleries of its size in the world.

* Includes masterpieces by Van Dyck & Tiepolo
* Comprehensive collection of Scottish paintings

Location
Off Princes Street, in city centre

Opening
Daily: 10am–5pm, Thu 10am–7pm

Admission
Free. Charges for some exhibitions

Contact
The Mound, Edinburgh EH2 2EL

t 0131 624 6200
w nationalgalleries.org
e enquiries@nationalgalleries.org

923 Edinburgh

National Portrait Gallery

2 hrs All year

The gallery provides a visual history of Scotland, told through the portraits of those who shaped it: royals and rebels, poets and philosophers, heroes and villains. All the portraits of Scots are by well-known artists, including Kokoschka and Van Dyck.

* Works by Gainsborough, Copley & Rodin
* Unparalleled collection of Scottish portraits

Location
At E end of Queen Street, in city centre

Opening
Daily: 10am-5pm, Thu 10am-7pm; 1 Jan 12noon-5pm

Admission
Free

Contact
1 Queen Street, Edinburgh EH2 1JD

t 0131 624 6200
w nationalgalleries.org
e enquiries@nationalgalleries.org

924 Edinburgh

Our Dynamic Earth

2 hrs All year

Explore our planet's past, present and future. You'll be shaken by volcanoes, fly over glaciers, feel the chill of polar ice, and get caught in a tropical rainstorm. New! Journey to the Earth's Core. New! Take your crew seat in the FutureDome and consider our planet's future.

* Live 4,500 million years in a day

Location
At foot of Arthur's Seat, adjacent to new Scottish Parliament

Opening
Please phone or visit website for details

Admission
Adult £8.95, Child & Concs £5.45

Contact
112 Holyrood Road, Edinburgh EH8 8AS

t 0131 550 7800
w dynamicearth.co.uk
e enquiries@dynamicearth.co.uk

925 Edinburgh

Palace of Holyroodhouse

1 hr All year

Originally founded in 1128 as a monastery, the Palace of Holyroodhouse in Edinburgh is the Queen's official residence in Scotland, and is no stranger to royalty, as Mary, Queen of Scots, among others, lived here. In fact, the palace has many associations with Scottish history.

* Queen's Gallery
* Features items from one of the finest art collections in the world

Location
At bottom of Royal Mile

Opening
Daily: Apr–Oct 9.30am–6pm (last admission 5pm); Nov–Mar 9.30am–4.30pm (last admission 3.30pm)

Admission
Adult £8.80, Child £4.80, Concs £7.80, Family ticket £22.50. (by timed ticket slots)

Contact
Royal Mile, Edinburgh EH8 8DX

t 0131 556 5100
w royalcollection.org.uk
e bookinginfo@royalcollection.org.uk

926 Edinburgh

Royal Botanic Garden Edinburgh

2 hrs All year

Founded in the C17 as a 'physic garden', growing medicinal plants, the Royal Botanic Garden is now acknowledged as one of the finest gardens in the world. It's a place to rest and relax, away from the city's hustle and bustle, and is home to unusual and beautiful plants.

* Guided & themed tours, refurbished Victorian palm house
* Queen Mother's memorial garden, opened by the Queen July 2006

Location
Off A902, 1 mile N of city centre

Opening
Daily: Mar & Oct 10am–6pm;
Apr–Sep 10am–7pm;
Nov–Feb 10am–4pm

Admission
Free. Charges apply to glasshouses

Contact
20A Inverleith Row, Edinburgh EH3 5LR

t 0131 552 7171
w rbge.org.uk
e info@rbge.org.uk

927 Edinburgh

The Royal Yacht *Britannia*

1 hr+ All year

Now permanently moored in Edinburgh's historic port of Leith, *Britannia* welcomes you to its visitor centre, located in Ocean Terminal, Edinburgh's stylish waterfront shopping and leisure development. Then step on board for a self-led audio tour of five decks.

* See royal apartments & the crew's quarters
* Children's audio tour

Location
At Leith Docks, signed from city outskirts

Opening
Daily: Apr–Sep 9.30am–4.30pm;
Oct–Mar 10am–3.30pm
Pre-booking is advised in Aug

Admission
Adult £9, Child £5, Concs £7

Contact
Ocean Terminal, Leith,
Edinburgh EH6 6JJ

t 0131 555 5566
w royalyachtbritannia.co.uk
e enquiries@tryb.co.uk

928 Edinburgh

The Spirit of the Tattoo

 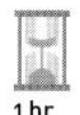 

1 hr All year

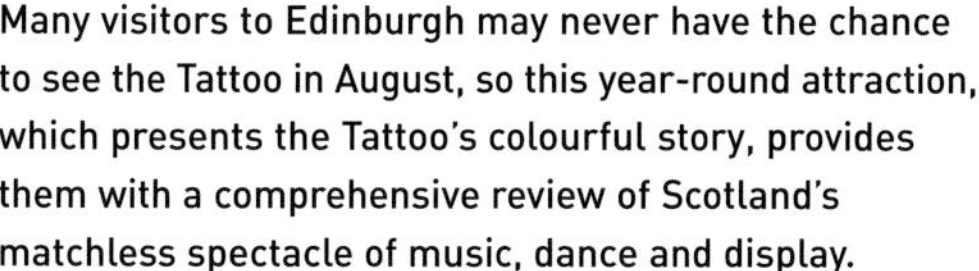

Many visitors to Edinburgh may never have the chance to see the Tattoo in August, so this year-round attraction, which presents the Tattoo's colourful story, provides them with a comprehensive review of Scotland's matchless spectacle of music, dance and display.

* Interactive exhibition & film theatre
* Rooftop café

Location
In city centre, on Royal Mile just below castle

Opening
Daily: Mon–Sat 10am–5pm,
Sun 11am–5pm
Winter opening times shorter, please phone for details.

Admission
Free

Contact
555 Castlehill, The Royal Mile,
Edinburgh EH1 2ND

t 0131 225 9661
w edinburgh-tattoo.co.uk
e administration@edintattoo.co.uk

929 Edinburgh

St Giles' Cathedral

 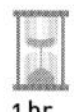 

1 hr All year

This is the High Kirk of Edinburgh and it has been at the heart of the city's spiritual life for at least 900 years. A living church with an active congregation, it also welcomes visitors who come to experience the unique atmosphere of continuing worship and age-old history.

* Mother church of Presbyterianism
* One of Scotland's most important buildings historically

Location
On Royal Mile, in city centre

Opening
Daily: May–Sep Mon–Fri 9am–7pm,
Sat 9am–5pm, Sun 1pm–5pm;
Oct–Apr Mon–Sat 9am–5pm,
Sun 1pm–5pm

Admission
Free, recommended donation of £1 per person

Contact
High Street, Edinburgh EH1 1RE

t 0131 225 9442
w stgilescathedral.org.uk
e info@stgilescathedral.org.uk

930 Fife

Scottish Deer Centre

2 hrs + All year

This 55-acre park is home to more than 140 deer representing 9 species. Other attractions include ranger tours, dramatic birds of prey demonstrations, a treetop walkway, viewing platforms, scenic pathways, and indoor and outdoor adventure play areas for children.

* Falconry displays
* Wolf wood now includes 2 European wolves

Location
On outskirts of Cupar, 12 miles from St Andrews on A91

Opening
Daily: May–Sep 10am–6pm; Oct–Apr 10am–5pm

Admission
Adult £5.50, Child (over 3) £3.95, Child (under 3) free, Concs £4.55

Contact
Bow-of-Fife, Cupar, Fife KY15 4NQ

t 01337 810391
w tsdc.co.uk
e info@tsdc.co.uk

932 Glasgow

Burrell Collection

 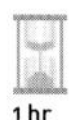 

1 hr All year

When Sir William Burrell gifted his collection of more than 9,000 works of art to Glasgow, the city acquired one of its greatest collections. He had been an art collector since his teens and the collection constitutes a vast array of works of all periods, from all over the world.

* Medieval art, tapestries, alabasters & stained glass
* Paintings by Degas & Cézanne

Location
5 miles S of city centre

Opening
Daily: Mon–Thu & Sat 10am–5pm, Fri & Sun 11am–5pm

Admission
Free

Contact
Pollok Country Park, 2060 Pollokshaws Road, Glasgow G43 1AT

t 0141 287 2550
w glasgowmuseums.com
e cls.glasgow.gov.uk

931 Glamis by Forfar

Glamis Castle

2 hrs+ Mar–Dec

Glamis Castle has a long and colourful history. It has a legendary association, at least according to Shakespeare, with the C11 Macbeth and has a place in C20 history as the childhood home of the Queen Mother.

* Rich variety of furnishings, tapestries & art
* Extensive estate & formal gardens

Location
On A94, between Aberdeen & Perth

Opening
Daily: Mar–Oct 10am–6pm; Nov–23 Dec 11am–3pm

Admission
Adult £7.30, Child £4.10, Concs £6.10, Family ticket £21

Contact
The Castle Administrator, Estates Office, Glamis by Forfar, Angus DD8 1RJ

t 01307 840393
w glamis-castle.co.uk
e enquiries@glamis-castle.co.uk

933 Glasgow

Gallery of Modern Art

  1 hr+  All year

GoMA is the second most-visited contemporary art gallery outside London, offering a thought-provoking programme of temporary exhibitions and workshops. The focus of the gallery is on contemporary social issues, often highlighting groups marginalised in today's society.

* Includes work by Bridget Riley, Scottish artists John Byrne & Christine Borland & photographer Sebastio Salgado

Location
In city centre, off Buchanan Street, close to Queen Street & central station

Opening
Mon–Wed & Sat 10am–5pm, Thu 10am–8pm, Fri & Sun 11am–5pm

Admission
Free

Contact
Royal Exchange Square, Glasgow G1 3AH

t 0141 229 1996
w glasgowmuseums.com

934 Glasgow

Glasgow Science Centre

  3 hrs+  All year

Shake hands with yourself, make a 3D image of your face and see how you will look in years to come. Enjoy more than 300 hands-on and interactive exhibits, take in a live science show, see the latest IMAX® fim, visit the Scottishpower planetarium and observe the stars.

* IMAX® cinema
* Several new exhibitions for 2007

Location
Opposite Scottish Exhibition & Crowne Plaza Hotel on River Clyde

Opening
Apr–Oct daily 10am–6pm; Nov–Mar Tue–Sun 10am–6pm

Admission
Adult £6.95, Child & Concs £4.95

Contact
50 Pacific Quay, Glasgow G51 1EA

t 0871 540 1000
w glasgowsciencecentre.org
e admin@glasgowsciencecentre.org.uk

935 Glasgow

Necropolis

 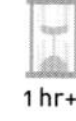 1 hr+  All year

The Necropolis stands on a hill to the east of Glasgow Cathedral, just a short walk across the Bridge of Sighs. The monument to John Knox, which was erected in 1825, dominates the hill. This Victorian cemetery was modelled on Père-Lachaise in Paris.

* Some of Glasgow's most noted people including architects, industrialists & religious leaders are buried here

Location
Near Glasgow Cathedral

Opening
Daily: 8am–4.30pm

Admission
Free

Contact
Cemeteries & Crematoria, 1st Floor, 20 Trongate, Glasgow G1 5ES

t 0141 287 3965

936 Glasgow

People's Palace

2 hrs+ All year

The People's Palace is Glasgow's social history museum and tells the story of the people and city of Glasgow from 1760 to the present day. There are paintings, prints and photographs displayed alongside a wealth of historic artefacts, films and computer interactives.

* Discover how a family lived in a typical single-end Glasgow tenement

Location
Short walk from city centre

Opening
Daily: Mon–Thu & Sat 10am–5pm, Fri & Sun 11am–5pm

Admission
Free

Contact
Glasgow Green, Glasgow G40 1AT

t 0141 271 2951
w glasgowmuseums.com

937 Glasgow

The Piping Centre

1 hr All year

Nothing makes a Scotsman feel more patriotic than the sound of a pipe band. This is the sound of Scotland, a haunting melody to lift the soul. At the Museum of Piping you can witness hundreds of years of Scottish heritage, played out before your eyes and ears.

* Outstanding collection of piping artefacts
* Study the history & origins of bagpiping

Location
In Glasgow, off junction 16 of M8 & along A804 towards the E

Opening
Daily: 9am–9pm, Sun 9am–5pm (closed Sun in winter)

Admission
Adult £3, Child & Concs £2

Contact
30–34 McPhater Street, Glasgow G4 0HW

t 0141 353 0220
w thepipingcentre.co.uk
e reception@thepipingcentre.co.uk

938 Glasgow

Scottish Football Museum

2 hrs+ All year

The world's first national football museum is housed at Hampden Park, the oldest continuously used international ground in the world. It is owned by Queen's Park FC, the oldest association team in Scotland (founded 1867) and one with an unrivalled history.

* World's most impressive collection of football memorabilia, covering 140 years of football history

Location
Take junction 1 of M77, on to B768 (Titwood Road), then right on to B766 (Battlefield Road), then Kings Park Road & left into Kinghorn Drive

Opening
Daily: Mon–Sat 10am–5pm, Sun 11am–5pm

Admission
Adult £5.50, Child & Concs £2.75

Contact
Hampden Park, Glasgow G42 9BA

t 0141 616 6139
w scottishfootballmuseum.org.uk
e museumInfo@scottishfootball museum.org.uk

939 Glasgow

Tall Ship in Glasgow Harbour

1 hr+ All year

Explore the tall ship *Glenlee*, one of only five Clyde-built sailing ships that remain afloat. Built in 1896, she operated as a long-haul cargo vessel before being bought by the Spanish Navy as a training ship. She has circumnavigated the globe four times.

* Exhibition tells the *Glenlee* story
* Children's events throughout the year, visitor centre

    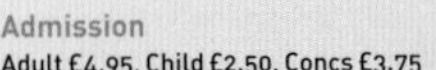

Location
Off M8 junction 19. Follow brown thistle signs

Opening
Daily: Mar–Oct 10am–5pm; Nov–Feb 11am–4pm

Admission
Adult £4.95, Child £2.50, Concs £3.75 (Adult price includes 1 child)

Contact
100, Stobe Cross Road, Glasgow G3 8QQ

t 0141 222 2513
w thetallship.com
e info@thetallship.com

940 Glasgow

Xscape – Braehead

2 hrs+ All year

Xscape is a fantastic adrenaline-filled entertainment complex. Try indoor free fall in the incredible fan drop, cruise the real-snow ski slope and test your nerve in the Skypark aerial adventure course or on the climbing wall. To relax, enjoy the cinema complex or bowling alley.

* Amazing choice of cafés, restaurants & bars

Location
Junction 26 (eastbound) of M8. A new motorway junction (25a) provides dedicated westbound access roads direct to shopping centre while new eastern link road connects to A8 dual carriageway

Opening
Daily: 9am–late

Admission
Please phone for details

Contact
Kings Inch Road, Braehead, Glasgow G51 4BW

t 0871 200 3222
w xscape.co.uk
e info@xscape.co.uk

941 Kinross

Loch Leven Castle

2 hrs Apr–Oct

The dramatic ruins of this castle stand on an island in Loch Leven. The late C14 or early C15 tower is infamous as the place where Mary, Queen of Scots was imprisoned in 1567. She escaped the following year, but her ghost is alleged to haunt the castle to this day.

* Loch is now a National Nature Reserve

Location
M90. Accessible by boat from Scottish Angling Academy in Kinross, signposted from A922

Opening
Daily: Apr–Sep 9.30am–5.15pm; Oct Mon, Wed–Thu & Sat–Sun 9.30am–3.15pm

Admission
Adult £4, Child £1.60, Concs £3

Contact
Kinross, Perthshire KY13 7AR

t 07778 040483
w historic-scotland.gov.uk

942 Kircaldy

Craigencalt Ecology Centre

1 hr All year

The Ecology Centre provides environmental education and information across a wide range of subjects. It is the home of the UK's first 'Earthship', a building created from waste and natural materials to be self-sufficient in energy and water.

* Community woodland & sustainable living display

Location
Take B923 off A921 between Burntisland & Kirkcaldy. Located beside Kinghorn Loch

Opening
Daily sunrise–sunset

Admission
Free

Contact
Craigencalt Farm, Kinghorn, Fife KY3 9YG

t 01592 891567
w theecologycentre.org
e admin@theecologycentre.org

943 Kirriemuir

Barrie's Birthplace

1 hr All year

J M Barrie, the creator of the eternal magic of *Peter Pan*, was born here in 1860. The upper floor is furnished as it was when Barrie lived here. The adjacent house, No. 11, features a new Peter Pan room where you can use your imagination and fly off to Neverland.

* For the young at heart, adults & children alike
* Audio programme in the wash house

Location
A901/A926 in Kirriemuir, 6 miles NW of Forfar

Opening
Sun all year 1pm–5pm;
Jun & Sep Sat–Wed 12noon–5pm;
Jul–Aug Mon–Sat 11am–5pm;

Admission
Adult £5, Child & Concs £4

Contact
9 Brechin Road, Kirriemuir, Angus DD8 4BX

t 01575 572646
w nts.org.uk/barrie.html
e barriesbirthplace@nts.org.uk

944 Linlithgow

Linlithgow Palace

1 hr All year

This magnificent ruin of a great royal palace is set in its own park, beside Linlithgow Loch. It was a favoured home of the Stuart kings and queens, from James I (1406–37) onward, and building work from the eras of James I, III, IV, V and VI can be seen, including the great hall and chapel.

* Birthplace of James V & Mary, Queen of Scots
* Oldest working fountain in Britain

Location
On A803/M9, in town centre

Opening
Daily: Apr–Sep daily 9.30am–6.30pm;
Oct–Mar Mon–Sat 9.30am–4.30pm,
Sun 2pm–4.30pm

Admission
Adult £4.50, Child £2, Concs £3.50

Contact
Kirkgate, Linlithgow, West Lothian EH49 7AL

t 01506 842896
w historic-scotland.gov.uk

945 New Lanark

New Lanark World Heritage Site

  2 hrs+  All year

The cotton mills of New Lanark were founded more than 200 years ago and the village became famous for the work of mill owner Robert Owen, who provided a decent life for the villagers. Today New Lanark has been restored and visitors can explore this fascinating place.

* Award-winning visitor centre
* Accommodation available at New Lanark Mill Hotel

Location
Off M74 junction 13, signed off all routes

Opening
Daily: Jun–Aug 10.30am–5pm; Sep–May 11am–5pm

Admission
Adult £5.95, Child & Concs £4.95

Contact
New Lanark Mills, South Lanarkshire ML11 9DB

t 01555 661345
w newlanark.org
e trust@newlanark.org

946 Newtongrange

Scottish Mining Museum

 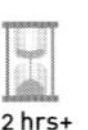 2 hrs+   All year

This museum is based at one of the finest surviving examples of a Victorian colliery in Europe, the Lady Victoria Colliery at Newtongrange. A fully accessible, three-storey visitor centre allows everyone to experience the atmosphere and noise of a working pit.

* 2 major exhibitions: The Story of Coal & A Race Apart
* Audio tour with 'magic helmets'. Big Stuff Tour (Wed & Sun)

Location
On A7, 9 miles S of Edinburgh

Opening
Daily: Mar–Oct 10am–5pm; Nov–Feb 10am–4pm

Admission
Adult £5.95, Child & Concs £3.95, Family ticket £17.95

Contact
Lady Victoria Colliery, Newtongrange, Midlothian EH22 4QN

t 0131 663 7519
w scottishminingmuseum.com
e enquiries@scottishminingmuseum.com

947 North Queensferry

Deep Sea World

  2 hrs+   All year

Explore the undersea world at the triple award-winning National Aquarium of Scotland. Situated on the banks of the Firth of Forth, below the Forth Railway Bridge, this fascinating attraction offers an absorbing day out for the whole family.

* Seal sanctuary dedicated to orphan & sick seal pups

Location
1 mile from M90 on N side of Forth Road Bridge

Opening
Daily: Apr–Aug 10am–6pm; Sep–Mar Mon–Fri 10am–5pm, Sat–Sun 10am–6pm (last admission 1 hr before close)

Admission
Please phone for details

Contact
North Queensferry, Fife KY11 1JR

t 01383 411880
w deepseaworld.com
e info@deepseaworld.co.uk

948 Perth

Scone Palace

  1 hr+  Apr–Oct

In a spectacular setting above the River Tay, Scone Palace has been the seat of parliaments and the crowning place of kings. It has housed the Stone of Destiny and been immortalised in Shakespeare's *Macbeth*, and it is regarded by many as the heart of Scottish history.

* One of the finest private collections of furniture in Britain
* Beautiful gardens, including Moot Hill

Location
Signed from M90/A9, between Edinburgh & the Highlands

Opening
Daily: Apr–Oct 9.30am–5.30pm (last admission 5pm)

Admission
Adult £7.20, Child £4.20, Concs £6.20, Family ticket £23

Contact
The Administrator, Scone Palace, Perth, Perthshire PH2 6BD

t 01738 552300
w scone-palace.co.uk
e visits@scone-palace.co.uk

949 Pittenweem

Kellie Castle & Garden

  2 hrs  All year

Now in the care of the National Trust for Scotland, Kellie Castle contains magnificent plaster ceilings, painted panelling and furniture by Sir Robert Lorimer. A special exhibition commemorates Hew Lorimer's life and work, and you can take an audio tour of the lovely garden.

* Fine example of domestic architecture
* Beautiful walled garden

   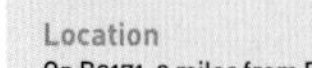

Location
On B9171, 3 miles from Pittenweem

Opening
Castle Daily: Easter & May–Sep 1pm–5pm
Garden Daily: 9.30am–5.30pm

Admission
Adult £8, Child & Concs £5

Contact
Pittenweem, Fife KY10 2RF

t 01333 720271
w nts.org.uk
e information@nts.org.uk

950 Pitlochry

Blair Castle

  1 hr+  All year

More than 700 years of Scottish history await you at Blair Castle. See displays of beautiful furniture, fine paintings, arms and armour, china, costumes, lace and embroidery, masonic regalia and Jacobite relics – all of which provide a colourful picture of Scottish life from the C16 to today.

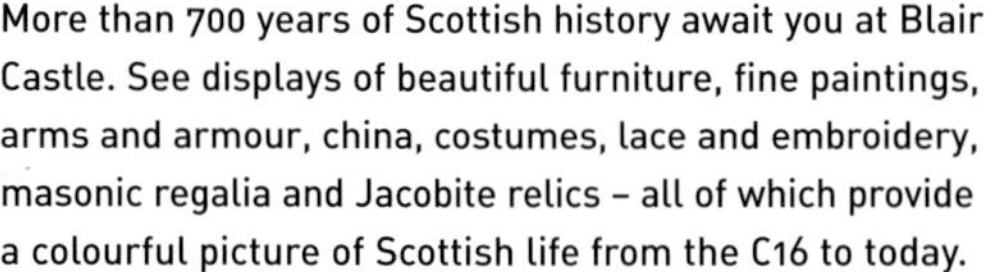

* Spectacular setting in the Strath of Garry
* Guided tours available for parties of more than 12

Location
At Blair Atholl, N of Pitlochry

Opening
Daily: Mar–Oct 9.30am–4.30pm; Nov–Feb Tue & Sat 9.30am–12.30pm

Admission
Adult £7.20, Child £4.50, Concs £6.20

Contact
Blair Atholl, Pitlochry, Perthshire PH18 5TL

t 01796 481207
w blair-castle.co.uk
e office@blair-castle.co.uk

951 Pitlochry

Killiecrankie Visitor Centre

  1 hr  Apr–Oct

In 1689 the Pass of Killiecrankie echoed with the sounds of battle, when a Jacobite army defeated the government forces. The spectacular gorge is tranquil now and a fine example of mixed deciduous woodland. The visitor centre explains the battle, natural history and ranger services.

* Site of Special Scientific Interest
* Visitors can watch birds nesting via a remote camera

Location
On B8079, 3 miles N of Pitlochry

Opening
Daily: Apr–Oct 10am–5.30pm

Admission
Free. Car park £2

Contact
nr Pitlochry, Perthshire PH16 5LG

t 01796 473233
w nts.org.uk

952 St Andrews

British Golf Museum

1 hr+ All year

Come to St Andrews to see the history of golf unfold before your eyes. Imaginative displays are enhanced by stunning interactives that add to the exciting and varied ways of looking at golf's past. A visit to the British Golf Museum is the perfect break from playing golf.

* Regular calendar of events
* Guided walks on the Old Course (summer only)

Location
Signed from town centre

Opening
Daily: Apr–Oct Mon–Sat 9.30am– 5.30pm, Sun 10am–5pm; Nov–Mar 10am–4pm

Admission
Adult £5, Child £2.75, Concs £4

Contact
Bruce Embankment, St Andrews, Fife KY16 9AB

t 01334 460046
w britishgolfmuseum.co.uk
e judychance@randa.org

953 St Andrews

Scotland's Secret Bunker

1 hr+ Apr–Oct

Discover the twilight world of the government's Cold War headquarters. Hidden for more than 40 years beneath a Scottish farm house, a tunnel leads to Scotland's Secret Bunker – 24,000 sq ft of secret accommodation on two levels, 100 ft underground.

* Built in complete secrecy in the 1950s
* Discover how the lucky few would have survived but you wouldn't

Location
On B940, between St Andrews & Anstruther

Opening
Daily: Apr–Oct 10am–6pm (last admission 5pm)

Admission
Adult £7.80, Child £4.80, Concs £6.20

Contact
Crown Buildings, Troywood, nr St Andrews, Fife KY16 8QH

t 01333 310301
w secretbunker.co.uk
e mod@secretbunker.co.uk

954 Stirling

Argyll's Lodging

1 hr All year

A superb mansion built around an earlier core in about 1630 and further extended by the Earl of Argyll in the 1670s. It is the most impressive town house of its period in Scotland. The principal rooms are now restored to their 1680 state.

* Beautiful furniture & furnishings
* Magnificent restoration

Location
Near castle

Opening
Daily: Apr–Oct 9.30am–6pm (last admission 5.30pm); Nov–Mar 9.30am–5pm (last admission 4.30pm)

Admission
Adult £4, Child £1.60, Concs £3

Contact
Castle Wynd, Stirling, Stirlingshire FK8 1EG

t 01786 431319
w historic-scotland.gov.uk

955 Stirling

Bannockburn Heritage Centre

1 hr+ Mar–Oct

Located at one of the most important historical sites in Scotland, this centre offers great insights into the Battle of Bannockburn, Robert the Bruce and William Wallace. Learn about the legendary battle of 1314 in which Bruce and his army defeated Edward II of England.

* Wars of independence exhibition
* Audio-visual presentation of the famous battle

Location
Off M80/M9 junction 9, 2 miles S of Stirling

Opening
Daily: Mar–Oct 10am–5.30pm

Admission
Adult £5, Child & Concs £4

Contact
Glasgow Road, Whins of Milton, Stirling, Stirlingshire FK7 0LJ

t 01786 812664
w nts.org.uk

956 Stirling

Stirling Castle

1 hr+ All year

Without doubt one of the grandest of all Scottish castles, both in its architecture and in its situation on a rocky outcrop. The great hall and gate house of James IV, the marvellous palace of James V, the Chapel Royal and the artillery fortifications are all of outstanding interest.

* Audio guides in 6 languages
* Regimental Museum of the Highlanders

Location
Off M9, in old town

Opening
Daily: Apr–Sep 9.30am–6pm; Oct–Mar 9.30am–5pm (last admission 45 min before close)

Admission
Adult £8.50, Child £3.50, Concs £6.50

Contact
Esplanade, Stirling, Stirlingshire FK8 1EJ

t 01786 450000
w historic-scotland.gov.uk

© Tony Stuchbury www.ajsphotos.co.uk

957 Stirling

Wallace Monument

1 hr All year

This is a chance to renew your acquaintance with Scotland's national hero William Wallace, popularly known as Braveheart and glorified by Hollywood, at the spectacular 220ft (67m) National Wallace Monument, completed in 1869.

* See the mighty two-handed broadsword
* Exhibition on the building of the Monument

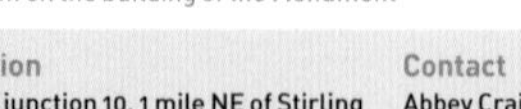

Location
Off M9 junction 10, 1 mile NE of Stirling town centre

Opening
Please phone for details

Admission
Adult £6.50, Child £4, Concs £4.90

Contact
Abbey Craig, Hillfoots Road, Stirling, Stirlingshire FK9 5LF

t 01786 472140
w nationalwallacemonument.com
e nwm@aillst.ossian.net

958 Aberdeen

Aberdeen Maritime Museum

1 hr+ All year

This museum tells the story of Aberdeen's long, close relationship with the sea. It houses a unique collection, covering shipbuilding, fast sailing ships, fishing and port history, and is the only place in the UK where you can see displays about the North Sea oil industry.

* Incorporates Provost Ross's House, built in 1593
* Offers a spectacular viewpoint over the busy harbour

Location
Overlooking the harbour

Opening
Daily: Mon–Sat 10am–5pm, Sun 12noon–3pm

Admission
Free

Contact
Shiprow, Aberdeen AB11 5BY

t 01224 337700
w aagm.co.uk
e info@aagm.co.uk

959 Aberdeen

Archaeolink

1 hr+ All year

This dynamic historical experience covers 10,000 years from the Mesolithic period to the Romans. Outdoor and indoor exhibitions, hands-on activities, workshops and guided tours really bring history to life in an exciting and interactive way.

* Special exhibitions throughout the year
* Re-enactments & spectacular events programme

Location
Just off A96 near Aberdeen

Opening
Daily: Apr–Oct 10am–5pm, Nov–Mar 11am–4pm

Admission
Adult £5, Child £3.40, Concs £4.50

Contact
Oyne, Insch, Aberdeen AB52 6QP

t 01464 851500
w archaeolink.co.uk
e info@archaeolink.co.uk

960 Aberdeen

Beach Leisure Centre

 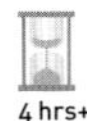  

4 hrs+ All year

This remarkable centre has a leisure pool with many water features, including waves, a fountain and rapids. There is a well-equipped fitness studio, saunas, a steam room and a double-sized sports hall, equipped for virtually every indoor game.

* Free crêche
* Ice arena

Location
Next to the beach at Aberdeen

Opening
Please phone for details

Admission
Facilities priced individually

Contact
Beach Promenade, Aberdeen AB24 5NR

t 01224 655401
w aberdeencity.gov.uk
e info@aberdeencity.gov.uk

961 Ballater

Balmoral Castle & Estate

1 hr+ Apr–Jul

The Queen's favourite home is still a thriving estate. A visit gives a marvellous insight into royal heritage and the life of a large estate, which provides employment and housing as well as working to conserve and regenerate the natural environment.

* Access to grounds, gardens, exhibitions, shops, tearoom & ballroom

    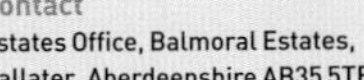

Location
Off A93, between Ballater & Braemar

Opening
Daily: Apr–Jul 10am–5pm (last admission 4pm)

Admission
Adult £7, Child £3, Concs £6

Contact
Estates Office, Balmoral Estates, Ballater, Aberdeenshire AB35 5TB

t 01339 742534
w balmoralcastle.com
e info@balmoralcastle.com

962 Dufftown

Glenfiddich Distillery

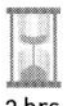
2 hrs

All year

Visit the home of the only Highland single malt Scotch whisky that is distilled, matured and bottled at its distillery. Whisky has flowed from the stills at this site since 1887. A must for all whisky connoisseurs.

* Distillery tours, shop, visitor centre, coffee shop & bar
* Special connoisseurs tour (£15)

Location
On A941, ½ mile N of Dufftown

Opening
Daily: Easter–mid-Oct Mon–Sat 9.30am–4.30pm, Sun 12noon–4.30pm; mid-Oct–Easter Mon–Fri 9.30am–4.30pm (closed Christmas & New Year)

Admission
Free

Contact
Dufftown, Banffshire AB55 4DH

t 01340 820373
w glenfiddich.com

963 Forres

Findhorn Heritage Icehouse

1 hr

May–Sep

Explore underground arched chambers built 150 years ago to store ice for packing salmon on the way to London. The chambers are now used to display all aspects of the salmon net-fishing industry. Visit the Heritage Centre where the history and ecology are graphically displayed.

* Junior quiz to complete
* See the unique Findhorn class yacht

Location
From Forres take B9089 to Kinloss, then B9011 to Findhorn & follow signs

Opening
May & Sep Sat–Sun 2pm–5pm; Jun–Aug daily 2pm–5pm

Admission
Free, donations welcomed

Contact
147, Findhorn, Forres, Moray IV36 3YL

t 01309 690659
w findhornbay.net
e s.eibbor@tesco.net

964 Fraserburgh

The Museum of Scottish Lighthouses

2 hrs+

All year

The history of Scotland's lighthouses is illuminated in the country's oldest example. There are multiscreen audio-visual presentations, and a guided tour to the top of the fully restored lighthouse where visitors can enjoy panoramic views of the Buchan coast.

* Largest collection of lighthouse equipment in the UK
* First lighthouse built on top of a fortified castle

Location
In town centre

Opening
Daily: Apr–Oct Mon–Sat 10am–5pm, Sun 12noon–5pm; Jul–Aug Mon–Sat 10am–6pm, Sun 11am–6pm; Nov–Mar Mon–Sat 10am–4pm, Sun 12noon–4pm

Admission
Adult £5, Child £2, Concs £4

Contact
Kinnaird Head, Stevenson Road, Fraserburgh AB43 9DU

t 01346 511022
w lighthousemuseum.co.uk
e info@lighthousemuseum.org.uk

965 Peterhead

Peterhead Maritime Heritage

1 hr+

Jun–Aug

This Heritage Centre, housed in an award-winning building, offers a historic look back at the Peterhead experience in sea-based industries. There are interactive displays on fishing, whaling and navigation and a brief exploration of the North Sea oil industry.

* Audio-visual displays on maritime life
* 3-star Speciality Attraction

Location
Overlooking Peterhead Bay & beside beach & marina. Reached via A90 or A950

Opening
Daily: Jun–Aug 10.30am–5pm, Sun 11.30am–5pm

Admission
Free

Contact
South Road, Peterhead, Aberdeenshire AB42 2YP

t 01779 473000
w aberdeenshire.gov.uk

966 Aviemore

Cairngorm Reindeer Centre

1 hr Feb–Dec

See Britain's only reindeer herd roaming free in the Cairngorm mountains. These extremely tame and friendly animals are a joy to all who come and meet them. Under supervision, visitors can feed and stroke the members of this 50-strong herd.

* Guided tours on the hills (weather permitting)
* Learn more about these fascinating creatures

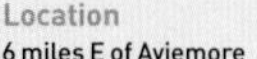

Location
6 miles E of Aviemore

Opening
Daily: Feb–Dec 10am–5pm; *Tours* Feb half-term, Apr & Oct–Dec 11am; *Tours* May–Sep 11am & 2.30pm

Admission
Adult £8, Child & Concs £4

Contact
Glenmore, Aviemore, Invernessshire PH22 1QU

t 01479 861228
w reindeer-company.demon.co.uk
e info@reindeer-company.demon.co.uk

967 Balmaha

Loch Lomond National Nature Reserve

3 hrs All year

Inchailloch, one of the most accessible of Loch Lomond's 38 islands, has a long association with Christianity. It is cloaked in oak woodland, with a wealth of bird life and flora, and there are several woodland trails giving fantastic views of the loch.

* Wonderful camp & picnic site
* Remains of a C13 parish church

Location
Inchailloch is reached by ferry from Balmaha boatyard off B837

Opening
Daily: wardens present Apr–Sep

Admission
Free

Contact
Loch Lomond & Trossachs National Park, Balmaha Visitor Centre

t 01389 722600/722100
w lochlomond-trossachs.org
e info@lochlomond-trossachs.org

968 Culloden Moor

Culloden Battlefield

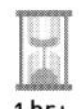
1 hr+

Feb–Dec

Few names in Scottish history evoke more emotion than Culloden, the bleak moor where, in 1746, Bonnie Prince Charlie's hopes were crushed and the Jacobite Rising was put down. The prince's forces were greatly outnumbered, but nevertheless went into battle with legendary courage.

* Permanent exhibition of the type of weapons used in the battle
* New £8 million visitor centre opening summer 2007

Location
On B9006, 5 miles E of Inverness

Opening
Daily: Feb & Nov–Dec 11am–4pm; Mar–May 10am–4pm; Jun–Aug 9am–6pm; Sep–Oct 9am–5.30pm

Admission
Adult £5, Child & Concs £4, Family ticket £14

Contact
The National Trust for Scotland, Culloden Moor, Inverness IV2 5EU

t 01463 790607
w nts.org.uk/culloden

969 Drumnadrochit

Loch Ness Monster Exhibition Centre

1 hr+

All year

Through photographs, descriptions and film footage, this exhibition presents the evidence about the existence of the Loch Ness Monster. It also highlights the efforts of various search expeditions, by both individuals and respected institutions, such as Operation Deepscan.

* Travel round the loch, view places & meet locals
* Exhibition cinema in 8 languages

Location
On A82, W of Inverness

Opening
Daily: Apr–Oct 9am–9pm
Nov–Mar 9am–5pm

Admission
Adult £5, Child £3.50, Concs £3.95

Contact
Drumnadrochit, Invernessshire IV63 6TU

t 01456 450342
w lochness-centre.com
e donald@lochness-centre.com

970 Fort William

The Jacobite Steam Train

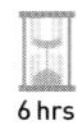
6 hrs

May–Oct

Described as one of the great railway journeys of the world, the Jacobite Steam Train leaves Fort William and travels on an 84-mile round trip. It passes Ben Nevis, then crosses the Glenfinnan Viaduct used in the *Harry Potter* films and arrives in Mallaig by the Atlantic Ocean.

* Leaves Fort William at 10.20am & returns at 4pm
* 1½-hour stopover in Mallaig

Location
Fort William railway station, in town centre

Opening
May–Oct. Please phone for details

Admission
Please phone for details

Contact
West Coast Railway Company, Warton Road, Carnforth LA5 9HX

t 01524 737751/737753
w steamtrain.info
e jacobite@wcrc.co.uk

971 Fort William

Vertical Descents

3 hrs+

All year

Located at Inchree Falls, this is Scotland's first and longest canyoning descent. Canyoning involves a combination of abseiling, swimming and sliding through water flumes, plus jumping into giant rock pools, as you make your way downstream. Try abseiling and fun yakking, too.

* Other activities include paintballing & white-water rafting
* All necessary clothing & equipment provided

Location
Off A82, 7 miles S of Fort William

Opening
Daily. (Closed Christmas hols)

Admission
£40 per person (half-day canyoning)
Activities priced individually

Contact
Inchree Falls, Inchree, Onich, nr Fort William PH33 6SE

t 01855 821593
w activities-scotland.com
e info@verticaldescents.com

972 Glencoe

Glencoe Visitor Centre

1 hr

All year

Some of the finest climbing and walking country in the Highlands is to be found within this area of dramatic landscapes and historical fact and legend. The infamous massacre of 1692 took place throughout the glen, one of the main locations being near the visitor centre.

* Summer events programme
* Display on the history of mountaineering in the glen

Location
On A82, between Glasgow & Fort William

Opening
Mar daily 10am–4pm;
Apr–Aug daily 9.30am–5.30pm;
Sep–Oct daily 10am–5pm;
Nov–Feb Thu–Sun 10am–4pm

Admission
Adult £5, Child & Concs £4

Contact
Ballachulish, Argyll PH49 4HX

t 01855 811307
w glencoe.nts.org.uk
e glencoe@nts.org.uk

973 Inveraray

Inveraray Castle

1 hr

Apr–Oct

Built 1745 and home to the Duke of Argyll, head of Clan Campbell, the castle's fairytale exterior befits its gracious interior. Marvel at a unique collection of muskets, axes, broadswords and swords from the Battle of Culloden, French tapestries and European furniture.

* Extensive grounds offer garden tours.
* Tearoom, picnic areas, gift shop & free parking

Location
On A83, on shores of Loch Fyne

Opening
1st Sat in April to last Sun in Oct Mon-Fri 10am–5.45pm, Sun 1pm– 5.45pm (last admission 5pm)

Admission
Adult £6.30, Child £4.10, Family £17.00

Contact
Castle Manager, Inveraray Castle, Inveraray, Argyll PA32 8XE

t 01499 302203
w inveraray-castle.com
e enquiries@inveraray-castle.com

974 Isle of Lewis

The Black House Museum

1 hr

All year

The site includes a traditional Lewis thatched crofter's cottage, or black house, with byre and stackyard, complete with a peat fire burning in the central hearth. There is also a restored 1920s white house and a visitor centre with fascinating information about Hebridean life.

* Green Gold Tourism Award winner
* 5-star Scottish Tourism Award

Location
Off A858

Opening
Please phone for details

Admission
Adult £4.50, Child £2, Concs £3.50

Contact
Arnol, Isle of Lewis, Western Isles HS2 9DB

t 01851 710395
w historic-scotland.gov.uk

975 Isle of Lewis

Calanais Standing Stones

 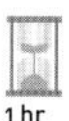 1 hr  All year

This is a cross-shaped setting of 50 standing stones. The site dates back to 3,000BC and the configuration, reminiscent of the larger formations of Carnac in Brittany, is unique in Scotland. The audio-visual presentation in the visitor centre tells their fascinating story.

* Visitor centre, shop & cafeteria
* Story of the Stones exhibition

Location
Off A859, 12 miles W of Stornoway

Opening
Site Daily
Visitor centre Apr–Sep Mon–Sat 10am–6pm; Oct–Mar Wed–Sat 10am–4pm

Admission
Exhibition Adult £1.85, Child 85p, Concs £1.35

Contact
Visitor Centre, Calanais, Isle of Lewis, Western Isles HS2 9DY

t 01851 621422
w historic-scotland.gov.uk

976 Isle of Mull

Hebridean Whale & Dolphin Trust

 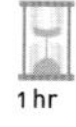 1 hr  All year

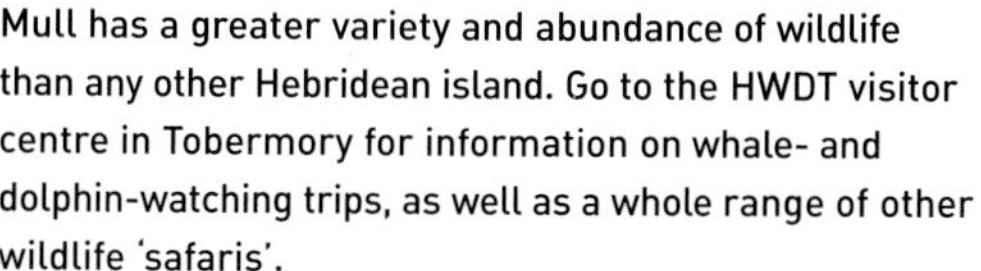

Mull has a greater variety and abundance of wildlife than any other Hebridean island. Go to the HWDT visitor centre in Tobermory for information on whale- and dolphin-watching trips, as well as a whole range of other wildlife 'safaris'.

* Huge variety of Scottish wildlife in its natural habitat
* Land & sea 'safaris'

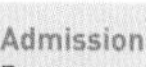

Location
To reach Mull take ferry from Oban to Craignure. Trust is opposite clock tower in Tobermory

Opening
Daily: Apr–Oct 10am–5.30pm; Nov–Mar 11am–4pm

Admission
Free

Contact
28 Main Street, Tobermory, Isle of Mull, Argyll PA75 6NU

t 01688 302620
w hwdt.org
e info@hwdt.org

977 Isle of Mull

Whale Watching Trips

  1 hr+  Mar–Oct

Climb aboard the *Alpha Beta* for a trip out among the Hebridean islands in search of minke whales, basking sharks, porpoises, dolphins, orcas and seals. You're also likely to encounter an abundance of sea birds such as kittiwakes, puffins and guillemots.

* Interisland cruises also available

Location
Croig (longer trips)
Tobermory (shorter trips)

Opening
Daily: Mar–Oct from 9.45am. Please phone for details

Admission
From £25 per person

Contact
Sea Life Surveys, Ledaig, Tobermory, Isle of Mull PA75 6NU

t 01688 302 916
w sealifesurveys.com
e info@sealifesurveys.com

978 Isle of Skye

Dunvegan Castle

  2 hrs  All year

Northern Scotland's oldest inhabited castle is also Skye's most famous landmark, having been the seat and home of the MacLeod chiefs for 800 years. Dunvegan Castle is a fortress stronghold in an idyllic lochside setting, surrounded by dramatic scenery.

* Many fine oil paintings & great clan treasures
* Picturesque woodland garden

Location
1 mile N of Dunvegan

Opening
Daily: Mar–Oct 10am–5.30pm; Nov–Feb 11am–4pm

Admission
summer Adult £7, Child £4, Concs £6
winter Please phone for details

Contact
Dunvegan Castle, Isle of Skye IV55 8WF

t 01470 521206
w dunvegancastle.com
e info@dunvegancastle.com

979 Isle of Skye

Family's Pride II Glassbottom Boat Trips

  1 hr  Mar–Oct

Frequent daily sailings provide an opportunity to see the stunning coastal scenery of Skye and marine wildlife (which may include dolphins, whales and seals), both above and below the waves through unique undersea windows, enhanced by an aquatic floodlight system.

* Trips on *SkyeJet*, a waterjet-propelled Rigid Inflatable Boat (RIB) also available

Location
In Broadford, Isle of Skye, 8 miles from Skye Bridge

Opening
Daily: Mar–Oct 10.30am–4.45pm

Admission
Adult £10.50, Child (under 12) £5

Contact
5 Scullamus, Breakish, Isle of Skye IV42 8QB

t 0800 783 2175
w glassbottomboat.co.uk

980 Kyle of Lochalsh

Eilean Donan Castle

  1 hr  Mar–Nov

Eilean Donan is located on a small island near Dornie, Rossshire. In a superbly romantic setting amid silent, tree-clad hills, it possesses a rare and dreamlike quality, but, in reality, is a fortress of solid stone and formidable defences. The Isle of Skye can be seen across the water.

* Visitor centre & gift shop
* Most photographed castle in Scotland

Location
On A87, 8 miles from Kyle of Lochalsh

Opening
Apr–Oct 10am–5.30pm; Mar & Nov 10am–3.30pm

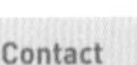 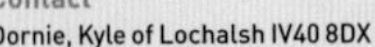

Admission
Adult £4.75, Child & Concs £3.75

Contact
Dornie, Kyle of Lochalsh IV40 8DX

t 01599 555202
w eileandonancastle.com
e info@donan.f9.co.uk

981 Nairn

Cawdor Castle

  2 hrs  May–Oct

A superb fairytale castle, Cawdor dates back to the C14. The imposing exterior gives way to a more intimate interior, with fine paintings, furniture and outstanding tapestries. Outside you can explore the three different gardens and the Big Wood.

* 9-hole golf course & gift shops
* Holiday cottages available

Location
Between Inverness & Nairn on the B9090 off A96.

Opening
Daily: May–Oct 10am–5.30pm

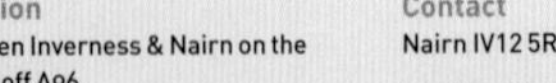

Admission
Adults £7.30, Child £4.50, Concs £6.30
Garden only £4

Contact
Nairn IV12 5RD

t 01667 404401
w cawdorcastle.com
e info@cawdorcastle.com

982 Oban

McCaig's Tower

1 hr All year

Undoubtedly Oban's most outstanding feature, McCaig's Tower was built in 1897 by local banker John Stuart McCaig to provide work for local stonemasons and a lasting monument to his family. The steep climb from the town centre is well worth the effort.

* Breathtaking views over Oban Bay to the Atlantic islands
* Peaceful gardens inside the tower

Location
Short, steep walk from town centre

Opening
Daily

Admission
Free

Contact
Oban Tourist Information Centre, Argyll Square, Oban, Argyll PA34 4AN

t 01631 563122
w visitscotland.com
e info@obanvisitscotland.com

983 Oban

Scottish Sealife & Marine Sanctuary

2 hrs+ All year

Located on the shores of beautiful Loch Creran, the sanctuary is home to more than 30 fascinating natural marine habitats containing everything from shrimps and starfish to sharks and stingrays. The sanctuary cares for many sick and injured seal pups every year.

* 3-Star Marine Attraction
* New displays added regularly

Location
10 miles N of Oban on A828

Opening
Please phone for details

Admission
Please phone for details

Contact
Sanctuary, Barcaldine, by Oban, Argyll PA37 1SE

t 01631 720386
w sealsanctuary.co.uk
e oban@sealsanctuary.co.uk

984 Spean Bridge

Monster Activities

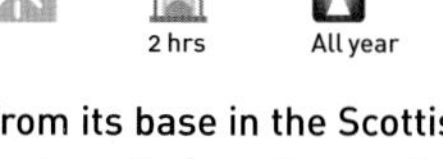

2 hrs All year

From its base in the Scottish Highlands, this sports centre offers outdoor activities of all kinds, including the country's most exciting white-water rafting. Not only does it offer instruction, hire, courses and short breaks, it also guarantees fun for the whole family.

* All kinds of outdoor activities on land & water
* All necessary equipment available for hire

Location
On A82, between Fort William & Inverness

Opening
Daily: 9.30am–5.30pm

Admission
Depends on activity, please phone for details

Contact
Great Glen Water Park, South Laggan, Spean Bridge, Invernessshire PH34 4EA

t 01809 501340
w monsteractivities.com
e info@monsteractivities.com

985 Tain

Glenmorangie Distillery Centre

1 hr All year

Tour the distillery in the company of one of the guides, who will explain the whisky-making process from beginning to end and introduce you to the Sixteen Men of Tain who make it, before a visit to the tasting room to sample the results of their industry and skill.

* Located in Glen of Tranquillity
* Regular distillery tours at 10.30am, 11.30am, 2.30pm & 3.30pm

Location
On A9, 1 hr N of Inverness

Opening
Tours Apr–Sep daily; Oct–Mar Mon–Fri
Shop Apr–Sep Mon–Fri 9am–5pm, Sat 10am–4pm, Sun 12noon–4pm; Oct–Mar Mon–Fri 9am–5pm

Admission
Adult £2.50, Child free

Contact
Tain, Rossshire IV19 1PZ

t 01862 892477
w glenmorangie.com
e tain-shop@glenmorangie.co.uk

986 Alloway

Burns National Heritage Park

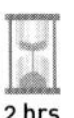
2 hrs

All year

Now fully restored to its original state, Robert Burns's cottage forms the heart of this attraction, offering a unique encounter with an exceptional Scot. Amid the delightful scenery of historic Alloway, this is the best opportunity to learn about Scotland's national poet.

* Unique authentic locations & artefacts
* World's most important Robert Burns collection

Location
On A719, S of Ayr

Opening
Daily: Apr–Sep 10.30am–5.30pm; Oct–Mar 10am–5pm

Admission
Adult £5, Child & Concs £3

Contact
Murdoch's Lone, Alloway, Ayr KA7 4PQ

t 01292 443700
w burnsheritagepark.com
e info@burnsheritagepark.com

987 Annan

Devil's Porridge Exhibition

1 hr

May–Oct

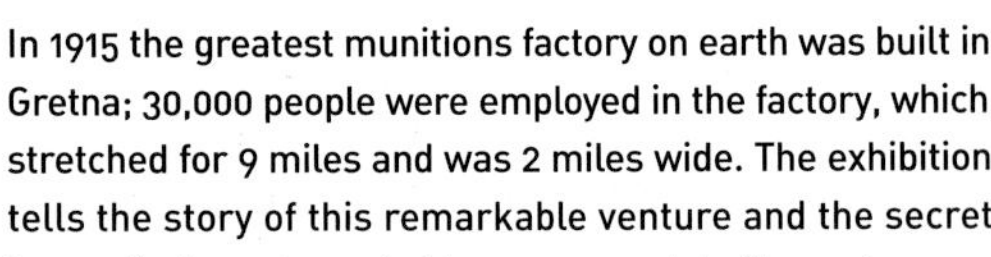
In 1915 the greatest munitions factory on earth was built in Gretna; 30,000 people were employed in the factory, which stretched for 9 miles and was 2 miles wide. The exhibition tells the story of this remarkable venture and the secret towns that were created to accommodate its workers.

* Learn about Britain's worst rail disaster
* Hear stories from WWII evacuees

Location
Follow A75 from Gretna, take Eastriggs turnoff & follow signs

Opening
May–Oct Mon–Sat 10am–4pm, Sun 12noon–4pm

Admission
Adults £2, Child & Concs £1

Contact
Dunedin Road, Eastriggs, nr Annan DG12 6QE

t 01461 700021
w devilsporridge.co.uk
e devils-porridge@tiscali.net

988 Ayr

The Electric Brae

 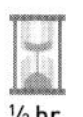 ½ hr  All year

A hill with a difference. While the views are spectacular, try placing a round object, like a ball, on the ground. In which direction do you think it will roll? Thanks to an optical illusion, the ball will roll upwards; let off the handbrake for a second and the car will move uphill!

Location
On A719 9 miles S of Ayr, 2 miles S of Dunure, 1 mile N of the A719–B7023 junction, NW edge of the hamlet of Knoweside

Opening
Daily:All reasonable times

Admission
Free

Contact
t 01292 678100
w south-ayrshire.gov.uk/tourism/around_dunure.htm

989 Caerlaverock

WWT Caerlaverock Wetlands Centre

  4 hrs+  All year

This 1,400-acre wild nature reserve is a must for bird lovers. The site has hides and observation towers linked by a network of screened approaches. The number of barnacle geese that fly from Norway to the Solway Firth each year is testament to the quality of the wetlands.

* Self-catering accommodation available
* Summer nature trail

Location
9 miles SE of Dumfries along Solway Coast Heritage Trail

Opening
Daily: 10am–5pm

Admission
Adult £4.40, Child under 4 free, Child (over 4) £2.70, Concs £3.60

Contact
Eastpark Farm, Caerlaverock, Dumfriesshire DG1 4RS
t 01387 770200
w wwt.org.uk
e info.caerlaverock@wwt.org.uk

990 Dumfries

Dumfries Museum & Camera Obscura

 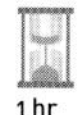 1 hr   All year

A treasure house of the history of south-west Scotland, the museum is centred on the C18 windmill tower that stands above the town. On the top floor there is a camera obscura and on the tabletop screen visitors can see panoramic views of Dumfries and the surrounding countryside.

* Lively programme of exhibitions & events
* Museum trails & fun activities for all ages

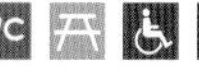    

Location
In town centre

Opening
Daily: Apr–Sep Mon–Sat 10am–5pm, Sun 2pm–5pm;
Oct–Mar Tue–Sat 10am–1pm & 2pm–5pm

Admission
Museum Free
Camera Obscura Adult £1.90, Child & Concs 95p

Contact
Rotchell Road, Dumfries DG2 7SW
t 01387 253374
w dumgal.gov.uk/museums
e dumfriesmuseum@dumgal.gov.uk

991 Eyemouth

Eyemouth Museum

  1 hr  Apr–Oct

This museum has a magnificent 15 × 4ft tapestry that commemorates the East coast fishing disaster of 1881 in which 189 local fishermen were drowned. It also has exhibitions on fishing, farming, milling, wheelwrighting, and blacksmithing.

* 3-star Visitor Attraction
* Exhibitions change throughout the year

Location
In town centre

Opening
Apr–Jun & Sep daily Mon–Sat 10am–5pm, Sun 10am–1pm; Jul–Aug daily Mon–Sat 10am–5pm, Sun 10am–2pm; Oct Mon–Sat 10am–4pm, (closed Sun)

Admission
Adult £2.50, Child free, Concs £2

Contact
Auld Kirk, Manse Road, Eyemouth TD14 5JE
t 01890 750678

992 Gretna Green

Gretna Green World Famous Blacksmith's Shop & Centre

1 hr+ All year

In 1754, it became illegal to marry under 21 but in Scotland it was, and is, still possible to marry at 16. Gretna Green is the first village across the border that many 'elopers' reached and the Blacksmith's Shop was the centre of the runaway marriage trade.

* Old coach collection
* Juicy stories of romance, intrigue & scandal

Location
On M74, just N of border

Opening
Daily: Apr–Sep 9am–early evening; Oct–Mar 9am–5pm

Admission
Exhibition Adult £3, Child & Concs £2.50

Contact
Gretna Green Group Ltd, Headless Cross, Gretna Green, Dumfries & Galloway DG16 5EA

t 01461 338441
w gretnagreen.com
e info@gretnagreen.com

993 Hawick

Drumlanrig's Tower

1 hr Apr–Oct

The Black Tower of Drumlanrig is an imposing landmark in the Scottish Border town of Hawick. The tower has borne silent witness to the savage cross-border warfare and bitter interfamily feuding that marked the town's turbulent past.

* Exhibition tells the story of the house
* Display of watercolours by the artist Tom Scott

Location
In Hawick high street

Opening
Daily: Apr–Oct Mon–Sat 10am–5pm, Sun 12noon–3pm

Admission
Adult £2.50, Child free, Concs £1.50

Contact
1 Towerknowe, Hawick TD9 9EN

t 01450 373457
w scotborders.gov.uk/museums
e museum@scotborders.gov.uk

994 Isle of Arran

King's Cave

2 hrs All year

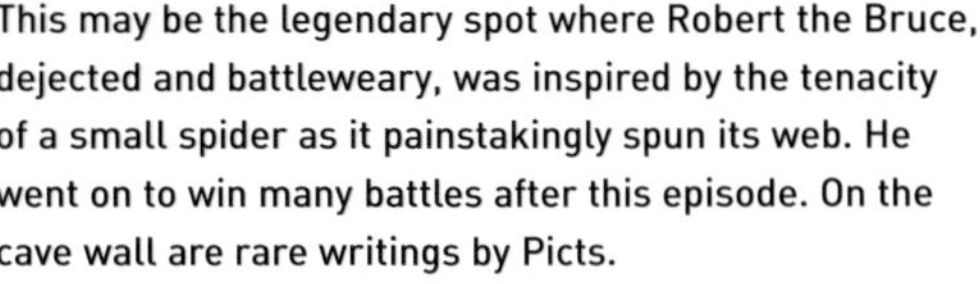

This may be the legendary spot where Robert the Bruce, dejected and battleweary, was inspired by the tenacity of a small spider as it painstakingly spun its web. He went on to win many battles after this episode. On the cave wall are rare writings by Picts.

Location
Off A841, near Blackwaterfoot, Isle of Arran, access by coastal path only

Opening
Daily: All reasonable times

Admission
Free

Contact
Blackwaterfoot, Isle of Arran

t 0845 225 5121
w showcaves.com

995 Kelso

Floors Castle

2 hrs Apr–Oct

Boasting fine views over the River Tweed to the Cheviot Hills, the castle has been home to the Roxburghe family since it was built by WIlliam Adam in 1721. It houses superb collections of art, tapestries and antiques and is set in parkland that abounds with flora and fauna.

* Exhibitions & events throughout the season
* Works by well-known artists, including Matisse

Location
On edge of Kelso

Opening
Daily: Apr–Oct 11am–5pm (last admission 4.30pm)

Admission
Adult £6, Child £3.25, Concs £5

Contact
Kelso, Roxburghshire TD5 7SF

t 01573 223333
w floorscastle.com
e marketing@floorscastle.com

996 Largs

The Viking Experience

  1 hr  Feb–Nov

This multimedia journey recounts the saga of the Vikings in Scotland, from invasion to defeat at the Battle of Largs. Meet the Gods and Valkyries in Valhalla, come face to face with Odin, the Viking god of war, and walk with him into the Viking world of 700 years ago.

* Regular shows
* Leisure facilities, soft play centre & theatre

Location
On Largs seafront

Opening
Daily: Feb & Nov Sat 12.30pm–3.30pm, Sun 10.30am–3.30pm
Apr–Sep 10.30am–5.30pm;
Mar & Oct 10.30am–3.30pm

Admission
Adult £4.10, Child & Concs £3.10

Contact
Vikingar, Greenock Road, Largs, Ayrshire KA30 8QL

t 01475 689777
w vikingar.co.uk
e info@vikingar.co.uk

997 Lockerbie

Carlyle's Birthplace

  1 hr  May–Sep

The Arched House, in which Thomas Carlyle was born in 1795, was built by his father and uncle in 1791. Carlyle was a great writer and historian and one of the C19's leading voices on morals and equalities. The house is now furnished to reflect Victorian domestic life.

* Collection of portraits
* Carlyle's belongings

Location
Off M74, on A74, in Ecclefechan, 5½ miles SE of Lockerbie

Opening
May–Sep. Please phone for details

Admission
Adult £5, Child & Concs £4

Contact
The Arched House, Ecclefechan, Lockerbie, Dumfries & Galloway DG11 3DG

t 01576 300666
w nts.org.uk

998 Melrose

Abbotsford

1 hr+ Mar–Oct

Abbotsford is the house built and lived in by Sir Walter Scott, the C19 novelist and author of timeless classics such as *Waverley*, *Rob Roy* and *Ivanhoe*. Standing on the banks of the River Tweed, the house contains an impressive collection of relics, weapons and armour.

* Rob Roy's gun & Montrose's sword
* Extensive grounds & walled garden

Location
On B6360, 2 miles W of Melrose

Opening
19 Mar–Oct Mon–Sat 9.30am–5pm;
19 Mar–May & Oct Sun 2pm–5pm;
Jun–Sep Sun 9.30am–5pm

Admission
Adult £6, Child £3

Contact
Melrose, Borders TD6 9BQ

t 01896 752043
w scottsabbotsford.co.uk
e enquiries@scottsabbotsford.co.uk

999 Melrose

Melrose Abbey

½ hr All year

Arguably the finest of Scotland's border abbeys, Melrose is a magnificent ruin on a grand scale with lavishly decorated masonry. It is thought to be the burial place of Robert the Bruce's heart, marked with a commemorative carved stone plaque within the grounds.

* Free audio tour & children's trail
* Museum with local artefacts found in abbey grounds

Location
Off A7/A68, in Melrose

Opening
Daily: Apr–Sep 9.30am–6.30pm;
Oct–Mar 9.30am–4.30pm
(last admission ½ hr before close)

Admission
Adult £4.50, Child £2, Concs £3.50

Contact
Abbey Street, Melrose, Roxburghshire TD6 9LG

t 01896 822562
w historic-scotland.gov.uk

1000 Melrose

Three Hills Roman Centre & Fort

1 hr+ All year

The most important Roman military complex between Hadrian's Wall and the Antonine Wall guarded and secured the crossing of the River Tweed at Newstead in the C1 and C2. Excavations have revealed much of what went on there. See finds from 1905 to 1910 and 1989 to 1998.

* See millennium milestone & timber tower
* Viewing platforms & information boards

Location
Market Square in Melrose

Opening
Daily: Apr–Oct 10.30am–4.30pm
Nov–Mar please phone for details

Admission
Walks Adult £3, Child free, Concs £2.50
Exhibition £1.50, £1, £1

Contact
Ormiston, Melrose TD6 9PN

t 01896 822651
w trimontium.net
e secretary@trimontium.freeserve.co.uk

1001 Newton Stewart

Galloway Red Deer Range

2 hrs Jun–Sep

This attraction has a viewpoint near the road from which beautiful red deer can be observed in their natural habitat. Visitors to the range can also walk among the deer, photograph them and even touch them, under supervision – a memorable experience.

* Guided tours in summer
* See & hear roaring stags during the rutting season

Location
On A712, 3 miles SW of Clatteringshaws Loch

Opening
End of Jun–mid-Sep Tue & Thu 11am–2pm, Sun 11am–2.30pm
Tours Tue & Thu 11am & 2.30pm, Sun 2.30pm

Admission
Adult £3.50, Child £1.25, Concs £2.50
Family ticket £8

Contact
Red Deer Range Car Park, nr Clatteringshaws, Newton Stewart, Dumfries & Galloway DG7 3SQ

t 01671 402420
w forestry.gov.uk/gallowayforestpark
e galloway@forestry.gsi.gov.uk

Index

Acknowledgements & picture credits

The publishers would like to acknowledge the important contribution the British Tourist Authority made to this publication through the use of images from its website, *www.britainonview.com.*

The publishers would like to thank the National Trust, the National Trust for Scotland and English Heritage, who kindly supplied photographs for use with their entries.

The publishers would also like to thank all contributors who provided information, and especially all those who kindly supplied photographs. Particular thanks go to Tony Stuchbury (www.ajsphotos.co.uk).

Compiled, edited and designed by Butler and Tanner. Edited by Libby Willis. Design and layout by Lyn Davies and Carole McDonald. Project Manager Nick Heal. Special thanks to Carl Luke, Jennie Golding and Dianne Penny.